Political Spaces and Global War

Political Spaces and Global War

Carlo Galli

Adam Sitze, Editor

Translated by Elisabeth Fay

University of Minnesota Press
Minneapolis • London

The translator thanks Timothy Campbell, Lorenzo Fabbri, and Andrea Righi for their help and support. The editor thanks Nicholas Pastan, Antonina Sanchez, and Lucy Zhou for their research and bibliographic assistance. We both thank Danielle Kasprzak, our editor at the University of Minnesota Press, for her guidance and advice, and Cynthia Landeen, our indexer, for her meticulous work.

Originally published in Italian as *Spazi politici*, by Carlo Galli, copyright 2001 by Società editrice Il Mulino, Bologna; and as *La Guerra Globale*, by Carlo Galli, copyright 2002 by Gius. Laterza & Figli. All rights reserved. Published by arrangement with Marco Vigevani Agenzia Letteraria.

English translation copyright 2010 by the Regents of the University of Minnesota

Published by the University of Minnesota Press
111 Third Avenue South, Suite 290
Minneapolis, MN 55401–2520
http://www.upress.umn.edu

Library of Congress Cataloging-in-Publication Data

Galli, Carlo.
Political spaces and global war / Carlo Galli ; Adam Sitze, editor ; translated by Elisabeth Fay.
    p. cm.
Translation of Spazi politici. Bologna : Mulino, 2001, and Guerra globale. Roma : GLF editori Laterza, 2002.
Includes bibliographical references and index.
ISBN 978-0-8166-6595-2 (hardcover : alk. paper) – ISBN 978-0-8166-6596-9 (pbk. : alk. paper)
1. World politics – 21st century. 2. Globalization. 3. Geopolitics. 4. Politics and war. 5. War on Terrorism, 2001–2009. I. Sitze, Adam. II. Fay, Elisabeth. III. Galli, Carlo. Spazi politici. English. IV. Galli, Carlo. Guerra globale. English. V. Title. VI. Title: Global war.
D863.G35 2010
327.1–dc22

                                    2010019698

Printed in the United States of America on acid-free paper

The University of Minnesota is an equal-opportunity educator and employer.

17 16 15 14 13 12 11 10   10 9 8 7 6 5 4 3 2 1

Contents

Preface to the English Edition

Readers of this work will encounter a way of thinking politics through philosophical tools that attempt to grasp it in its *complexity*, which is to say, with reference to the epochal dimension and the radical contingency from which politics (the thought that thinks it, the institutions that organize it) originates.

The thesis developed in these pages is that every political thought and institution hosts a spatial dimension within itself, be it implicit or explicit. Political thoughts and political institutions, I shall argue, come into being as relatively stable and durable (epochal) regulating responses to concrete perceptions of the structures of space and their transformations.

My aim has been to reconstruct the fixed link between political theory and spatiality in its specifically epochal articulation, or, in other words, in terms of the great destructions and reconstructions that articulate Western history. In particular, I wanted to show that the categories of modern politics (the public and the private; citizen, society, and state; war and law) depend on two prior spatial pairings: the internal and external, on the one hand, and the particular and the universal, on the other. The spatial determination contained in these categories is a "modern" spatiality that is disenchanted and deprived of its traditional qualitative characteristics, and that, as such, demands and provokes the regulating action of sovereignty to cut and divide it. It was also clear to me that the processes and dynamics of the contemporary world ("globalization") presented a challenge, requiring us to rethink the relationship between space and politics in terms that are specific to the global age, an age which, in disagreement with those who maintain that it has been present since the origins of capitalism, I recognize in its epochal discontinuity. In the global age, I shall claim, the relationship between space and politics places itself beyond the State (the principal modality of the spatialization of politics in the modern age), beyond the two late-modern world empires that faced off from 1945 to 1989, beyond the United Nations' illusion of institutional universalism, and beyond economic liberalism's ability to bring peace to the world. The challenge was to understand what kind of space global space was, and what kind of politics was suited to it; what concepts could think it and what regulating institutions could govern it; and, finally, what significance we could find in the world's new radical disorder, in the new and ungovernable political centrality of contingency that globalization has brought.

I wrote *Political Spaces* in 2000, before the attacks of September 11, and *Global War* in 2002, before the invasion of Iraq. In both books, it was clear to me that global space is a paradoxical space, lacking an exterior and run through by infinite fractures and mobile contradictions that put every point on the globe in contact with every other point. In global space, the relationships between particular and universal, contingency and totality, cease to have rational-linear or dialectical forms, and take on completely new, random, and changing ones. In the second book in particular, I maintain that Global War—violence that eludes every traditional conceptual or spatial link between war and politics—is not a sudden disorder or an unexpected interruption of the global age's peaceful dynamics, but is the other face of globalization, an essential property of global space. Global War is, in other words, verification that the global age exists outside the modern way of thinking and organizing the relationship between politics and space, and that Global War is not thinkable as a specification of the relationship between war and the State.

These books contain the discovery of the crucial theoretical and political significance of globalization's intrinsically conflictual spatiality. I was not able to discuss the ways in which the contingency of the global age has since evolved (such as, for example, the American effort, after the phase of the "global war on terrorism," to respatialize politics and war through the construction of a new imperial *limes*[1] in central Asia [the military base strategy], or the new "pluralistic" phase of the global age, the global crisis of capitalism and the delineation of many worldwide political "poles" ["near-empires"] emerging from the jumble of globalization). Nor will readers find mention of the electoral setback that has been occurring in Europe in the interval, which has so far disappointed hopes for a new and effective postmodern political space.

My impression, however, is that even the new spatializations of politics that seem to be emerging today (the new geopolitical areas where power seems to be building in the world) are marked by a contingency so radical and of such evident fragility and criticality that it is not yet possible to say that the relationship between space and politics has found new concepts, new institutions, and new configurations. Global mobilization still seems to challenge our capacity to understand and to order the link between space and politics.

If the reflection contained in these pages can contribute something to this understanding, I believe I will have not worked in vain, and the generosity and talent of those who have wanted and worked to make this work available to an English-speaking audience will not have been wasted. I offer my sincere thanks to two very important scholars, Professor Alberto Moreiras and Professor Adam Sitze, and to Elisabeth Fay, my excellent translator.

Carlo Galli
Bologna, March 2010

Editor's Introduction

Carlo Galli is one of the world's leading authorities on the German political thinker Carl Schmitt (1888–1985).[1] In 1996, Galli published a monumental study of Schmitt that has been called, with good reason, "the most complete, comprehensive, and insightful account of Schmitt's thought ever published."[2] At the close of the present work, however, the reader will find the provocative assertion that, in the global age, "Schmittian political thought is exhausted."[3] The purpose of this introduction is to outline the counterintuitive itinerary through which Galli came to this conclusion. How does it come to pass that one of the thinkers who has most exhaustively thought through Schmitt is today claiming that Schmitt's thought is exhausted? And what might we have to learn about the global age from a scholar who describes himself, curiously, as a *non-Schmittian Schmittologist*?[4]

The Thinkability of Politics

Carlo Galli is today *professore ordinario* in the Department of Historical Disciplines at the University of Bologna, where he teaches the history of political thought. Trained in the Frankfurt School tradition of critical theory, Galli's approach to the history of political thought focuses on the impasses and contingencies that trouble from within the basic concepts of modern political thought. The point of this focus is to reveal that the institutions and practices that are founded on those concepts are neither as coherent nor as necessary or inevitable as they might appear, and that it is thus both possible and desirable to think politics outside of the terms and concepts of modern political philosophy.[5] "Those who lack imagination cannot imagine what is lacking," read graffiti in Paris in May 1968. For Galli, what is most lacking today is the ability to produce the new "figures"—the new paradigms, schemata, or diagrams—that will allow us make sense and order out of the chaos of the global age.[6]

Like Theodor Adorno and Max Horkheimer, Galli has pursued his ambition through intellectual projects that are cooperative in character. With the philosopher Roberto Esposito, Galli is co-editor of the *Enciclopedia del pensiero politico. Autori, concetti, dottrine* (Encyclopedia of Political Thought: Authors, Concepts, Doctrines), which was first published in 2000 and was reissued in 2005.[7] Like its French counterpart, the 2004 *Vocabulaire européen des philosophies: Dictionaire des intraduisibles* (European Vocabulary of Philosophies: Dictionary of Untranslatable Terms) edited by Barbara Cassin,[8] and its precursors in Italy (the 1976 *Il dizionario di politica* [Dictionary of Politics] edited by Nicola Matteucci and Norberto Bobbio[9]) and Germany (the 1972–1977 *Geschichtliche Grundbegriffe: Historisches Lexikon zur politisch-sozialer Sprache in Deutschland* [Basic Concepts in History: A Historical Dictionary of Political and Social Language in Germany] directed by Reinhart Koselleck[10]), the *Enciclopedia* is an Enlightenment project in the best sense of the word. Against the assumption that political philosophy should be limited to a cloistered, esoteric conversation between initiates, the *Enciclopedia* presupposes and addresses itself to any and all readers who dare to know—who have the courage to use their own understanding. It is an attempt to enable philosophical understandings of experiences that would otherwise risk being interpreted by the attitudes of authoritarianism, prejudice, and reaction—or, in Adorno's phrase, the "nonpublic opinions"[11]—that quietly persist even, especially, in the most Enlightened of publics.

The *Enciclopedia* fulfills this aim by fostering a style of erudition that is distinct from that of its worthy counterparts and predecessors. Koselleck's "Historical Dictionary" limits its focus to the emergence of modernity in Germany alone, and to that end places special emphasis on the various sorts of discontinuities that differentiate the basic concepts of modern German politics (most notably the period from 1750 to 1850) from those of earlier phases in German history (classical antiquity, the Middle Ages, the Reformation). This does not make it a parochial work; by limiting itself to the horizon of German conceptual history, the "Historical Dictionary" allows the reader to particularize German political concepts and to grasp the difficulty of generalizing or translating those concepts into other languages and political experiences.[12] Cassin's "European Vocabulary of Philosophies" also takes up the problem of translation, but in a slightly different way. By elevating the untranslatability of philosophic terms to the level of an explicit problem for philosophic thought, it seeks to avoid sacralizing any given language into a philosophic metalanguage, and instead foregrounds the endless work of translation itself as one of philosophy's essential energies. But even as the "European Vocabulary of Philosophies" emphasizes the "deterritorialization" of philosophic languages (pointedly including, for example, Arabic and Hebrew in its etymologies), it nevertheless accepts a certain iteration of European space as the horizon for the pluralist and comparative cartography it claims to offer.[13] This horizon remains for the most part unproblematized; perhaps because the creation of a "European Vocabulary" is its explicitly stated hermeneutic aim, the "European Vocabulary" contains no entry for "Europe" itself.

Galli and Esposito carry out a much different project in their *Enciclopedia*. They problematize the epistemic space of Europe from the outset, defining the horizon of their concern as the *diffusion* of Western political thought.[14] "Europe," for the *Enciclopedia*, is not, then, the fundamental horizon *for* the project of encyclopedic knowledge; it is simply one among many topics *within* that project, one that moreover cannot be understood in the absence of imperialism.[15] Even though the *Enciclopedia*, like Cassin's "European Vocabulary of Philosophies," retains an emphasis on what it calls "the West," the understanding of Western political thought it presupposes is thus, as Dipesh Chakrabarty might put it, provincialized.[16] The reader of the *Enciclopedia* consequently will find entries not only on Plato, Aristotle, Avicenna, Maimonides, Hobbes, and Kant, but also on François Toussaint L'Ouverture, Símon Bólivar, Gandhi, Frantz Fanon, and Amartya Sen. The reader also will find that while the *Enciclopedia*, like the "European Vocabulary," focuses on the inadequacies of received political lexicons, it measures those inadequacies not with reference to the untranslatability of philosophic terms, but instead to the incommensurability of the modern age with the global age.[17] Thus, for example, whereas Phillipe Raynaud's entry on "*politique*" in the "European Vocabulary of Philosophies" concludes by summarizing Schmitt's concept of the political, and arguing that "the concept of politics is without doubt part of the common ground of contemporary philosophy,"[18] Galli's entry on "*politica*" in the *Enciclopedia* closes with a review of authors (Michel Foucault, Richard Rorty, Jacques Derrida, and Roberto Esposito) who each recognize, albeit in very different ways, the unintelligibility of the concept of "politics" in and for contemporary experience.[19] Similar differences distinguish Galli's entry on *"politica"* from Volker Sellin's entry on *"politik"* in the "Historical Dictionary" (which also concludes with a summary of Schmitt) and Norberto Bobbio's entry on *"politica"* in the "Dictionary of Politics" (which emphasizes the relation between politics and ethics, and concludes with a section on politics as group ethics).[20] Whereas the latter both operate on the assumption that the concept of "politics" will continue to have sense and meaning in the contemporary world, the hypothesis underlying Galli's entry is that modern political theory has turned into a "sad science" that is devoted less to the comprehension of its present than to the mourning of its "lost object."[21] In a sense, Galli's entry on *"politica"* can serve as a metonym for the project of the *Enciclopedia* as such; taken as a whole, this is a book that prepares its reader to think politics within a newly open horizon—within the horizon of an unpredictable and unstable future, of a world that is undergoing "globalization," but that has only recently, and quite belatedly, started to devote serious thought to what "globalization" might mean for the concept of "politics" itself.

A similar intellectual task governs the work of the journal *Filosofia politica*, which Galli co-edits with Esposito and historian of political thought Giuseppe Duso. Housed at the University of Bologna since its founding by Nicola Matteucci in 1987, *Filosofia politica* has served as a forum for rethinking the "epochality of the modern" outside of the explanatory paradigms and hermeneutic horizons according to which modern political thought prefers to evaluate itself.[22] Although the essays that appear in this journal often share historiographical concerns and methods with historians of political thought in Germany and England (mainly Koselleck's school of *Begriffgeschichte*, though also, albeit to a much lesser extent, the "Cambridge School" of Quentin Skinner and J. G. A. Pocock[23]), the scholarship of *Filosifia politica* is generally distinguished from its counterparts by an approach to the terms and concepts of modern politics that is specifically critical, deconstructive, and genealogical in character. It springs from the editors' consensus that, as Galli put it in 2007, modern political thought has degenerated into mere moralism—into simple expressions of what "ought to be"—because it has failed to fully think through the problems posed by the experience of globalization.[24] As an antidote to this malaise, *Filosofia politica* seeks to publish scholarship that takes the global age as a point of departure for a rethinking of the most basic premise of political thought itself—the very notion that there is indeed something called "politics" that, in turn, can and should be "thinkable." As Galli summed it up in 2007, in a difficult formulation to which we shall return:

> Political philosophy should now assume the task of thinking anew
> the thinkability of politics, finding it once again in the most com-
> plete immanence and at the same time—this is the key point—in
> non-conciliation with that immanence, which is to say, through
> the radical critique of immanence, made without recourse to
> transcendence.[25]

As a part of this intricate task, each issue of *Filosofia politica* contains a section that is called "Materials for a European Political Lexicon," but which, as Nicola Matteucci observed soon after the journal's launch, might be more accurately called "Contributions for a Definition of Political Philosophy."[26] The articles collected under this rubric, despite their very different shapes and styles, nevertheless share a specific aim and function. They bracket modernity's preferred self-definitions of its basic terms and concepts in order to think through its unthought, to open it up to immanent critique, to write its genealogy, and to deconstruct it. The point of the history of political thought today, at least in the unusual iteration of it that *Filosofia politica* seeks to foster, is not, then, simply to clarify the terms of modern political thought by situating them in their appropriate historical and linguistic contexts. Nor is it to revive the classic works of political thought in the present by asserting the timeless relevance of the questions they pose. It is to rethink the basic terms and concepts of political thought by explicating the limitations imposed upon their coherence by their implicit epochal horizons, and by revealing their inability to illuminate the crises that define contemporary experience.[27] "We need a new political lexicon," Adriana Cavarero has written, "a new political theory that does not limit itself to reorganizing modern categories in a different way to adapt them to new scenarios, but that registers their collapse to radically rethink the matrix of politics itself."[28]

The aim of *Filosofia politica* is not, then, to engage in an "antimodern" destruction of modern politics (which would be one of modernity's own standard narratives, that of conservative "negative thought"[29]). It is to understand contemporary experience (or, in Galli's phrase, "the global age") as the disjunctive synthesis of the incommensurable epochs that preceded it (the ancient, medieval, and modern ages). It is to seize upon this disjunctive synthesis—this nonidentity of the present with itself, this unpredictable and unstable assemblage of times and tenses, this contemporaneity—as a chance to gain critical distance from the terms and concepts of "the present."[30] It is, in short, to invent a set of philosophical concepts that, as Esposito has put it, "can keep pace with the events that involve and transform us."[31]

A Divided City

The University of Bologna is, to say the very least, an interesting place to begin thinking about the inadequacy of modern political thought in and for contemporary experience. Located in the center of a city called "the red one" (*la rossa*) not only for its scores of red-tiled roofs but also for its innovative experiments in left politics,[32] Bologna is the oldest university in Europe. Founded in 1088, it was from the twelfth to the mid-thirteenth century the site of a decisive intellectual event the force of which remains in effect even, especially, today. It was in Bologna that a school of scholars who would come to be called the "glossators" systematized Roman Law by applying to the then recently rediscovered Digest of Justinian a set of hermeneutic methods that hitherto had been applied only by theologians to the Bible. At first, these scholars only inscribed their *glossæ* ("glosses") on the margins or between the lines of the Digest. Gradually, however, they began to generate long, self-standing texts consisting of rigorous analytic commentaries on cases from all branches of Roman Law.[33] In the ensuing centuries, the scholarly study of Roman Law spread from Bologna to universities throughout Europe, eventually giving "all Europe (including England) much of its basic legal vocabulary."[34] Never without resistance, contestation, or alteration, this renewal of Roman Law gradually created the conditions for, among other things, new conceptions of the relations between royal and imperial power,[35] the rise of a "scientific jurisprudence" capable of questioning kingship itself,[36] and the "names, battle cries, and costumes" through which the revolutionaries of 1776, 1789, and 1848 would misrecognize their time and their desires.[37] For Carl Schmitt, meanwhile, the rediscovery of Roman Law in the twelfth and thirteenth centuries constituted nothing less than the genealogical origin of modern European identity. As Schmitt would put it in the 1943 lecture he came to call his "testament," the rebirth of Roman Law was the "first-born child of the modern European spirit, of the 'occidental rationalism' of the modern age."[38] The Roman Law revival was, in Schmitt's view, an event the impact of which was "overwhelming not only on the history of European jurisprudence, but on the history of European science and the European spirit as a whole."[39] For Schmitt, in other words, Bologna is not one among many "political spaces." It is a name for the genealogical origin of the concept of jurisprudence to which he, by his own account, committed his life's work.

It was here, of all places, that Galli began his encounter with Schmitt's thought. A student at the University of Bologna from 1968 to 1972, Galli wrote his *laureato* on Adorno's interpretation of Hegel under the guidance of the philosopher Felice Battaglia (a neo-Hegelian with a marked interest in the Frankfurt School).[40] In 1973, this work culminated in the publication of an essay detailing the reception of the Frankfurt School in Italy, and criticizing the misreadings that had informed that reception.[41] During these same years, Italian politics was undergoing significant political transformations, and these transformations would, in turn, create the conditions under which Galli would bring his Frankfurtian sensibilities to bear on the interpretation of Schmitt. Just as the Italian student revolt of 1967 to 1968 spurred greater and more enduring social transformation than did comparable revolts elsewhere in Europe, so too was the reaction to it more extreme.[42] Beginning with the massacre at Piazza Fontana in Milan in 1969, the neofascist right and their police sympathizers organized a set of violent acts that came to be called the "strategy of tension."[43] Its goal was to destroy the political, legal, and social accomplishments of the student movement (in the areas of workers' and women's rights[44]) by sowing panic in the Italian public and creating the conditions for the government to declare martial law. As a means to this end, neofascist cells assassinated leftist leaders and activists and placed bombs in cities known for their strong leftist leanings, while their counterparts in the police tried to pin the violence on anarchists.[45]

Compounding this crisis was the political remedy proposed for it by the Italian Communist Party (*Partito Communista Italiano* or "PCI"). In a series of articles published in October 1973, PCI general secretary Enrico Berlinguer proposed that the Party's path to institutional power lay in a "historic compromise" with its traditional adversary, the Christian Democrats (*Democrazia Cristiana* or "DC"). If Italy was to resist the neofascist "strategy of tension" and escape the fate of Salvador Allende's Chile (where a similar "strategy of tension" had a month earlier culminated in a successful right-wing *coup d'état*), Berlinguer argued, the PCI needed to accept the grim reality that it not only lacked the votes to take control of Parliament and govern Italy from the left, but also could not even hope to govern on its own (even if they did have the votes). Under conditions defined by the Cold War and by Italy's dependence on NATO, geopolitics set the limits for national politics; the United States, it was said, would never countenance communist leadership in Italy.[46] What was more, according to Berlinguer, there was virtue in this necessity. By joining forces with the DC, the PCI could broker a marriage between Catholic and communist values that, in turn, could instill in Italians a spirit of sacrifice and austerity capable of resisting the nihilism of consumer capitalism. Thus it was that at a moment when broad segments of the Italian left were emphasizing sexual liberation (rights of abortion and divorce, equality in education and work, wages for housework), workers' autonomy (democratic self-governance outside of union bureaucracy in the cause of equal pay raises for all, an end to piecework, reduction of the working week, and better pensions), and civil liberties (limits on preventative detention and police authority, prison reform), the PCI adopted and ran on an electoral platform grounded in a moralistic emphasis on the traditional values of family, hard work, and law and order.[47]

Berlinguer's "historic compromise" did indeed produce electoral gains for the PCI in 1975 and 1976, and nowhere more than in Bologna, which Franco "Bifo" Berardi called "the city of the realized Historical Compromise."[48] These electoral successes were in fact, however, a profound failure. At the very moment that a set of unprecedented events made imaginative politics more necessary than ever, the PCI achieved parliamentary power precisely by abandoning any specifically emancipatory political practices (and this not despite but because of their fidelity to the thought of Antonio Gramsci, whose theory of "hegemony" the

PCI interpreted to imply the necessity for compromise in "conquest of the state").[49] Its theoretical poverty came at a high cost for those whose interests the PCI claimed to represent. In May of 1975, for example, the PCI did not oppose the Italian Parliament's passage of the *Legge Reale*, an old set of laws resurrected from the years of Italian Fascism that allowed the police to fire without warning upon striking protesters (militant workers in particular).[50] The PCI's achievement of a governing majority also made it easier for the International Monetary Fund (IMF) to achieve its longstanding goal of restructuring Italian labor policy on the basis of neoliberal economics; to keep the PCI in power, trade unions now felt obliged to consent to the very wage cuts they had opposed only a year earlier, when proposed by their adversaries in the *Banca d'Italia*.[51] In the PCI, in other words, the Italian left was confronted with the spectacle of a revolutionary party whose theoretical emphasis on a Gramscian "war of position" amounted, in practice, to nothing more than "a harmonious and non-conflictual management of politics."[52] "For the first time," Sylvère Lotringer wrote of PCI governance during his 1979 visit to Bologna, "young workers and students saw what 'Socialism' looks like: acute unemployment, living costs higher than anywhere else, and the hypocritical image of a benevolent PCI."[53]

Betrayed by their ostensible representatives in Parliament, threatened by extraparliamentary violence from the neofascist right, and sobered by the theoretical impotence implicit in PCI governance, significant parts of the Italian left began to organize themselves outside of the PCI. The critique of bureaucratic state communism, which a number of Italian intellectuals had been developing at least since the Soviet Union's invasion of Hungary in 1956,[54] now came into its own as a political movement. This movement raised sharp and searching questions that extended well beyond simple criticisms of the PCI's leadership, its concrete policies, its cynical parliamentary maneuvers, and the reformist interpretation of Gramsci that guided its thinking.[55] Some on the radical left (most notably the Red Brigades) resolved their doubts with a strategy of violence that, however anti-statist in theory, was nevertheless thoroughly statist in practice. These radicals sought to strike at the "heart of the state" by assassinating persons who represented state power (such as magistrates and elected officials), on the assumption that the high drama and visibility of these acts would gain the radical left a quotient of the representation denied to it in Parliament. But even before this strategy culminated in the Red Brigades' May 1978 assassination of Aldo Moro (former prime minister and then-president of the DC), which by all accounts strengthened the Italian state in ways that the DC on its own could not possibly have accomplished,[56] many other radical left intellectuals had already been engaged for years in lines of inquiry and critique that broke with the Red Brigades' guiding assumptions.[57]

Working with a new intensity and energy, these intellectuals questioned the very notion that the institutions and practices of the State, together with the modes of thinking, doing, and being associated with those institutions and practices, were and ought to remain the center of political life. They sought to understand the imaginative experiments in politics that flourished above all in Bologna, where the "creative wing" of the student movement opposed the PCI and DC in a manner that was at once non-violent, joyful, and effective.[58] From this perspective, the fatal flaw of the Red Brigades was that their anti-State violence ratified rather than rejected the assumption that the State is the fundamental horizon orienting all viable political thought and action.[59] Working both outside and inside the PCI, thinkers such as Mario Tronti, Massimo Cacciari, Paolo Virno, and Antonio Negri attempted to invent schemata of the political that rejected both the historic compromise, on the one hand, and terrorism on the other. They sought to renew the classic Marxist critique of the State-Form by turning to theoretical sources outside of the Marxist tradition, and their search indeed ranged far and wide.[60] They did not hesitate to appropriate philosophers who had in the past figured centrally into the thinking of the political right, such as Søren Kierkegaard, Friedrich Nietzsche, and Martin Heidegger.[61] And perhaps because, as Norberto Bobbio noted in 1982, Italy's precarious political situation in the 1970s bore more than a passing resemblance to the "crisis of parliamentary democracy" of the German Weimar Republic,[62] one of the thinkers whose theoretical relevance seemed obvious or self-evident was that most forceful critic of Weimar of all, Carl Schmitt.

Occasio

In 1972, the Bolognese publishing house Il Mulino released a new Italian translation of the second edition of Schmitt's *Der Begriff des Politischen* (*The Concept of the Political*).[63] This translation, as Galli would later put it, marked the "return" of Schmitt within Italian political thought after three decades of silence.[64] The debates it spurred provided the occasion for Galli's first work of scholarship on Schmitt, a long 1979 article called "Carl Schmitt in Italian Culture (1924–1978): History, Assessment, and Views of a Problematic Presence." In this text, which amounts to exhaustive symptomal reading of the entire Italian reception of Schmitt's thought, beginning with the first commentaries on Schmitt's work in the 1920s (in the fascist journal *Lo Stato*) to the renewed debates that took place over Schmitt after 1972, Galli methodically worked through the silences, omissions, censures, and misinterpretations that marked each of the very different interpretations of Schmitt in Italy since the 1920s (ranging from fascist and Catholic to liberal and Marxist).[65] The central claim of Galli's essay was that none of these readings had been able to interpret Schmitt on his own terms, to offer a coherent account of the unity and basis of Schmitt's thought as a whole, or (in what really amounts to the same thing) to understand how the peculiar "contradictoriness" of Schmitt's *oeuvre* is intrinsically related to the thing Schmitt thinks.

In particular, Galli opened up a critique of the appropriation of Schmitt by thinkers on the "post-workerist" left, such as Mario Tronti and Massimo Cacciari. Galli noted that what thinkers such as Tronti and Cacciari most wanted from Schmitt was insight into the "autonomy of the political," which is to say, an understanding of political conflict outside of the institutions and practices of the State.[66] The trouble with this reading, Galli noted, was that it remained silent on the disturbing necessary condition of the political in Schmittian thought. As Galli explained, Schmitt's notion of the "autonomy of the political" could not be separated from a second Schmittian concept, one to which no egalitarian intellectual can or should consent: the decision on a public enemy, and the exclusion of that enemy from the space of politics.[67] Galli's critique is not, to be clear, moralistic; he does not, as did Jürgen Habermas, view the post-workerist turn to Schmitt as an attempt to "drive out the Devil with Beelzebub."[68] In his view, the problem it is subtler than that; it lies in the way the post-workerist use of Schmitt remained marked and constrained by the engagement with Schmitt inaugurated by Karl Löwith in 1935. In order to truly appropriate or deconstruct Schmittian thought—or, more modestly, even simply to come to terms with the "problematic presence" of Schmitt within Italian political thought—it would be necessary, Galli argued, to rethink the terms on which Löwith posed Schmitt's writings as a problem for philosophy.

Among the enduring claims of Löwith's 1935 text was his argument that Schmitt's decisionism had a philosophic provenance, namely, that it was derived from the work of Marx and Kierkegaard.[69] But, Löwith noted, whereas both Marx and Kierkegaard attempted to justify their decisionism in the name of some transcendent being or higher "court of appeal" (history for Marx, God for Kierkegaard), Schmitt's decisionism attempts no such justification; it is a "decision for decision's sake," Löwith observed, that affirms no transcendent being at all.[70] As such, Löwith argued, Schmitt's thought is destined to fail to accomplish its own aim. The point of Schmitt's decisionism, Löwith argues, is to counteract the age of "neutralization and depoliticization" inaugurated by liberal individualism and humanitarianism by retrieving criteria (such as the friend-enemy distinction) that could *give* measure and form *to* politics.[71] But, Löwith observed, Schmitt's decisionism in fact could not but *receive* its measure and form *from* politics. In the absence of a commitment to any norm but decision itself, Löwith argued, Schmitt's decisionism is incapable of giving form or measure to anything, and the content of any given decision must necessarily remain dependent on whatever accidental political situation happens to prevail at a given moment.[72] Even though Schmitt might then polemicize against the "endless dialogue" of what he calls the "political romantic," Löwith concluded, Schmitt's decisionism thus nevertheless shares with political romanticism a foundation in nihilistic "occasionalism." Exactly like the political romanticism to which it opposes itself, Löwith stated, Schmitt's decisionism derives its innermost substance from nothing more than accident, opportunism, and caprice.[73]

For Löwith, this explains why Schmittian thought could veer so wildly from topic to topic: Because of its occasionalism, Schmitt's work was incapable of not only rational self-justification but also (and indeed relatedly) internal self-consistency. It moreover explains why Schmitt's thought could have assumed no other form but polemic: In the absence of any higher norm, Löwith argues, Schmitt is constrained to derive the "correctness" of his arguments from the enemy against whom he happens to be attacking.[74] And it finally explains why Schmitt was obliged to abandon even, especially, the most distinctive hallmark of his own thought: In a situation where (as in 1935) the disorder presupposed by his decisionist thought would undermine not an enemy (liberalism) but now a friend (Nazism), Schmitt would abandon not only decisionism but also polemic itself, no longer writing as a critic of the State but now as its main apologist, a *Kronjurist* whose specific bureaucratic function is, in the worst Hegelian tradition, to explain the rationality of the real, and so to justify the irrationality of domination.[75]

The problem with Löwith's criticism of Schmitt, in Galli's view, is that it does not apply Löwith's own secularization thesis to the very criticism it itself practices. Löwith's 1935 essay, like his 1949 book *Meaning in History*, is centered on a claim about the insufficiency of modern criticism in relation to its own present. Criticism that lacks a measure outside of history by which to criticize the course and events of history, Löwith there argues, also will lack any grounds for resisting or opposing political evil in its present. Modern political thought, however, is grounded in a philosophy of history that not only secularizes Christian eschatology, but also abandons any notion of an otherworldly basis for judging good and evil in worldly events. Because of this abandonment, Löwith concludes, there is in modern (and not just Schmittian) political thought a disquieting inability to object meaningfully to the emergence of political nihilism. What's odd about this argument, however, is that Löwith does not consider the possibility that the very premise for his critique of modern nihilism—the very notion that the responsibility of the critic can and should be to stand outside of history in order to pass judgment on it—might owe its own genealogy to the same "immanentization of the *eschaton*" (as Galli sums up Löwith's secularization thesis[76]) that Löwith otherwise traces so assiduously.

If Galli's immanent critique of Schmitt may be considered a *recapitulation* of Löwith's 1935 essay on Schmitt—if it is, in other words, a repetition of Löwith's criticism that recuperates its unactualized potential and thus also redoubles its force—it is because Galli's point of departure implies an immanent critique of Löwith on precisely the question of "criticism" itself. Turning to the genealogy of modern criticism set forth by Reinhart Koselleck in his 1959 book *Critique and Crisis: Enlightenment and the Pathogenesis of Modern Society*, Galli argues that Schmitt's occasionalism is not the sign that Schmitt lacked a philosophy of history, but the mark of Schmitt's retrieval of a theological experience of criticism that had been secularized by the modern philosophy of history. According to Galli, the *occasio* that is at the root of Schmitt's occasionalism is both the precursor for, and incommensurable with, the concept of the "event" in the modern philosophy of history. As distinct from the concept of the event within modern historiography, however, the *occasio* in Schmittian thought is an opportunity in the grand sense of the word. It is not merely one among many interesting or significant happenings, but is an ecstatic experience—an experience of *kairòs*[77]—in which the infinite irrupts within the order of the finite. This irruption not only throws into question the coherence and self-evidence of sequential temporal order (the mathematized and static time of *chronos* that is the primary measure and indispensable condition for the modern philosophy of history), but also, and in that same gesture, establishes a point from which it becomes possible to relate *to* a given historical moment on terms, and in a mode, that do not derive their intelligibility *from* that moment.

The experience of the *occasio* is not, then (as Löwith argued), a surrender to the immediate demands of a given historically determined situation; it is not a version of Hegel's "the real is rational." In the form it assumes in Kierkegaard's writings, for example, the *occasio* is rather a nondialectical relation between the finite and the infinite, an irruption in which the infinite fully presents itself inside the finite, exceeding and enveloping the finite from within.[78] Implicit in this experience of the *occasio* is a much different relationship between thinking and being than the relationship between critic and history Löwith finds lacking in Schmitt. The "critic" is here not the one who must strive to stand *outside* of history in order to render a juridical or moral verdict on it. This, as Koselleck shows, amounts precisely to a repression of the political in the Schmittian sense.[79] The critic is rather the one who remains so completely open to the experience of crisis—of the irruption within the order of historical time of that which historical time cannot contain—that he comes to occupy a position of *interior exteriority* with respect to historical time. The "exteriority" that irrupts in a crisis of this sort is *an either-or*: It is a need for decision that is so exigent, so stark, and so demanding that it exposes *a representational deficit* in the hermeneutic horizons that, taken together, would ordinarily allow for the possibility of comprehending a judgment as a "rational" or "judicious" act. Understood in this sense, criticism is not an act of rendering "impartial judgment" upon this or that crisis; it is not the work of a historian who stands outside of this or that event in order to mediate and evaluate it with reference to the equally transcendent schematas of the particular and the universal. It is an immanence of the critic within the crisis that is so complete and so extreme that it *therefore—because* and *by virtue of* this immanence—leaves the critic without any immunity to the representational deficit that is the core of any crisis worthy of the name. *Immanence of the critic within the crisis, excess of the crisis within the critic*: The more the critic enters into the crisis, the more the crisis enters into the critic, the more the crisis exceeds, from within, what Kant would call our "schemata"—the "rules" or "measures" in accordance with which we are able to imagine general concepts, and which, as such, allow us to judge, classify, evaluate, and otherwise make sense of our experience.[80]

Criticism is not here an act at all; it is an experience of passivity. It is an openness to the element of unimaginability and unnameability that is intrinsic to any true crisis; it is a vulnerability to the irruption of an epochal lack into one's ability to judge, speak, and act. The more complete this passivity, the more fully this epochal lack will irrupt into and disrupt from within the schemata that ordinarily would be available to us for the purposes of orienting our thinking, judging, speaking, and acting. "Criticism" is here a name for the difficult task of *reflecting upon* and *giving voice to* this experience of irruption, and "critic" a name for the one who suffers to undertake that task. To read Schmitt's criticisms of modernity on their own terms—for, as Galli has recently noted, Koselleck's book on crisis and critique originates in Schmitt's 1938 book on *Leviathan*[81]—is to understand Schmitt as a critic in this precise sense: a thinker who is exterior to his time only and precisely to the extent that he internalizes its innermost crises.[82]

The Political and the Polemical

The question of Schmitt's occasionalism, as Roberto Racinaro has argued, is the true crux of all Schmitt interpretation,[83] and Galli's recapitulation of Löwith's criticism of Schmitt on this point indeed allowed Galli to find a way to rethink Löwith's interpretation of Schmitt as a whole. Galli's rethinking of the *occasio* in Schmitt first of all enabled him to put forward a new interpretation of the "contradictoriness" that Löwith so easily (perhaps *too* easily) demonstrated in his critique of Schmitt. Arguing that "the dual value of Schmittian concepts has been accepted only in part" by Italian readers of Schmitt,[84] Galli concluded his 1979 essay with a call for a systematic reading of Schmitt that would take account of this contradictoriness by refusing the clear and distinct division that had emerged in Italian Schmitt scholarship between thoughtless polemical works, on the one hand, and works of political thought, on the other.[85] In the case of the reading of Schmitt advanced by the post-workerist left, this amounted to a very direct criticism; there is no way, Galli warned, to extract from Schmitt's text the ostensible "acceptable" (because of its status as political thought or even political science) concept of the "autonomy of the political" without also dragging along the "unacceptable" (because of its status as propaganda and ideology) concept of the sovereign's designation and exclusion of the public enemy.[86] These two concepts are at once distinct and inseparable; they are two parts of a single insight into the double-sided origin of the politics.[87]

The purpose of Galli's claim about the indistinction of politology and polemology in Schmittian thought was not, then, to urge relativistic indifference to these distinctions. Rather, it was to reveal the sense in which the equivocal *content* of Schmitt's political thought—that, precisely as Löwith put it, there is, for Schmitt, no political relation that is not rooted in some warlike intensity or potentiality[88]—was *also* the hermeneutic key to understanding the equivocal *form* of Schmitt's *oeuvre* as a whole. But whereas Löwith attributed the polemical quality of Schmitt's thought to an occasionalism that amounted to *a lack* of a philosophy of history, Galli attributes it to the occasionalism of a critic who is internal to the crisis. For if, as Galli argues, Schmitt's occasionalism implies a critic who enters into a specifically unmediated and immediate relation with the crisis he thinks, such that the subject of thought by definition reproduces in his thought the schema of the either-or that confronts him in the crisis,[89] then the critic who thinks the epochal crisis of modernity—which, as we shall see in a moment, is its ruination from within of the same sovereign peace that is the central justification for its institutions and practices—will remain troubled by a trace of the same latent "polemicity" (as Galli would put it) that troubles modernity as a whole. Any and all truly critical political thought will, on these grounds, retain the potential to revert to polemic.

Having thus rethought Schmitt's occasionalism, Galli was also able to interpret Schmitt's Nazism in a way that departed from Löwith. To the prevailing reading of Schmitt's Nazism (which pivots on the question of how to "periodize" Schmitt's Nazism, and more often than not dissolves into microscopic bickering over historicist and biographical details), Galli offers a simple but bold hermeneutic alternative: There is only a single synchronic caesura that runs throughout Schmitt's entire *oeuvre*, a single "immanent risk" that marks *all* "phases" of Schmittian thought.[90] Galli draws out the dialectic of this risk by seizing upon a remark by Schmitt in his preface to the 1972 Italian edition of *Der Begriff des Politischen*. There, after a short précis of his theses on the criterion of the political, Schmitt addresses the question of the hermeneutic horizon within which his theses ought to be interpreted. The impulse of his theses, Schmitt insisted, is scientific (*scientifico*), in the sense that "they do not make any move to situate themselves in the right and to push their adversaries into non-right. On the other hand, 'science is but a small power' [English in the original], and in the ambit of the political the freedom of independent thought always entails a supplementary risk."[91]

It is essential to understand that even though, on Schmitt's own terms, this "supplementary risk" is antithetical to scientific thought as Schmitt understands it, there is nevertheless no way to rid or purify Schmittian scientific thought of that risk. The inconsistency of Schmittian science with itself—its permanent and constitutive openness to polemic, ideology, and propaganda—is utterly consistent with science in the Schmittian sense; it is the manifestation, in Schmitt's own criticism, of the crisis Schmitt thinks in and through his genealogy of the political, of his discovery that modern political institutions are radically incomplete in relation to its own attempts at peace, security, and reconciliation. "The objectivity of conflict," as Galli pithily put it in 1986, "implies the non-objectivity . . . of science."[92] Or, as Galli has put it in his most recent book on Schmitt,

> Schmitt's intellectual presentation is born in, and is characterized by, a polemical impulse, a positioning that is existentially oriented and militant: it is *thanks to* this impulse and this positioning—and

> not *despite* it—that Schmitt is capable of a radical analysis of
> politics . . . . Ideology is the *porta Inferi* [the "gate of hell"] that
> leads Schmitt to knowledge of the "political," and it is the dramatic
> and irritating condition thanks to which Schmitt is not only an
> ideologue but also an important thinker.[93]

If Schmittian "political science" is science not *despite* but *because of* its polemical and ideological character, then political science that is *not* plagued by the risk (and perhaps temptation) of its own polemicity is *not political thought at all*. It is thought that, to the contrary, *suppresses* the political, that stands outside the crisis it criticizes, that seeks to immunize itself from the crisis that the "political" itself is. Political thought that does not seek to immunize itself from the political, however, will suffer from a very different risk. It will share with modern politics a certain tragic susceptibility to dissolve itself from within. It will reproduce, now in the mode of thought, the constitutive risk that troubles all modern political institutions: It will be unable to become what it is without also supplementing itself with a polemicity that threatens to undermine its form, coherence, and integrity as thought. But just as political thought that fully *suppresses* its polemicity is not truly political thought, neither is political thought that fully *succumbs* to this immanent risk. By Schmitt's own account, it becomes something else: polemic, "an attempt to push its adversary into non-right," or, put simply, the epistemological equivalent of the destruction of the unjust enemy, the unbracketed hostility that Schmitt regarded as a plague upon the house of the modern.

On these hermeneutic grounds, the task of reading Schmitt is not to quarantine his Nazism to the period from 1933 to 1936 in order to liberate the rest of his work for neutral analytic "use" or even for leftist reappropriation. Nor is it, on the basis of a deeply ambivalent logic of taboo, to treat the whole of Schmittian thought as if were tainted, as though Schmitt's anti-Semitism were somehow so powerful and mysterious in its ways that it is akin to a contagious and communicable disease, an incurable illness against which the only possible safeguard is complete and total immunization. It is to understand Schmitt's Nazism as the extreme actualization of a potential for regression and domination that is internal not only to Schmittian thought, but also, as Horkheimer and Adorno argued, the

Enlightenment itself.[94] The immanent risk of Schmittian thought, Galli wrote in 1979, is "the risk of transforming scientific exposition into propaganda, of surrendering to the polemicity (*polemicità*) implicit in the discovery of the political in order to support, historically, a contingent political practice."[95] That, according to Galli, "Schmitt fell into this risk precisely when he 'used' the general form of the 'political' in a pro-Nazi sense"[96] does not, however, mean that this development of Schmitt's thought was either necessary or inevitable. Parting ways with Löwith on this point, Galli argues that

> if it is true that Schmitt's Nazi phase fully realized all of the risks inherent in the structure of Schmittian thought, it is also true that this realization is ultimately a betrayal—both theoretical and practical—that does not occur necessarily or automatically, but that instead requires a conscious personal will, dictated primarily by opportunism, and academic and political ambition.[97]

Here, where Galli's understanding of Schmitt seems to be at its most "forgiving" (for having abstained from polemic), it is, in fact, at its most damning. Phrased in its sharpest possible terms, Galli's point is not only that Schmitt is personally responsible for his Nazism (he was not, in other words, held "hostage" by the Nazis), but also that Schmitt's evil was banal in the Arendtian sense of the word. It was an evil not of the exception but of the norm, the evil latent in a *paterfamilias* who limits his care and concern to his career, his security, and the security of his family.[98] It follows that Schmitt's evil is not to be sought in his thought, but rather in what Arendt might call his "thoughtlessness" (her later, more philosophical term for the "banality of evil").[99] In the Arendtian sense, thoughtlessness is not the same as a simple *lack* of thought; it does not imply that Schmitt became a Nazi in a fit of absentmindedness. It implies that Schmitt's Nazism is the complete actualization of the polemicity that Schmitt could not fail to think if he was to remain loyal to his insight into the "political," yet to which he could not fully succumb if his insight into the "political" was to retain its character as thought. It is a sign that Schmitt's thought is, as Adorno might say, "non-identical" with itself.[100] And this, in turn, has a startling implication: Another realization of Schmitt's thought is possible, one to which Schmitt the person would not consent, but to which his impersonal thought cannot but yield.

A Genealogy of Politics

The consistency, focus, and depth with which Galli proceeded to pursue this immanent critique of Schmitt in the ensuing decade is nothing less than extraordinary. Between 1981 and 1991, Galli, now teaching at his *alma mater*, translated into Italian a number of important yet oddly neglected texts by Schmitt, including Schmitt's *Political Romanticism* (1919), *Roman Catholicism and Political Form* (1923), and *The Leviathan in the State Theory of Thomas Hobbes* (1938). He realized the program he announced in 1979 not only in his comprehensive introductions to his translations (as well as to Simona Forti's 1983 Italian translation of Schmitt's 1956 *Hamlet oder Hekuba*), but also in a series of essays on Schmitt's relation to Ernst Jünger, war, and Catholicism (among other topics).[101] And in 1996, Galli's labor culminated in the publication of his monumental 936-page *Genealogia della politica. Carl Schmitt e la crisi del pensiero politico moderno* (Genealogy of Politics: Carl Schmitt and the Crisis of Modern Political Thought).

Written with a hermeneutic rigor and sustained analytic attention that reminded one reader of "the august tradition of the great philological monographs of the classics,"[102] Galli's *Genealogia* is quadruply systematic. It is, to begin, a "historico-critical . . . reconstruction of the internal logic of Schmittian argumentation" that accounts for all of Schmitt's writings, in the mode of a symptomal reading, and that has as its aim a claim on the essence and basis of Schmittian thought from within its own immanent horizon.[103] Because no such reading could avoid paying attention to the crises to which Schmittian criticism is internal, Galli also engages in an "external contextualization" of Schmittian logic, discerning in the contradictoriness of Schmitt's texts the traces of select and pivotal events.[104] This contextualization is not, however, historicist; it does not seek to undercut the autonomy of Schmittian thought with reference to its determinants in its immediate cultural and political context. Galli argues that the fundamental crisis to which Schmittian thought is internal is not limited in place and time to the Weimar Republic or to Nazi Germany; it is instead an epochal crisis, the crisis of modern mediation as such. To support this claim, Galli situates Schmitt in the history of modern political philosophy, explaining how Schmitt inherits a crisis in philosophical mediation that begins with Hegel and Marx, reaches its turning point in Kierkegaard and Weber, and dissolves in Nietzsche.[105] In the process, Galli engages in a systematic overview of the secondary literature on Schmitt in German, Italian, Spanish, French, and English. The critical apparatus that results from this labor (Galli's footnotes alone take up nearly three hundred pages) does not, however, merely communicate bibliographic information; it adds up to a second book, an extension of Galli's 1979 "symptomal reading" of Schmitt commentary in Italy to Schmitt commentary worldwide.

The central claim of Galli's *Genealogia* is that Schmitt's accomplishment was to have opened himself to, in order to radicalize, the crises that together constitute the origin of the modern epoch (where "origin" is understood as *Entstehung* or *archē*).[106] Schmitt is consequently, on Galli's read, a specifically genealogical critic of modernity: Schmitt's single-minded focus, according to Galli, was to grasp the origin of the strangely double-sided energy he perceived in the institutions and practices of modern politics. Schmitt's discovery, Galli argues, was that this energy derived from "an originary crisis—or, better still, an *originary contradiction*—which is not a simple contradiction, but, rather, the exhibition of two sides, two extremes," such that "the origin of politics is not, in either of its two sides, an objective *foundation* for politics, but rather its *foundering* or *unfounding* (*sfondamento*)."[107] The "political" is Schmitt's name for this originary crisis, this free-floating energy that undermines the very institutions and practices it simultaneously founds, that deforms the same political forms it produces, and that disorders the very systems of thought to which it gives rise. By fixing his gaze on this origin, Schmitt realized that modern political thought (and consequently too the liberal democratic institutions and practices whose modes of self-justification it grounds and sustains) is divided against itself in a nondialectical manner. At the same time that it emerges from and even implicitly feeds upon a crisis it is incapable of resolving, modern political thought also accounts for this incapacity by suppressing the symptoms of the crisis, compensating for own incoherence with ever more moralistic reaffirmations of the unquestionable necessity of its own explicit goals.

The core problematic of Schmittian thought, Galli will consequently argue, cannot then be reduced to any one of the themes of Schmitt's various texts (the distinction between exception and norm, theology and politics, decision and discussion, friend and enemy, constituting power and constituted power, land and sea, limited and unlimited warfare, European center and colonial frontier, and so on). It is Schmitt's discovery that all of the forms of modern politics share a common trait, a birthmark that, in turn, attests to their common origin; despite the many and various differences between modern political thinkers—indeed as the silent but generative core of those differences—the epochal unity of modern political thought derives from its distinctive doubleness, its simultaneous impossibility and necessity, or, in short, its "tragicity."[108] This doubleness, Galli argues, is the hermeneutic horizon within which it becomes possible to grasp the systematicity of Schmitt's contradictory *oeuvre* as a whole. Schmitt's *oeuvre* unfolds in such a way, Galli argues, that

> beginning precisely with its contradictions—taking those contradictions, as it were, seriously—it is possible to reconstruct, in a non-extrinsic mode, a better part of the argumentive and conceptual machine of Schmitt in the various phases of his thought, thus pinning down the Chameleon into a form and forcing the Sphinx to reveal its face and its enigma.[109]

The "essential theme" of his book, Galli continues,

> is that the many apparently contradictory aspects of Schmitt's thought are in fact the manifestations of the work of a problem, and that this problem is consubstantial with an intellectual and political space that is definable in a general sense as "the modern epoch," and that this problem—which is shared, albeit in other forms, in the scientific experiences of the main legal and political thinkers of the first half of our century—permits us to perform a rereading of Schmittian thought that illuminates not only its greatness, but also its limitations and its miseries.[110]

Galli's name for this problem, which according to him is the real source of the contradictoriness of Schmitt's writings,[111] is the "origin of politics." Developing claims he had already announced in 1979,[112] Galli argues that the specificity of Schmitt's genealogical insight derives from the *occasio* at the core of Schmittian thought. Schmitt wrote at a juncture in European politics in which inside and outside, peace and war, civil and military, enemy and criminal were entering into the gray of a twilight, and in which a certain warlike polemicity was consequently emerging as the normal mode of being for political institutions and practices the explicit and definitive aspiration of which was reasonable discussion, transparent representation, and rational mediation.[113] Instead of interpreting this crisis of representation from modernity's own various privileged points of internal self-understanding (the State, the Subject, Society, or Reason), Galli argues, Schmitt instead sought to understand it with reference to the catastrophe from which modernity itself emerged, namely, the dissolution of the specifically Christian form of representation that governed political order in medieval Europe.[114] To give a name to this lost form of representation—this peculiar and specifically imperial ability to embrace any and all antitheses (life and death, Heaven and Earth, God and Man, past and future, time and eternity, good and power, beginning and end, reason and nonreason, etc.) in order to absorb them into one unified form—Schmitt took a term from the medieval Catholic thinker Nicholas de Cusa: *complexio oppositorum*. According to Galli, Schmitt understood the *complexio* neither as a dialectical synthesis (a simple coincidence of opposites), nor as an eclectic relativism (a jumble of plural and variegated qualities), but rather as "a form in which life and reason coexist without forcing," a single hierarchy the integrity of which derives, above all, from the way it reconciles and preserves many different, even opposed forms of life in the single "glorious form" of Christ's Person.[115] For Schmitt, Galli argues, the genealogical significance of the *complexio* is not theological but political: Schmitt is interested in the *complexio* because of the way in which its mode of representation—the extreme publicity and visibility through which all opposites coincided in the immediate mediacy of Christ's Person—in turn called into being a relatively stable and enduring political order.[116]

It is on the basis of this capacity for a mode of representation to constitute a political order (or what Galli calls "morphogenetic power") that Schmitt understands the modern. With the events that together opened the modern epoch (such as the Copernican Revolution, the Wars of Reformation, and the conquest of America), the *complexio* and the Order of Being it sustained could no longer be treated as a self-evident "given" that could be presupposed *by* political thought. In the absence of a coherent and integrative Idea in which opposites can coincide without conflict—indeed, under the unprecedented conditions of theological civil war in which the Person of Christ was no longer the basis of European *peace* but was now precisely both a source of and a stake in European *conflict*—political and juridical Power became disconnected from theological and moral Good, and the question of how to mediate opposing forces and qualities through representation suddenly emerged as an anxious and explicit question *for* political thought.[117]

According to Galli, Schmitt understands modern mediation to originate as an unwitting, precarious, and partial response both to this question and to the epochal catastrophe that occasions it. Modern mediation marks the attempt, on the part of a European subject who suddenly finds himself alone in the universe, to accomplish a set of morphogenetic tasks bequeathed to him by the *complexio*—such as the creation of order, the reconciliation of opposites, and the accomplishment of peace on Earth—but now without the support of a *Gestalt* in which everything, however opposed, had its place—now, in other words, only through an ad hoc use of his own immanent powers.[118] In modernity, in short, the European subject is faced with the task of producing *ex nihilio* the political form, peace, and reconciliation it once could presuppose in the *complexio*. It pursues these aims through, on the one hand, instrumental reason (the mathematization and technical mastery of nature, up to and including human nature), and, on the other, through a new form of representation, which seeks to mediate contradictions between opposing forces, but which also recognizes, without also fully realizing why, that its attempts at mediation are somehow already destined, in advance, to failure. The reconciliation of opposites, the *complexio* achieved felicitously with reference to the Person of Christ, is now the work of an unhappy consciousness, a person in the juridical sense who is capable of peace, reconciliation, and order only at the cost of a ceaseless and restless reflection on division and disorder.[119]

The State is modernity's solution to this predicament. In the place once occupied by the hierarchical *complexio* of the Catholic Church's "glorious form," Hobbesian political philosophy proposes the egalitarian simplicity of a new beginning—a revolutionary *tabula rasa* that articulates the rational necessity of peace, and establishes the impersonal laws of the

State, through a manifestly geometrical deduction.[120] But the impersonal laws of the State can only produce political form and exercise morpho-genetic power in an ungrounded manner, by presupposing the complete separation of Power from the Good. Indeed, the strength of impersonal law (its principled insistence on the formal equality of all persons before the law) is predicated on a displacement of the morphogenetic power of the *complexio* (a hierarchy centered upon the Person of Christ). In the absence of a felicitous use of morphogenetic power, the State finds that law alone is insufficient for accomplishing the aims it inherits from the *complexio*, and discovers itself to be in need of supplements for its impersonal law. The State discovers this supplement by placing instrumental reason (which is to say, the neutralization of conflict through *dispositifs* of discipline, governmentality, and security, but also, if necessary, through the use of military and, later, police forces) at the service of repeated sovereign decisions that reproduce a semblance of the unity and integrity of Roman Catholic visibility and publicity by setting aside the impersonality of law (with its insistence on formal equality) in order to fabricate a public enemy, whose schema can then serve as the point of reference for the formation of the unity and integrity of a newly secular public.[121] In short, the State achieves the aims bequeathed to it by the *complexio* to the extent that it now includes exclusion.[122]

Both of these techniques, however, repeatedly undermine the end to which they aim. The State's attempt to create political form and maintain order through the use of force results in an "armed peace" that, in the concrete, amounts to a constant preparation for the next war, while its attempt to produce and maintain public unity and integrity through decisions on a public enemy constantly reintroduces into the internal space of the State a trace of the same unlimited hostility, the suppression of which is (as in Hobbes's elimination of the *bellum omnium contra omnes*) the main justification for the State's existence in the first place.[123] The means for resolving conflict within Christian Europe turn out to be plagued by a similar infelicity, only now acted out on a global scale: Europe attempts to expunge and expel the trace of unlimited hostility by instituting the *jus publicum europæum*, which creates an order of limited hostility (formalized warfare, distinction of criminal and enemy) within Europe only by demanding and justifying an order of unlimited hostility toward Europe's exterior (in the form of colonial conquest and genocide). In every case, in other words, modern political order discovers that it *must aim at*, but *cannot attain*, a set of goals—peace on Earth, mediation and reconciliation between opposites, the production of political form—that have been set for it, and indeed bequeathed to it, by the very form of medieval representation it also aggressively displaces. Modern political mediation therefore finds itself in a position where it can only fully legitimate its existence with reference to a set of inherited concepts to which it is also especially vulnerable. It discovers that it is fated to attempt a set of tasks (the *ex nihilio* creation of political form, peace, and reconciliation) that is both *necessary* (because the *complexio* is now missing, because opposing forces remain, and because peace and reconciliation provide the modern state with its *raison d'être*) and *impossible* (because, above all, in the thoroughly secularized modern epoch, there is no equivalent to the theological concept of miraculous creation; there is only making, fabrication, production—or instrumental reason, the work of *homo faber*).[124] To even approximate the realization of its inner aims—which are, to repeat, not its own, but those it inherits from the *complexio*—modern mediation seeks to forget the medieval origin that is at once indispensable for it and unsettling to it, and to that exact degree leaves itself exposed to destabilization by a genealogy written from a Catholic standpoint.

But though Schmittian thought is thus, indeed, for Galli, a Catholic genealogy of the modern,[125] Galli also cautions that Schmitt's relation to Catholicism not be misunderstood as one of religious belief or even nostalgia. When Schmitt thinks the emergence of modern mediation with reference to its secularization of the *complexio*, he does not suppose that a return to the *complexio* is either desirable or possible.[126] Nor, on Galli's read, does Schmitt really even mourn the passing of the *complexio*. Schmitt's achievement is rather to have occupied that standpoint *from which* a thoroughly secularized modern mediation genealogically derives its innermost aims, *through which* a thoroughly secularized modern mediation refuses to understand itself, and *to which* all of its institutions and practices are thus especially vulnerable.[127] Schmitt's idiosyncratic reading of the *complexio* is, in other words, a way to think the "origin of politics" outside of the standard points of self-understanding that modernity privileges in its own self-justifying historical narratives of its emergence.

It is an attempt to name a crisis in which the old order (the *complexio*) has irreversibly dissolved and in which the new order (the modern State-Form) cannot accomplish the goals it inherits from the *complexio* (reconciliation and peace).[128] Schmitt does not, then, analyze modernity from the standpoint of a fully intact Catholic faith or ideology; nor does he really even presuppose that his account of *complexio* is accurate (which is why empirical or historicist refutations of Schmitt miss the mark). The *complexio* is simply the blind spot of modern mediation, that concept that enables us to grasp in genealogical terms the reconciliation at which modern mediation must aim but cannot achieve.

Here, indeed, because of the manifestly tragic character of the crisis Schmitt thinks, we need to clarify the limits of our earlier comparison of Kierkegaard's *occasio* to Schmitt's. For Schmitt, the crisis that the *occasio* imposes upon the thought and being of the critic is not the plentitude of an infinity. It is the poverty of a Nothing. It is the utter privation of order, an unsayable opacity internal to the critic's knowledge that is not a "trauma" in the psychoanalytic sense, but simply an absence of form-giving speech, the lack of any language that can resolve or even just describe the unprecedented crises of the modern, the intrusion of the nameless into the order of the named. Indeed, it is this vacuum, this "inability to explain," that then serves as the inexhaustible resource for the prolixity of the critic's criticism.[129] And while it would be tempting to make sense of this epochal crisis-event by calling it an *interregnum*, Galli does not, to my knowledge, do so in any of his writings, perhaps because this would be to use a juridical concept, and to give juridical form, to an experience and an event that, to the contrary, mark the *failure* of all juridical forms, both modern and medieval, and that consequently would be more properly characterized as an epochal anomie or, as Galli would later write, *chaos*.[130]

A Hermeneutics of the "Political"

Chaos is also the word that many readers would choose to describe Schmitt's *oeuvre*—and not without reason. Read alongside one another, Schmitt's terms and concepts seem to form nothing but an incoherent maze, a jumble of shifting terms that veer from the archaic to the pragmatic, from the systematic to the oracular. What indeed is the relation between the idiosyncratic theory of "irruption" Schmitt sets forth in his 1956 *Hamlet or Hecuba* and the obnoxious defense of Raoul Malan he lays out in his 1963 *Theory of the Partisan*? Between the crisp decisionist thesis he formulates in his 1922 *Political Theology* and the critique of decisionism he offers in his 1934 *Three Types of Juristic Thought*? Between the systematic analysis of "constituting power" he outlines in his 1927 *Constitutional Theory* and the rambling rant he addresses to his daughter in his 1942 *Land and Sea*? Given this jarring conceptual excess, many Schmitt scholars have simply abandoned altogether the ordinary but indispensable hermeneutic task of inquiring into the common horizon and specific unity of the Schmittian *oeuvre*. In the absence of this inquiry, the reading of Schmitt has taken place largely by way of synecdoche, where a handful of random but fashionable concepts (decision and exception, friend and enemy, *nomos*, etc.) stand in as names designating the essence of the strange and forbidding heterogeneity of the Schmittian *oeuvre*, and where Schmitt's own person becomes a synonym for a series of mutually exclusive political categorizations.[131]

Galli's approach to Schmitt in the *Genealogia* provides a way to exit this maze. On Galli's read, Schmitt's *oeuvre* amounts to a single metonymic chain, an integrated series of attempts to name a crisis for which modernity itself has no name: the real contradiction that is the origin of modern politics.[132] Consider, for example, Galli's reading of Schmitt's famous 1922 utterance, "sovereign is he who decides the exception."[133] In many commentaries on Schmitt's *Political Theology*, this formulation has been extracted from Schmitt's text with few, if any, worries about interpretive perplexity—as if Schmitt's remark on the decision were somehow magically exempt from the standard problems of hermeneutics—and then abstracted into the sort of sterile logical puzzle that is ordinarily limited to certain traditions of analytic philosophy. The questions that result from this process of abstraction quickly terminate in paradox: If an exception becomes a norm, is that exception still an exception? Is the norm still a norm? Does the norm then become an exception to the exception?[134] It is in no small part thanks to the "relevance to current events" promised in and by this procedure of extraction and abstraction that Schmittian thought became popularized in the years after September 11, 2001. During this time, an ostensibly Schmittian "logic of the exception" became a self-evident or obvious way to put a name to the Bush administration's long train of abuses and usurpations. Was it not, after all, George W. Bush himself who referred to himself as "the decider"? Is this not a perfect example of the "logic" we see in Schmitt?[135]

A much different picture emerges once we interpret Schmitt's phrase within the hermeneutic horizon Galli proposes. In Galli's view, Schmitt's 1922 formulation of the exception cannot be understood apart from his 1923 inquiry into the "political Idea" of Roman Catholicism.[136] According to Galli, Schmitt seizes on the concept of the *complexio* in 1923 in order to put a name to the representational matrix that gave shape and form to medieval politics. On Galli's read, Schmitt's interest in the *complexio* is not that of a believer; it is genealogical in character, and as such it presupposes the interpretive field opened up by Nietzsche's criticism of Christianity as "Platonism for 'the *Volk*.'"[137] In Platonic political philosophy, as in the medieval *complexio*, the Idea is a strictly visible phenomena. According to Heidegger (whose work is, on Galli's read, at once very close to and very distant from Schmitt's[138]), the Idea is, for Plato, not a "mental" or "cognitive" activity, but rather the "outward look," "appearance," or "aspect" according to which something shows or reveals itself to thought, and which provides thought with a pattern according to which thought may then measure its own order and coherence.[139] The highest of all Ideas, for Plato, is the Good; it is that unchanging and unchangeable pattern in the light of which everything can be seen and understood.[140] In *The Republic*, the Idea of the Good is a paradigm for the undivided soul and city, and the thought that measures itself with reference to the visibility or perceivability the Idea provides also finds itself empowered to liberate itself from the dark and bewildering "cave" of a world governed by contradictory and ever-changing appearances. In Schmitt's account of the *complexio*, Christianity's Platonic inheritance is central, if inexplicit; the "political Idea" that is so central to *Roman Catholicism and Political Form* is, like its Platonic precursor, a paradigm for undivided order, only an order that now *realizes* the Idea of the unchanging and undivided Good, rendering it visible in and through the Person of Christ.[141]

Interpreted within this horizon, Schmitt's 1922 utterance has a meaning very different than the "logic" so often ascribed to it today. The exception now comes into view as an answer to the genealogical question that frames all of Schmitt's text without also being explicitly stated in any one of those texts. This question does, to be sure, involve a certain sort of "logic," but not in the analytic sense of the word. Framed as a problem for genealogy, the theoretical interest of the exception is not that it violates the ostensibly timeless law of noncontradiction; it is that the exception originated as a makeshift technique for artificially miraculating "glorious political forms" in an age defined by the sudden lack of an integrative Idea in which opposites could coincide without conflict.[142] Understood in these terms, the exception gives rise not to an abstract formal logic, but to a concrete logic of form; unlike the Idea it seeks to replace, and against whose lived and felt absence it tacitly measures its efficacy, the exception can reconcile opposites and fabricate political form only contingently and infelicitously, by deciding on an enemy, and thus too by constantly reintroducing a trace of the very polemicity its "armed peace" was designed to exclude. The exception is therefore contradictory to the core, for it unmakes the same political forms it strives to make; but the core of its contradictoriness cannot but remain constitutively opaque to the procedures of formal logic, for modernity's very reliance on this sort of formal rationality is *itself*—like the exception, which is indeed both its direct opposite and its mirror double—an incomplete and ad hoc response to modernity's own catastrophic origin.

> On the one hand, the concrete exception is a conflict that negates all order and all self-enclosed form. On the other hand, the concretization of the exception can be thought only in terms of form, which is to say as a "concrete" superimposition of a "logic," of the power of the absent Idea (this is precisely the *logic of the concrete*). And this originary contradiction of politics—its being suspended between contingency and Idea—is insuperable and irreconcilable: it is *not* removable, and it remains *internal to* every order.[143]

Because the contradictoriness of the exception is the symptom of a conflictual energy that is at once *pervasive within the institutions and practices of modern politics* and *inaccessible to the basic concepts of modern political thought*, it cannot be resolved simply by criticizing it as "illogical" or "irrational." As Galli reads Schmitt, it can be illuminated only by revealing, in genealogical terms, the absent Idea that constitutes the unstable origin of modern politics as such.

It is this permanent and originary contradiction that furnishes the political energy that renders order effective, which in turn remains possible only through the *political* intensity that springs from the "difference in potential" between exception and Idea. Order is therefore historical and concrete, not tautological or formalistic, only because of the action of this complex origin—which is to say, only because the concrete historical crisis from which it originated has continued to provide energy, so much violence and vibrant polemicity, which it retains, contradictorily, only as awareness of the necessity and obligation of form. However, the origin is, at the same time, the fatal destruction of order, one that can occur in two guises. On the one hand, even if the origin of politics is not recognized and controlled, it nevertheless speaks anyway, but in a destructive modality: its exceptional side becomes absolute hostility, and its regulating side becomes inert and shapeless formalism. But even if the source is fully acknowledged, a consciously political practice that opens up the political crisis as its origin will itself be necessarily traversed by contradiction: it will be, that is to say, effectual but unstable, perpetually exposed to mobilization, to a political intensity that, at least potentially and in advance (and even against Schmitt's own intentions), destructures any form that claims to be transparent and closed in on itself. The origin both determines and also undetermines [*indetermina*] every order, rendering it both practical and incomplete, both possible and indeed indispensable as much as it is contingent and menacing. The originary contradiction thus acts within order with as much *intensity* as it does *opacity*, and therefore prevails over all forces of understanding and active formation. In sum, political orders find in concrete historical crisis their home, their political energy, but also their potential order.[144]

By explaining the "logic of the exception" in terms that are concrete and genealogical rather than abstract and formalistic, Galli is able to reveal its constitutive relationship to another of Schmitt's more prominent concepts: the *nomos* of the Earth. Some readers of Schmitt, operating on the basis of a non-Schmittian understanding of history, have interpreted Schmitt's concept of the *nomos* as a new and discontinuous phase of Schmittian thought—a postwar turn "away from" concerns of domestic law and "toward" those of international law. Other readers, operating on the assumption that *nomos* is simply a name for any especially broad conjunction of space and law, interpret the concept of *nomos* as little more than a sweeping methodological device—a totalizing concept somewhat akin to the *episteme* in the early work of Michel Foucault or the mode of production in Marxist thought. On Galli's read, by contrast, the *nomos* of the Earth is simply the last in a long chain of attempts by Schmitt to put a name to the unnameable origin of modern politics.[145] Like Schmitt's 1922 formulation of the sovereign exception (with which it is, in fact, nearly contemporaneous, for Schmitt's first discussion of *nomos* took place in his 1928 book *Constitutional Theory*[146]), his theory of *nomos* presupposes the absence of any political Idea—the absence, that is to say, of a measure for space rooted in a sense of enduring proportion and undivided harmony.[147] It is a theory of the process or action by which the political Idea, which in modernity can only be forced into being through techniques of artificial miraculation, now renders itself concrete in and through specific techniques of appropriating and dividing up the Earth. In grammatical terms, "*nomos*" is surely therefore a concrete noun, for it refers to the "brute geographical fact of *Landnahme*."[148] But, as Schmitt points out, *nomos* is crucially also an *action noun*, a name for an event, deed, or process,[149] and as Galli reads Schmitt, a *nomos* of the Earth comes into being precisely in and through the act of a cut, a "decision" that confers political form onto a space that otherwise lacks it; by dividing space into an inside and outside, the articulation of a *nomos* precisely also allows for the fabrication of the same sorts of political forms that sovereign exceptions attempt to produce (such as those between friend and enemy, police and military force, criminals and enemies, internal war [*stasis*] and external war [*polemos*]).

In this sense, Schmitt's "later" theory of *nomos* is not discontinuous but continuous with his "early" discussion of the "logic of the exception." The former, like the latter, is a name for the nonjuridical origin of modern juridical order, and for modernity's contingent and ad hoc techniques for ordering the disorder produced by the absent Idea at modernity's origin. It is "a theory of the origin of politics—a theory that, while 'enlarged' in comparison to the paradigm of decisionism, is consistent and compatible with that paradigm."[150] This consistency and compatibility extends to include the exception's infelicity and tragicity as a technique for the production of political form; on Galli's read, Schmitt's theory of the *nomos* is also, like his "logic of the exception," a name for a deed that is simultaneously also the source of its own undoing. Because the apparatus that produces the jurisdiction of the modern state rests on and responds to non-statal foundations, the space of the modern state is constitutively vulnerable to events that are not themselves directly statal in character (such as the emergence of revolutionary new technologies, like those of aerial warfare, that appropriate and divide space much differently than does the State), and it cannot respond to those events without also exceeding the very juridical theories and practices it is committed to preserving. "Space," for Schmitt, is not, then, "a neutral dimension in which the power of the political can actualize itself."[151] As Galli understands it, Schmitt's theory of the *nomos*, like his earlier writings on the "logic of the exception," is an attempt to understand how and why certain transformations in techniques for the production of space acquired the ability to undermine juridical institutions that are, within the horizon of their own self-understanding, completely self-determined and self-enclosed.

Nomos is not, then, for Schmitt, a conceptual instrument designed to conjoin or harmonize the fields of geography, jurisprudence, and political philosophy, or to put new empirical and descriptive powers at the disposal of those fields. It is not, that is to say, a tool for improving interdisciplinary cooperation and unity. It is a critical and genealogical term; it is made for cutting. Its purpose is to bring to light a tragic dynamic of structuring and destructuring that shadows all attempts by modern politics to achieve form and order, but which the disciplines of geography, political science, and jurisprudence, in the placid confidence of their quests to accurately represent their respective, discrete disciplinary objects ("space," "law," and "politics"), are alike fated to misrecognize. It is a name for modern thought's epochal failure to name the co-constitutive and antagonistic relation that has existed between space, law, and politics from the very inception of modern politics itself. *Nomos* is not, then, a lens; it is a catachresis.[152] For Schmitt, Galli argues,

> *nomos* is also, and at the same time, "antinomian." This is because it is a "cut," a decision (a *nomen actionis*) which also contains in itself a possibility, albeit an aporetic one, for measure, form, and order; because it is a "constitutive" event that is also structured as a constituent power; and because here, as always, the concretization of an order is given by its conscious insistence on its own unfounding [*sfondamento*].[153]

That both the "logic of the exception" and the *nomos* of the Earth are derivative of a more fundamental conflictual intensity or energy—a more originary or abyssal contradiction—does not, however, mean that these concepts can be reduced to a simple expression of a prior essence. Unlike Heidegger, for whom there is no *polis* that is not essentially grounded in the polarity of *polemos*, Schmitt does not, on Galli's read, ontologize war.[154] As distinct from Carl von Clausewitz, whose central question was war and for whom (as the cliché would have it) "politics is war pursued by other means," the term "war" is not, as Galli sees it, conceptually decisive in Schmitt.[155] Galli indeed will refer repeatedly to the problem of a certain polemicity in Schmitt's thought, but only in order to differentiate Schmitt's approach to war from *polemos* "as such." As Galli interprets it, Schmitt's emphasis on war is not ontological; its point is simply to show that the modern rational project of peace cannot complete itself on its own terms—that it cannot but include within itself a certain trace of conflict, a trace that is not representable precisely because it is the mark of the incompletion of modern political representation, and that is not an essence because it only comes into being when and where there is no longer any possibility of grounding it with reference to an Idea.[156] On this read, Schmitt's writings on war are thus neither an apology for war, nor an affirmation of the simple coincidence between war and politics. They amount to the discovery that modern political order is rendered possible by a radical disorder that brings with it a potential for war that is a permanent and constitutive possibility of modernity's technicized peace—this "armed peace" in which neutrality is impossible, because neutrality itself only gains its meaning by entering into conflict against conflict.[157] War is no more capable than the exception of serving as a synecdoche for the metonymy of Schmittian thought.

Indeed, on Galli's read, Schmitt's political thought ultimately cannot be limited to any single term or concept. Schmitt's achievement, as Galli sees it, was instead to have invented a gaze that was appropriate to the "doubleness" of modern politics. According to Galli, it was this gaze that allowed Schmitt to discern in the institutions, theories, and practices of modern politics the disturbances and disruptions created by an originary contradictoriness that Schmitt then called "the political." As Galli has summed up in his most recent book, Schmitt's *oeuvre* amounts to

> a political theory of the nexus—of the compulsion and at the same time the impossibility—between origin and form, between energy and order (decisionism, the "political"); an anti-progressive epochal theory of modern history as secularization (political theology); and an anti-universalistic theory of political space as *nomos*. The whole amounts to a genealogy of the Modern—of modern European politics—that renders itself possible in its early twentieth century crisis. This is a genealogy that consists in grasping the other side of the Modern, in saying the unsaid (the origin) of its *logos* and of its narration, of interpreting it not in its customary motives (the conflict between subject, society, and state, the struggle of ideologies), but according to the profound logic of its origin and its end. Schmitt's theory is a double gaze on the double face of the Modern.[158]

To put a name to this double gaze, Galli turns to a figure from Roman mythology whom Schmitt mentions, in passing, in *Roman Catholicism and Political Form*, to describe the "diversity and ambiguity" of the Roman Catholic Church: Janus.[159] For Ovid, Galli reminds his readers, "Janus symbolizes the double aspect of things, the passage from inside and outside, and the transmutations and the determinations of the elements that emerge from the primordial Chaos (and "Chaos," don't forget, was Janus's ancient name)."[160] As such, Galli suggests, Janus can serve as a fitting interpretive key to illuminate the unspoken core of Schmitt's restless genealogical inquiry into the "doubleness" or "contradictoriness" at the origin of modern politics.

> Schmitt, after all, had the same ambivalent ability to see the two sides of the "political." Schmitt was able to capture the transition between the formless and form, between chaos and order, between war and peace; he was also able to capture their fatal reversibility, which is to say, the new transition between form and crisis. But Schmitt's theory—a "vision" that, in his case, was also an "experience"—was designed to fit with the double face of the Modern. It was designed to fit with the simultaneous *disconnection* and *co-implication* between Idea and contingency that generates and courses through the Modern; and it was designed to fit both with the epoch's compulsion for order and with the impossibility of that order. Its wisdom allowed Schmitt to see in modern politics both God and the absence of God; it allowed him to think politics as that energy which at once establishes boundaries and transgresses them, which generates not only revolutions but also constitutions, which produces both decisions and forms.[161]

Skeptical though he may be of interpretations of Schmitt's political thought that reduce its theoretical metonymy into terminological or conceptual synecdoches, Galli thus affirms the possibility and even desirability of putting a name to the theoretical viewpoint that renders that metonymy visible. The point of this affirmation, however, is not simply to read Schmitt on his own terms. It is to train Schmitt's double gaze on a crisis in relation to which its constitutive blindness cannot but come into view.

The Challenge of Carlo Galli

It is not uncommon these days for readers of Schmitt to interpret *Concept of the Political* in perfect isolation from *Theory of the Partisan* and *Nomos of the Earth*, to criticize the overt anti-Semitism of *Three Studies on Juristic Thought* and *The Leviathan in the State Theory of Thomas Hobbes* while withholding comment on the analytic taxonomies of *Constitutional Theory*, to reread *Political Theology* without reference to *Roman*

Catholicism and Political Form, and so on. From a Gallian standpoint, this compartmentalization of the Schmittian *oeuvre* is lacking in both sense and purpose. Picture a group of Freud scholars each writing separately about distinct problems in psychoanalysis (one on sadism and masochism, a second on the death drive and the pleasure principle, a third on repression and sublimation), but all without a single mention of the unconscious, or a set of Marxist thinkers taking on distinct questions within historical materialism (commodity fetishism, use value and exchange value, base and superstructure), yet without also referring to labor. Strange though it may sound, an arrangement of precisely this sort very much pertains in Anglophone Schmitt scholarship today. While many intelligent studies have appeared in recent years on various elements in Schmitt's thought (such as the exception and decisionism, secularization and political theology, the distinction of *hostis* and *inimicus*, the *nomos* and the *katechon*, and above all Schmitt's Nazism, his anti-Semitism, and his relation to the Weimar Republic), very few, if any, have attempted to put a name to the common hermeneutic horizon from which all of these elements gain their singular sense and force. Tempting though it may be, however, to conclude that Galli does for Schmitt's *oeuvre* what Jacques Lacan did for Freud's and Louis Althusser for Marx's (Galli does, after all, perform something very much like a "return to Schmitt," explicating the textual principles on the basis of which alone the specific unity of Schmitt's theoretical formation may then come to light), Galli's rereading of Schmitt is ultimately very different from Lacan's return to Freud or Althusser's return to Marx, for it is not an attempt to renew or revive Schmitt's teachings. The true precedent for Galli's study of Schmitt is Adorno's immanent critique of Heidegger: Galli's great achievement is to have dissolved Schmitt's conceptual apparatus by "reliquefying" the *occasio* that is the innermost core of Schmittian thought.[162]

Look again at the crisis in relation to which Galli began reading Schmitt. Although the 1970s in Italy are often called the "years of lead" (*anni di piombo*), it is far from clear to what this name refers. Some commentators understand the "lead" in this phrase to be a reference to "bullets," whereas others understand it to suggest the decade's "heaviness" or "gravity." Matters do not become any more coherent once we shed cliché and euphemism for theoretical analysis. According to Lucio Castellano, the polemicity that emerged in Italy during the 1970s called into question not only the distinctions between peace and war (and thus, too, between army and society, soldier and civilian), but also the entire concept of politics associated with the State. "To erode the distinction between peace and war," Castellano wrote in 1979, "means placing oneself on the terrain of the critique of the State; it means doubting the principles of legitimization of political power, which affirms a distinction between 'State' and 'society,' 'public' and 'private,' 'general' and 'private.'"[163] For Norberto Bobbio, by contrast, the situation involved no categorical confusion whatsoever. In Bobbio's view, the 1969 Piazza Fontana massacre "marks a decisive turning point in the history of the First Republic, for with it the terrorist makes his first appearance as a political actor—an actor who has yet to disappear from our country's political scene."[164] His certainty notwithstanding, Bobbio's categorization and periodization were thrown into question by the very administrative body created by the Italian Parliament in 1988 to inquire into the events of the 1970s. Called the Parliamentary Commission of Inquiry on Terrorism in Italy, this body was the institutional counterpart to Bobbio's sense of philosophic and historical certainty, for its very title reflected its agreement with Bobbio that the polemicity of the 1970s could be adequately periodized and characterized in terms of "terrorism." After almost a decade of investigation, however, the head of the Commission, Giovanni Pellegrino, came to a much different conclusion; the "years of lead," Pellegrino argued, really should be understood as a revival of the conflicts of the 1940s, and its "terrorism" as "a sort of civil war, albeit one of low intensity."[165]

Years of lead, strategy of tension, armed struggle, guerilla warfare, terrorism, civil war — this metonymy is a mark of the difficulty, even impossibility, of settling on the name for the mode of polemicity that emerged in the 1970s. Conflict over the naming of a war is not, of course, unprecedented: It is a convention in modern warfare not only for wars to be retroactively named, but also for warring parties to enter into discord over the names of war, such that the end of war regularly coincides with the beginning of a "war of words" over the name of the wars they wage.[166] The events of the "years of lead," however, stretched this convention to its breaking point. Here we encounter not merely a conflict over the name of this or that war, but *a conflict over the basic concepts according to which it is even possible to give shape and form to conflict itself.* Not least because there are coherent reasons why each of these very different, even mutually exclusive, concepts should serve as a comprehensive name for the mode of polemicity that emerged in Italy during the 1970s, none of them has succeeded in becoming the comprehensive name for the sort of conflict that took place during these years, and the crisis of the 1970s has extended to include a crisis in the very schemata according to which its polemicity can become intelligible.

This "inability to explain" was not merely epistemological in character. In the late 1990s, Italy was riven by renewed polemics over the question of whether the Italian Parliament should offer amnesty to those who had been implicated in the violence of the 1970s. Amnesty had been a topic of hot dispute in Italy since at least 1979, when Lanfranco Pace and Franco Piperno published a controversial article arguing that the Italian state should offer release without prosecuting the thousand or so "communist fighters" who had been arrested and imprisoned under the charge of "terrorism." According to Pace and Piperno, these fighters committed their violent acts in the name of an "armed struggle" that, in turn, originated in and derived its legitimacy from enduring social problems, and as such they were neither terrorists nor common criminals but "political prisoners" who should be amnestied by the Italian state.[167] At the time, no less a thinker than Massimo Cacciari rejected this argument on the grounds that "it makes no sense at all to serve an amnesty to the politics that kills democracy."[168] But Cacciari's own rejection, which was predicated on the assumption that something like democracy even existed in Italy at the time, was itself symptomatic of a certain sort of senselessness. In a short 1997 essay on the topic of the return of the amnesty question in Italy, Giorgio Agamben pinpointed a paradox in the Italian government's stance on amnesty. At the same time that the government continued to insist that those who were implicated in the "years of lead" must be tried as common criminals, Agamben observed, the emergency measures (or "Special Laws") passed by the Italian government during the 1970s still remained in force. In Agamben's view, this was a telling inconsistency, for in juridical terms the very act of suspending law is already itself an implicit recognition of the existence of a civil war. Were the Italian government to choose to "preserve" the rule of law by insisting on prosecution instead of amnesty, Agamben thus concluded, it would not only *remember what it should forget* (the "civil war" of the 1970s); it would also *forget what it should remember* (its own normalization of the exception).[169] In Agamben's analysis, at least, the return of the amnesty question in Italy revealed a state whose very demand for the "rule of law" both disavowed and unwittingly confirmed the existence of civil war—which is to say, the absence and negation of any and all law. By the late 1990s, it would then seem, there were signs that the categorial crisis of the 1970s had blossomed into a juridical crisis as well.

Schmitt, to be sure, was no stranger to the fragility of the distinctions between peace and war, police and military force, public authority and private individuals, criminals and enemies, and norm and exception. Writing at a juncture in the twentieth century when these distinctions were already weakened, Schmitt seized on their occasional collapses as chances to expose and criticize the ineliminable trace of polemicity internal to all institutions, theories, and practices of modern politics. Crucially, however, Schmitt's exposures of these traces of polemicity always also presupposed the continued existence of the same modern politics he criticized. As Galli argues, Schmitt's criticisms of modern politics never failed to interpret every irregularity or exception with reference to some prior regularity or normality internal to modern politics.[170] Exemplary in this regard is the short criticism of the Allied "denazification" campaign Schmitt published in the Italian weekly *Il Borghese* in November 1951. Arguing that "denazification" was a clear case of a victorious military power using law to criminalize its defeated enemy, Schmitt faulted it for confusing war and peace, and for turning the administration of justice in postwar Germany into what he called "a cold civil war" (*una guerra civile fredda*). This malaise, Schmitt then proceeded to claim, was not without remedy; in his view, there existed a clear alternative to denazification, one that could be brought to light by recalling the origin of modern politics. In the history of humanity, Schmitt asserted, all civil wars that have not ended with the total destruction of the enemy have concluded with an amnesty, which he understood as "the restoration of normality" (*il repristino della normalità*) in which "no one can be persecuted or punished simply for having been on the wrong side of a conflict." Reminding his reader that modern

England itself came into being in and through an amnesty—the English Revolution of 1660, as Schmitt noted, ended with a law of indemnity and forgetfulness—Schmitt concluded by counseling his reader not to forget that "amnesty" is one of the original meanings of the word "peace."[171] Here, as elsewhere, Schmitt's political thought amounts to a volatile mix of genealogical insight, anti-Anglo-American polemic, and self-serving bombast (Schmitt himself, remember, was banned from teaching in 1945 under denazification directives). And here, as elsewhere, even as Schmitt identifies a point at which the conceptually double machinery of modern politics "short-circuits" itself in tragic contradiction (because denazification, in Schmitt's view, involves a criminalization of the enemy, it introduces an element of "civil war" into the very peace it attempts to establish), Schmitt's thought also remains thoroughly internal to the horizon of modern politics itself (amnesty in general, and early modern amnesty in particular, here provides Schmitt with the "normal" criminal-enemy distinction on the basis of which he criticizes the confusion at work in denazification). This is why, as Galli puts it, Schmittian thought amounts to a "modern anti-modernity": Precisely because Schmitt gained his critical insight by positioning himself at the extreme limit of the same epoch he also denounced, his thought also remains thoroughly dependent on that epoch for its continued intelligibility.[172]

The critic who opens himself to the crisis of the "years of lead," by contrast, will find himself in a much different position. The more loyal this critic is to the Schmittian *occasio*, the more he will be obliged to confront in the "years of lead" an incipient mode of polemicity that differs from Schmitt's concept of the "political" not only in degree but also in kind. The faceless, frontless, and formless bombings and killings that took place during the "years of lead" implied such a prolonged short-circuit of the distinctions between peace and war, police and military force, criminals and enemies, and public authorities and private individuals that it pointed not simply to their symptomatic confusion, but now to their *complete fusion*—to the meltdown of modernity's doubled-up machinery into a single molten mass. Whereas Schmitt interpreted the short-circuits of modern politics on the assumption that there can and should exist forms of normality in relation to which any and all exceptions can and should become intelligible, the "years of lead" involved (as Bobbio pointed out in the early 1980s[173]) a conjunction of norm and exception so thorough that it resulted in a situation of "anomie" (as Paul Virilio called it in 1977[174]), in which the assumption of any juridical norm, up to and including the declaration of any amnesty, was but a nostalgic fantasy. What comes into crisis here is not simply modern politics, but also the very possibility of using the "doubleness" of Schmitt's Janus-faced gaze to make sense of, and give form to, the specific sort of polemicity that materialized in the "years of lead."[175] Indeed, even the tragicity of Schmittian political thought appeared to come into question during these years. The "end of politics" declared by Bolognese youth activists in the late 1970s had nothing to do with apolitical apathy or melancholic loss. It was a rubric for the flourishing of a novel sort of "creative intelligence," for experiments in the production of political form (such as Radio Free Alice), for an exploration of non-statal modes of antagonism and emancipation, and for new theories and practices of political space (the political slogan of the Bolognese youth was, as Lotringer notes, "The Margins at the Center").[176] In Bologna, at least, the infelicity and crisis of modern politics was not at all a cause for lament and mourning; it was an occasion for festival and imagination. Its declension was not tragic; it was concretely utopic.

We would not, of course, want to carry the point too far. The "creative intelligence" that began to emerge in Bologna in the 1970s did not mark a total break with the schemata of modern politics; its experiments with modern political space remained hemmed in by the *katechon* of the Cold War, and it could still be interpreted according to its optics.[177] For the same reason, the faceless and shapeless violence that marked the "years of lead" cannot be said to be the same as the apocalyptic terrorism that Galli identifies in and with the global age. Although the random bombings of the 1970s contained more than a trace of nihilism (aimless to the same degree that they were unaimed), they cannot be said to have been motivated by what Galli in this book calls "extreme theology"; these bombings were still intelligible according to the logic of instrumental reason (they could still be understood, however remotely, as "means to the end" of attaining or retaining political power), and thus remained within the interpretive horizon of the modern age. It also must be said that Italy was hardly the only country to experience a crisis in the categories of modern politics during this decade. Similar confusions had been latent and even manifest in many parts of the world for some time, most notably in Europe's former colonies—these political spaces where, as Ashis Nandy memorably put it, modernity appeared in its "armed version,"[178] where modern distinctions between police and military force seldom, if ever, emerged in the first place,[179] and where the theorists and practitioners of counterinsurgency explicitly abandoned these distinctions as meaningful guidelines for their use of violence.[180] In the European metropole, meanwhile, modern political categories began to disintegrate for a different set of reasons. In the early 1970s, the political economy of Europe was shaken by the dissolution of Bretton Woods institutions, the devaluation of the dollar, stagflation, the oil crisis, and the end of a long postwar boom dating from 1945. The "years of lead" were, in part, a distorted and indirect reaction to this radical transformation in capitalism—this "sea-change," as David Harvey has called it—that, in turn, created the conditions for the spatiotemporal dynamic we today call "globalization."[181] In this respect, especially, the amorphous polemicity that emerged in Italy during the 1970s was not at all exceptional. It was the shape of things to come: it was the violent, reactive, and inchoate manifestation, in Italy, of an emergent form of anomie that, in the global age, would increasingly become the norm.

The point here, then, is not that the phenomena Galli would later call "the global age" and "global war" were already somehow uniquely in full effect in Italy during the 1970s. It is that the crisis which was the occasion for Galli's immanent critique of Schmitt *already itself heralded* the incipient crisis of Schmittian political thought. To read Galli on his own terms—to understand his relation to the "years of lead" in the same way that Galli himself understood Schmitt's relation to Weimar—is to realize that Galli's thought originates in a repetition of the Schmittian *occasio*—the immanence of the critic in the crisis—that is *so completely Schmittian*—so loyal to the innermost spur of Schmittian thought—that it *therefore* finds itself obliged to be *completely non-Schmittian*.

Schmitt scholars, whether critical or affirmative, have sometimes referred to Schmitt's thought as a "challenge."[182] Galli's reliquefication of the Schmittian *occasio*, however, issues its own challenge. If Galli's scholarship is any example, it would seem that the fewer Schmittian texts we read (the more we limit our reading of Schmitt, say, to *Concept of the Political* or *Political Theology*), and the more carelessly we read these texts (the more our hermeneutic encounter with Schmitt's texts is limited to the extraction of timeless and abstract "logics"), the more acutely we will suffer from the illusion that Schmittian thought is adequate for thinking through contemporary experience, and the more we will be inclined to prolong "Schmittian logic" past its own immanent expiration date. Conversely, the more deeply and widely we read Schmitt's writings, and the more loyal we remain to the kernel of Schmittian thought in our own thought, the more we will realize just how pointless are Schmitt's categories in an epoch in which Schmitt's contradictory *oeuvre* no longer sustains a relation to the *occasio* from which alone it originates. The use of Schmittian categories to interpret the global age not only betrays what was most alive in Schmitt's thought; it also allows us to comfort ourselves with the reassuring knowledge that contemporary crises will so resemble those of modernity that the critique of the latter will retain purchase on the former as well. The challenge of Carlo Galli is to read Carl Schmitt so completely, so carefully, and so loyally, that we *therefore* close the book on him, turning instead to face a set of crises about which Schmitt has, precisely, nothing to say.

A Genealogy of the Global Age

This challenge is the point of departure, as well as the unstated hermeneutic horizon, for the volume you hold in your hands. *Political Spaces and Global War* combines into a single edition Galli's 2001 book *Spazi politici. L'età moderna e l'età globale* (Political Spaces: The Modern Age and the Global Age) and the short 2002 book Galli penned in the wake of the attacks of September 11, 2001 (*La guerra globale* or "Global War").[183] Taken together, these two texts mark an intensification and extension of Galli's non-Schmittian Schmittology: They designate in "positive" terms the same epochal crisis that Galli had already outlined "negatively" in and through his immanent critique of Schmitt. Indeed, for Galli, *the emergence of the global age* and *the desuetude of Schmittian thought* are two names for one and the same epochal turning point. The global age is that epoch whose novelty we become able to recognize to the precise extent that we allow Schmitt's thought to negate itself, using its insights into the modern age in a way that lets those insights confirm their own increasing uselessness.

Conversely, our very loyalty to the Schmittian *occasio* obliges us to realize that the polemicity that Schmitt wanted to designate with the term the "political" has today exploded into a conflict that cannot be understood on Schmittian terms, such that any truly rigorous Schmittologist today must become a non-Schmittian critic of a "global war" that is specific to the "global age."

The analysis of contemporary experience that results from this non-Schmittian Schmittology is, to say the least, quite unusual. In Galli's view, the global age is defined first and foremost by a new and worrisome mode of mediation, namely, the "immediate mediacy" of economic globalization, which in turn emerges in and through the terminal crisis of the distinctions—between inside and outside, and particular and universal—that allowed modern politics to confer shape and form upon space.[184] For Galli, as for Schmitt, modern political space is not a stable and self-conscious system. It is an intrinsically unstable and precarious equilibrium of forces the continued existence of which depends on the montage of colonial and geometric "figures" that it invented in order to stabilize space, neutralize conflict, and create political order. To clarify the crisis that gives rise to the unstable origin of modernity, Galli outlines premodern political space in a reading that has affinities to Alexandre Koyré's 1953 Hideyo Noguchi Lecture on "the sky and the heavens" and Michel Foucault's 1966 discussion of "resemblance" in *The Order of Things*.[185] Galli argues that space in premodern political thought is "qualified," in the sense that space itself is understood to possess intrinsic, objective meanings (such as the Order of Being or the Idea of Justice) that then provide firm grounds for political order.[186] Modern political thought, Galli then suggests, needs to be understood as a response to the crisis and dissolution of this space, and thus too of the political orders founded on it. For Galli, as for Schmitt, modern political thought is not, then, an autonomous and self-legislating philosophic system; it is a precarious equilibrium that came into being as a response to the loss of intrinsically qualified grounds for politics. If, in the premodern age, *space gave the measure to politics*, in the modern age, it is *politics that gives the measure to space*.[187] Unlike the "political geography" of premodern political spaces, in which various *qualities* understood to inhere in space provided the grounds for political orders, the "political geometry" of the modern age construes space primarily as an undifferentiated *quantity*, as an abstract and measurable plane, a blank surface that can be apportioned and used at will.[188] Modern space is thus, for Galli, what modern time is for Walter Benjamin[189]: empty and homogeneous, it is a passive blank slate that makes itself available to the gaze of the State and offers no resistance to the State's projects of instrumental reason.

Much in this account resembles similar claims in the work of not only Koyré and Foucault but also, more recently, James Scott.[190] Galli's difference from these thinkers consists in the centrality that his genealogy, like Schmitt's in *Nomos of the Earth*, confers upon the colonial origins of modern political space. In Galli's rendering, the "empty space" that defines modern political space is not the pure or simple result of autonomous geometric abstraction. It is rather the reiteration, in geometric terms, of a prior political space, namely, the "empty space" of America, the space of colonial conquest.[191] In Galli's account, modern political geometry originates in a principle that is not itself geometrical; it comes into being through the "geometrization," we might say, of a prior colonial space. It follows from this that modern political thought cannot understand its own origin; its own self-explanation cannot adequately account for the circuitous route in and through which it acquires the figure of "empty space" that allows politics to become thinkable for it. It depends for its coherence on a figure of emptiness that it discovers first in America, this "land without people," and which it *then* transposes to and misrecognizes as an empty geometric plane. And this, in turn, gives rise to a crucial complication. Once modern political space "geometrizes" the "empty space" of America, it not only forgets this space's genealogical origin; it also then converts that now-mathematized "empty space" into the basis of the *jus publicum europæum*, which is to say, a political order that demarcates the inside of Europe (where distinctions of war and peace pertain) from its outside (where colonial conquest and occupation is not only possible but desirable and necessary). The emergence of Eurocentric political space here reveals itself to depend upon Europe's unwitting internalization of the very figure of external space it also authorizes itself to dominate.

In Galli's telling, then, modern political space is not a cathedral; it is an intricate, improvised, and fragile lean-to. Its founding demarcation is not clear and distinct (on the model of geometry); it is torqued and opaque, and contains from the very beginning the seed of its own destruction.

It is precisely the instability of modern political space—and not, as the neoliberal narrative would have it, its strength—that gives rise first to the totalitarianism of the early twentieth century, and then to the globalization of the late twentieth century. For Galli, there is complementarity between these two collapses of modern political space. Whereas totalitarianism, in Galli's view, emerges from an *implosion* of modern political space, globalization results from its *explosion*.[192] This explosion is novel in many ways; it has created new experiences of political borders, new modes of statuality and subjectivity, and new frontiers between public and private. What is more, Galli argues, the global age has, for the first time in the history of humanity, realized the unification of the world (which is not at all, Galli emphasizes, the same as the *unity* of the world[193]). For all of its novelty, however, the global age is not, in Galli's view, a pure and simple break with the modern age. Galli's own name for the despatialization that takes place in this epoch ("global mobilization," a variation on what Ernst Jünger called "total mobilization"[194]), implies that he sees in it a survival of some of the worst dynamics of the modern. Most important of all, Galli does not at all assume that global mobilization is an inevitable phase in the development of modern politics; its domination of contemporary experience does not at all imply that it was the only or best way for modern political space to come undone. Global mobilization is, in Galli's view, simply one among many possible collapses latent in the unstable and unpredictable equilibrium that was constitutive of modern political space from its very inception. Its vicious torque may be the only closure of the modern with which we are familiar today, but it is no more necessary or rational than were any of the other possible completions of modern political space, and it owes its contemporary dominance only and exclusively to a set of contingencies or accidents that easily could have turned out otherwise.[195] For Galli, as for Adorno, "the real" is not at all "rational."[196]

Like modern political space, global political space implies its own mode of conflictuality: "global war" (a version of which some readers will have already encountered in Antonio Negri's and Michael Hardt's 2002 book *Multitude: War and Democracy in the Age of Empire*).[197] For Galli, "global war" is simply that mode of polemicity that corresponds to the "space" of global mobilization. Just as the phenomenological character of global mobilization is borderlessness, so too is global war deprived of the borders specific to war; it is a war without fronts, war deprived of the possibility of face-to-face or forward-facing conflict, war without war-time (it does not begin with a "declaration of war" and cannot end with a "peace treaty"). Global war is war whose form is structured by the same space-time compression that defines economic globalization (ubiquity, punctuality, and instaneity). To be clear, none of this implies that Galli presumes that modern warfare will somehow magically cease to exist. Like the global mobilization of which it is but a mode, global war implies a claim on the Earth that is unitary but not homogenous or unified. As such, the emergence of global war neither precludes nor is contradicted by the continued existence of residual modes of war. Nor should we understand Galli to suggest that global war is somehow equally distrib-uted over the Earth. Just as globalization intensifies inequalities between the North and the South, the rich and the poor, and the center and the periphery, so too may we expect global war to manifest itself unequally, in a distribution of life zones (where the residual existence of modern political spaces retards the dominance or even emergence of global war) and death zones (where global war rages not only through the internal displacement of peoples, the chronic permanence of low-intensity con-flict, the indefinite prolongation of counterinsurgency campaigns, and the operation of the penal state and its police forces, but also through the hostile governmental exposure of certain populations more than others to risk, accident, inclement weather, pollution, and disease). Finally, Galli's claims about the emergence or even dominance of global war should not be mistaken for claims that global war is a radical novelty that somehow emerged promptly with the fall of the Berlin Wall in 1989. Just as global mobilization is not the result of a pure and simple break with political modernity, but rather a development of political modernity's tensions and equilibriums in a particularly extreme direction, so too is the emergence of global war the result of the intensification of certain dynamics, disequi-libriums, and tensions that were already latent in modern warfare—only now in a new and radical direction, past a new and irreversible threshold. Global war is not, then, fully discontinuous with the mode of polemic-ity that plagued the modern from within. It is that same polemicity, only now unconstrained by any *nomos* and resistant to the forms what would be imposed upon it by any single decision or "decider." It is, put simply, the mode of polemicity that corresponds the generalized anomie that has washed over the Earth with the emergence of the "sea" of globalization.

This has significant implications for the way in which Anglophone readers think about the place and function of "terrorism" in contemporary experience. Many American readers in particular may feel that they are already familiar, even overfamiliar, with the sort of juridical and political indistinctions that Galli proposes to analyze in his 2002 text. What else, after all, defined the period of political reaction following the attacks of September 11, 2001, except the confusion of criminal and enemy (in the Presidential Military Order of November 13, 2001, with its category of "illegal enemy combatant"), of norm and exception (most notably in the passage of the U.S. Patriot Act, with its authorization of "indefinite detention"), of public authorities and private persons (where the United States supplements its armed forces with mercenaries to "hunt down" and "smoke out" specific individuals who represent no state or public authority), and of inside and outside (not only in the attack itself, but also in the Bush administration's response to it, their "global war on terrorism" that implies the existence of battlefronts everywhere)? To the comprehension of this experience, Galli makes a number of pivotal contributions.

To begin, Galli's analysis of the attacks of September 11, 2001, implies an emphatic rejection of the "presentist" hermeneutic horizon that dominated the Bush administration's reaction to the attacks ("everything is different now"), and that has insinuated itself into far too many analyses and critiques of the Bush administration (in the specific form of the mistaken assumption that the inflation of emergency power in the United States only began after 2001).[198] Galli's genealogy, by contrast, reveals that neither the attacks of September 11, 2001, nor the Bush administration's confused response can be said to mark the advent of something new or unprecedented. For Galli, these phenomena are simply the most spectacular manifestation of a mode of polemicity that corresponds to a political space (the "glocal"), and to a form of mediation ("immediate mediacy"), that originated well prior to 2001, with the emergence of "global mobilization" itself. The corollary of this genealogy is a critique of legal liberalism that, in its basic gist, extends and intensifies the critique of legal positivism that Schmitt himself issued in the 1940s and 1950s.[199] If Galli's analysis and periodization are not off the mark, then the juridical and political confusions that surround "terrorism" are themselves neither juridical nor political in origin, but derive from a more fundamental and concrete dynamic, namely, the explosion of modern political space that has been under way for at least a decade, if not longer. It follows that a mere insistence on the rule of law alone—however forcefully moralistic in tone, however fiercely faithful to the great principles of modern politics (we *should not* confuse enemies and criminals, we *should not* allow exceptions to the norm, we *should not* confuse internal police force with external military force, etc.)—will constitute an empty, ineffectual, and even counterproductive response to contemporary polemicity. Galli's genealogy of global war, by contrast, does for space what William Scheuerman has done for time: Whereas Scheuerman shows that the erosion of the division of powers in contemporary political liberal democracies cannot be understood without reference to the prior teletechnical and economic conditions that today produce the general social acceleration of time,[200] Galli teaches us that global war cannot be restrained unless and until we treat its punctual and ubiquitous mode of conflict (i.e., "terrorism") as the symptom of the prior anomie—the spaceless sea—that global mobilization has set into motion.

Needless to say, Galli's interpretation of contemporary violence sharply contradicts those who still persist in viewing economic globalization as though it were guided by a silent but purposive plan—as if it were, in true Kantian fashion, the providential precursor for the gradual spread of cosmopolitanism and democracy over the face of the Earth. Interpreted within this reassuring historical horizon, contemporary polemicity cannot but be interpreted as an aberration. Indeed, the dominance within contemporary political discourse of a concept derived from the modern age—"terrorism" is a term that was first used in English in 1795—implies that the violence of global war is somehow "out of place" in the global age, a "throwback" to an earlier era, a residue of the past that blindly and unreasonably "retards" the progress of an economic globalization that is supposedly not only inevitable but also profoundly good, our last and best hope for "perpetual peace."[201] Galli's concept of "global war" (not unlike Virilio and Lotringer's concept of "pure war,"[202] though according to an entirely different scholarly itinerary) allows us to resist the disavowal at work in this interpretation. Global war, in Galli's view, is not "out of synch" with the global age; it is its uncanny double and alibi. It cannot and will not be pacified by economic globalization; economic globalization itself calls it into being. Global war is not anomalous to economic globalization; it is the normal mode in which polemicity manifests itself under conditions of "glocality," war in which every point on Earth is—in principle, if not in fact—immediately and directly exposed to the global flux of violence without the intervening mediation of the State.

This response to 9/11 also, of course, cuts sharply against the grain of the abstract and extractive reading of Schmitt that became popular in the aftermath of the attacks of September 11, 2001. For many scholars in the Anglophone humanities and social sciences writing about politics during these distressing years, Schmitt's logics and categories seemed a perfect fit with the "post-9/11" moment.[203] Leading American presses responded to this unexpected demand by bringing to market a number of new translations and new editions of Schmitt's works, and Schmitt seemed well on his way to being the theorist *du jour*.[204] Galli's response to 9/11 calls this "turn to Schmitt" into question. For Galli, the attacks of September 11, 2001, mark the emergence of a mode of warfare in which all of Schmitt's key distinctions have fused together and are, as such, inoperative.[205] On this reading, it is a profoundly consoling illusion to treat the attacks as a chance to see, in the relation between Schmitt and "9/11," a perfect coincidence of thought and being. For Galli, the attacks are instead an occasion for realizing the impossibility of using Schmittian categories for grasping the origins of the real crisis at hand.[206] Only by exiting Schmittian thought for "an opening, a new space," as Galli has more recently put it,[207] will we be able to form a sober perception of the global war for which the metonyms "9/11" and "global war on terrorism" are but symptomatic disavowals.

In the end, these two sides of Galli's approach to contemporary experience—his turn from Schmitt and his break with the presentist account of 9/11—issue from one and the same source. Just as Schmitt arrived at his genealogical insights into the "double-sided" origin of modern politics by occupying a position internal to the passage of the premodern to the modern, so too does Galli write the genealogy of the global age by situating himself in the passage of the "political" into "global war." The critical gaze that gives rise to *Political Spaces and Global War* derives from precisely the same immanence of critic and crisis that is the submerged but active kernel—the same *occasio*—that is, in Galli's view, responsible for spurring Schmittian thought in its unity and singularity as a theoretical formation.[208] With one vital exception: Galli's genealogy of the global age so thoroughly activates Schmitt's *occasio* that it ends up fully exhausting Schmitt's thought. Not *despite* but *precisely because* he is loyal to Schmitt's *occasio*, Galli is able to define the global age as that epoch which is defined by the complete and irreversible desuetude of Schmittian thought.[209]

For Galli, of course, the converse holds as well: the dialectic in and through which Schmittian thought negates itself—the principle according to which it is ultimately Schmitt's own *occasio* that compels us to recognize the crises in relation to which the use of Schmittian thought is no longer either "useful," "thoughtful," or even "Schmittian"—is simultaneously *also* that dialectic which opens up the horizon inside of which alone the true novelty of the global age can come to light. And this, no doubt, will give some readers pause. Isn't "non-Schmittian Schmittology" an unwieldy, idiosyncratic, arbitrary, and even politically undesirable point of entry for the understanding of a global age that is, by Galli's own account, mainly the product of economic globalization? Won't a non-Schmittian approach to problems of geopolitics and geophilosophy (as Étienne Balibar has characterized Galli's *Spazi politici*[210]) be significant only for readers who were already interested in Schmitt to begin with? How exactly would a genealogy of this sort have any meaning at all for scholars of the global age who were never Schmittians in the first place, who do not regard Schmitt as a serious interlocutor, and who therefore do not view the invention of a non-Schmittian Schmittology either as an intellectual challenge or an intellectual achievement?

To respond to this sort of skepticism from within the Gallian horizon, we first need to restate one of the basic principles of the Frankfurtian tradition of critical theory that provides Galli's genealogy with its specific shape and force. For Horkheimer and Adorno, Enlightenment thought "seals its own fate" to the precise degree to which it does not include within itself critical reflection upon its own susceptibility to, or even drive for, the sort of regressive self-destruction of the modern exemplified by Nazism and fascism.[211] To this end, as Adorno wrote in 1951, one of the tasks confronting contemporary thought is that of placing reactionary arguments against the Enlightenment "in the service of progressive Enlightenment."[212] It is no doubt tempting to suppose that we would be able to comprehend the passage from the modern to the global age without also including the worst dimensions of modernity as essential elements in our understanding of modernity itself. This sort of approach would allow us to regard Nazism and fascism, not to mention imperialism, as nothing more than aberrations of an otherwise rational project; it would fully justify us to remain disengaged from a thinker in whom, as Adorno once said of Schmitt, "National Socialism attained historical consciousness of itself."[213] But if Horkheimer and Adorno are not off the mark, the beautiful soul who wants to study the global age without also being "tainted" by a confrontation with modern reactionary thought will also unwittingly prepare the soil for the return of the weed itself, staying "clean" only at the cost of preserving the subjective and objective conditions in which reactionary thought, having survived the transition into the global age unchallenged and unscathed, can then reestablish itself.[214] From a critical theoretical perspective, then, a confrontation with Schmitt is not one among many methodological "options" for the scholar of the global age; for Enlightenment thought that wants to outlive the demise of the epoch of its birth, it is nothing less than a dialectical imperative.

From this standpoint, there is a very concrete reason why the immanent critique of Schmitt can and should today serve as a privileged point of departure into our comprehension of the global age. Certain key tenets of Schmittian thought were, from the beginning, already internal to the work of the same neoliberal thinkers whose paradigms of free market capitalism dominate the globalized world. Schmitt's writings on the crisis of parliamentary reason and on the strong, decisionist state provided political theoretical premises not only for German ordoliberals like Alexander Rüstow, but also for the Austrian neoliberal Friedrich A. Hayek, who spearheaded the formation of the Mont Pèlerin Society in 1947, and who was a catalyst for the formation of the neoliberal theories and practices that are today associated with the Chicago School of Economics.[215] Naomi Klein is not, then, free-associating when she cites Schmitt's infamous decisionist maxim in her detailed analysis of the Chicago School's endorsement of political authoritarianism as a means to the end of forcing neoliberal economic theories into practice.[216]

Nor is William Scheuerman when he draws precisely the same connection.[217] There is a distressing and concrete sense in which it is already too late for the genealogy of the global age *not* to be Schmittian in origin and in character. Here, too, the immanent critique of Schmitt is not one among many methodological "choices" or "preferences." It is a critical theoretical task we avoid only at the cost of misrecognizing the genesis, and thus too the essence, of the global age itself.

Where is "Political Space"?

Even the reader who accepts the Gallian challenge—who understands not only why any true Schmittology must culminate in a non-Schmittian genealogy of the global age, but also why any real genealogy of the global age cannot do without non-Schmittian Schmittology—might find *Political Spaces and Global War* challenging in yet another sense. *Spazi politici*, as Antonio Negri perceptively noted, is not intended as a conventionally academic book.[218] As such, even the most sympathetic reader might struggle to understand how exactly Galli's concept of "political space" figures into the study of space and politics today. The most straightforward way to resolve this difficulty is to say that for Galli, as for Agamben, the term "political space" is simply a gloss of Schmitt's concept of *nomos*.[219] Galli's concept of "political space" is not, then, a methodological instrument geared toward the implicit goal of adequate perception; it is not an "optic" that is supposed to allow us to measure the accuracy or inaccuracy with which various political thinkers "represent" the physical geography in which they find themselves. Thus, although Galli is extremely interested in the way in which a certain profile of "America" figures into Hobbes's text, his aim will not be to correct this profile on the basis of empirical information from anthropology, ethnology, or history. Nor, however, is Galli's "political space" a name for the way that political thinkers use spatial tropes or spatial rhetoric in their argumentation. In his reading of Hobbes, for example, Galli forgoes a textual exegesis of Hobbes's metaphors of law as a riverbank (in which law's purpose is to direct, without blocking, the flow of human action) or hedge (in which a natural growth, passion, is shaped into a culturally recognizable form, a boundary).[220] Galli's *Political Spaces and Global War* does not, then, participate in the "spatial turn" in humanities scholarship, in which a preoccupation with the "poetics of space" or with "spatial metaphors" has tended to predominate over, even cancel out, the tasks specific to metatheory.[221] Nor, finally, does Galli seek to define "political space" with reference to the sort of research that one often finds today in the field of critical geography, where there is often an emphasis placed upon the tangible particularities and material complexities at work in various case studies of globalized space. Although Galli openly pronounces his debt to critical geography, and in particular to David Harvey's thesis of time-space compression, his approach to the problem of space derives from a theoretical source that is almost completely absent from scholarship on space today.[222]

To throw Galli's concept of "political space" into sharper focus, it is surely necessary to line it up with Schmitt's concept of *nomos*; but because political thought for Schmitt is always also polemical thought, the student of space and politics will only fully grasp Schmitt's concept of *nomos* once she brings it into conflict with its two main theoretical adversaries: the concept of *nomos* in Plato's *Laws*, and the concept of *lex* in Cicero's *De Legibus*. Explaining Galli by way of a detour through Plato and Cicero may at first strike the reader as circuitous and digressive; in fact, it will allow us a concise summary of the way in which Galli's non-Schmittian Schmittology confers upon his concept of "political space" its unique dialectical thrust.

Plato and Cicero

In Book 4 of Plato's *Laws*, the place where historians of jurisprudence have often claimed to find Plato's most definitive statements on law,[223] the Athenian Stranger ("in whom," Gadamer observes, "more than anyone Plato has most obviously hidden himself"[224]) offers up a formulation of *nomos* that Schmitt will both *draw upon* (in *Nomos of the Earth*[225]) and *oppose* (in his esoteric polemic against Johann Huizinga[226]). Law (νόμος/*nomos*), the Stranger says there, should be understood as a name for the dispensation (διανομήν/*dianomēn*) of thought (νοῦ/*noû*).[227] This formulation involves an intriguing tangle of interpretive problems, not the least of which is the "wordplay" that binds it together. In his footnote to this passage in his 1926 translation of the *Laws*, the classicist R. G. Bury would observe that the Stranger's definition consists of a "double word-play: νούς (*nous*) = νόμος (*nomos*), and διανομάς (*dianomas*) = δαίμονας (*daimonas*). Laws, being the 'dispensation of reason,' take the place of the 'daemons' of the age of Cronos: The divine element in man (το δαιμόνιαν [*to daimonian*]), which claims obedience, is reason (νούς [*nous*])."[228] But the Stranger's play (or, as Eric Voegelin put it in his commentary on the same passage, his "pun") is perhaps even triple in character.[229] The Greek word that the Stranger uses to name the relation between *nomos* and *nous* is *dianomēn*, which translators have rendered with terms as different as "dispensation," "apportionment," and "edict." *Dianomēn* is proximate not only to *nomos* (its root is *nemein*, which designates precisely the "distribution" or "division" that Schmitt would connect, in his postwar writings, with *nomos*[230]), but also to *dianoia*, which is the word Plato uses in *The Republic* to name the modality of mathematical thought that alone can provoke or awaken thought as such.[231] The Stranger's formulation of law is thus governed by an odd and beautiful play: Each of the names in his definition shades into and joins with the others.

Interpreted within the horizon of Platonic political philosophy, this play is not at all arbitrary. In Book 7 of the *Laws*, the Stranger pauses to reflect upon the dialogue in which he and his interlocutors have been participating since dawn. Their own dialogue, the Stranger acknowledges, is not only itself *akin to* a form of tragic poetry; it is also, he asserts, the very "paradigm" (παράδειγμα/*paradeigma*) for the sort of discourse that ought to govern the guardians' education of the young *instead of* tragic poetry (which the Stranger will then proceed to exclude from the political community).[232] This self-reference gives us the interpretive key we need for understanding the meaning of the Stranger's wordplay between *nous*, *nomos*, and *dianomēn*. Interpreted as a part of a paradigm for "true law" (νόμος Ἀληθής/*nomos alēthēs*, which is the name the Stranger will eventually give to the sort of discourse that takes place in the *Laws*[233]), the very pattern of letters that appears there on the page now comes to light as an *exemplar* of the same harmonious juridical and political order the Stranger describes. In their close concordance with one another, the communication between the words *nous*, *nomos*, and *dianomēn* is *itself* a blueprint that allows the reader to see what it would mean for "thought," "law," and "space" to coexist in agreement with one another in an undivided political community governed by the Idea of the Good.

The relation between *nous* and *nomos* in Plato's *Laws* cannot, then, be interpreted as a relation between "mind" and "matter," between the two discrete "substances" of *res cogitans* and *res extensa*. There is no hint here of an "internal" thought that is active and the purpose of which is to inscribe its juridical blueprints upon the passive blank slate of "external" space. In fact, between *nous* and *nomos* we would appear to find no relation at all. We seem to find only a peculiar sort of community (or *koinoia*), a subtle but nevertheless definite participation of *nous* within *nomos*, an intimate proximity of names that, in its approximation of the paradigm of indivisibility rendered visible by the Idea of the Good, *itself* exemplifies the sort of intimate proximity that would exist in the best possible political community. Plato's *Laws*, which contains the assertion that man (Ανθρωπον/*anthropon*) is the "plaything" (παίγνιον/*paignion*) of the gods,[234] is often interpreted as the origin of political theology.[235] The Stranger's formulation of law needs to be seen in this light; interpreted on Plato's own terms, the wordplay that joins *nomos* and *nous* is no accident; it is a sign of divine order.

One can then understand why Cicero, in his interpretation of Plato's *Laws*, would define "*lex*" as the written expression of the "right reason" that is common not only to all humans but also to all gods, and that therefore binds the entire universe into a single commonwealth (*civitas*).[236] For Cicero (as, it would seem, for Plato), the purpose of law is to render immanent the transcendent unity (which is not the same thing as a "higher law"[237]) that only philosophic thought (*nous* for Plato, *recta ratio* for Cicero) can properly comprehend. As distinct from Plato's *nomos*, however, Cicero's *lex* is unburdened by any reference to the concrete distribution and partition of space. *Lex*, as Cicero writes, has a signification that is closer to "choice" or "selection."[238] As part of his attempt to create a new form of wisdom (which Cicero calls "*jurisprudentia*") that surpasses that of Greek philosophy,[239] Cicero's *lex* therefore implies a jurisdiction for reason that cannot be limited in spatial terms, that is indeed literally universal in scope. Because "right reason" is, for Cicero, shared by humans and gods alike, and because it binds the universe into a single *civitas*, the law that expresses this right reason must also be, by definition, spatially unlimited. A particularized *lex*, a law that was not in some way universal, but valid only for a spatially limited concrete distribution of lots and land, would be a contradiction in terms; it would not be law at all.

Schmitt

For Schmitt, the universalism of Ciceronian reason is not a model for modern republicanism; its spacelessness is a source of modern nihilism. To the extent that jurisprudence succeeds in its Ciceronian ambitions, all of the distinctions that Plato understood to be implicit in the concept of *nomos*—not only the inside–outside distinction, but also the friend–enemy distinction and the *stasis–polemos* distinction[240]—are at risk of dissolution. The broader and more abstract the *lex*, the more inclusive it becomes, the less it becomes able to ground a concrete *nomos*, and the less too it is able to distinguish between inside and outside, between criminal and enemy, between *polemos* and *stasis*. Universalism in law is not, then, as is so often assumed, a basis for imperial power; it is the root cause of political impotence. For Schmitt, the impotence intrinsic to *lex* reaches a crisis point with the development, in modernity, of the science of legal positivism.[241] The more that legal positivism establishes itself in Europe as the basic horizon for the interpretation of law, the more the forgetting of *nomos* becomes complete, and the more that Europe unwittingly consents to the disintegration and deterioration of the concrete spatial order that is the true foundation of its jurisprudence. For the more that Europe begins to orient its juristic thinking not with reference to the act of land-appropriation and colonial occupation that confers upon Europe its true and concrete juridical form, but now only with reference to "the rule of law," the more Europe will be unable recognize the absolute necessity of its lawless colonial exterior (in which, as Galli puts, it "everything is possible") for the creation of its intensely hierarchical internal political and juridical order (in which, in Galli's phrase, "nothing is possible"). The more Europe tries to define its juridical order in universal and spaceless terms, in other words, the less Europe will understand itself, and the more it will uproot itself from the concrete spatial origin that silently sustains it—the more too, therefore, it will unwittingly condemn itself to wither and fade away.[242]

It is this epochal crisis that caused Schmitt to declare war on legal positivism, and thence too to retrieve the concept of *nomos* from its oblivion. In 1957, Schmitt wrote that Cicero's translation of *nomos* into *lex* was "one of the heaviest burdens that the conceptual and linguistic culture of the Occident has had to bear."[243] But, as Schmitt noted in 1950, a misreading of Cicero's type is already latent in Plato's own discourse on *nomos* (which, Schmitt noted, already "deteriorates" *nomos* into nothing more than a "mere rule"[244]). In his 1950 *Nomos of the Earth*, therefore, Schmitt would attempt to think the concept of *nomos* outside of the Platonic tradition altogether, through a contentious interpretation of the pre-Socratic poet against whom Plato directed his most forceful and productive censorship: Homer.[245] The result is a jolting understanding of the relation between *nous* and *nomos*. Whereas Plato emphasizes continuity between *nous* and *nomos*—demonstrating through wordplay how *nous* shades harmoniously into *nomos* by way of *dianomēn*—Schmitt finds between the two terms a deadly serious discontinuity.

On the standard translation of Homer's *Odyssey*, Schmitt notes, Homer's opening passage says of Odysseus that "[m]any were the men whose cities he saw and whose minds [*noos*] he learned."[246] The problem with this translation, Schmitt observes, is that it imposes onto Odysseus the modern conception of a social psychologist whose main interest is to chart and describe the various "spirits" or "minds" that distinguish various "peoples." However genial this translation may be for modern readers, Schmitt insists that it remains logically impossible. Pointedly leaving open the question of whether or not *nous* and *nomos* are etymologically related,[247] Schmitt proceeds to accept the premise that *nous* is that which is common to all humanity, but only then in order to point out the absurdity in the notion that Odysseus's travels somehow could have given him the chance to witness and learn "different" *noos*. Precisely because *nous* is common to all of humanity, Schmitt argues, the opening of *The Odyssey* can only make sense if, in place of the conventional *noos*, we instead read *nomoi*: "Many were the men whose cities he saw and whose customs or conventions [*nomoi*] he learned." On this read, Homer's passage would signify "something walled or enclosed, or a sacred place, all of which are contained in the word *nomos*," which Schmitt then interprets as "precisely the divisional and distinguishing orders whose particularity necessarily would be of interest to a perceptive and 'very wily' seafarer."[248] The opposed and conventional understanding—the claim that Homer never used the word *nomos*—is, for Schmitt, so inconceivable that he will call it "one of the most extraordinary phenomena in the intellectual history of mankind."[249] The only way to explain the persistence of this philological error is by writing its genealogy, and here, as elsewhere,[250] Schmittian genealogy ends up ferreting out a Jewish thinker as the origin of the plague upon the house of the West. The substitution of *noos* for *nomos*, Schmitt argues, was introduced into Western thought by the medieval Platonist Philo of Alexandria, who was only able to comprehend *nomos* within a hermeneutic horizon governed by the post-exilic distinction between Jewish law and Christian grace, and who therefore remained wholly unable to grasp the spatial dimension from which alone the concept of *nomos* receives its substance.[251]

The effect of Schmitt's turn to Homer, according to Galli, is to turn the Platonic approach to *nomos* on its head.[252] Not *despite* but *precisely because of* the way that *nous* is shared by all of humanity, there can be no universal *nomos*. To the extent that *nous* is common to all humanity, it demands of us political orders that exist only and precisely to the extent that they divide and distinguish, include and exclude, and carve out boundaries between inside and outside—boundaries that, quite contrary to the post-exilic interpretation of *nomos* that has been perpetrated upon the West by Philo, are prior to any distinction between law and grace, and are therefore also constitutively sacred in character.[253] On this view, the most humanity can share are the untouchable barriers that divide and separate it from itself. Schmitt's philological turn to Homer is here, as elsewhere, a polemical and genealogical return to the origin: It pits itself against the layers of willful blindness, philological error, interpretive violence, and simple forgetfulness that Europe has inflicted upon itself through its commitment to Platonic political philosophy (Philo above all), Ciceronian republicanism, and the "science" of modern legal positivism. And here, as elsewhere, Schmittian genealogy generates an account of politics that is not philosophical (emphasizing the possibility of bringing Power into contact with the Good), but tragic and antiphilosophical (emphasizing the absence of the Good, and the inevitability of conflict and division within the city).

Originated in the 1920s and 1930s, but only fully fleshed out in the late 1940s and 1950s, Schmitt's theory of the *nomos* answers a classic Kantian question—for what may we hope?[254]—but now in non-Kantian terms, with no reference to providence, with polemical fury against the "particular universalism" of Anglo-American humanitarianism, and perhaps even with silent comment upon the crises of his present. The years in which Schmitt developed the concept of *nomos* were decades in which "peace" was pursued by means of political theological separation: the partition of Ireland in 1921, the partition of India in August 1947, the United Nations' partition of Palestine in November 1947, and the onset of formal apartheid in South Africa in May 1948. The theory of *nomos* implies that we indeed may hope for an end to a world of openly declared war, but only and precisely to the extent to which we consent to a world of sacrosanct walls.

Galli

This detour, which seems to take us far afield, in fact gives us a precise way to clarify the provenance and stakes of Galli's concept of "political space." With this term, Galli in effect proposes to study the same relation that is *harmonic* in Plato (in and through the play on the words *nous*, *dianomēn*, and *nomos*), that is at once *universalized* and *obliterated* by Cicero (in the spacelessness of his translation of *nomos* as *lex*), and that is *torn asunder* by Schmitt (through his retrieval of the tragic and antiphilosophical concept of a sacred *nomos* grounded in nothing but decision). "Political space" is a way to study the relation between *nous* and *nomos* no longer as a problematic stirring silently *within* the history of political thought, but now—given the time-space compression that is the singular *occasio* of the global age—as an open and anxious question *for* the history of political thought. The relation that Plato understood to be *continuous*, that Cicero inadvertently *discontinued*, and that Schmitt revealed to be *discontinuous*, is for Galli *an explicit task for thought*: Under conditions of globalization, the problem of the "implicit spatiality" of political thought has come to the fore as source of deep disquieting perplexity, revealing itself to be newly questionable in and for any and all political thought that takes seriously the "thinkability of politics" in and for contemporary experience.

Thus framed, Galli's approach to "political space" may be distilled to two central propositions, and thence too to a single dialectical tension. The first is that *there is no political thought that is unmarked by political space*. In order for thought to come into its own *as* thought—in order for *nous*, the "eyes of the mind,"[255] to cast its gaze beyond its *nomos*—it must in some way "withdraw," as Arendt might put it,[256] from the concrete political space within which it comes into being. In the absence of an Idea, however, thought has no unchanging and unmoving paradigm of the Good with reference to which it can "turn itself around" (as in Plato's allegory of the cave) and establish its full autonomy from its political space (and do not forget that *nomos*, in its declension as "custom" or "convention," is that in part from which Plato's prisoners must be freed[257]). Schmitt, as we have seen, thinks the political precisely in the absence of any Idea, and with reference to the contingencies that ruin political form from within.[258] As such, there is for Schmitt no thought that can succeed in entirely ridding itself of the trace of the concrete political space from which it separates itself in order to become thought.[259] Precisely because this space constitutes the negative horizon with reference to which thought then orients itself in its attempt to come into being *as* thought, there is no *nous* that is not also marked and shaped by the *nomos* from which it emerges. There is no thought, in other words, that is not also, even primarily, a thought *of* some or another political space—that does not in some way *originate in*, *derive from*, and *belong to* some or another political space. As such, all political thought worthy of the name will, by virtue of its genesis, be marked by a trace of political space. Political space is not here the passive and external backdrop (or, in Straussian terms, the "setting"[260]) within which political thought takes place. It is instead internal to political thought as its innermost form, as the unspoken but generative "fore-structure" (as Donald Kelley once put it[261]) that determines the way in which political thought shapes, and attempts to resolve, the questions it poses for itself.

This proposition, which outlines in the terms of non-Schmittian Schmittology the sort of claim that many readers will be inclined to associate with Gilles Deleuze and Félix Guattari's approach to "geophilosophy" or Donna Haraway's call for "situated knowledges,"[262] must be held in dialectical tension with a second proposition, one that may be less familiar to readers of Deleuze, Guattari, and Haraway: *Political space hosts a tragic dynamic that ruins political thought from within.* Because every *nomos* is always already undone by its own antinomian force—because there is no Idea with reference to which we can measure the decisions that create the *nomoi* that orient the gaze of our *nous*—the aspiration to delocalized generality that, per Arendt,[263] governs any genuine thought will be vulnerable to the contingency intrinsic to the concrete political space that all political thought cannot but presuppose. In this proposition, there is certainly, as Galli suggests, a certain "complementarity" between his own work and the work of the scholarship he calls "political geography," but there is an important difference as well. Whereas David Harvey argues that "the *insertion* of space . . . into any social theory . . . is always deeply disruptive of its central propositions and derivations,"[264] Galli seeks to explicate the way in which political space is always already—*prior to* any "insertion"—internal to and disruptive of political thought. Galli's attempt to explicate the "implicit spatiality" that is the unspoken but generative core of all political thought is, in other words, an effort to bring to light the unstable iterations of *nous* and *nomos* that have always quietly roiled political thought from within. It is an attempt to bring into the open a tragic drama that, however subtly or imperceptibly, has been playing itself out in the history of political thought since its very inception: "politics" can only become thinkable for political thought insofar as political thought grounds itself tacitly in a figure of political space; but political space itself acquires its figure only through a "decision"—an ungrounded "cut" into space that is constitutively thoughtless, that takes place without reference to any Idea, and that consequently also threatens to undo thought from within.[265]

As an exemplary example of this dialectic, consider the figure—the friend–enemy distinction—that gives shape to Schmitt's concept of the "political." Schmitt's friend–enemy distinction is not, of course, an attempt to give an accurate and adequate account of the empirical world (such that we could then criticize that distinction by exposing inaccuracies and inadequacies in this or that representation of the enemy). It is instead a "schema" in the specifically Kantian sense of the word: a rule on the basis of which our imaginations can create a synthesis between the manifold phenomena we encounter in our everyday empirical experience, on the one hand, and the transcendental categories of time and space, on the other hand.[266] The "rule" that governs the Kantian schema is not simply receptive and theoretical; it is also practical and productive. In order for transcendental understanding to remain consistent with itself—with what Kant calls its own "felt need of reason"[267]—Kant holds that it must realize the infinite and unconditional inside of the limits of the finite and conditional; it must somehow body forth, within the temporal and spatial constraints of the empirical world, the transcendental categories it comprehends in their purity as noetic forms. It is to achieve this paradoxical duty that transcendental understanding creates schemata—figures that synthesize the transcendental categories and actualize them in our experience in a tangible form. This creative power is what Kant calls the "imagination." Its purpose is to create—or, as Gilles Deleuze puts it, to "embody or realize"[268]—the patterns that bind together, that confer order and form upon, our otherwise chaotic and manifold empirical experience. The "friend–enemy" distinction is not, then, a matter the truth of which can be settled with reference to empirical experience; it is a question about the criteria on the basis of which it is possible to make sense of—in the generative sense of the word, where "making sense" is equivalent to a mode of *poesis* or production—empirical experience in the first place.[269] It is, as Galli argues, a response to the problem of *morphogenesis*, which is to say, the specifically modern question of how to create political form in the wake of the dissolution of the medieval *complexio*.

The various figures of political thought to which Galli refers throughout *Political Spaces and Global War* are, in this strong Kantian sense, "products of the imagination." Whether in a form that is "double" (such as the distinctions between inside and outside, universal and particular, criminal and enemy, the personal and the impersonal) or "single" (the pirate, the forest, the savage), Galli's figures may be understood as Kantian schemata that are prior to any empirical experience, and that allow us to make sense of empirical experience, with an emphasis on *make*; figures are blueprints for the *fabrication* or *production* of form where none would otherwise exist. And while Galli's emphasis on figures might be a source of a disappointment for the reader who expects to find in this book yet another set of empirical case studies detailing the "complexity" of this or that global space—who presupposes, let us say, that the proper place of "political space" is "out there in the world" and not "in here in my thought"—it is worth underlining that this very expectation is *itself* nothing more than the unselfconscious product of a prior set of interpretive schema. After all, we can remain certain in our assumption that this sort of knowledge is adequate to the global age only to the extent that we first fail to recognize its dependence not only upon the figure of modern Cartesian space (in which "space" becomes intelligible and measurable on the basis of a deeply questionable distinction between *res extensa* and *res cogitans*), but also upon a secularized iteration of the early modern figure of the *complexio* (for indeed much research today, even in critical geography, culminates in the bland conclusion that space in the global age is a privileged concept for rendering intelligible the "complex" or "complicated" coincidence of all sorts of opposed categories, such as psychic and the material, the personal and the political, and so on—the more inclusive, the better, just as in the *complexio*). The problem is not, then, that Galli's "merely theoretical" study of the global age is insufficiently empirical; it is that the merely empiricist scholar of the global age is insufficiently Gallian—or, more to the point, that the merely empiricist scholar of the global age will remain trapped in a vicious hermeneutic circle, doomed to endlessly report upon new "case studies" that in fact amount to nothing more than byproducts of obsolete schemata with no relation to the global age.

To this disconnect between political space and political thought there are very high stakes indeed. The political forms generated by the figures Galli describes are not at all abstract; they enable the "thinkability of politics" not only in the writings of political theorists but also in the concrete practices of political institutions. These same figures, however, are the principal sites for the crisis that is specific to the global age—an epoch in which very specific concrete events (such as time-space compression) have rendered inoperative almost all of the "implicit spatialities" from which classical and modern political thinkers took their bearings. And herein lies the importance of Galli's *Political Spaces and Global War* for the contemporary student of space and politics. Galli adopts a relation to the basic concepts of modern political philosophy that is not instrumental but, like Schmitt, tragic. Galli does not, that is to say, use the fundamental figures of modern political thought merely as a "means to the end" of seeing our situation more clearly. He instead understands those figures *themselves* to be historical artifacts or products; they are, for him, the deposits, residues, or sedimentations left in our political theoretical imagination by the crises of prior iterations of *nous* and *nomos*. The more we insist upon "using" these schemata today, the more we will blind ourselves to contemporary experience; the more our political thought will degenerate into the mere moralism of claims of what "ought to be," and the less capable we will be to generate a *nous* that is capable of cobbling together a livable *nomos* in and for the contemporary world.

In this, *Political Spaces and Global War* differs from one of the very best empirical analyses of globalization to emerge in recent years, Saskia Sassen's 2006 book *Territory Authority Rights*. Sassen, like Galli, understands globalization to be an "epochal transformation," and finds that she can only explain its significance by rethinking, as does Galli, the thesis of a clear and distinct discontinuity between the premodern and modern epochs.[270] Sassen, again like Galli, understands the modern nation-state to be not a formal self-enclosed totality but rather a precarious assemblage, an apparatus composed of a contingent set of institutions and practices, chief among which is colonial conquest.[271] Finally, Sassen, like Galli, argues that the global age has emerged not because the nation-state has been the "victim" of radically new global processes, but rather because of the nation-state's undoing of itself; in a different way than for Galli, Sassen thus holds that globalization is the radicalization of certain dynamics or unstable equilibriums within the nation-state itself (or what she calls its "denationalization").[272] Sassen, however, seeks to interpret globalization with reference to three "transhistorical components" that are, she claims, found in almost every society: territory, authority, and rights. These three components are, in Sassen's analysis, invariables; they are the constants on the basis of which Sassen interprets the change that is globalization.

As Peter Sahlins has noted, the historiographical dimension of this project is contradictory to the core: Sassen's book amounts to an attempt to narrate fundamental epochal transformations on the basis of components that somehow themselves remain transepochal and untransformed.[273] Indeed, Sassen's three components acquire their capacity to explain epochal transformation to the precise degree they remain exterior to, untouched by, and immune from that transformation. This form conveys a content that runs counter to Sassen's overarching claim. At the same time that Sassen wants to argue that globalization is a radically new age, the mode in which she presents her argument implies that globalization is no different than any other age; the emergence of the global age, just like the transformation of the premodern to the modern epoch, may be explained with reference to concepts that are themselves unchanging. This, in turn, offers us a deeply consoling fantasy: No matter how profound are the epochal changes we today seem to be witnessing, these changes are not so profound as to alter either the basic political space of modern political thought (territory) or the experiences of politics (authority and rights) this space enables us to think.

Nothing could be more different than Galli's genealogy of the global age. Instead of immunizing his own concepts from the epochal crisis he narrates, Galli instead lets his thought enter into an immediate or unmediated relation with that crisis. He adopts the innermost figures of the modern state—the inside–outside distinction, and the distinction of particular and universal—but not as "lenses" through which to view, as if from the outside, the emergence of the global epoch. He adopts them instead with the understanding that they are finite, epochal patterns that, under pressure from the crises specific to the global age, can and do dissolve from within. In *Political Spaces and Global War*, Galli uses figures of modern political thought in order to embody and realize their unusability; he enters into the internal logic of these figures in order to enact and perform their disappearance. Whereas Sassen seeks to narrate the collapse of the modern age on the basis of concepts that somehow remain outside of that collapse, Galli understands the crisis of space in the global age as an occasion to question the inner coherence of the most basic schemata that link *nomos* and *nous* in contemporary disciplinary reason.

In 1962, Schmitt famously declared that the enemy is "the figure of our own question."[274] The enemy, in this Fichtean formulation, is the prior *Gestalt* on the basis of which I *then* acquire the ability to pose the political as a problem for thought, such that there is no political thought that is not already shaped in some way by the silent force exerted upon my thought by the enemy's outline or profile.[275] Implicit in *Political Spaces and Global War* is a reversal and a displacement of this formula. For Galli, we might say, the global age poses *the question of our own figures*. It is that age in which a set of contingent and concrete events has exacerbated and aggravated a relation to space that, for modern political thought, was always difficult in the first place.[276] It is that age in which the "implicit spatialities" on the basis of which classical and modern political thinkers oriented themselves in thought are no longer capable of producing form or order, but are now open and exposed, intolerable impasses that pain all truly self-conscious attempts to think contemporary experience. It is an age that calls upon us to invent new figures of political space—figures that have the binding quality and synthetic force to keep pace with the events that involve and transform us.

"Necessary" Bologna

Focused as he is on the nexus between *nous* and *nomos*—on that inconspicuous bond that links political thought to the implicit spatiality that both supports and subverts it—Galli reveals that the history of political thought amounts to a history of political spaces that undo political thought from within. Depending on the thinker and the epoch in question, this undoing can take place in a wide variety of ways, according to much different vectors of torsion, planarity, measure, and movement. The image of thought that emerges from Galli's telling is neither that of an esoteric "quarrel" between the ancients and the moderns, nor that of a set of detailed, historically specific "contexts" enabling the use of this or that political term. It is a jagged, almost cubist portrait, a vast canvas of broken angles, a space in which war and peace have long since shaded into gray, a *Guernica* of epochal proportions.

To this image there is undoubtedly a "tragic quality," one that moreover resembles that of Schmittian thought. But Gallian tragicity is ultimately very different from Schmittian tragicity, and to understand how we need only consult Galli's introduction to the 1997 Italian translation of Horkheimer and Adorno's *Dialectic of Enlightenment*.[277] There Galli acknowledges the resemblance between, on the one hand, the "critical theory" of Horkheimer and Adorno and, on the other, the "negative thought" of Heidegger and Schmitt; both train a tragic and genealogical gaze upon the origins of Western reason.[278] For Galli, however, this resemblance is not at all an identity. It is instead the site of a disagreement in the most radical sense of the word. Whereas Schmitt argued that political order was impossible but necessary, Horkheimer and Adorno argued that the tragedy of modern domination was that it was *not* necessary.

And this consciousness of the nullity of the pure, real omnipotence of *Herrschaft*—of the non-fatality of its claim to destiny, of the falsity of its truth—unfounds [*sfonda*] the categorical horizon of domination and demonstrates the possibility of material freedom in the recuperative remembrance of the concrete being of one and all, beyond the deforming screens of power. The freedom of all is possible precisely because it is *not* necessary, precisely because it is *not* deducible from the present.[279]

The desire of critical theory, as distinct from negative thought, is thus

to deny the necessity of the continuity of history and . . . to think revolution not as progress, but as a qualitative leap beyond the progression of *logos*. Freedom is here not deducible from a concept or a project. It is instead the difference between concept and reality—it consists, in other words, in the opacity of the real. It opens up a "possibility" that *itself* puts an end to the necessity of domination, identifying the non-necessity of it. This is a possibility that is given to, and for, the imagination: it is the ability of all humanity to understand the self-evident irrationality of reason, as well as the urgency of thinking differently, of exiting from the categorical compulsions perpetrated upon them by the metaphysics of *logos*.[280]

Whereas Heidegger (and Schmitt too) "criticize reason in the name of nonreason," critical theory criticizes nonreason in order to demonstrate that "*the necessity* of domination is, in fact, a *nonnecessity*."[281] The result is an entirely different way of thinking through the tragic quality of the impasses of modern political order.

The *Dialectic of Enlightenment* does not oppose the necessity of *ratio* to its impossibility, as does negative thought—which, in so doing, of course denies the very possibility that there can be a rational society. Instead, it opposes the necessity of *ratio* to the rejected possibility, the gap and the leap, that emerge from thinking otherwise, outside the horizon of domination.[282]

Galli's *Political Spaces and Global War* (which, like *Dialectic of Enlightenment*, is not directly a philosophy of history but rather a "philosophic reading of history"[283]) is tragic in this precise sense. Consider, for example, Galli's emphasis on the importance of colonization for the formation of modern political space. Galli and Schmitt are in agreement that, absent colonization, modern political space would not have come into being at all; they are also in agreement that decolonization is an event of the highest importance for modern political space. Galli disagrees with Schmitt, however, over the sense in which modern political space may be considered "tragic." Schmitt understood the tragedy of the *jus publicum europæum* in a conservative declension: For Schmitt, it is the tragedy of a political order that so profoundly misunderstands its own irrational origins that it then proceeds to create a set of rationalistic theories and practices (humanitarianism, legal positivism, the criminalization of warfare) that, in turn, end up undermining the foundation for its own concrete order and orientation. For Schmitt, the *jus publicum Europæum* was—however riddled with aporias and impasses, however irrational at its core—nevertheless necessary to preserve.

Galli's *Spazi politici*, like Schmitt's *Nomos of the Earth*, also narrates the rise and fall of the *jus publicum europæum*. But it does so on the basis of a declension of the tragic that is incommensurable with Schmitt's. For Galli, the *jus publicum europæum* was tragic not because it was "impossible but necessary," but to the contrary because it was *never necessary in the first place*, and because its *false* necessity foreclosed upon a host of other theoretical, institutional, and practical possibilities for politics. The intellectual task that follows from this "critical theoretical" (or, as Roberto Unger might put it, "anti-necessitarian"[284]) declension of tragicity has nothing in common with the self-pitying bombast Schmitt generated during the postwar period (when he called himself "the last conscious advocate of the *jus publicum europæum*" and compared himself to the tragic hero of Herman Melville's 1855 short story *Benito Cereno*[285]). It is the specifically emancipatory task of recuperating the paradigms of thought and action that were consciously and forcefully suppressed by the advocates of the *jus publicum europæum*. Gayatri Spivak is right to call attention to the nuanced way in which Galli refers to "necessity" in his discussion of "'necessary' Europe."[286] The subtle lexical difference between "the *necessity* of Europe," on the one hand, and "the 'necessity' of Europe," on the other, implies an entire subterranean dispute; it is the point on which Galli most sharply rewrites the fatalistic genealogy of the *jus publicum europæum* that Schmitt offers in *Nomos of the Earth*.

This difference extends to include the very term Galli uses to gloss Schmitt's concept of "*nomos*." Galli, like Schmitt, breaks with Platonic political philosophy; both "political space" and *nomos* amount to attempts to think through the space of contemporary politics in a manner that is at once *completely immanent* (both concepts illuminate the relation between *nous* and *nomos* without also making any reference to a timeless Idea or to the universality of right reason, without recourse to what Galli in 2007 called "transcendent norms") and also *radically critical of the immanent* (both concepts provide ways to think through the relation between thought and space without supposing the possibility of a coincidence between thought and being). Taken to its logical conclusion, however, the same commitment to the principle of immanence that attracts Galli to Schmitt's concept of *nomos* also compels him to pass beyond Schmitt altogether. For Schmitt, remember, there can be no *nomos* of the Earth that is not constitutively sacred, and European political space, in particular, is a space the inside and outside of which is demarcated by a manifestly political theological decision.[287] In Galli's concept of "political space," by contrast, not only is any reference to the sacred quality of *nomos* conspicuously suspended, but Galli emphatically distinguishes his call for "new borders" from the forms of exclusion that were so essential for Schmitt.[288]

These two differences between Schmitt's *nomos* and Galli's "political spaces," we should note, are not unconnected. As Agamben has pointed out, the thought of the sacred and the practice of separation are two sides to the same phenomena. "Not only is there no religion without separation," Agamben writes, "but every separation also contains or preserves within itself a genuinely religious core."[289] Agamben's philosophical project involves an attempt to bring to completion the "profanation of the holy" that capitalism itself has already set into motion; he invites us to deactivate the salvational and sacrificial devices that govern our relations to life and law, not in order to completely erase their defining separations, but in order to free up those separations for new uses in a classless society.[290] To an extent, a similar ambition is at work in Galli's immanent critique of Schmitt's *nomos*. Galli, we might say, carries to its logical conclusion capitalism's "dissolution" and "disenchantment" of modern political space (its "sweeping away," we might say, of "fixed, fast-frozen relations, with their train of venerable prejudices and opinions"[291]), but *not*, however, in order to affirm the annihilation of political space as such: *Political Spaces and Global War* is not a vague embrace of a world of "flows" or simple "deterritorialization."[292] For Galli, globalization is nothing more and nothing less than an occasion "to rethink the thinkability of politics itself," and it is as a part of this rethinking that he asks us to imagine a new use for the concept of the *nomos* of the Earth. Galli's concluding call for a "secular promised land" may be understood as a "new use" of just this sort; even as its use allows us to realize the unusability of Schmittian categories, it also enjoins us to invent new forms of equilibria between particulars and universals, new figures of subjective emancipation, and, above all, a dialectical redefinition of the very meaning of "border" itself—a border that is desacralized and that is *therefore* no longer a relation of exclusion.[293] On a strict Schmittian understanding of *nomos*, a border of this sort would be a simple contradiction in terms. For a non-Schmittian Schmittologist, it is a task for thought.

Today, in the aftermath of the financial crisis of 2008, this task has become more exigent than ever. At a moment defined by the failure of all of the "shields" created by European jurists in the late 1990s to guard against financial crisis,[294] the populations of Europe are exposed today as never before to the sea of globalization (abandoned, in Balibar's stark rendering, like "carcasses floating along the stream of a river"[295]), and the very possibility of a "European Union" has been placed into question. "Unless it finds the capacity to start again on a radically new basis," Balibar warns, "Europe is a dead political project."[296] If the European Left is to respond to this crisis without also collapsing into what Balibar has elsewhere called "European apartheid,"[297] it clearly will need to articulate a theory and practice of political space that rejects the figures of partition in both root and branch.

Galli's "'necessary' Europe" is one of a range of contemporary philosophic concepts that could help the Left rise to this occasion. In 1955, Aimé Césaire declared that Europe's "great good fortune" was to have found itself at the crossroads of various ideas, philosophies, peoples, and cultures. Because exchange between civilizations is, in Césaire's memorable phrase, the very "oxygen" of civilization itself, the accidental but definitive attribute of European political space—its capacity to place civilizations in contact with one another—also conferred upon it the ability to serve as a locus for the "redistribution" of civilizational energy, a sort of "coefficient" capable of multiplying human vitality. The epochal tragedy of modern Europe, on these terms, was its failure to actualize this contingent but essential capacity; because of its embrace of racist theories of humanism and practices of colonial domination, modern Europe deprived itself of realizing of this, its innermost possibility.[298] Galli's concept of "'necessary' Europe," which construes European political space as a desacralized site for the reciprocal and unmediated exposure between individuals and populations, amounts to a recuperation of the "rejected possibility" Césaire describes. The "multicultural humanity" Galli imagines living in this space is neither the hierarchified humanity of the eighteenth-century Enlightenment (in which various "natural" cultures are "put in their place" by the mediations of a universal European mind[299]) nor the diversity of "repressive tolerance" (in which the necessity of preserving civil peace becomes an alibi for the oppressive management of cultures[300]). It is simply whatever humanity will emerge in a place where it is no longer possible to synthesize multiplicity with reference to the schemata of modern political space (inside and outside, particular and universal). As Galli sees it, this will be a humanity whose profile will come into view not on the basis of the mediations of this or that "concept" or "category," but only through the uncertain, contingent, and interminable work of mutual translation. Within this space of reciprocal unmediated exposure, to be sure, no one will be immune from a certain sort of conflictuality; but this will also be a space in which there is no need, indeed no grounds, for conflictuality to assume the modern form of hostility between friend and enemy.[301] On this view, in other words, Europe's current crisis is an *occasio* to imagine a political space that would be—in the strictest possible non-Schmittian sense—"unpolitical."[302]

For Galli, then, the global age is not merely a source for new forms of domination; it also contains a chance for an emancipatory "leap" into new and different practices of space and thought. It is worth underlining just how far this "leap" takes Galli from his point of departure in Schmittian thought. For Schmitt, as we know, the systematization of Roman Law that began in Bologna was not only "the great recurring event in the history of jurisprudence,"[303] but also the very foundation for the unity and community underlying the diversity of European traditions. "The cultural edifice built by the European spirit," Schmitt argued in 1943, "stands on this common foundation created by a common European jurisprudence. Its significance is no less than that of those great works of art and literature usually identified as the sole representatives of the European spirit."[304] Long before Galli ever began thinking through Schmitt in Bologna, in other words, Bologna itself was already implicit in Schmittian thought; more than any other, Bologna was the figure of political space that enabled Schmitt to define in genealogical terms the identity, centrality, and necessity of modern Europe. By Schmitt's own account, however, Bologna will also have been a *nomos* like any other; it will have contained the potential not only for order, form, and measure, but also for an antinomian energy that undoes the very *nous* to which it gives rise. Galli's achievement is to have set this dialectic back into motion, liberating the Schmittological antithesis of *nomos* and *nous* from the reification imposed upon it by Schmitt's attempt to freeze Europe into a timeless concept. Occupying the political space of Schmittian political thought on Schmitt's own terms, Galli drives Schmittology on toward a horizon Schmitt resisted, treating Schmitt's Bologna no longer as a source of identity, but now as a figure for a political space that, in the strictest possible Schmittian sense, subverts the very political thought it supports. "Bologna" is, to be sure, the name for the political space implicit in Galli's own political thought; but the Bologna that confers shape and form to Galli's non-Schmittian Schmittology is incommensurable with the Bologna that allowed Schmitt to theorize the supremacy of European jurisprudence. The Bologna implicit in Galli's thought is no longer the navel of modern European law and politics; it is a site for the crisis of the modern State (up to and including the managerial banality of bureaucratic state communism), for the dissolution of modern political space (which established "peace" in the center by pushing war to the margins), and for the emergence of a new sort of "creative intelligence," a practice of imagination that fixes its sights on the creation of unprecedented forms of concrete egalitarian politics.

In the strict Kierkegaardian sense, as Adorno wrote in 1933, the knight of faith leaps while also standing perfectly still: the *kairòs* in and through which the knight of faith leaps out of time, and that accounts for his absolute difference from his time, coincides with perfect immobility in space. In the Kierkegaardian leap, in other words, there is an immediate and paradoxical join between complete *kinesis* and complete *stasis*.[305] The leap that animates Galli's non-Schmittian Schmittology is no different. Galli's thought pivots on a repetition of the implicit spatiality of Schmittian thought, where "repetition" is understood, in strict Kierkegaardian terms, as a torsional force that creates turning points in history (or what Benjamin would call a leap in "the open air of history"[306]). To trace the genesis of Galli's genealogy of the global age to its origins in his non-Schmittian Schmittology is thus to arrive at a destination that is no less surprising for being implicit, all along, in the very premises of Galli's thought. With the audacity that characterizes all immanent critique, Galli's gloss of Schmitt's *oeuvre* reveals that Schmitt's "testament" can be executed in a manner that liquefies everything Schmitt ever willed. From the Nazi thinker of *nomos*, it is possible to inherit a concept of European political space that is no longer Eurocentric, a schema of the border that is no longer synonymous with political theological partition, and a photographic negative of a world in which plans for peace will no longer entail the globalization of war.

I

Political Spaces

Introduction

Ich verliere meine Zeit und gewinne meinen Raum: "I lose my time and win my space."[1] This is how Carl Schmitt expressed himself after the catastrophe of the Second World War, when—by then hostile to his own time, with the untimeliness of a "vanquished man writing history"— he believed that he had grasped the secret of the spatiality of politics. He believed that, with the concept of *nomos*, he had hit upon the interpretative key that would once again allow him to think the gene- alogy of modern politics—the real connection between appropriation and partition, order and orientation, and law and violence—against the liberal-democratic and communist universalisms that were then victo- rious. During the first period of *mondialization*—which was juridical, taking form at the start of the century when an international law, no longer completely Eurocentric, was being built between Geneva and the Hague—these universalisms were bringing about the second period of ideologico-military *mondialization*. With the destruction of the fascist hypotheses of a planet articulated in enclosed *Großraume* (or "greater spaces"), this second *mondialization* turned the planet into an arena of confrontation between individualist, capitalist liberal democracy and planned, collectivist communism.

But the third *mondialization*—which was techno-financial, and today goes by the name "globalization"[2]—needs to be interpreted according to principles different from Schmitt's, which were born at the extreme edge of the modern age, are sometimes ideological or mythological, and, more important, have little value outside the horizon of modernity.

Because today a serious discontinuity between the modern age and the global age is clearly perceptible, our navigation of this sea must be performed with other instruments, other compasses, and other maps.

Objectives, Hypotheses, and Method

The objective of this book is to observe globalization's manifold phenomenology with eyes that can perceive, above all, the fact of novelty. Our desire is to contribute to the specification of the categories through which we can comprehend globalization's new spatial principles (assuming there are any) as well as the new relationship between space and politics that is immanent to these categories. To fully measure this *novum*, we must first enter into a long circumnavigation through the political spaces of the West. This voyage will be much more tortuous than some presumed plan of progressive steps that proceed from City to Empire, State, Universal, and then, finally, to the Global—or, from a theoretical point of view, from the complex space of tradition to the geometric space of modernity and then to the formless space of globalization. Our voyage between the various political spaces of the West will involve turns, returns, and delays; above all, we will need to pay very close attention to the traps of modern political spatiality. With its complex structures and contradictory architectures, its Chinese box joints, its precarious equilibriums between internal and external, particular and universal, order and movement, form and conflict, Utopia and design, realism and idealism, figures of political geometry and universalistic dynamism, discipline and freedom, Continental states and Anglo-American political forms, modern political spatiality is the antecedent of globalization, even if today it is "surpassed" by it. Indeed, our analysis of modern political space—the space that is, today, distorted and revolutionized—will allow us a first comprehension, in the negative, of global political space.

The space that shall interest us is a specifically *political* space. It is, even more precisely, the space of the *implicit spatial representations* in and through which political thought supports itself. Our first hypothesis in this work, in fact, is that space is one of the inescapable dimensions for politics; it is through specifically spatial representations, that is to say, that political theories form their concepts, arrange their actors, organize their actions, and devise the aims of politics in terms of collaboration and conflict, order and disorder, hierarchy and equality, inclusion and exclusion, borders and freedom, sedentariness and nomadism, marginality and centrality. In our emphasis on space, we are dealing with a dimension that is much less conspicuous than time; there have been many more methodical and sophisticated reflections on progress, secularization, or the end of history than on the relationships between space and politics. Once we have explicated the relation of space to political thought we may find that we become able to throw at least a partially new light on certain sections and internal articulations of the history of political thought.

Our second hypothesis is that the spatial representations that are implicit in political thought derive from the concrete perception and organization of geographic space as experienced by a given society. The implicit spatial representations of political thought, in other words, refer back to the explicit displacements of space realized by the concrete articulation of power and of powers on the world stage; they respond to real historical challenges, supporting, criticizing, and refusing the modalities with which a determined epoch takes control of space, and, in so doing, creates its own political, economic, and cultural spatiality.

To say that space is important for politics is not, to be clear, to suggest that space dictates the rules or bends politics to its own internal "necessity." It means only that politics cannot but measure itself with space, that the control of space is one of the stakes in the game of power (along with the control of time, the symbolic, and production).[3] It is, in other words, *politics* that arranges *itself* in space and that, moreover, arranges *space itself*, determining it, not only insofar as it represents space in thought, but also because it politicizes, produces, and structures space in reality. As such, we may say, the (implicit) spatiality of politics is also the (explicit) politicity (*politicità*) of space. If political thought constructs itself in and through spatial representations, this is because politics concretely organizes the spaces of liberty, citizenship, law enforcement, and institutional efficacy. Politics extends the spaces of dominion, traces lines of exclusion, designs internal and external borders, determines the center and the peripheries, the "highs" and the "lows," and articulates the spaces of production and consumption.

Our third hypothesis—illustrated through examples, which will not be exhaustive, of the different spatialities implicit in modern political thought—is that modernity entertains a particularly difficult relationship with space, in which the dominant element is politics (centered on the Subject, State, and Society), and not space understood in a natural sense.

On the basis of this hypothesis, we will then argue that the politico-spatial categories that animate modernity and its institutional and political self-representations—the distinctions, that is to say, between internal and external, universal and particular, public and private, and cosmopolitan and local—are contingent and unstable geometries that are moved from within by internal dynamisms and dialectical universality.

Finally, our fourth hypothesis—and the one from which this work is specifically generated and oriented—is that the politico-spatial categories of the Modern are no longer usable today. Because globalization— understood as the immediate relationship between local and global— entails both the fulfillment and the dissolution of modern categorical structures, it will remain incomprehensible to us to the extent that our thought remains governed by those categories. In short, globalization not only changes the real organization of political space and its social and cultural perception, it also changes the implicit representation of space in political thought.

The method and the thematic limits of this work derive from the aforementioned objectives and hypotheses. In a sense, our task is the complementary reverse of the political geographer's, of those who— having digested Fernand Braudel's teaching that every social reality is, above all, a spatial reality[4]—pursue the geographic comprehension of political processes and the geographic interpretation of politics.[5] Or, we might say, it is the complementary reverse of the work of the legal historian who—knowing that space is internal to society, and not an empty and inert dimension external to it—characterizes, recalls, and interprets the concrete modalities with which, throughout civilization, organized human communities have explored geographic space, lands, and seas, and have rendered it productive of economic and political orders.[6] Or again, we could call it the complementary reverse of the work of a political expert with historic sensibility, such as Stein Rokkan, who designs a geo-political map of Europe by crossing the cleavage of city and country (East and West) with the cleavage of state and religion (North and South).[7]

Our concern, then, is with the other side of this same constellation, this same meeting, of space and politics. We want to understand how political thought has historically thought, and today thinks anew, the spatial dimension of organized human existence. We want to grasp the way in which political thought reacts to and modifies space, reflecting it or, on the contrary, orienting it and even making it possible. As such, this work will not deal with the history of scientifico-natural or philosophical ideas about space.[8] Nor will it advance a historical reconstruction, or a deconstruction, of geographical ideas about space (those which could be described as different "images of the world" in a realistic sense).[9]

The object of this work is not, in short, *the thought of space*. Rather, we must repeat, it is *the space in thought*, or, more precisely, the space that is at work in the history of political thought. We will not, then, engage in an analysis of the various spatial metaphors that are employed in and by political discourse (for this would be too vast and undetermined a theme). Nor will we limit ourselves to a consideration of the explicit thematizations of the link between space and politics, in the form of geo-politics[10] or the ontologies of Land and Sea, and the symbols of the House and the Ship[11] (for this would ultimately be reductive with respect to our intention). We do not even intend to offer the features of a history of the concept of political space (a concept configured in the modern age that presumably continues to configure itself, in a new way, at the dawn of the global age), if by this we mean, in the traditional way, the analysis of a theme or a *topos* of thought.

Put in positive terms, we may understand the work that follows as a contribution to the history of the concept of "political space" only if it is clear that this "concept" is sought and found even, and in some ways especially, *where it is not explicitly thematized*—only if it is clear, in other words, that what we are engaged in here is (in accordance with our first hypothesis) *the interpretation of space as a category for the thinkability of politics*, where space is understood as an inescapable dimension for the concepts in and through which political thought then, in turn, constructs its own concepts. In fact, the result of our treatment is that it will become clear that political thought actually organizes its own concepts by relating itself to space. "Democracy," "freedom," "sovereignty," "state," "empire," "globalization," "Europe"—all of these concepts are structured according to an implicitly spatial dimension, which is to say, they all implicitly return to a political representation of space. Our aim is to render these implicit representations explicit.

As we analyze the intellectual side of the historico-concrete relationship between space and politics, and clarify its implications as far as political concepts are concerned, it is essential that we remember our second hypothesis, namely, that the spatialities implicit in political thought relate to the real forms and deformations of political space, to conflicts born from dynamics of inclusion and exclusion, belonging or expulsion, and to antagonistic determinations of identity and alterity, subalternity, and domination. We can only understand space as a category of political thought insofar as we also consider space as an arena of *praxis*, as a theater of real power.

If, in the end, the development of our various hypotheses in this work culminate in a overall thesis, we might put it like this: Because modern political spaces emerged as a response to a challenge, they have configured themselves in very precarious and contingent terms. But because these same spaces are also capable, for better or worse, of housing within themselves the mobilizing forces of subjective and social liberty, it is necessary today to confront the great crisis of globalization—the fulfillment of the Modern's contradictions—with a new spatializing intent. In fact, if liberty in the Modern was that subjective action that proposed opening the State's closed space, today liberty probably lies in the search for new borders— certainly not, we would hasten to add, to realize the sort of closures that are dictated by a fear of open space or of new encounters, but precisely as new orientative guidelines that are capable of demarcating the spaces in which new encounters between new forms of subjectivities, both with themselves and with others, may become both possible and sensible.

Ours, therefore, is a political intent. We will support it with a work that is disenchanted enough with modern political geometries—with their by now worn-out tensions between freedom and order, between the "universal particularities" of subjectivity and the "universal particular" of the State—that it does not seek to reintroduce them today, unchanged, as though nothing had happened. This does not, of course, mean that our work will have as its objective a proposal for some sort of definitive New Order. It means only that we will use what energy we have to effectively delineate, in the midst of this *mare magnum* the Earth has today become, the space of new liberties for new, twenty-first-century subjectivities. Our task—a task that is political precisely because it is inevitably spatial— is to form, in new figures, a new equilibrium between particulars and universals.

1

Premodern Political Spaces and Their Crises

Even if it involves unavoidable brevity, let us begin by sketching an outline of premodern spatialities. This outline will have a simple purpose: to measure the disparity between premodern and modern space.

Political Geographies

The category that allows us to render premodern spaces intelligible is *political geography*. With this term, we certainly do not refer to the scientific discipline we know today, but to the political *quality* of geography or, better, the intrinsic politicity (*politicità*) of space that unites and separates human groups made different, as if by fate, because of their natural geographical location. We will outline this originary qualification of space with a brief *excursus* that runs from the large scale to the small scale (from Indo-European spatiality, to Europe, to the City and its internal struggles) and then returns again to the large scale (to Empire and Christian universalism).

Antiquity: Cities and Empires

Anthropology tells us that it was only with the Neolithic revolution that the forms of human coexistence passed from predatory to productive, from hunting and nomadism to agriculture. These forms then became territorialized, abandoning the mobile patterns of extended family belonging[1] and "inventing" a permanent and monumental type of civilization, namely, the *City*.

The City is born representing itself and organizing itself as a "world" that reproduces the sacred order of the universe on a small scale.[2] The City is undoubtedly a concentration of functions that were previously dispersed throughout the territory: it is a machine for accumulating power and wealth, first in the person of the king, then in the persons who compose the society. More important, however, the City is a sacred space made inhabitable not only—or not completely—by the work of technics (although this strengthens it in its interior), but more so by sacred acts (omens, auspices, conjurations, deprecations, sacrifices), which define the interior by comparing it to external space—by positively qualifying, that is to say, the latter's negative, or at least dangerous, qualities from within an enclosed space. These are acts of complex rituality that render order "productive," concentrating, in different ways for different subjects, the violence that "animates" the natural sacrality of space and separates order from chaos. It is not by chance that the space of the City—beginning from the Bible, which indicates Cain as the first city founder, and the myth of the founding of Rome and the establishment of her borders—incorporates homicide within itself.[3] Introduced within a naturally qualified spatiality, the City is the first form of political space and is extraordinarily long-lived and effective. In sum, we may accordingly say that the political space of antiquity was essentially a space of the City.

The first Indo-European civilizations, in particular, present a specific spatiality of political thought: the spatiality implicit in the representation of a *Trinitarian society*.[4] The functional tripartition of divinities in the sphere of the heavenly cosmos into regal, combatant, and productive (each function, in its own right, divided into positive and negative, creative and destructive) in reality acts as a model for the "micro" sphere of human society; it is within this "full" and organic space that Indo-European civilizations articulate and hierarchize themselves.

Within the sacred and political interpretation of space articulated by oppositions and hierarchies and among the many differences therein, we witness the emergence of a qualitative difference: Europe becomes conscious of itself as a land of *difference*. This difference is expressed both as an opposition toward the exterior, toward Asia (and, according to Aristotle, toward the North[5]), and as the difference at its own interior, which is intrinsically plural.[6] Greece is Europe's originary nucleus, and the differences between Orient and Occident, Greeks and barbarians—though they have been expressed in other ways—are qualitative before they are physically marked; the border is here the material expression of a quality of space. In general, every spatial difference reveals the Order of Being, which thought supports and reflects: it is space, qualified naturally, that has in itself the measure that then, in turn, legitimates its politics.

In the Greek world, political space is determined in many ways: sometimes as a pyramid of command (essentially on the battlefield), sometimes as a circle of the elders' council,[7] and sometimes as a space of participation inside the *polis*. It is here that political spatiality appears in its eminent sense: The *polis*—not as a space defined by the physical border of walls but as a group of citizens who meet and act in the "high" places of politics, the *agora* and the theater[8]—establishes the criteria of belonging (that which makes us "*polites*") and of exclusion (that which is not allowed) toward both the interior and the exterior. The *polis* also determines the quality and modalities of the relationship between citizen and foreigner, asserting, for example, the rights of autochthony (which, in Rome, would become much more binding than not). Moreover, the space of the *polis*, being qualitatively different and superior, contains the domestic space of production and need, which is not political as such.

But despite the compactness of the *polis*, a tension emerges within it between the idea of equality and democracy, on the one hand, which seems to refer to a smooth political spatiality, and on the other hand, the hierarchical idea of aristocracy and supremacy by birth. What is more, already in the first surviving example of Attic prose—the *Athenaion Politeia* of pseudo-Xenophon[9]—democracy is associated with thalassocracy, the needs of the fleet, and finally, the smooth element of the sea; while the aristocracy, the element of birth, and the verticality of command by the "finest" is associated with hoplitic war, the needs of the military, and land. This distinction appears, we should note, in a text that is not at all inclined to mythology or symbolism—a text that, indeed, is so severely realistic that it grasps with shocking force the idea that democracy is not peaceful coexistence, but a civil war waged by the people against the "finest," the idea that equality implies difference and that smooth space is in reality marked by a lacerating wound. But even here we can ascertain that, in Greek thought, political space is at root a *qualified space*—a space, that is to say, that is intrinsically and naturally endowed with a meaning that then, in turn, reverberates in politics.

Of the two ways in which Greek philosophy elaborates its theories on space—on the one hand, the neutral, empty, and homogenous space of the atomists; on the other, the full, objective, animated, organicistic, complex, hierarchical, and qualitative space of Plato's *Timaeus*[10]—political space in its true sense belongs, from the very beginning, to the second. In the classical age, political space is a qualified space, the logic and borders of which take precedence over the work and will of man.

The Greek City universalizes itself only with difficulty, in alternate and ephemeral attempts at hegemony. To aspire to the universal, Greek civilization must leave the City and make itself into an Empire, more Macedonian than Greek. Only at this price is the Hellenistic *oikoumēnē*[11] born. The City of Rome, on the other hand, thanks to its superior permeability toward the outside[12] as well as its predominantly juridical, and not ethnic, connotation of citizenship, is able to make itself into an Empire. But the universalism of Rome's Empire is also an example of political geography, intrinsically qualified spatiality.[13] Indeed, find as we may in this Empire every variegated mix of cultures and every porosity of borders—for the borders of the Empire certainly do not display the rigidity typical of modern nation-states—similarly and to a greater degree than in Hellenistic *oikoumēnē*, we do not find spatial indifference. The opposition between Occident and Orient, between the Olympians and "barking Anubis,"[14] is in fact the origin of Empire, knowingly imagined by Octavian as an alternative to Antony's Asian politics. Empire, moreover, is a universal space of the world of civilized men (whose *limes*, rather than excluding barbarians, attracts them, exhorting them to cross the threshold of humanity), and as such has a center of gravity, a curvature that qualifies it. It is, in short, a space with an inborn founding authority,[15] more *centering* than *central* (as Rutilius Namatianus writes at the beginning of the fifth century in *De Reditu Suo*, to summarize and praise a more than millenarian history: "*Fecisti patriam diversis gentibus unam*" [You made one fatherland from diverse nations]).[16] Classical spatiality is qualified even when configured as a global dimension. The Roman *ecumene* is not indifferent space; it is *patria*.

Even the cosmological Egyptian and Eastern Empires, albeit in more compact and less articulated forms, put forth the claim that the space of politics is a "cosmos." In fact, those Empires claim to represent celestial order on Earth, to organize the spatiality of the interior in analogy with Heaven, to express the Order of Being within themselves.

Their imperialistic teleologism derives from this claim, as does their tendency to think that the entire globe, chaotic in and of itself, must become a single space submitting itself to a single universal authority.[17]

Christianity and the "Res Publica Christiana"

Christianity does not really refer back to a space in any strict or proper sense. Indeed, the placement of mankind's *patria* in Heaven[18] is, in principle, indifferent to geography and politics. Instead, it reveals the abysses of the soul's inner life, transcendence, and the absolute verticality of God. Of course, Christianity addresses the question of the relationship between Heaven and Earth in an obvious and immediate way, but not as a relationship between two spaces, only as a continual critical and deforming opening exercised by the historically unattainable perspective of the City of God upon the events of the Earthly City. And yet, even though the relationship between Heaven and Earth is not then directly spatial, it nevertheless affects the representation of space in thought.

Political space now constitutes itself because Christianity brings onto the world stage a saved people—an *ekklēsia*. This people, whether inhabiting the underground space of the catacombs or triumphing with Constantine, resides—even if in the mode of a "*peregrina in sæculo*" (a stranger in the secular world)[19]—in an originary and ineliminable public dimension: "[T]he Church of Christ . . . is *in* this world. That means: it is localized and opens up a space; and space here means impermeability, visibility, and the public sphere."[20] This intrinsic public dimension, in short, gives the Catholic religion its spatial and juridical quality, which, until the Gregorian reform, was the forerunner and matrix of the Western juridical experience.[21]

Christianity's originary publicity and spatiality also explains the ease with which both Eastern Christianity and its Western counterpart, Catholicism, related positively to the qualified, objective, and hierarchical spatiality of classical Greece, as well the universal and imperial Roman spatiality, with its notion of authority—though, in the end, Christianity places this in God, and not in Rome or the universal mission of the *imperium populi romani* (imperial Roman people). Of course, the difference between Orient and Occident, in this case, is that in the European

Orient, the relationship between space and politics assumes the form of the imperial theology of *the One* devised by Eusebius of Caesarea, while in the Occident, political spatiality is implicitly arranged, from Gelasius onward, by *the Two*, which is to say, by the permanent conflict between *auctoritas* and *potestas*, *sacerdotium* and *imperium*.[22] This religious border within Europe is of the utmost historical importance and contributes to the determination of the different qualities of political cultures. In the Occident, where a lasting hegemony of one principle over another has never been known, and where Empire (and then State) and Church (followed by church*es*) have always been competitively compared, political cultures are predominantly critical. The European Orient, used to more than a millennium of "symphonic" collaboration between Empire and Church, to one voice, has more compact and dogmatic political cultures.

In the Occident in particular, the universality of Catholic space is thought in the modalities of a "pontifical" mediation between Heaven and Earth, or rather, of an objective *auctoritas* (the universal and supreme truth of salvation) that has its own center on Earth—the throne of Peter—and its own sphere, the *res publica christiana*, a qualified space that is rendered as such not by geography, but by religion.

The *res publica christiana*—from a concrete historical point of view, the European space of feudal lords, monasteries, and, later, of commercial cities—is pluralistic and at the same time, in principle, hierarchical at its interior. It is a space that is not smooth, within which the spaces of countless political realities are added and embedded[23]—it is a space of vertically organized difference, which, from a political point of view, fully legitimates the aristocracy. It is no accident, therefore, that Montesquieu would say that the principle of honor is responsible for the nobility of the father and the son; it is on honor, on the difference of quality between men as an organizing principle of political space, that the aristocratic system is based.[24] This system, in Christian Europe, founds its own hierarchical interior not only on differences of birth, but also, in the last resort, on a God who is creator and guarantor of this "stereometric" spatiality and organized plurality.

Because Christ is present wherever people gather together in his name, the *res publica christiana*, when compared with non-Christian spaces, is also marked by a qualitative difference toward the exterior. This difference is more transitory than permanent, as even these spaces are destined to be evangelized; Catholic universalism is in this sense objective and missionary, following the command of Jesus, *"euntes docete"*[25] (to spread the Word). But this logic—according to which the universal objective has the right and duty to fulfill itself—also founds the crusade, the "just war" based on the moral and ontological difference between the contenders.[26] As such, Catholic universalism is the originary matrix of all of those universalisms that qualify themselves in and through opposition.

However, the juridico-Roman element and specific religious elements are not the only competitors who seek to qualify the political space of Europe; there is also a strong Greek legacy. In fact, Plato's *Timaeus*, which itself informed the high medieval world, furnishes Catholicism with the idea that a complex, organic, and objective Order of Being exists. Within this space, we observe legendary voyages, extraordinary navigations, fabulous geographies, knightly wanderings, pilgrimages along the sacred roads of Europe, merchants' routes, fantastic and fearful landscapes[27]—all manifestations, from the ices of Ultima Thule to the sands of Libya, from central European wilderness to ocean shores, of the world's fullness and diversity.

From a political and juridical point of view, the plan of this ordered world would then be formalized by the culture of the middle and late medieval period through the notion of "Justice" (in which, to be sure, the "ordered world" was perceived in a much less fabulous and much more rationalized way, namely, through Aristotelianism). Justice provides a coherent and harmonious spatial picture, in which all things, actions, persons, and hierarchically superordinate and subordinate spaces of angelic, ecclesiastic, and political cosmology find a place and reveal themselves to be "good." In this space ordered by Being, politics is able to "do Justice" because it is submitted to and connected to Divine Justice. In fact, the Good Government—depicted best in Siena's Palazzo Pubblico[28]—protects both City and countryside with its Justice, derived as it is from Divine Justice through various mediations and through the guarantee of order. With a concreteness created by the opening to Transcendence, the Government transmits the Good (of the civil variety, while the religious is, obviously, entrusted to the Church's mediation) from Heaven to Earth. Thus, the qualitative and intrinsically hierarchical representation of space coexists in Christianity with a capacity to rationalize it (one example would be the cathedral).

This categorical picture does not at all entail a politics of appeasement; at its interior, there is space for Dante's Empire, for Marilius's City, and for the power of "the first deliberately nonlegitimate and revolutionary political association (*politischer Verband*)," the "*popolo*" of the "Plebeian City"[29]—in short, for that medieval commune whose internal rate of conflict, but also of political participation, created a political space that would contribute to the genesis of Machiavelli's politico-spatial model.

The Spatial Crises at Modernity's Origin

Modern politics has its origin in a set of catastrophes that are also, in effect, *spatial revolutions* that reveal the qualitatively differentiated spatiality and hierarchical stereometry that had structured the traditional Order of Being to be impossible. In modernity, space is no longer the bearer of politics, nor is it organically full of complexity. It is instead dequalified and undifferentiated—empty of any measure. As it begins to come into its own, it is not yet universal in the modern sense, but it is no longer universal in the traditional sense.

Crisis

Put simply, modern political space is a space of *crisis*.[30] Of cosmological crisis, due to the "Copernican Revolution" and the disorientation it causes in man, whose Earth loses its central place in the universe. Of geographical crisis, provoked by the discovery of America, which, among other things, paved the way for the Mediterranean's centrality to be supplanted by the Atlantic's and the shift of Europe's center of gravity from South to North (a shift much more revolutionary than the barbarian invasions or the Arab, and later Turkish, advances). Of the crisis of *economic spatiality* (the passage from "open fields" to enclosures and the beginning of capitalist primitive accumulation, which resulted in the expulsion of the poor into the cities and the redefinition of new rural and urban landscapes). Of categorial crisis—originating in nominalism—within the traditional apparatuses of thought, the hierarchical relationships between different spheres (theological, political, economic), the idea of Justice, and the qualified space that gives measure to everything, receives everything, in which everything takes root. Above all, modern political space is the theo-political crisis of the *res publica christiana* spurred by the Lutheran Reformation. One fundamental effect of these crises is the liberation of the individual subject from the weight of spiritual *auctoritas*, and the gradual disappearance of political spaces' organic plurality. By setting the inessential space of exteriority against the infinite abyssality of an inner life that is, by definition, devoid of space, the Reformation produces a subjectivity that is, in effect, liberated from space. More precisely, it produces a Protestant subject who, when projected outside himself, is able to place himself anywhere, to take control of any land, precisely because he is not at home in any place.[31] Religion here loses its own objective relationship with space, and the sectarian borders within European space overlap and intersect, torn apart by religious civil wars. On the whole, we find ourselves before a catastrophic "crisis of European conscience," a "loss of center" for the traditional man—even though, as we shall see, it is precisely this social, economic, and political uneasiness that will give Europe the energy to place itself at the center of world politics until at least the end of the nineteenth century.

We will stress that modernity derives its origin from the destruction of the spaces of tradition, responding to these crises with multiple spatial projections and countless artificial borderlines. The many spatial criteria of modern politics, along with the many spatialities implicit in its forms of thought and its institutions, reveal that it has an arduous relationship with space—that it is, more precisely, no longer able to identify any spatiality that is *immediately* political. In short, in the Modern, it is not space that exhibits an intrinsic political measure; it is politics that determines space.

The New World

Among these challenges, the "discovery" of America—which was also, of course, "invention" and "conquest"—is, with the Reformation, the most radical, as it produced the breakup of the ordered plan of Being, forcing European humanity to reorient the spatiality implicit in its own political and moral thought. This occurred in many ways.

On one hand, the discovery of America—the event in which the Old World, as Montaigne said, found another[32]—gave birth to a vast tradition of thought in which the "newness" of the American world differentiated it from the Old World through youth and immaturity, but also through decadence and coarsening, through excessive closeness to nature and distance from civilization, and through excessive distance and aberration from the paradigms of natural humanity.[33] Europe's attempt to react to the disorientation implicit in the experience of difference contains the origin of that relationship of opposition between "us" and "the others" (the so-called problem of the "savages") that structures so much of modern political thought.[34]

Of course, the pillaging and extermination of the Mexican at the hands of the Spanish, or the "redskin" at the hands of the Anglo-Saxon colonizer, included an initial moment of reciprocal misunderstanding. But, however political thinkers consider the figure of the "savage"—better, worse, or equal to Europeans, even in their diversity—this figure (which is analogous, moreover, to oppositions between Europe and America) is constructed with strategies that are useful precisely because they give meaning, through opposition, to a space that, in itself, is "empty" and that therefore, in its infiniteness, inspires vertigo. For Europe, then, the "savages" are political figures—not of spatiality, but of the *absence* of spatiality in its qualitative and originary sense. They are figures born from the West's need to reassure itself of its own identity and capacity for domination, which it found shaken by the traumatic experience of the Other.

The perception of spatial dequalification and moral undifferentiation was already at work in Montaigne who, in his 1578–1580 essay "Of Cannibals,"[35] does not place America in qualitative opposition with Europe, but rather on the same plane as it. In Montaigne, the judgment of "barbarism" is, all things considered, completely reciprocal, though in the ingenuous and childlike world of the Americans, the barbarism seems due to a lack of civilization,[36] while in Europe, it stems from an excess of artifice (*artificio*).[37] This discovery of the relativity of systems and of morals—for which, as Pascal will later say, "a meridian determines the truth"[38]—is the opposite of a new spatialization qualified by politics. Space here still determines variations of politics and morals, but now with the critical difference that these variations are now random—they are indifferent differences, differences devoid of quality. Where space is still that which determines politics, but no longer in the sense of a qualitative determination, this means that space has become, in reality, that which *un*determines politics—that which, precisely, *relativizes* it. This undetermined space certainly gives rise to an attitude of tolerance, but it also involves great standardization and indifference: it is an opening to the Other, but only insofar as the Other has already been "decided" as our equal.[39]

It is no accident that the tendency toward skeptical inner life begins here, with the subject's withdrawal from an external space that is now senseless into a sort of private utopia—an escape that is almost opposite, in its libertine results, from Thomas More's "public" moralistic–authoritarian escape (which is, in turn, quite distant from Thomas Hobbes's Utopia). It is from this inner utopia that the mature bourgeois individualist[40] shall emerge, looking to reconquer the very space he had previously escaped. In the course of this *reconquest of space* that is modernity, and that is made possible by the discovery of America, space assumes a sort of "perspectival" value[41]: the initially relativized and senseless space of absolute alterity becomes a space "for us," a space newly legible, but only from the point of view of Europe's new artificial and scientific rationality.

Opposition (but now dequalified) and relativization are, then, two of the modalities through which European thought faced the discovery of America. But, according to a different interpretation by Catholic historian Alphonse Dupront,[42] America was "invented"—within a humanist Renaissance culture—as singularity, alterity, and novelty, an object of *curiositas* and admiration.[43] Read through these classical intellectual coordinates,[44] the discovery of another space, of new men and new morals, also allowed the discovery of another time, in an attempt to return, through the "savages," to the origin of humankind. This was a return that could not succeed, but it led to the recognition, through the figure of American alterity, of a natural common order of humankind, a shared foundation for the progress of the species.[45] However, it was not only on time, and on the myth of origin and progress, that the new American space acted; above all, for Dupront, it is in America's limitless space that modern man both finds his liberty and loses his way. In the infinite opening of nature to the gaze and its new availability as possession, we see the origin of the bourgeois scientific will to power that will soon be deployed all over the planet. We also see the universal foundation of truth, the root of a potential *consensus omnium* (agreement of all) which finally realizes the fullness of the human condition, a fact already noted by Francisco de Vitoria, who theorizes the moral and material unity of the world through the American Indians.[46] The discovery of America, according to this Catholic historian, presents a challenge for the humanism of old Europe, which first constructs and then suffers alterity. Furthermore, through the experience of the duality of spaces and worlds, it not only produces relativization, but also allows humankind to reach the unity of a global space, qualified by a new, concrete humanism.

With these scenarios of nonqualitative opposition and of relativization, of newness and unity, we must now include the thesis of a very different kind of Catholic: Schmitt. For Schmitt, as distinct from Dupront and de Vitoria, America is neither a space characterized by its status as an object of relativistic discovery, nor a humanistic invention of alterity and, later, vehicle for the reunification of humanity. Rather, because it is deprived of Statehood, it is an object of conquest and division—which are, for Schmitt, the only logical result of discovery—for the European States.[47] The modern space revealed by the discovery of America, for Schmitt, is not full of *mirabilia* (miracles). It is essentially empty, homogenous, and dequalified. Its destiny is not to bring unity to humankind, but division.

2

Responses from Political Thought

Without laying claim to the completeness required by historical erudition or theoretical modeling, let us now analyze a few of political thought's reactions to the different spatial crises (in addition to the discovery of America) with which modernity begins.

Machiavelli

In Machiavelli, we witness the exhaustion of the hypotheses of an ordered plan of Being or of a Justice that supplies the objective measure of human action. Politics, whether individual or collective, now becomes a "virtuous" operation. It also, however, and in this same movement, becomes excessive and over-the-top, taking place in a space that is neither ordered nor qualified by natural characteristics. The space implicit in Machiavelli's political thought is most explicit in the fourteenth chapter of *The Prince*,[1] where Machiavelli interprets landscape and space in military terms, and where he reads the "nature of sites" from the point of view of a war that almost coincides with politics, due to the reciprocal reversibility of "good laws" and "good arms."[2] The substance of space and its ontological order here disappear, transfigured by a specifically practical knowledge of politics (a knowledge arising from the particular, Tuscany, that nonetheless makes itself universally usable through "certain similarities with other provinces"), which translates both space and order into a new code within a different horizon, in which what matters to the Prince is "how to find the enemy, how to pick quarters, to lead armies, to arrange battles, to besiege lands to your advantage."[3]

However, what emerges from the crisis of traditional space is not the formless uniformity of a fully available and potentially scientific space (as will happen in Hobbes). Furthermore, even though he lives in the midst of the Renaissance, Machiavelli does not adopt the reading of space promoted by Italian humanism, which seeks to reorder space in terms that are simultaneously objectively Platonic and anthropocentric.[4] As far from the spirit of the Renaissance world as it is from the scientific and individualist, modern image of the world, Machiavelli's space is instead determined by potential politicity (*politicità*) and latent conflicts. Space is here crossed by vectors of conflict, by the always-changing theater of the "virtuous" operation, and this conflictuality is, for Machiavelli, space's paradoxical qualification, one based on neither boundary lines nor moral differentiations, but simply on the search for glory.

This link between conflict and glory is the very opposite of the link that rationalism would later institute between conflict and order. Machiavelli thinks a logical and spatial continuum between contingency and political action, a "natural" affinity between fortune and virtue that arises from his intuition that chance and contingency are, in the last resort, ungovernable by even the most capable human work. Of course, as Machiavelli writes, we must build quays and embankments to contain the river of fortune,[5] but sooner or later, these too will be swept away by circumstances that even the most virtuous man cannot foresee. Machiavelli's "spatial" metaphor on the topic of good and evil, which states that the Prince must "know how to *enter into* evil when he needs to,"[6] reveals that politics does not consist in escaping reality (and, in this, Machiavelli is distinct from what both More and Hobbes, albeit in opposing ways, will maintain). On the contrary, it is played out within the specifically tragic dimension of contingency, a dimension in which conflictual political action is able to qualify as "glorious" but without also, however, finding itself able to "modify" the world in a constructivist sense. Machiavelli is incapable of "construction" because he lacks not only the modern notion of the Subject who is able to represent himself and his powers in the State, but also, and more important, the logic and the regulating finality that sustain modern rationalism's entire political thought.

Nonetheless, distant though he may be from the ordered spatiality of State modernity, Machiavelli's space is already expressly modern, for it does not dictate the rules to politics, or present an antecedent measure to politics. Rather, it is a space that receives energy from politics, and it can be said to possess a "quality" only insofar as it is political (which, for Machiavelli, is true of any sphere of reality).[7]

We see this nonobjective, purely political qualification of space emerge in the *Discourses*. There Machiavelli seeks the "scientific" predictability of political events not only in the "cyclical" succession of political forms,[8] but also in the analogy between ancient and modern, in the constancy of human passions and their spatial distribution.[9] Space here is the foundation of a kind of "geography of virtue" that changes from one province to another, from one people to another, but is due less to objective causes than to the "form of education" of the populace, whose "national constants" are thus political and not natural.

It bears repeating that because Machiavelli's universe of discourse is neither rationalist nor constructivist, the fact that space here exists *for the sake of* politics does not mean that space is *indifferent to* politics. Rather, even though space here does not bring "measure" to politics, it does constitute a variable in the expression of the energy of politics. The importance of space for politics is demonstrated in Book Two of *Of the Art of War*, where Machiavelli describes what we might call "the cycle of virtue."[10] The victorious expanse of the Roman Empire, Machiavelli there argues, concentrated every political virtue within itself, pushing it toward Europe, Asia, and Africa. After the decadence of Rome, virtue was no longer revived for various reasons; because the large dimensions of modern States keep them safe from the fear of "ultimate ruin" after defeat in war, they no longer pushed their inhabitants to fight with the same passionate virtue as citizens of small, ancient republics (which could be annihilated in a single defeat).

Here, let us note, we find a negative judgment on the "bracketing of war" that is typical of the *jus publicum europæum*,[11] and in Machiavelli there is also a kind of anticipation (but now in the positive) of the republican emphasis on the "small State." This does not mean that Machiavelli objectively prefers small dimensions (for, on the contrary, he elsewhere condemns those aristocratic republics that remained prudent "in the short term," accusing them of suffering from "avarice," a mentality dominated by acquisition and fear of "tumults" and "infinite dissensions," which are actually "the causes of expansion,"[12] as they generate the energy of virtue in people). Rather, it means only that political virtue is once again the standard and the objective of Machiavelli's discourse, which is not oriented around a State-owned space in which politics is *represented* (as in

Hobbes), but around a municipal political space, one that may extend across a given region, but that is nevertheless always able to allow its citizens political *participation*. This is not due to the quantitative dimension of political forms' geographic expansion, but to the specific political spatiality of Machiavelli's thought, or rather, to the coordinates with which he interprets political space. These are not coordinates of order, but of energy, and they are modern because they imply a perception of nature's lack of a spatial and ontological Order of Being. To the extent, however, that these coordinates render space intelligible as a vector of conflict and a variable of virtuous action, they situate Machiavelli laterally with respect to geometric representations of modern statuality (*statualità*).

More

The opposition between Machiavelli's politics of power and Thomas More's political moralism is, to be sure, a well-worn interpretative *topos*.[13] Nevertheless, where implicit spatiality is concerned, it must be said that the two presentations are, indeed, quite distant from each other. More—in his classical moralistic rationalism and his model Catholicism—reacts primarily to the crisis of Justice as an Order of Being, to the "topsy-turvy world" that England has become, in which every measure is lost, and no one and nothing remain in their proper place. His egalitarian communism, which lets neither private property nor the differences between city and country subsist, is an explicit polemic against the spatial revolution brought about by the enclosures.[14] Utopia—in the specifically "public" sense More gives to the term—is therefore a double space. On the one hand, it is a space (namely, the space of order) that, in the concrete, *is not there*, but which, in the abstract, *should be there*. On the other hand, it is a space which, in the concrete, *is there*, but which, in the abstract, *should not be there* (and which, in any case, cannot have ontological consistency). The political reality of disorder and injustice, despite its existence, is therefore, for More, a "non-place," a realized absurdity to which More's Utopia (an ideal non-place whose opposite is a real non-place) diametrically opposes itself, in an immediate negation of negation.

There is thus an initial alterity in Utopia and in the way it does not "take place" in the space of the world. Utopia is an island of Ought and morality, and only in Utopia is the Order of Being, Justice, operative (without, however, having any apparent relationship to Being or to the disorderly and iniquitous sea of reality). Utopia is both elsewhere and nowhere, and as such it is a rock against which the waves of history are powerless. But this insularity is less a sign of hope than a sign of desperation. After all, the same nomenclature More uses in his Utopian work (Utopia, Amaurot, Anidron, etc.) also governs the self-denying paradox he develops in analogy with Erasmus's nearly contemporary work, *In Praise of Folly*: on the one hand, More dismisses the givenness of empirical reality as utter unreality (as nothing more than a dream of reason), while on the other hand, he sarcastically and resignedly accepts, as an utter impossibility, the possibility that Justice could truly realize itself in the space of Being.

But since More's rational abstraction reflects, like a play of mirrors, the concrete and irrational deformation of the space of Justice, and since the island of Utopia is actually the opposite of England, Utopia becomes the other face of the Modern, not its radical alterity. Modern Utopianism is characterized not so much by an opposition between "full" rootedness and "empty" uprooting as by two modalities of uprooting: on the one hand, the historic, concrete, chaotic uprooting of the first proto-capitalist agrarian revolution, and, on the other, the uprooting of rationalistic planning, here declined in a specifically Utopian form, which wants to transform that disorder into order. For his part, the order More seeks is "transparent," and not without pedagogical authoritarianism, and the modalities of establishing it can only be described as an escape from an implicitly corrupt "state of nature"—a moralistic retreat into the island of Ought.

The duplicity of Utopia—suspended, as it is, between alterity and specularity compared with the Modern—makes even its implicit spatiality double. On the one hand, More makes reference to a differentiated space and clearly distinguishes between good and evil, allowing hardly any contact between these two realities. From this perspective, Utopia is an absolute "reserve," a pure potentiality, a "message in a bottle" entrusted to future centuries in a gesture of hopeful desperation. But on the other hand, More implicitly thinks the space of "bad" reality as completely destructured, uniform, and undifferentiated. He perceives it, in short, as a dimension that is fully and integrally available for modification by the forces of good, by the "moral politics" of Utopia. Even though it is impossible to know how or when, Utopia therefore retains the capacity *to overflow*, to leave its own "reserve" whenever it likes and to strike out against its "unjust" enemies in a just and humanitarian war[15]—as an Ought tends to do, wherever and whenever it transforms itself into Being. Even if it does not have a coherent strategy to realize itself, then, More's Utopia is nevertheless, paradoxically, *a concrete plan*: It is a plan for *a non-place* that, *in nuce*, contains within itself artifice, desperation, and hope.

Scholars from Gerhard Ritter to Hans Freyer saw in Utopia this dimension of smooth space not only in its interior (in the form of moral and political equality) but also in its exterior (in the form of just and humanitarian war); they saw that this undifferentiated spatiality is available to a moralizing intent, this possibility that within Utopia there hides an oppositional universalism, a spirit of crusades and of "just war."[16] They saw a metaphor for a mode of power inclined to conceal its status *as* power, and to present itself instead as a universal, as an essentially ubiquitarian form of Justice. They saw the metaphor of English naval powers presenting their particular power politics in moralistic and universal terms (and England, for them, was what the United States is today, though in the United States, the Protestant legacy is in play alongside the inheritance of the British Empire). This sort of politics does not hesitate to move war across the world "for the world's own good." At the very least, it envisions the world as a smooth space, available to "good" or "useful" powers—to powers, that is to say, which industriously use commerce, marine forces, communications, and electronics, along with aerial and spatial technology, to mold the world in their own image.

Hobbes

More's "naval" and "moral" response to modern spatial revolutions finds its counterpart in Hobbes's "terrestrial" and "realistic" response (even with all the reservations that must accompany such a definition[17]). In Hobbes, we observe a "Utopian" escape similar to More's—but this time it is an escape from a nature that is, paradoxically, naturally unlivable, in which Justice has never occurred. Hobbes's aim is to "return" after this escape—to revisit natural space after having just left it, but now in order to dominate what before was dominant, to institute an order more artificial than moral, a mechanical and individual order that it constructs rationally, an order that is rigid externally to the precise degree that it is able to contain the dynamism of the modern Subject internally. Though we recognize the distinction between the political models of order and conflict,[18] our observation regarding the link between space and political energy in Machiavelli is also valid for the Hobbesian relationship between space and order, for both think *determinations of space by politics* and not *political "measures" that emanate from space*. It is in this respect only that the two can be associated within the rubric of "political realism." As far as everything else is concerned, Machiavellian politics (which emphasizes conflict) is exactly what Hobbesian politics (which is centered on order) combats and denies. Between the two greatest modern political thinkers there is, therefore, an unbridgeable distance: a distance which, from the point of view of concrete historicity, is equal to the passage from City to State, from municipal conflicts that make the City the high place of politics to their neutralization in the extended spatiality of the State, in which the City becomes, at most, the capital—in other words, just a function, even if a central one.

From the standpoint of the implicit spatiality of politics, Hobbes's revolutionary gesture—which opens a "new world" to politics at least as far as the discovery of America is concerned—consists first in his substitution of the traditional "pontifical" link between transcendence and immanence with the rational link between nature and artifice (*artificio*); and second in his substitution of naturally articulated and hierarchical space with homogenous, disorderly, and uniform space, which can, however, be ordered through the power of reason. The radical assumption Hobbes makes, through his embrace of materialistic atomism, is that natural space is "empty" and not open to any "beyond" relative to itself—and this, of course, implies that space has no quality. Because every stereometric, organic, and qualitative structure of space is alien to Hobbes, so too does he refuse every natural hierarchy among men,[19] deny that Justice exists in nature as an Order of Being, or accept the notion that it is possible to "*unicuique suum tribuere*" ("to give each his due").[20] For Hobbes, Justice is, if anything, simply *the logic of the pact*, which by definition must be respected by anyone who is not "stupid." This thesis finds its appropriate spatial representation in Hobbes's assertion that America is the "state of nature." Implicit in this is that, for Hobbes, America is not a more or less corrupted alterity, but the beginning of the construction of our own State, and also our immanent risk—our end—should we find that we are unable to construct political artifice (*artificio*) or should we run that artifice to ruin.[21] Hobbes's "Other" is therefore an equal: we ourselves *are* the "savages"—at least potentially. The differences in civil development between "us" and "them" do not protect us from the risk of plummeting back into nature, a risk we fully run with religious civil wars (which are, of course, the real historical challenge to which Hobbes's political thought responds). Hobbes here leaves behind the skeptical relativism of Montaigne; in the undifferentiated uniqueness of world space, he discovers a unique, undifferentiated human nature. He discovers that, in nature, there is no such thing as a good savage or a bad savage. Rather, there is everywhere, and in everyone, the same natural and dangerous mix of reason and passions.

Above all, Hobbes performs a spatial simplification. The space he thinks—the "state of nature"—is completely deprived of any intrinsic measure. It is uniform in its multiform diversity and its endless conflict. It is a space he thinks not because he supposes an authority will emerge naturally from it, but rather because it shows him the logical cogency of transitioning (or rather, "leaping") into the artifice (*artificio*)[16] that must order space, thereby eliminating the concrete danger which runs through it: mankind's incapacity to collaborate, their violent interaction. With this, Hobbes reinterprets contingency, the unpredictability of the world, and the conflicts of existence, reading them now from the standpoint of the Subject's need to have a safe life, to eliminate the mortal danger of noncollaboration and aggression, and to guarantee man his necessary security. For Hobbes, in other words, violence does not "animate" space; it is only a mortal danger to be avoided. For him, the City cannot incorporate bloody sacrifice, but must banish it (perhaps at the price of the bloodless sacrifice of the Subject's natural freedom), and *as such* must become a State.

It is not important, now, that the objective of excluding the contingency of political space had already failed in the *Leviathan*, and that contingency naturally infiltrates internal space from the exterior.[22] Instead, we must remember that implicit in Hobbesian thought there is, in the first place, a space that can be abandoned; that Hobbes interprets nature as a Nothing from which to escape or to manipulate in the interests of security; and that Hobbes understands politics as a partition between associated life and the external Nothing—a sort of bulwark placed between us and death.[23] This is the archetype of modern politics, oriented toward saving the life of the Subject even at the cost of his natural freedom, which is primarily a freedom of movement, a hostility toward boundaries, and an indifference to space.[24] However, Hobbes also abandons the other aspect of natural freedom—the "freedom of," which is to say, the "power of governing oneself"—if for no other reason than that such freedom in nature is, like the first (of which it is only a specification) both absolute and impossible. Both freedoms, in fact, return to the same formless and available space, even though this space is not anthropomorphic, even though it is not, therefore, immediately "made" for man, and even though it will indeed soon reveal itself to be completely uninhabitable. As such, these freedoms refer to a space of danger, in which anyone may be free and dominant, but at their own risk. The "freedom from" relates itself to this space in the mode of uprooting and through the absolute mobility of the Subject; the "freedom of" relates itself to this space in the mode of the expansion of the Self.

This abandonment of natural space, as we have noted, makes even the "realist" thought of Hobbes literally Utopian. But Hobbes's peculiar Utopianism implies that the Subject, in a typically modern fashion,[25] reacts to disorder and the uninhabitability of natural space by representing himself in an artificial space, the State, which is built according to coordinates originating from the Subject's viewpoint, defining a space fully available to subjective reason and its effectiveness, to *technology*. This space is "artificial" because it is constructed, and not natural; but it is actually quite real, represented but effective, and clearly limited. Thus, even though it is made by man, it is incompatible with his natural liberty; it is the result of both his desire for security and his vocation for manipulating nature. But, as we will see, even though the modern Subject still needs this artificial limitation, he retains a reluctance toward borders—an anxiety over freedom from political space and an anxiety over productive expansion of the Self—that will manifest itself in the construction of "universals" out of forms that are not immediately political, but economic and moral.

Hobbes's thought thus refers to a space that is neither natural nor anthropomorphic. It is, above all, an artificial representation available to "geometric" intervention—Hobbes's analogical reference to Cartesian mathematics is obvious, even more so than in Spinoza—by the macro-Subject, the *sovereign*. Our use of the term "geometric" here is not metaphoric. The spatiality of Hobbesian thought consists in the application of a constructive rigor to the artificial space of politics. This rigor is analogous to the rigor employed by the only science that, according to

Hobbes, God bestowed on us,[26] the only science capable of measuring up to natural space: geometry. If politics is to make itself "absolute," it must make itself an exact and rational science, like geometry, and it does so by clarifying its own definitions and defining its own actors, and ends with a rigorous nominalism that excludes every claim to transcendence. From this foundation of desperate optimism and a growing awareness of the world's desolation, but also faith in the constructive capabilities of subjective reason, Hobbes sees the political problem as tantamount to an algorithm of compatibility, the correct solution to which will point the way to the rational path (the method and the technological instrumentation) that leads, in turn, to cooperation between individuals (who Hobbes construes as equals arranged on the same horizontal space). This path is one that renders effective the rational laws of nature, laws which are naturally present, but not immediately operative, in every particular individual. Modern politics is therefore indifferent to space—not because it can set space aside, but because it makes space into whatever it wants.

The first result of this techno-geometric political science is the construction of the artificial representation of citizens—the *sovereign*—who is able to order space and make it secure, or better, who is able to unify a portion of it by confining conflict, by neutralizing the civil war of religion at the interior and driving it to the exterior. This contractual, representative, and artificial sovereignty that brings unity, order, and peace to the people within its perimeter (and which, in fact, creates them as political subjects), is obviously vertical compared with the horizontal space it defines, establishing borders and compulsory rules while simultaneously reserving the right to break them, controlling transgression and exception. The smooth, planar space of politics is here clearly contained—as Schmitt demonstrated—in the volume of a "crystal."[27]

Within this State, we are therefore able to speak about "high" and "low"—and even about the center (which is also the perimeter, the form, the Whole, the *sovereign*) and of periphery (the constituent parts of the Whole, the *citizens*)—but only if we remember that, from a logical and categorical point of view, we are not dealing with qualified, ontological, stereometric, or organicistic spatiality. In fact, the verticality of modern sovereignty is quite distant from that of traditional authority; it is a rational mediation, and not a foundation or a pontifical mediation between Heaven and Earth.[28] Better: modern sovereignty is only the exertion of a rational and functional power. The sovereign who is depicted in the frontispiece of *Leviathan*—who is quite different from contemporary effigies of the absolute sovereign as "Sun"—is not engaged in "Good Government," and lacks any relationship with Heaven. His work is not pontifical but representative, and it is through representation that he is constitutive of the people.[29] Despite the frontispiece image of the *makroanthropos*, however, sovereignty is not describable through the traditional organicistic image (a head compared to the limbs, etc.). Instead, it generates a functional, one-to-one correspondence between State and Citizen, between particular and universal, who are dependent on each other even in their antagonism. The space of the State, though it is therefore the space of sovereignty, is thus also, and at the same time, the space of Citizenship. The figure and form of the sovereign are thus necessary to determine the figure and form of a neutralized space, exempt from conflict, on which politics imposes its own law. This law is *jus soli* (a "right of the soil") and not *jus sanguinis* (a "right of blood"). It is internal to a space that is ordered politically, not naturally: *taxis*, not *cosmos*.

From an internal point of view, the space determined by the sovereign is a smooth, unitary, neutralized, and peaceful space, founded on the prohibition of civil war and on the legal equality of its citizens, more so than on their natural freedom of movement. This positive law, structurally determined both by the sovereign act that sets it and the territory where it is valid and effective, takes the place of traditional Justice and functions as a new canon—at once absolute and limited—of justice understood as "conformity to law."

It is critical to note that the "citizens," despite having knowingly renounced their natural mobility as "humans" and their freedoms "of" and "from," are not attached to the ground inside the State. Though preceded by an originary geometric operation on the part of the sovereign to establish the borders of land ownership, individual mobility remains, but it is devoid of its absolute and natural dimension, which generates conflict. The State, in short, serves the purpose of giving cohabitation stability, but it does not impose fixity or rootedness on the Subject; its artificiality renders its space not only horizontally ordered, but also "without quality."

If, from a political viewpoint, this is a residual liberty which finds expression only in spaces where the law of the sovereign is silent, from the individual Subject's viewpoint, it nevertheless reveals itself as a possibility for laboring activity and for the individual mobilization of the *homo faber*,[30] who takes his freedom to produce well beyond every limit in the spaces granted him by the State. He construes this "freedom of"—this freedom to produce himself and to expand himself—in a tendentially universal mode. He becomes a producer of goods, critical thought, and moral and juridical freedom.

From an external point of view, meanwhile, there is implicit in Hobbes's thought a political spatiality that foresees that statual (*statuale*) space only differentiates itself qualitatively (by area, population, and wealth) in relation to other States, which are different in practice but equal in their artificiality. As each State-owned space is placed, like the others, in the state of nature, it thus becomes an island of artificial order immersed in a great sea of political Nothing, of disorder. On these terms, the universality of modern reason presents itself only as a "universal particular"—as a State among a plurality of States. The State's essence and principle of order is not so much reason as its border, its boundary, its relationship with other States. Though he never quite explains why (and instead takes the naturalness of this multiplicity for granted), Hobbes claims that even though States have a plural life, they are, at the same time, closed entities. Each State, within its own self-interpretation, is thus incapable—despite the rationality from which the State, in Hobbes, emerges—of opening itself to any universal reason that goes beyond its survival and its quest for power. To put it another way, if "the Law of Nations, and the Law of Nature, is the same thing,"[31] then the State's exclusive objective—vital but limited—of putting an end to internal civil war means that the enclosed space of the State will remain open to the ever-present possibility of wars between States. For Hobbes, then, rational peace and security are limited to the interior of the States, while the exterior remains dangerous and subject to the possibility of war. Nonetheless, given the ontological parity between the contenders, war turns out to be limited and not "just," or rather, neither absolute nor discriminatory.[32] This is why Hobbes is a "realist": His Utopianism, which manifests itself as constructivist rationalism, stops short of the State's external borders. Outside those borders, there is war. And this is the intrinsic limit of a peace that (at least when judged with the yardstick of medieval political space) is not *vera* but *apparens*, not *opus justitiae* but *opus rationis*—a peace that Kant, from the perspective of the same modern reason, will also find contradictory.

The homogenous, undifferentiated, and amorphous space of nature is thus differentiable and formable by politics and States. If the political space implicit in More is smooth at both the interior and exterior, Hobbes's space is smooth at the interior but striated at the exterior by the existence of other States. Unlike the island of Utopia, Hobbes's State is not then a "reserve." It is not structured by a moral Ought that is able to unconditionally extend itself across the globe according to a universalist logic, but only by the modern sense of duty, which amounts to imperative for the individual to have a safe life. Hobbesian political space is an artificial construction that rises out of an indeterminate space (the "state of nature"), but which accommodates and demands the determination of individual sovereignties. The state of nature is potentially the same throughout the world, even if there are empirical differentiations. Even political reason is universal, but not extended; it is instead contracted, limited, and concentrated in those "universal particulars" that are modern States. This theoretico-practical model is also at work in Rousseau, although he—in the republicanism he derives from Machiavelli—places modern, dequalified (Hobbesian) spatiality beside direct political relevance of space, through the theme of the "small State," which only makes sense in the political universe of virtue and participation, and not that of abstract representation.[33]

Quite significant, then, is this idea of politics as a science that is capable of calculating the representative construction of power, or the forms of universal collaboration (between particulars, which is to say, actors who are individual, equal, and rational) in a smooth space that is devoid of history and given authorities—a space that, as such, becomes rationalizable and constructible according to the whims of instrumental reason. It is precisely because of this concept that implicit spatiality in Hobbes's thought crosses into that broad section of modern and contemporary political thought that takes up the mutual exclusion between political space and conflict as its object and, indeed, dogma.

Montesquieu

Having examined the skeptical thought of Machiavelli, More, and Hobbes, we cannot fail to mention the spatiality implicit in another great author of modern political thought: Montesquieu. Montesquieu demonstrates a capacity for thinking space in a way that is more concrete and articulated than our other moderns, one that is removed from the logics of opposition between artificial politics and natural space. But the fact remains that even in his nonconstructivist viewpoint—in which politics does not dominate space, but where space undoubtedly has more weight than politics—space cannot be defined as "qualitative" and objective. If anything, Montesquieu's discussions of the ways in which climates and geography influence customs and politics are the object of an extensively scientifico-political evaluation. Space is here the dimension that contains the "coordinated diversity" that, according to Kristeva,[34] is the authentic cipher of Montesquieu's thought. It is a space that presents traits quite different from the formless and indifferent "availability" to form that characterizes space in Hobbes's thought.

It is within this way of thinking space that the opposition between East and West takes shape—an opposition Montesquieu shares with a large part of eighteenth-century thought. This opposition allows Montesquieu to differentiate the political principle of despotic fear from that of republican virtue and monarchic honor. But let us not fail to note that, at root, this difference derives from the qualitative spatial opposition we discussed in the prior chapter: the opposition, instituted by classical culture, between the plurality of free political forms in Europe and the uniform vastness of Asiatic despotisms. This opposition was so effective that it would be used even up until our century (for example, in the work of Karl August Wittfogel).[35] Conversely, however, this opposition also permits the emergence of an eccentric perspective that highlights the corruption and crisis of Europe (which also, on these terms, is different from the East precisely because of its political freedom). But even though it refers to a space that seems politically relevant rather than indifferent, Montesquieu's opposition addresses civilizations first, and spaces second: It prioritizes politics over geography. It is an opposition of liberty to despotism, and although Montesquieu *develops* this political opposition with reference to oppositions grounded in the physical characteristics of space, it is not *determined* by those oppositions. In short, we must conclude that thinkers who, like Montesquieu, present the theme of qualitative difference between Asia and Europe are not as interested in a comparison between different political systems as they are in interpreting this theme within the categories of European politics, and that the reference to the alterity of spaces and civilizations is functional to the needs of European political polemics. The ultimate purpose of Montesquieu's discussions of the Persians—like his discussions of the Huron, the Chinese, the Egyptians—is not to describe an authentic, differentiated spatial and political reality. It to express a critical point of view on France and on Europe. To Montesquieu, it almost does not matter whether the occupants of this space are Persians or extraterrestrials like Micromégas.

3

Political Geometries

Modern spatial logic, we must insist, is Hobbesian—or, if you will, Cartesian—in character. It is governed by available, amorphous natural space (devoid of "places," concrete bonds, and meaning) and by the Subject's need to define rationally the smooth, artificial space of politics for himself. This spatial logic is a dimension of thought that, in its pure form, was never realized in history (although the French Revolution came close), but it nonetheless contains, *in nuce*, the political logic of modernity. Modern spatial logic, we may say, is not the theory of the absolute State. It is the absolute theory of the modern State.

In our examination of this spatial logic, we will demonstrate that inherent in its spatial simplification there is, paradoxically, considerable complexity. We will emphasize that, in the *void*[1] of desolate modern land without quality, space does not give meaning to politics, at least in principle. Rather, it is politics that gives meaning to space—cutting it into portions and striating it according to the various modalities, the mobile borders, and the many figures of *political geometry*.

With the term "political geometry," we shall refer to the spatial dimension implicit in modern rational mediation, the topological and figurative matrix of political form in the Modern. The term thus designates the architecture of modern political thought, and in particular those rational political acts that artificially establish internal and external borders, ceilings, intersections, distances, inclusions, and exclusions, as well as the actions and reactions of the various figures (the Subject, the State, the "universals") that enter into modern political space. Political geometry is to traditional political geography what political theology, the matrix of modernity's political temporality,[2] is to traditional political theology; between political geometry and political geography, there is at once a *formal continuity* (because both represent politics as inserted into a spatiality that is endowed with meaning) and a *substantial discontinuity* (with regard to the ways in which space is rendered politically meaningful). Modern political space is geometric because, unlike traditional space, it is a space determined by politics—because, in other words, it was represented in such a way as to enable it to welcome into itself artificial political figuration, and, as such, to be organized by figures that we can accurately define as the *spatial categories of political modernity*. These categories are a response to the crises at the beginning of the Modern, above all to the discovery of America (which inaugurated the categories of "external" space that are implicit in modern political thought) and to religious civil wars (which founded the categories of "internal" space implicit in modern political thought). This response is certainly directed toward neutralization (to the construction, that is to say, of a neutral political "crystal"[3]), but this neutrality is also "oriented" to safeguard a new human type: the modern Subject, who is, for political geometry, a presence at once *necessary* and, strangely, *unwelcome*.

Why? The modern Subject constitutes itself as a *particular* who exists within, and is therefore subservient to, a political *universal*, the State. At the same time, however, the Subject is also, as we are about to see, a "*universal* particular" (who strives to cross borders and cast himself outside the State) and the State is a "*particular* universal" (it is, as we have seen, incapable of true, unconditional universality). Even so, the State remains able to bend and redirect the universal impulses of the Subject so that they remain within the sphere of the State's logic (an operation that continued until the end of the twentieth century). Modern political space is that space in which State and Subject coincide, each with its own universality and its own particularity. It is a space *of* movement; but it is also, as we shall see, a space that is itself *in* movement.

Despite the modern claim that political geometries are stable and certain, the presence of the Subject and his universal projections reveal that the spatial categories of modern politics are actually unstable and changing. The Subject's "free" action mobilizes him, even if he is unable truly to liberate himself from the State and is instead shaped and disciplined by it. This instability is also due to the fact that the State's political space is nothing other than the provisional, artificial organization of a dequalified, natural space, which, as we have already said, is also "available." The combination of these two elements—the presence of the Subject and the unsuccessful ontological foundation of modern space—reveals that the external borders between States, and furthermore, the borders that exist between the figures populating the internal space of modern politics (Subject, Society, State), are mobile and crossable in all directions. Indeed, the State cannot quite manage to "stay still," to close transparently political space. Instead, it is always occupied with the task of subduing and interfering with subjectivities. Conversely, as we will see in the next chapter, the Subject is unable to truly develop his many energies in a fully universal sense. As such, we may say that modernity is a precarious and unstable equilibrium between the Subject's universal movement and the particular political figure of the State; between the Subject's politico-economic action (which moves toward opening) and the State's disciplinary action (which favors closure). The contingency that modern politics hoped to exclude here, to the contrary, reveals itself to be one of modern politics' originary components, and it acts as a force of instability at the very interior of modern political space. We say this without disapproval; indeed, it is only in the contingency and constitutive contradiction of political space that a condition of liberty comes to exist for the moderns.[4]

Internal/External

The first category of modern political geometry is the link between *internal* and *external* in the sphere of State relations. This link marks the overcoming of religious civil wars; within the ambit of a spatiality determined by politics, and as the eminent example of that space, the modern State forms itself precisely in order to expel war to the exterior and to delimit a pacified space at its interior.

The clearest historical example of the modern link between internal and external is the logic of *cujus regio, ejus religio*,[5] the principle of internal politics that governed European politics from the second half of the sixteenth century, and which received an even clearer formalization in the mid-seventeenth century. We should stress that by this point, Europe was no longer centered politically and economically in Italy, but had found a center of gravity in the areas opening onto the Atlantic. The *regio* that determines religion, and consequently peaceful political belonging, is not, for the most part, a "natural" space. It is, however, determined by the sovereign's contingent decision (from a conversion, a succession, etc.) and by the object of the sovereign's government.[6] Historically, the centralizing spatiality of absolute monarchy has manifested itself through the theory of national interest and "police"[7] practices, and still refers to a plural and hierarchical "cosmos" to be governed (the aristocracy persists as organized difference) rather than a smooth and unitary space to be represented. It likewise projects itself on a *theatrum mundi* ("theatre of the world") organized by God and does not, therefore, imply that space is an arena available to geometric representation. However, even though the centralizing spatiality of absolute monarchy does not then coincide with Hobbesian philosophical categorization, it is nevertheless marked by a spatial crisis that no organicism can truly save.

The plurality of States as "particular universals" and the link between internal and external acted as a basis for the organization of the international side of modern politics, the *nomos* of the Earth in the period of the *jus publicum europæum*. As Schmitt has shown, contesting Hobbes, the efficacy of the *jus publicum* within modern politics puts the lie to the idea that modern States exist in a "state of nature" relationship with one another. To be precise, this idea is only true in the negative, in the sense that there is no mega-State ordained from above that dictates binding rules of behavior to the others. Their relationship, in this "natural" sense, is, however, a relationship between sovereign political artifices (*artifici*) that recognize one another as such. This is proved by the modern limitation of interstate war: a war that is not natural, but a somewhat "artificial" measure between sovereign States, in which both parties are *justus hostis*.[8] This "small" difference in the relationship between equals implies the political determination of a space, Europe, in which the typical "state of nature" principle ("anything is possible, anywhere") is not then in effect. European space so construed—space as it is arranged in the "Westphalian" system of modern statuality and "war in form"—gives rise to various modalities of organization. These run from equilibrium between States and the alliance games this equilibrium generates to attempts—present in war throughout the modern age—on the part of a State (sometimes Spain, France, Germany, or Russia) to impose a hegemony on other States. This, however, implies neither the annihilation of the hegemonized States nor a "natural" qualification of space, whose partition remains entrusted to purely quantitative power relationships.[9]

It is precisely political orders and their borders that differentiate the formless and uniform space on which modern politics insists. At its inception, then, modern political space is defined by an internal space in which *nothing is possible* (the internal sphere of the State, which has been depoliticized and made "smooth" and safe) and an external space, Europe, in which *everything is not possible* (which involves, that is, a relatively ordered external space). This difference may be noteworthy, but it is still relatively small—after all, European States are qualitatively homogeneous—and it, in turn, enters into the much greater difference between Land and Sea. To avoid ontologisms and mythologisms, let us immediately clarify that the Land–Sea distinction refers, more precisely, to the equilibrium between the politico-military logics of territorial powers and those of naval powers like England (an equilibrium that, according to Schmitt, also needs to weigh the interests of private citizens who are pirates,[10] which is to a certain extent polemical bias on Schmitt's part, even if modern England truly does achieve a meeting of private logics and naval logics). But behind this equilibrium, there is a more fundamental one yet: the equilibrium between limited war and absolute war, between power that is openly and explicitly pursued and power that pursues its ends by "moralizing"—in short, the equilibrium between smooth space and striated space, between Atlantic political civilization and Continental political civilization.[11] Ultimately, both the difference between European States and the equilibrium between continent and sea register the profound difference between Europe and the rest of the world, between those inside and those outside the planet's political center. Outside Europe, European powers can give themselves over to conquest because they do not encounter any other *justus hostis*, that is, any other State. This conquest can take many forms—crusades which advance Christianity, or the civilization of the European Enlightenment—and since there is no relationship between States involved, but only "just war," everything is possible.[12] In short, to use Deleuze and Guattari's terminology,[13] the State "captures" the "nomadic" power of war, but it only fully fixes it to the ground within the European continent. Elsewhere, at sea or outside Europe, it cannot or will not employ war which is completely "in form."[14]

Modern politics, with its epicenter in Europe, thereby determines itself through growing spatial differences that are put into place by politics itself. As radical as these differences are (there is a big difference between being a citizen of a European State and being an inhabitant of extra-European lands), they do not arise from an intrinsic quality of space. Modern political space is not, for the most part, a matter of the opposition between barbarians and Greeks, or Christians and infidels; space is rendered meaningful, above all, by the presence or absence of the State-Form. If, in the premodern age, space gives the measure to politics through the Order of Being and the Idea of Justice, in the modern age, it is thus politics that differentiates space through its agent, the State. Even the distinction between Land and Sea, we must stress, is not a natural ontology, but only a politically decided destiny (a choice between two spatialities).[15] Politics here determines the space of inclusion and exclusion, and it allows a portion of world space (Europe) to establish itself as a political order, differentiated from natural disorder, but also made possible by it. The point of origin for modern politics is the fact that, for the Subject, "peace" is a good that is appetizing but scarce. This principle is spatially represented by the meagerness of land in which war is limited; the European order of States establishes itself as the eye of the storm of international politics, its rational order made possible by a precise orientation[16] to differentiation and the imbalance between Europe and the rest of the world. Here, of course, the universal only presents itself as "opaque" and "particular."

Finally, we must remember that the spatial logic that distinguishes internal from external, or the *jus publicum europæum*, also leads to the distinction between enemy and criminal, military intervention (external) and police intervention (internal), not to mention the distinction between citizen and foreigner. These last two categories in particular are determined with increasing clarity based on the *jus soli*, that is, on the political strategies of inclusion and exclusion within a space that is not "natural," but defined and bordered by sovereign power.[17]

Particular/Universal

Next to and intersecting with the spatial representation that distinguishes between internal and external, another equally powerful representation exists in modern political thought and institutions. Regarding internal politics, this spatial representation places the link between Subject and order within the relationship between particular and universal, which also includes the relationship between public and private. This relationship is at least as unstable and prismatic as that between internal and external, despite Hobbes's attempts to secure it in the figure of a "universal" Leviathan that is firmly constituted by "particular" individuals. It is a relationship that inheres to a politics thought not as organic, but rather, as artificially constructed and therefore opposed to premodern tradition, with significant differences from Atlantic political civilization.

Indeed, if the strategic difference between the *external* spatiality of the continental States and England resides in the opposition between Land and Sea or State and Empire (as we shall explore more in Chapter 4), at the interior, we must distinguish between two forms of sovereignty. On the one hand, we find the continental State's sovereignty (in the Hobbesian theoretical model), geometrically represented and inhabited by "individuals" who are only made a "people" by this sovereignty. On the other hand, there is the sovereignty of England, which is the real corporeity of the country, incarnate in the crown and in the concrete person of the monarch, inhabited by a plurality of "corporations."[18] As distinct from the artificial political space of Hobbesian thought (which is by nature exclusive and absolute because the very existence of organized politics depends upon it), this complex political space will allow for the emergence of the originally Anglo-Saxon strategy of power limitation: constitutionalism.[19] This strategy will extend to the United States, although there it will manifest itself with a significant difference: In the United States, it is not the country but the people who concretely exist and who, even though the Constitution is organized around the rights and the actions of the individual Subject, constitute themselves as a political "us" that can never be completely absorbed into the logic of political form.[20]

Within the sphere of Anglo-Saxon political, juridical, and institutional culture, then, the space of politics—which is quite removed from the logic of rationalistic statualism and the determination of sovereignty as an artificial construction on a *tabula rasa*—is designed not only by the State, but also by a preexisting plurality of Subjects, which is to say, by a *Civil Society*.[21] In these contexts, the transition from an internal political spatiality that is *complex* to a political spatiality that is *simplified* in a modern, individualistic sense can take place in a relatively nontraumatic way. This is because the transition is not carried out according to logics of revolution, but of evolution, or perhaps of constitutional revolution. Here, too, we find the democracy of modern subjectivities, which, unlike the continental State's political spatialities, are not determined exclusively by the State, but by Civil Society as well.

In general, Anglo-Saxon political forms are characterized by a *non-closed spatiality*, whether it be the sea outside the State's borders or the frontier within (as with westward expansion into the borderless space of America). These open political forms are compatible with a mobility that is not just public, or "imperial," but also "private." In this sphere, space is truly nature that is available to conflict, adventure, and the domination of pioneers and pirates.[22] It is also open to the conquest of a naval pioneer such as Robinson Crusoe, who re-created the same industrious everyday life of the *patria* in the exotic space of a remote island, through the hard work of a "bourgeois" completely lacking in imagination.

Meanwhile, on the continental side, we see a much different sort of political space take shape. After the phase of libertine skepticism (which, thanks to Montaigne, saw modern subjectivity lose its relation to an external qualified space, only to then seek refuge and salvation in the infinite and elusive space within the conscience), the Subject, even though he thinks of himself as an "atom," turns out really to need space. Even though he frees himself from natural, given spaces and collocations, from qualified births and organicisms, and even though he manages to liberate himself as well from the senseless, measureless space of nature, he is nonetheless the emissary of an urgent demand for a new space. Unlike the space of nature, this space is smooth, uniform, and also amorphous, and here the Subject is able to make his individual, natural rights count. Paradoxically, however, these natural rights extend completely only within the artificial space of the State and its representative sovereignty. As such, we find in the Modern a curious compulsion toward political order that consists—from a spatial perspective—in a *figural coaction*, in the necessary dialectics of two figures: the particular and the universal. On the one hand, the particular (the Subject) has the duty of the political universal, namely, the necessity of willing, along with the State, its universal space. But on the other hand, of course, the Subject also has the duty of the particular, which is to say, the necessity of willing the space of the citizen.

(In the relation between these two duties, of course, we find the "freedom of" and "freedom from" in the sense we have already outlined and will discuss further in the next chapter.) Put simply, the identity of the individual demands the space of identification—the State—in order to be effective, while the State cannot keep up with the times if it fails to enable the realization of the individual's identity. Public space must make private space possible; this is the principle of modern legitimacy.

To be clear, the State's enabling of the individual is certainly not a "standing aside." To the contrary, it is an educating and a disciplining. Indeed, from this perspective, in the historical *praxis* of the absolute State, the defining feature of modern politics is that the government's "police" work—even though this continues to fall under the moral sign of "prudence"—demonstrates the power of discipline that transforms man into citizen and producer, identified within the State and by the State. In order to make him into a "Subject," the State molds him as the object of a power that actually extends to the private, intimate spheres of custom, mentality, and belief in a three-century colonization of vital worlds.[23] This systematic process of exceeding the limits of public power is constituted by inclusions and exclusions, but also by the use of lateral places like Foucault's "heterotopias." It demonstrates that it is historical reality, and not mere political theory, that the internal spatial distinction between public and private turns out to be not only mobile and reversible, but at the same time internal to a single logic of power: the geometric logic of the availability of space for politics and its order.

If this ability to accommodate the Subject within its own space and choosing not to suffer or repress him, but rather to form him, is the power and the novelty of modern politics, it is also true that there is an obvious contradiction at work. To subsist effectively, the individual person in fact needs the impersonal—the State—to impose the law (and the State, in turn, is a sovereign person, assuming a truly juridical personality at the peak of its trajectory).[24] Thus, although from a historical standpoint private law predates public law, we have to reinterpret private law in the modern age from a political standpoint as having been made possible by public law. Modernity's rational mediation does not, after all, bring about a "governmental" management of Justice (along the lines of pre-modern political thought). It creates an order of artificial political spaces that coincide in the public dimension of citizenship, in the universal smooth space bounded by the State, inhabited by equal "particulars," and regulated by the law.

From a theoretical viewpoint, there are only two players in the political game of statual and continental modernity: the individual and the State. Society, in this model, does not constitute (or, at least, *should* not constitute) a problem. On principle, it should have neither an autonomous existence nor a separate basis, but should amount only to the sum of its citizens, united and arranged in the form of the State.[25] "Society," in this conception, is only the depoliticized side of the political State. As such, it is a space in which Subjects realize forms of coexistence that are oriented more toward a juridical distance between individuals than to a "warm" proximity between them—or, in short, toward a democracy of "atomic" individuals. Indeed, to the extent that these Subjects are conceptually adequate to the conditions of modern statuality, they are by definition individual subjects. The collective subjects that possessed autonomous political relevance during the long middle age (such as, for example, corporations) have difficulty finding a place in the modern State, and do so only through important juridical redefinitions of their own nature. The fundamental quality of the modern State is that, despite the multiplicity at its exterior, it insists upon unity in its interior, and as such cannot tolerate alternative centers of power. Religion in particular loses its own external space (in theory, at least), and makes itself "private." This privatization poses more of a problem for the Catholic Church and its emphasis on "publicity" than it does for Protestant churches (which, on the Continent, appeal to the conscience of the faithful, whereas in the English world, by contrast, where statuality does not assume a closed form, the faithful present themselves as subjects of public importance, as "constituted churches"). Insofar as there is any encounter at all between the Catholic Church and the State, this takes place only late in the modern period, through the juridical form of the Concordat,[26] which realizes the coexistence of two independent, public spatialities on the same territory.

We can see, then, that under conditions of modernity, legitimate political power conceives of itself, and indeed organizes itself, in forms that are neither natural nor universal, but particular. These particular forms are bound to a precise performance of rational efficacy within a specific, artificial space—within the space, that is to say, that has been created by the politico-geometric gesture of sovereignty, which determines political space because its virtuality alone cannot be effective, and because, as such, it needs a space in which it can manifest itself. Sovereignty, in other words, can only achieve its validity as a universal command within a particular space, a space it has first rendered smooth and orderly.

Within this political space that is so devoid of natural differences and handed-down authority, the forms of government that turn out to be most adequate are those that give free reign to individual political subjectivity (although those founded on the equality of individuals and on their power within secure State borders also prove suitable). This space is, in short, the condition for *democracy*. To be sure, Rousseau's understanding of democracy as a political form demands that sovereignty exist in the people and not only, as Hobbes would have it, in the institution that represents them (Spinoza's theory of the constitutive *power* of the people, meanwhile, is another thing altogether[27]). But as a political dimension adequate to the conditions of modern individualism,[28] in the form of a "democracy of individuals," democracy is unquestionably the result of the smooth spatiality of the continental State.

It would take de Tocqueville, however, to recognize that whereas "[a]ristocracy had made of all citizens a long chain that went from the peasant up to the king, democracy breaks the chain and sets each link apart."[29] It is precisely because democracy comes into being within the monistic and artificial space of the State, in other words, that it intrinsically knows such serious limitations, none so grave as its inability to institute between the individuals who comprise it a social bond that is more than just extrinsic. This flaw is even more aggravated in the continental version, while in the English version, it is subject to correction and substantiated by social pluralism. Worse, whenever this democracy wants to make itself concrete (from Emmanuel-Joseph Sieyès onward), it brings into the smooth spatiality of the State a lacerating conflict against the "internal enemy," thus undermining from within the fundamental task and objective of modern statuality: peace.

Variable Geometry

This political geometry is also a specifically *variable* geometry; in it, we can also see the reality of modern and contemporary political struggles, the intrinsic instability of the State's supposedly "static" geometry.

The political space of the interior is a space devoted to the neutralization and confinement of conflict. Nonetheless, within this framework, we can observe a sort of "dynamic of attrition"—a set of conflicts that are not intended to be destructive—among the spaces of the State, the Subject, and Society. This dynamic originates in the various ways in which modern political space allows itself to be mobilized in a universal direction (which we will discuss in the next chapter), on the one hand, and in the State's disciplinary intervention in these mobilizations, on the other.

From the standpoint of the "geometric" political space we are outlining here, we can interpret this "dynamic of attrition" as the result of a set of conflicts dedicated to the realization of spatial preferences or spatial "reserves" (we cannot really say of modern politics, as we could of premodern politics, that it is governed by spatial "hierarchies" in any strict or literal sense of the word). They are conflicts, that is to say, that seek to define, widen, or restrict the ambits of private liberty, social initiative, public intervention, the franchise, or State authority. In essence, we are dealing here with conflicts between two groups. On the one hand, we have those who, in the name of the State and its "coactional" vocation for the production of order, think the smooth space of internal politics as a territory available to the gaze of the State, which controls and secures the Subject in rigid order (or, in other words, those who promoted the *Panopticon*[30] to stabilize politics within the formal limits of its existing institutions). On the other hand, we have those who are involved in various political "mobilizations"—mobilizations that affirm the primacy of the Subject, the autonomy of social space, and the economic production that particular actors together perform. Within the space of the State, the border between individual, Society, and State (as well as that between the private, the public, and the statual), thus proves to be, as we have already noted, a *frontier*[31]—a place of struggle, advances, retreats, and, in every sense of the word, *movement*.

Of course, beyond these variations of modern political space, between their different measures and excesses, we also find *revolution*.[32] This is a term that will quickly cease to signify the *ab integro* reintroduction of a *Magnus Ordo*,[33] and come to signify instead the radical modification of political space—the end, however momentarily, to the confinement and neutralization of conflict. With the French Revolution, the spatiality of the old regime (which was still partially stereometric, organic, and hierarchical—in short, classist), is transformed into the smooth, modern spatiality of internal equality and, generally, of democracy. Furthermore, as we will see, revolution triggers a new, ideological universalism, which exports to the State's exterior a conflict born at its interior. From this moment forward, there emerges a constant possibility that the geometries of the Modern will be subjected to political mobilizations.

In short, through the long, historic struggles of social movements that pushed so that certain classes or groups from the periphery of the system might win access to its center—or, more to the point, might win equality and citizenship on one and the same plane—we see a dynamic in which reformism overcame various phenomena of exclusion from full citizenship (on the basis of wealth, religion, age, sex, or class). Yet historically important though these phenomena may be, we must nevertheless observe that they did not correspond to the concept of the modern State, which implies a smooth space, not a discriminatory space. This space fully came into its own only when the State truly began to function at its full potential, that is to say, in the nineteenth and second half of the twentieth century.

In the end, we can see that the absence of natural coordinates for internal political space is the characteristic that allows for the segmentation of the Modern into right, center, and left. This is a division, in other words, that is not necessarily ontological or a mark of "civilization." It is a functional division, one that establishes itself in the unitary, spatial *continuum* internal to the State.[34]

Alternative Spaces: The "Small State" and the Federation

In contrast to the State logics and political geometries we have delineated here from a theoretical standpoint, there are a set of other political spaces in the modern era that have a life that is purely imaginary, residual, or polemical.

Let us begin with Tommaso Campanella's dream of a universal Catholic monarchy.[35] Implicit in Campanella's thought is a qualified, homogeneous global political space of the religious type, where a sort of eschatological spiritual renewal of humanity is realized. This space is itself, of course, anachronistic, and is only interesting in this context as a symptom of the recognition that the "peace" established in and by European political space is increasingly problematic. Read in this way, Campanella's thought amounts to an implicit criticism of the State-Form and its inability to avoid the destiny of war. His dream, we should add, is clearly marked by providentialism, founded on an interpretation of the universalistic and millenarian prophecies in the Book of Daniel,[36] which would also be the source of Jacques-Bénigne Bossuet's historical reflection on universal monarchy.[37]

On the opposite end of the spectrum, at least in terms of size, we find the much more felicitous thematic of the "Small State." The very existence of this thematic is itself evidence that under certain conditions, and even in modernity, political space has been thought in such a way that it does not appear indifferent and artificial, but rather, still "natural" and capable of bearing intrinsic measures for politics. At the very least, the Small State appears as a space whose natural characteristics are not indifferent to politics, but influence politics. To be clear, however, we need to remember that even in this case, we are dealing with the political determination of space, and not the spatial determination of politics. Nevertheless, this is still a politics that diverges wholly or partially, where logics and objectives are concerned, from the statualistic Hobbesian politics that we have presented as paradigmatic of the Modern. In short, the Small State is a model of alternative political thought with regard to specifically statual spatiality, throwing its *aporiae* into relief and responding to them with a set of ostensibly "geographical" modalities that are, in reality, political and polemical, where the polemic in question is conducted in the name of ancient republican ideality.

In the *topos* of the Small State (one that is, we might add, quite typical of republican thought), what in fact manifests itself is a resistance, on the part of the political space of the City, to the State's attempt to "subsume" it within its own political space. To be precise, the survival of the Small State thematic demonstrates that, even in the age of representation (in the sphere of political philosophy) and monarchical States (in historical reality), the drive to political participation in the public life of a free and virtuous City does not die quietly (and, indeed, has not died). The Small State is, in fact, primarily a classical City (say, Sparta or Athens, or republican Rome), in which the political myth (perpetrated by Livy,

Cicero, Plutarch, and Thucydides) is employed by many authors, from the mid-sixteenth century onward, against European monarchies, with particular attention paid to the opulence, inequality, corruption of custom, and spirit of conquest that characterizes those monarchies. Those who prefer Athens tend to be more careful about civilization's commerce and profits (but always with the exclusion of luxury) while those who think of Sparta and republican Rome will imagine a poorer, more military society (which is not, however, simply a conqueror). This theme is already present in Montesquieu with an anti-monarchical (but not philo-feudal) valence (until, that is, having conceded the impossibility of realizing it in a modern European context, he recognized the monarchy as the form of State and government best able to manage the new commercial reality of Europe[38] with equilibrium and without allowing Society to be destroyed), but it was, of course, only fully developed by Rousseau.

The "modern" structure of Rousseau's thought—which is centered on artificial sovereignty, even if it resides in the contractually self-constituted people, and not in the representative institution—emerges clearly in foreign politics, which is conceived, as we have noted, as a confrontation between States. As far as internal political space is concerned, Rousseau diverges significantly from the Hobbesian model. In fact, Rousseau thinks a political subject who not only obeys the law but also is capable of loving it as an expression of General Will—a subject who is, therefore, not only "honest" in the prevailing modern legalistic meaning,[39] but also pure of heart. Rousseau thinks a social bond that is not just mechanical but also spiritual and emotional, and a political end that is not just avoiding the *summum malum*, death, but also tapping into a *summum bonum* in a positive sense (even though natural innocence has been lost forever): the General Will. Rousseau achieves this through a supreme contractarian alienation that is, at the same time, an opportunity for supreme reconciliation. It consists in a supreme liberty that is properly located only in the total presence of the political body—a liberty that is, in other words, at the same time artifice and substance.

In this finality of politics, we observe Rousseau's need to recuperate elements of republicanism and to make those elements coexist with the contractual and democratic system of his thought. Indeed, the republican tradition outlines a citizen who is not tied to the State as much as he is to the "City" (though not in its capacity as "capital"), where politics occurs not through its representation, but through virtuous participation in public life.[40] Thus, in the second book of his *Social Contract*, after having spoken about people in relation to time (which is to say, about the level of civilization that has been reached by a given people), Rousseau examines physical space and its constraints, positing the necessity of equilibrium among people, extensions of the State, and forms of government. He argues that "[t]he more the social bond stretches, the looser it grows, and in general a small State is proportionately stronger than a large one,"[41] and that the large State collapses under its own weight.[42] The goal of this search for "equilibrium" between space and politics is to determine the best form of State and government for every people and, in this way to outline the uniqueness of each people. Thus, it is not exempt from a strong, clearly ideological element of "right to citizenship" couched in terms of "national character." All this makes Rousseauian political space an antecedent, if not of the "community," then certainly of the "place" that we shall discuss in Chapter 5.

The theme of the Small State and everything connected to it is expressed in its most celebrated form in Rousseau's *Constitutional Project for Corsica*. Here we see Rousseau voice his appreciation for the relative poverty and mountainous isolation of the Country, as well as his preference for subsistence agriculture removed from the market and commerce. Here we find his theorization (of clear Machiavellian origin) of an inverse relationship between military valor and civic virtue on the one hand and money on the other. Here, too, we should note, Rousseau revives the polemic against the City as the "capital" of a modern State, and emphasizes the direct relationship between physico-geographic nature and national character.[43] This is a theme that he would only amplify in his *Considerations on the Government of Poland*, where he writes that "almost all small States, republics as well as monarchies, prosper simply because they are small," while, on the contrary, the vastness of States is "the first and principal source of the miseries of humankind," given that excessively large States demand a despotic-bureaucratic government, and that the lack of mutual recognition among citizens within them impedes sincerity, participation, and love of *patria*.[44]

The alternative between the politics of virtue (the small State) and the politics of power (the large State) is certainly similar to the alternative between qualified space and indifferent space, or the alternative between political geography and political geometry, but they do not completely coincide. Indeed, differences between various political aims will remain the true criterion on which differences in the evaluation of spatiality depend. In any case, it is an alternative that can only be avoided, as Rousseau maintains, if we resort to what might be defined as a kind of *tertium genus* of spatiality, that is, "the system of federative Governments, the only system which combines the advantages of large and of small States, and hence the only one that can suit you."[45]

The *federation* is truly the model of an alternative politics, a politics born from the contract but not from the logics of individualism. Moreover, it is the model for a Society that is not merely the depoliticized side of the State, but that is also, autonomously and originarily, a set of subjectivities that are already political in and for themselves. But federalism does not simply re-propose premodern organicism and its spatiality (qualified and open to transcendence), by setting it against modernity's artificiality. In federalist thought, man is still a truly political animal who lives "naturally" among others and who does not need a Leviathan to be united with his peers. However, the circles that naturally form come together, through free act of will, forming larger and larger circles in a political body that is not the abstract and formal unity of equal singularities, but the free unification of different parts and secure identities. Excluding politics—that is, modern sovereignty—as artifice does not invalidate the coexistence of the organic with the "manufactured."

Johannes Althusius presents a clear example of this difference with regard to both tradition and modernity.[46] In the nonatomistic society he outlines, people and class circles position themselves *opposite* to the representative; they are not constituted by him or incorporated within him. The political body, in which intermediate bodies freely participate, is born in the laws and morality of God, and not in the will to order of single individuals. Politics is therefore "symbiotic," or rather, a simultaneously horizontal and vertical association in which power is still manifested as Government communicating Good in a complex space. The "stereometry" of this space, however, is not only an expression of the Order of Being, but of pactional will.

The complexity and alternativeness of this federate space was clear to Daniel Elazar,[47] who shows that the federal model of political community—inasmuch as it is different from a simple league of sovereign political forms—implies a space that does not take the form of a pyramid (organized according to a logic of high and low) or of a circle (organized according to a relation of center to periphery). It is a space that is neither purely traditional and stereometric, nor purely modern and geometric; a space that recognizes neither the hierarchical "levels" of traditional space nor the compulsory unity (despite the separation of power) of modern sovereignty. Nevertheless, it is not mere disorder, for it is a *matrix*-like space, in which "the distribution of powers implies different skills in different arenas for different ends." For Elazar, federal space is differentiated according to different objectives (defense, education, finance, land conservation, etc.), which politics engages with different political functions (states, cantons, regions, federations, etc.) by employing an explicit and revocable negotiation between the system's components. The result is a flexible and pluralistic space, crossed by formal and informal lines of communication, able simultaneously to attain and preserve political unity and identitary diversity.[48] In short, it is a space in which power manifests itself in dialogue rather than in representation. This does not, perhaps, render the space Utopian, but it does present a sure alternative—with the extremely important exception of the United States—to continental and State-based modernity,[49] and does so in such a way that only in the postmodern can it find any degree of plausibility.

4

Modern Universals

The spatiality of the State and the Subject—that unitary yet double geometry of modernity—is, with its internal mobility, actually a *battlefield*, a theater of conflict. Subjective energies rise out of modern political space, causing its geometries to change and, more important, mobilizing those geometries so that they open up to specifically universal dimensions. These dimensions are not, at first, vehicles for spatial order. To the contrary, they have the capacity to destroy any closed political space. As such, throughout modernity, the State as a "particular universal" (which is to say, as a disciplinary machine) will be challenged by other spatialities—spatialities that are in essence limitless (even though the most aggressive of them happen to be born within the State) and that claim to be much more radically "universal" than the State. Besides being contradictory at their interior (as we have seen in the previous chapter), these universalities also create vectors of contradiction with regard to State geometries. The tension that results—between the *closed space* of the State, on the one hand, and the universal or *limitless space* of the Subject, on the other—will not be explosive in the modern age. Instead, as we have observed, the Modern will remain constituted by precarious equilibriums that serve, in turn, as vehicles for social mobilization and for the achievement of individual and collective liberty. However, this tension always runs the risk of being exposed as an aporia—an inconclusive and endless journey through modern categories.

Empires and State

In historical practice, the State's sovereign power (in its absolute form rather than its theoretical "Hobbesian" form) gains control of its own internal space thanks only to concrete power relationships that turn out to change in its favor—thanks, that is, to alternate conflicts against historical competitors and their political spatialities. To be precise, control is gained not only through conflicts against the particularisms and plural hierarchies of feudal or city aristocracy, but also through conflicts against the different and preexisting universalisms of Church and Empire.[1]

The Hapsburg Empire—which did not disappear in the modern age but instead followed the tradition of the Holy Roman Empire[2] until the beginning of the nineteenth century—brings a universalism that is still partially premodern, consisting, since the time of Charles V, in a combination of the Catholic principle of missionary universality and the colonial dynamics of the *jus publicum europæum*. Its spatiality is thus qualified and marked not by the centralization of political power but, rather, by the centrality of an *auctoritas* legitimated on the basis of a universal, and not territorial, principle manifesting itself in a political command capable of preserving and protecting a *plurality* of subordinate political realities.

The naval and commercial empire of Anglo-Saxon nations is also pluralistic. This is valid both at the interior—where the State's space does not claim to coincide fully with society's—and at the exterior, where space is seen as a natural parameter effecting political forms that change depending on the space's function. This "responsiveness" to space is not, however, a naturalistic and ontological requalification of space; it is a different way of "treating space" politically in a mode that is effective but not (as in Hobbes) constructivist. Here, the form through which political space relates to its exterior is governed not so much by the State as it is by the naval empire with open geometry. This is an empire founded not on closed territory or religious universalisms, but on military and commercial oceanic courses, above all in the Atlantic. Despite England's attempts to apply a quasiterritorial logic of closure to its home seas—pitting John Selden against Hugo Grotius, Holland's champion—England creates an open naval spatiality that also manifests itself in the organization of its complex imperial territoriality. The independence of the North American colonies is a response to the motherland's centralization, which is itself a reaction to the growing complexity that came with the empire's geographic expansion.[3]

Unlike these competing imperial and universal spatialities (and, of course, unlike the different particularisms of the City and the Fief), the State's defining feature is the *centralization*, both symbolic and otherwise, of command and administration over territory, which is thought as homogenous and equally exposed to the regulating power of the sovereign and his law. But while the State's space certainly contains a "center" and many "peripheries," the issue at stake is one of spatial determinations that are politically modifiable in history, and not the subsistence of autonomous and independent political entities within its territory. Centralization is therefore the State's disciplinary subsumption of political and existential spheres, and vital worlds, in a single political space. On an historical plane, centralization turns out to be the equivalent of modern politics' indifference to traditional spatial qualifications on a theoretical level, as both are founded on modern space's openness to taking a geometric form from political action.

Even in its external relationships, despite the fact that it derives its existence from a complex system of spatial differences, the continental State regards and attempts to realize itself—without completely succeeding—as a centralized, stable, and closed space. External relationships within Europe occur in the form of alliance treaties and wars, whereas outside Europe they occur through "expeditions" and missions of discovery or conquest.[4] It is important to note that these dynamics and logics apply not only to extra-European continents but also to the Eastern borders of the European order of States. These borders are not the object of war between *justi hostes* (given the substantial deficiency of Russia and Poland's State dimension), but are rather the object of constant redefinition and contention between Slavic and Germanic powers.

The Universal Categories of Modernity and Their Contradictions

In addition to the challenges presented to them by their external relations, modern spatialities also must confront a set of challenges from within. And these, which originate from the elements of universality, turn out to be far more complex.

When we turn our attention to the interior of modern political geometries, we find logics and practices of limitless spatiality that originate from the modern Subject's capacity for freedom, on the one hand, and individual mobilization of freedom, on the other (or, in other words, both "freedom from" and "freedom of," which, as we will see, always go together, and which, as residues of the condition of the Subject *prior* to the constitution of the State, the State can neither allow nor provide *after* it has come into being). These limitless spatialities are implicit in the universals of *criticism*, *economic production*, and *moral duty*. The economic universal will unite itself, as we shall see, with the Empire's "naval" political form, resulting in a very effective configuration of power. To be clear, however, these universals are not ontologically distinct from or opposed to closed spaces (as occurs in the "elemental antithesis" of Land and Sea). The real defining feature of the modern universals is rather their *subjective origin*—for in this they depart from premodern and, above all, Catholic universals, which are and remain *objective*—and their ability to transform individual mobilization into social mobilization. Unlike premodern universals, modern universals are thus able to rearticulate the borders between individual, Society, and State. Furthermore, because they are able to project the Subject's energies (which are born at the State's interior), first to the exterior of society and then, potentially, worldwide, they become factors of liberty for the Subject, and at the same time, factors of risk for modern political geometry.

Now, in the dialectic of universals and in their contradictions, modern political spatiality reveals itself to be *intrinsically unstable* and *profoundly indeterminate*. These contradictions will completely explode in the age of globalization, but they emerge well within the limits of modernity.

The first contradiction is that even though the universals of modern politics originate within the State, they polemically turn against the "borders" within which they originated—the very "borders" that made their emergence possible. In other words, the struggle between the Subject's "open" liberty and the State's closed space—the most obvious level for a reading of modern political events—takes place at the interior of the State. Civil and political liberty tends to assert itself primarily as a "freedom from"—from the State, above all—but is never truly able to leave that "from" aside, making the freedom from borders a specifically *confined* freedom. The free Subject, in this sense, always *needs* the State, if for no other reason than to maintain an effective guarantee of his own liberty and rights. The State is also necessary either as a point of departure or as a resting place from which the Subject then may project himself outside, expanding his "freedom of" in a borderless liberty. There are therefore two ways in which modern universals are "particular": either because they retreat into the logic of sovereignty as a result of their need for defense and affirmation, or because they come into being through the projection, into the space outside of the State, of a Subject who is born in its interior. In the global age, this dialectic will become even more pronounced; universals will be perceived as worldwide projections of the logics and values that are specific to Western culture.

We may also note another contradiction: after the mostly nineteenth-century phase of equilibrium between freedom and State, the result of the universal projection of the Subject's energies in the twentieth century will be the formation of *supersubjective constellations*—constellations, that is to say, of objective and impersonal logics that are estranged from, even hostile to, subjectivity, and of spaces that are uninhabitable by individuals. Neither of these contradictions can, in themselves, be overcome.

Criticism and Rights

Within the space made smooth by the State, we witness the formation of the problematic space of *Society*. Initially, Society is little more than the neutralized side of the State, but eventually, it also becomes the space where universal, individual, and collective energies manifest themselves. These energies reveal themselves to be capable of crossing and destructuring the closed space of politics, and of eroding the borders between its spheres. In short, they reveal themselves as *counterforces* that have the power to oppose political regulation.

One of these energies is *criticism*, the genesis of which is quite complex. The modern Subject, in fact, does not limit himself to his self-constitution as a holder of rights who depends on the State even while combating it. The Subject also introduces the dimension of his "inner reserve"—of the freedom hidden in the conscience that, like a non-place, evades the State's spatiality.[5] The emergence of this non-spatial, private dimension (which is, of course, extremely politically important) is the result of the neutralizing action of State sovereignty, which relegates political energies generated by religious conflict to the Subject's interior in order to render them politically inoffensive. Thus, within every State, we see the formation of a relation of internal to external that is completely different from the similar relation formed in international space. This is because here the "interior" in question is not the space surrounded by the borders of political form, but the intimate space of the individual—the Subject's initially secret conscience. This interior contests the State and its politics not by *exceeding* the State's space, but by *subtracting* itself from that space—an "interiority that has fled into the exterior"—with strong "critical" responses from a specifically *moral* point of view.

The critical power of extremist Protestantism draws strength from a subjective conscience in which divine Transcendence erupts without mediations, breaking up every spatiality and every institutional perimeter system, and thereby granting the Subject the ability to perform radical negations of the present, as well as the will to redesign political space from its foundations and to realize the Utopia of a community of saints on Earth. In England (from 1640 to 1660) and with greater success in America, this critical power found—though not without effort or internal compromises—open spaces in which to experiment with the realization of its revolutionary political theology in the social and political sphere.[6]

However, in the continental State, where political space is bordered by sovereignty, religious impulses of this sort were neutralized and the Subject was guaranteed only a limited "freedom from," a freedom confined to the interior of the law and to its interstices. This situation quickly gave rise to a new demand and aspiration: to exercise a positive "freedom of" speech and criticism. Initially secret and private though these critical subjective energies might have been, they came to constitute the *public sphere*, the voice of public opinion that strives to be free and open and that promptly acquired the attributes of the Enlightenment, giving rise to a specifically *rationalistic* universalism. This universalism is no longer Catholic and providential; it is now instead subjective and generically human. It is perhaps best illustrated with Voltaire's "total" history in *Essay on the Manners and the Spirit of Nations*, which, in contrast to Bossuet's "universal" history, extends the historian's gaze toward Eastern space.[7] The critico-rational universalism of the Enlightenment tends to be reformist—gradual in its pursuit of political change—and to remain within the limits of existing State forms. But, like all modern universalisms, it is also capable of slashing up political space by tracing potentially destructive lines of conflict between reason and nonreason, barbarianism and civilization, enlightened society and obscurantist State. It is this universalism (as we have already noted) that will give rise to the revolution that, in turn, codifies the universal impulse of subjective reason in the polemical assertion of the Rights of Man, the universality of which then would have to find a way to coexist with the particularity of the Rights of the Citizen.[8]

This coexistence, to say the least, soon revealed itself to be problematic. In fact, the affirmation of rights, far from being universal, has historically been one of the principle vehicles of reinforcing and legitimating sovereignty (that is to say, the "particular universal" of the State). For the entirety of the nineteenth and twentieth centuries, the logic of individual rights and the logic of sovereignty would at once *reinforce* and *combat* one another. To be sure, all of those political figures and thinkers (from Maximilien Robespierre to Camillò di Cavour to Vladimir Lenin) who affirmed "rights"—be they civil, social, or national in substance—had the more or less clear intention of limiting the State's sovereign power. Nevertheless, the State consistently revealed itself to be the most appropriate and historically effective instrument to implement those rights. By implicitly extending the domain of its own efficacy in this manner, the State gained what it had, perhaps, lost (but really, only in proclamations of intent) in intensity and absoluteness of command. Beyond the territorial determination of law, the State thus also produced a territorial determination of rights.

In its initial stages, then, revolution remains that movement within the State's political space, which, rather than destroying that space, pushes it to adapt to its own concept. In other words, revolution renders the State's political space capable of accommodating the Subject's liberty within itself, while its intrinsically universal reach (which, in principle, really should force the particular spatiality of the State to "liberate" the entire world) remains purely theoretical. From a practical point of view, without even needing to mention Stalin's doctrine of "revolution in only one country," even the initial, paradigmatic instance of the French Revolution demonstrates that "universal" liberation was actually limited to the space of Europe. We need only consider the events in Haiti between 1791 and 1804, and the difficulties that black leader Toussaint L'Ouverture[9] experienced there while struggling against slavery in the name of revolutionary ideals, to appreciate how much the differences between Europe and the rest of the world still mattered, even—especially—in the space of revolution.

In any case, the transformation of criticism into revolution gave rise to the newly unitary and smooth space of the bourgeois State, in which "opinions" could confront one another in terms that were not destructive but, necessarily, relative. However, as soon as criticism began to turn into *ideology*—that is to say, not simply a manifestation of the Subject's anxiety for freedom, but an assertion of objective and absolute Truth (as happened with eighteenth- and nineteenth-century ideologies)—it acquired a new capacity to break the State's spatiality into pieces, at which point it began to radically destructure modern subjectivity as well (even though ideology was also, of course, an expression that *originated in* modern subjectivity).[10]

Nonetheless, the totalitarian result of rationalistic universalism is not its ultimate expression. In the second half of the twentieth century, it would develop into new political spatialities (such as, for example, the social State), and at that point, the Subject would attempt to remove the theoretical and practical nucleus of this universalism from the State's control, and to fully assert it in the global age. This nucleus is, of course, the universality of human rights, which was solemnly declared in 1948 in the wake of a barely finished war.[11]

Finally, we must mention a peculiar figure of modern criticism and its claims of universality, which in reality enter into tension with the State's spatiality: the *potestas indirecta* of the Catholic Church. In modernity, the Church will no longer pursue the chimera of direct political universalism, and will consign its universal force instead to the theory of *potestas indirecta* (as advanced, for example, by Roberto Bellarmino in his 1610 *Tractatus de potestate Summi Pontificus in rebus temporalibus*—a text that would, not by chance, be the object of polemic from Hobbes). *Potestas indirecta* is the appeal of the Church to the interiority of conscience removed from the direct power of a secular sovereign. It brings about a short-circuit of State-determined political space, presenting itself as a sort of modernization of Catholic universalism, in which the subjective side (criticism of political power to the point of active disobedience) is partially modern in its critical effects, but still argued according to coordinates with Thomistic origins that refer to the "Order of Being." Here, as in medieval political space, the subjective element ultimately ends up serving the traditionally objective element of Transcendence, as interpreted through pontifical *auctoritas*.

The Economic Universal

In its tendency to consider natural space as infinitely "available" for design and planning, *technology* is, to be sure, the very horizon of the Modern. It is the indispensable condition for the creation, formation, and inhabitability of modern political space. But only in the twentieth century will it manifest itself as a "universal" that is capable of breaking open the State's closed spatiality and imposing its own subjectivity on the Subject in the twentieth century. Alongside technology, and in some ways prior to it, we can observe another power manifesting itself in society: the limitless power of work and production, in which modern individual mobilization becomes, even more clearly, social mobilization.

Despite the long historical life of the political and organizational model of the *oikos*,[12] which extends into the Modern, the space of production in modernity is, from a theoretical standpoint, not qualitatively separate from politics (as it was, for example, in the ancient domestic dimension). Despite numerous attempts, even in the modern age, to maintain the distinctions between Society and State, economy and politics, modern production is undeniably an activity that is regulated by private law, and that originates from the same subjectivity that seeks the construction of a "particular universal" for the State and for public law. According to the rationalistic Hobbesian model, politics enables the creation of a smooth space in which, under protection of law and in the spaces freed by law, the economic activity of the Subject and his "freedom of" are able to find safe expression, allowing the Subject to produce himself and his own existential condition in the interior of civil society.

Of course, the State cannot permit economic activity—work—to limit itself to competition; nor can it permit economic energy to fragment radically the unity of internal politics (although in this case, the denial would come only later, in the twentieth century). Already in Locke, however, it is plain that politics and economics both have the same subjective origin, and that both refer to two spatialities that cannot be distinguished from each other using ontological precedents or preestablished hierarchies. Indeed, we could even hypothesize a logical precedence of economics over politics, so long as we interpret the economic, if not as a "necessary evil," then certainly as a secondary function for the Subject and for the space of his many liberties, including economic liberty.[13]

Yet even though it is ontologically inseparable from politics, the economy also tends toward the limitless and expresses a borderless liberty. In fact, in the ostensibly limited and "internal" space of competition and production, the Subject and his work trigger a manifestly universal logic, a universalism of profit that, despite being completely centered on the individual Subject, enables the Subject (assuming, of course, that it is "in moderation") to encounter other Subjects on the same ground in a potentially universal chain of particularity; the search for profit is, as such, an indirect universal, an "invisible hand." In this way, within the "particular universal," within the smooth, determined space of the State, we see the emergence of a "universal particular," namely, the smooth, indeterminate space of the market. The former spaces are artificial, the latter supposedly "natural." Though they are not destructive at first, the dynamism and movement that are generated within modern political space do have the potential to enter into conflict with the stability of the State. Here, as in the case of subjective liberty, mobilization and limitlessness are born within a space that is limited by institutions, but which they then overcome in a world space. This world space is specifically smooth in its form, constricting little by little precisely to the degree that the domain of traffic, commerce, production, and universal consumption expands. Thus, even though property is traditionally related to the gesture of fencing in land (as, for instance, Rousseau writes in the *Second Discourse*), in the modern age, economic space is founded on property—but not, strangely, on borders. It is instead configured as one of modernity's most powerful universalisms, which, beginning from its specifically private base, characteristically extends into a smooth world space. Unlike the Hobbesian model, international space here is not dangerous and amorphous; it instead is qualified by the "good" of the universal circulation of wealth that is proposed by the anti-protectionist and anti-colonialist model of classical political economics. In the balanced increase of profit lies the potential for the progress of civilization, which, in substance, measures itself by legal guarantees, the spread of commerce, and private international law.[14]

Market spatiality is therefore the spatiality of "sweet commerce." It is, according to a line of thought that runs from Adam Smith to Herbert Spencer, an alternative to the fragmentation of international space that is caused by States—and that, in turn, causes war. The implicit space of the market acquires its "qualification" not by differentiating itself from other coeval spaces (the qualified space of the market is, in other words, not the same as the "qualification by opposition" that is implicit in and generative of the *bellum justum*), but through its difference with respect to *other times*; the market, that is to say, becomes a qualitative space in and through *progress*. As such, whenever it finds that this progress is being impeded by outmoded spatial forms (such as, for example, the closures of "protectionism"), even the universal spatiality of the market can, its difference from the space of the *bellum justum* notwithstanding, become polemical and oppositional. In theory, this smooth space of international economics can also shatter itself in another way, namely, when its constitutive imbalances aggravate themselves and, in so doing, generate a space that is anything but "smooth." In this case, the smooth space of the market becomes the premise for "wars of economic liberation" that do not generally present themselves as such, and that justify themselves instead in terms of "national liberation."

Let us not forget, however, that even though from Locke onward we see various attempts to make economics independent of politics, this "economic universalism" is nevertheless, in the end, born from subjective impulses that come into being within a political space that is determined by States, and the dynamics of which States have controlled now for nearly two centuries. We should also bear in mind that Locke openly predicts that the external space between States will assume the form of a "Hobbesian" state of nature[15]—and not, as one might imagine from an "economic universalist," an economic and commercial unity of the Earth. In any event, the world-wide system of capitalism,[16] which formed in the modern age, would not become decisive for a long time; its universal spatiality may be persistent within modernity, but it is certainly not the only form of modern political space. To the contrary, the political spatiality of the State (in both its continental and its Anglo-Saxon political forms) would remain preeminent for quite some time. So too, therefore, would the State remain able to impose controls on the economic dimension, and to prevent the social mobilization that is triggered by individual mobilization from becoming, in turn, political mobilization (which is to say, revolution).

Different States would, of course, exercise these controls in different ways. The main Anglo-Saxon powers (such as England and the United States) would join the internal freedom of individual and social production (arranged according to the capitalist model) with the external freedom of the seas and free commerce. They would not hesitate to supplement their control of the market with politico-military force (we may think here of the way in which the United States, in the nineteenth century, forced Japan to open itself to the world market). As such, we see in these States the realization of an overlap between, on the one hand, the universal spatiality implicit in the market and, on the other, the universal spatiality implicit in their naval empires (whether formal or informal). Though it would be an exaggeration to suggest that "the expansion of England in the seventeenth century was an expansion of society and not of State,"[17] the success of the naval and capitalistic Anglo-Saxon powers to merge these two universals—one economico-social and the other politico-imperial—will nevertheless constitute a permanent, structural, and autonomous element of modern political spatiality.

The continental States offer an alternative to Anglo-Saxon political space. They generally seek to maintain a more explicit form of control over the economy, and as such they remain tied to a political spatiality founded on clearly demarcated borders (and we may think here, for example, of Johann Gottlieb Fichte's closed "commercial State," the autarchic imperialism of the fascist powers' *Großraume*, or the Soviet model's "command economy," which openly defined itself in opposition to the market economy). Today, the market economy, despite having triumphed over its communist enemy, nevertheless persists in carrying out precisely the dialectic we have just described: It discovers that it actually has realized a universal that is not subjective, but objective. The logics of the market, even though their rather "particular" order and orientation continue to be plainly recognizable, have by this point transcended individual will and subjective interests, imposing themselves according to automatisms that they deduce from one another and reciprocally reinforce, often without regard for the various subjectivities involved. This dynamic, which dialectical thought grasped in purely schematic terms, is precisely what realizes itself today in, and as, globalization.

The Juridico-Moral Universal

Alongside the universalisms that came into being through criticism, rights, and economics, there is in modern rationalism another universalism, one that is direct rather than indirect. This is the Kantian universal of *duty*—the duty that is, to be precise, entailed in and by "the concept of perpetual peace" itself, and that is juridical-political without being in disagreement with morality.[18] This universal presents itself as "objective," but not at all in the "substantialist" sense in which premodern universals presented their claim to objectivity. The objectivity of Kantian duty is instead derived from the self-evidence of reason in the form of law. In effect, Kant seeks to force and to overcome the spatiality of modern liberty (which, as we have seen, is at once "bordered" and "borderless," at once a "freedom of" and "freedom from") in order to assert that freedom is a "fact" that is, in and of itself, its own law (and which, depending on whether we are referring to the "phenomenal" man or the "noumenal" man, will manifest itself as an "apodictic law of practical reason"[19] or as an "unconditioned practical law,"[20] as regulated or absolute liberty). In this sphere, Kant sees law as the joining of theory and practice, as the natural disposition and destination (or duty) of man to live according to liberty. This theoretical difference—which grounds Kant's rationalism in law as duty and not in rights—generates Kantian political spatiality through its differences from modern rationalism's spatiality.

We must point out that despite the objectivity of Kantian universalism, it is the individual Subject who constitutes the warp and weft of the rational universal (which is, remember, nothing but free, rational, and responsible communication between human beings). The Kantian Subject thus remains a particular individual who does not, however, enclose his own liberty within the limits of the "particular universal" (of the State) but instead, by ceasing to favor the logics of his own security and of the State's political power, takes his place at the height of his dignity and universal moral vocation, as well as the rational uniqueness of the world. The Kantian Subject's universal vocation, therefore, is as much the complete truth of Enlightenment universalism as it is one of the sources of contemporary "liberal" universalism.

This universalism makes Kant more than just a "reformist" who intends to rationalize the State's internal space. Kant is a "revolutionary,"[21] precisely because he presents the necessity and possibility for the universal to go beyond modern political spatiality, as an unconditioned moral duty, however, that cannot be in opposition to the conditionalities of political order, but only in convergent distinction to them.

For Kant—as he says plainly enough in the "Preliminary Articles" to his 1795 essay "Toward Perpetual Peace"[22]—politics cannot remain a "particular universal." Nor can it be marked by an opacity that removes itself from reason and its practical projection, law; for Kant, there can be no motive (apart from the moral and intellectual laziness of those who do not wish to leave a guilty minority) for peace and reason to be limited within the borders of only a few States, so many islands of imperfect reason staining an irrational, global space. There can be no motive, moreover, to content ourselves with mere "armistices" between sovereign States in Europe, who are otherwise free to wage limited war on the old continent and to conquer the rest of the world in the meantime. Kant therefore breaks with the order of modern political space according to which (as we saw in Chapter 3) *not everything* can happen *within* Europe and *anything* can happen *outside of* Europe. Kant opposes the limitless, moral, rational duty of universal peace (even if only as a federation of States and not yet as a *civitas gentium*[23]) to the political representation of a limited rational space (the State). This duty becomes concrete within the universal juridification, or better, rationalization of politics, that Kant understands to have been made possible by the progress of nature.[24] This allows mankind to escape the situation in which war is the permanent possibility of politics, and to instead establish rational universal communication between political forms, which—having overcome the State's enclosure of its own reason (as happens in Hobbes) without acceding to "humanitarian"[25] interference (as happens in More)—can now lose their self-referentiality and their exclusive sovereignty. In short, by transforming the logic of rights into a logic of duty, and transforming the freedoms "from" and "of" into freedom as a single unconditioned "fact," rationalism escapes the dialectic that causes modern universals to turn themselves into particulars, and to enter into conflict with them.

Kant's image is that of a smooth (juridified) political space, primarily at the interior. The republican political form he outlines in the "First Definitive Article" of his "Perpetual Peace" implies the political liberty and juridical equality of citizens in a total structure of "state of law." This implies that politics cannot have something particular like State power as its objective, nor can it employ sovereignty's method of self-interpretation removed from its citizens' public rationality (even if, empirically, coercion founds public law). The same agreement between politics and law is also valid, without any caesura, in the exterior. In his "Second Definitive Article," Kant will therefore imagine a space that is universal but not formless, empty of objective order but teleologically prepared by nature and its evolution to accommodate human rationality in its juridical form, and thus intrinsically qualified. It is, in other words, the image of a positive universalism. But we must hasten to add that this universalism is not at all Utopian. It is, to begin, not an escape. In Kant, the state of nature does not need to be avoided, given that it is already, if we so choose, behind us. Moreover, Kant decisively asserts the applicability—here and now—of the Ought to Being. According to this principle, there should be no space—whether at the State's interior, among the States of Europe, or between Europe and the rest of the world—in which power is able to determine all (or, in short, in which "everything is possible"). Above all, by confirming the sense in which the State's logic of including citizens and excluding foreigners does not exhaust all political possibilities, the cosmopolitan law Kant sets forth in his "Third Definitive Article" (and, remember, this is distinct from the international law of the federation of States that Kant sets forth in his "Second Definitive Article") points to the universal efficacy of modern individuality; Kant will thus guarantee the right to visit everywhere, while also denying the right to colonization.[26]

Yet although it does not intend to justify interventions of just any kind, although it abstains from any kind of power politics, and although it is in principle independent from historico-political institutions in their empirical realities, Kantian universalism nonetheless has a critico-mobilizing effect and contains the possibility, as Heinrich Heine had foreseen, to "mercilessly tear up the soil of our European life, with axe and sword, in order to destroy the past to its very roots."[27] Kantian universalism, that is to say, contains the risk—typical of all universalisms—that the universal will want to assert itself at any cost (and with good reason) against every "particular" that removes itself from its universal destination. This is a revolutionary possibility that—from the standpoint of someone like Schmitt, who is strongly oriented toward the spatialization of politics[28]—contains the risk of abstraction, as it renders Kant's theory available for the revival of discriminatory war, the *bellum justum*, or, at the very least, renders itself incapable of stopping that revival in its tracks.

5

Dialectics and Equilibriums

Modern political geometries are, as we have seen, full of contradictions—which are concentrated in the universals and in their relationship with political space—that seem aporetical. Dialectical thought will take up some of these contradictions, conceptualizing them and "surpassing" them in theory, while also generating hypotheses about their resolvability in practice. Other contradictions, however, will present themselves as "natural" and inevitable, and as such will remain structurally implicit in modern political spatiality.

Dialectical Thought

In dialectical thought, the particular no longer has, as it does in Kant, a solely universal destination (despite Hannah Arendt's suggestion, in *The Life of the Mind*,[1] that we see in Kant's *Critique of Judgment* a new relationship between particular and universal, one that is much more politically centered on the individual's action). Instead, the particular is now the necessary "obstacle" for the universal (or, more precisely, its *determinate negation*). In this arrangement, the universal is certainly the most general of the two terms, but its wealth and truth nevertheless rest in the particulars—in its concrete determinations and in the real contradictions that run through them. In some ways, then, dialectical thought reengages at least one aspect of Machiavellian spatiality, which consists in seeing vectors of conflict, and not geometries, in political space. Of course, the conflict under discussion here is anything but the struggle for power and glory, as it was in Machiavelli; it is rather the result of individual, social, and political mobilizations that grow within modern geometries to the point of deforming them. Dialectical thought does not, then, assume the tasks of constructivism and geometrization; it does not seek *to remake* space in the image of politics. Instead, it seeks *to adhere to* the logical structure of political space—in all of its roughness and ruggedness, its solidity and concreteness—as it actually configures itself in the course of history. In Hegel, the purpose of this exercise will be *to bolster* political space. In Marx, it will be *to break its back.*

Hegel

From the perspective of political spatiality, dialectical criticism (and criticism, remember, is not the same as rejection) of the conceptual apparatuses of modernity is central to Hegel's thought. This is especially true of his central thesis—namely, that it is the Subject who represents, arranges, and organizes political space. Thanks to this criticism—which he also extends to the abstractness of Kant's universal duty—Hegel believes he can master the contradictions inherent in universals and their relationships with the closed forms of politics (which produce destructive effects on any thought which is—like rationalism—only "intellectual" and subjective, and not dialectical).

A late example of this theoretical attitude, which is visible even in his early work, can be found in Hegel's *Elements of the Philosophy of Right.* Here, Hegel demonstrates that only by beginning with the space (the "dimension") of the State—which, for him, is also a "particular universal," that is to say, a concrete and determinate entity—can we fully understand subjectivity and its claim to constitute the primary cell of politics. Hegel does not theorize State politics as a "full" premodern space that is removed from the Subject's availability. Instead, he understands the Subject to bring an inflection of freedom to politics[2]—an inflection that is, moreover, necessary in its negativity if the State is to realize itself in its ethical fullness. For Hegel, internal political space is consequently more "uneven" than smooth. It is certainly not hierarchical in any premodern sense, but rather polydimensional. Above all, it is a *total space*. In contrast to the internal space implicit in political rationalism, Hegel's internal political space is neither closed nor constructed by the geometric composition and juxtaposition of the various figures of politics (the subject, the family, civil society, the state, and so on), or even by universals and particulars. It is, in short, a space that is historically constituted in its entirety and crossed by these figures, which then present it with its own concrete contradiction. As such, it is a dialectical totality, a political space that also contains its own negations: historical time, the Subject's non-spatiality, and the universal mobilization of society.

Once we approach Hegel from this angle, we can see that he has, in effect, set for himself the task of understanding the dynamic and mobilizing elements—criticism and work—that, under conditions of political geometry, threaten to exceed from within the interior of modern political space. Hegel thinks these elements not only by attending to the way the Subject's mobilizing capacity passes from interior to exterior[3] (which is, of course, typical of the Modern more generally), but also by focusing on the space of civil society and on the universal dynamics that, true to form, cause it to go outside of itself,[4] and, finally, by tracing the dialectic through which the State, far from configuring itself as a closed space, in fact constitutively opens itself up to its own historical dispersal.[5] To be clear, Hegel understands these dynamics only insofar as they are moments of a dialectical totality—the logical figure of modern politics—that amounts to a system of political relations and contradictions that is simultaneously real and rational. Hegel's "dialectical totality" is, consequently, a system that precedes its own components; to suppose that the Subject precedes the State and creates it through a contract is therefore, for Hegel, a "bad abstraction."

This is not, of course, to suggest that Hegel's "dialectical totality" necessarily realizes itself in a cramped and compressed system of political security (or, worse yet, as a "totalitarian" political form). Our point is simply that it is only thanks to the perspective of dialectical totality that Hegel is able to interpret the relations among individual, family, civil society, and state in a way that allows him to see in those relations more than just a set of contradictions, or a system of reciprocal threats, in which the Subject is threatened by the State and the State by the Subject. Dialectical totality, for Hegel, is the concrete "true universal," the *Wirklichkeit* ("actuality") in which unity and differences are present together, and the theoretical and practical freedoms of the Subject and State include one another and concretely reveal themselves to be historical determinations of substantial freedom.[6]

Thanks to this perspective of dialectical totality, Hegel can understand the *soziale Bewegung* ("social movement"), which modifies the borders between the figures and spaces of politics, as a threat, perhaps, to the constituted order, but not as a catastrophe (and in this, Hegel is quite different from a counterrevolutionary thinker like Karl Ludwig von Haller).[7]

Even from a standpoint that considers the exterior of the State, spatiality plays a complex role in Hegel's thought. Hegel explicitly makes space into a theme for philosophical reflection (though only, to be clear, at the level of the objective Spirit, given that the Absolute is evidently free from empirical determinations). In his 1830 *Encyclopædia of the Philosophical Sciences*, Hegel designs a topology of the Spirit that moves away from the Earth as the overall environment of humankind. In its progressive conquest and rationalization of nature, Spirit is, for Hegel, determined (and not merely "conditioned") by geography. This is true both from a subjective standpoint (where the rise of Spirit as the spirit of a given people, or in the spiritual configuration of ethnic groups, reproduces the geography of the continents) and from an objective point of view (in its historical development).[8]

In Hegel's *Lectures on the Philosophy of History*,[9] meanwhile, the universality of the Spirit's space is even more explicitly determined by particularity. Relying on the historically based geography of Karl Ritter, and in (mutual) opposition to the physical geography of Alexander von Humboldt, Hegel describes the journey of *Logos* in geographically determined and spatially limited ways. The historico-geographical linearity of the path taken by Spirit—which proceeds along the privileged Mediterranean vector from the East to the West, from Asia to Europe—implies a verdict of exclusion for Africa and America (which may have the future, but not the past) from this geographical "foundation" of *Weltgeschichte* ("world history"). This, in turn, denies the universality of the human thought as it was configured in the Enlightenment, and instead concentrates self-assured Reason only in a determined time and space: the Germano-Christian world. Here we witness the final destination of an itinerary that began in *Phenomenology of Spirit*, where we see the alleged abstractness of French revolutionary reason pass into the concreteness of Germany, which Hegel then construes as the "region of self-conscious Spirit" and as the space, at once limited and universal, in which Reason finally becomes sure of itself.[10] Even from the spatial point of view, the particular can be given universal content only once it has completed a long, historical journal.

Since Europe is this "particular universal," the link Hegel makes between geography and history in his *Elements of the Philosophy of Right* will construe the spatiality of international politics in a way that is still Eurocentric—that is still differentiated according to the logics of the *jus publicum europæum*, expressed in terms of civilization and barbarism (in an evolutionary, perspective sense, and not an ontological one).[11] As such, Hegel criticizes the representative and constructivist perspectivism of modern rationalism, as well as Kantian universalism. For Hegel, universal political space is neither the limited (statual) space constructed by the Subject, nor the limitless space prefigured by rational duty. It is the historical and concrete space of the Spirit of world history, which accommodates its own real negation within itself.

Marx

In Marx, we find a complication of modern logics and spatial representations that is somewhat analogous to Hegel's. From the point of view of internal political spatiality, Marx's theoretical work (like dialectical thought more generally) minimizes the importance of the "bourgeois" conflict between the space of the Subject and the space of the State. Marx emphasizes instead the way in which the "particular universal" of the State—which ostensibly defines the smooth space of citizenship and enables the limitlessness of production—is in fact immediately involved in a class conflict that is generated in and by the space of economics and labor, which, correctly interpreted from a standpoint that substitutes "class conflict" for Hegel's "dialectical totality," reintroduces the laceration of civil war within statual political space.

In short, for Marx, political space does not coincide with statual space; it also includes economics. Indeed, Marx understands the State to be determined by precisely the same economic forces that, on the terms of political geometry, were thought to be contained within the State's universality, but that now instead—even from the viewpoint of internal politics—turn the State into a particular (which is to say, a function of class). Economic contradictions (the radicality of which the "bourgeois" State refuses to acknowledge), here arrange the border and the frontier of politics not at the State's *external edges* but rather in its *interior*. The system of political and social relations that was, for Hegel, a "dialectical totality" thus reappears in Marx as a fracture of political space. Even more pronounced is Marx's separation from modern rationalism: Marx radically revokes the geometry of modern politics, and the politics that hoped to exclude conflict is, as such, forced to confront it. It follows from this that the distinctions between internal and external, enemy and criminal, are no longer valid (and, indeed, that they have never been valid). The same dialectical particularization is valid for the modern Subject, whose universality can be traced back to "bourgeois" partiality. For Marx, the Subject (whether bourgeois or proletarian) does not, through his work, produce *himself*; rather, he produces his own *alienation* from himself.

Marx's dialectical thought, like Hegel's, does not reject the categories of the Modern, but only their subjective and "geometric" self-comprehension. Here, as elsewhere, dialectical thought thus implicitly exhibits a spatiality that is, first and foremost, an adequation to the uneven and rugged profile of the real. However, in Marx, this adequation is at the same time a critical rupture of that space, for Marx's thought expresses an emancipatory interest, a way out of that space (one that, at least in its intentions, is not utopic but scientific), an exit in the direction of another, truly smooth space: communism. And while Marx's destructuration of modern political geometry does, of course, continue to work with the "spatial" concepts of particular and universal, Marx's concept of the universal does not arise from a geometric extension of the *makroanthropos* State of the logics of the Subject (which, in Marx's terms, would be the abstract "bad universal"). Rather, Marx's concept of the universal comes into being through a *determinate negation*, namely, *revolution*, the radical subversion of political space. Revolution, in the dialectical context, is not understood in a "bourgeois" and democratic mode (which proposes to smooth out and equalize a space striated by privilege and traditional hierarchy). Rather, it is understood through the mode of class, with the objective of developing the contradictions of the *abstract* universal (the bourgeois) and the practical overturning of these contradictions into a new, *concrete* universal at the hands of that part which is truly the whole: the proletariat.

Marx, like Hegel, thus sees political space as historical, concrete, and complex—even if, in principle, it retains the potential to turn itself into the smooth, indeterminate space of communism once it has reached the maximum of its complexity and contradiction.

From the standpoint of external political spatiality, it must be said that Marx's recognition and acceptance of the modern Subject's universality is much more explicit than Hegel's. Marx recognizes that the Subject, even in his particular bourgeois form, has a universally mobilizing vocation that crosses state borders in a capitalistic universalism that, in turn, sets the practical and theoretical pace for proletarian universalism. Marx is, furthermore, very careful to emphasize the formation of the nation-state around the economic interests of the bourgeoisie and to recognize the space of its worldwide economic power; he sees clearly that "the bourgeoisie drags even the most barbarous nations into civilization."[12] Once it is overturned, the "bourgeois" universalism of profit becomes a true *internationalism*, the first conscious political projection of a universal that does not originate from Catholic or imperial logics. Even so, this new open spatiality that directly opposes itself to the State's closed space is nevertheless born from the same "modern" spatial logics that give birth to the State; this space is a unilateral interpretation of these modern logics, but it does not escape them. The State and the international are two sides of the same political-geometric coin—which Marx rethinks in terms that are dialectical rather than static. At base, in other words, Marx presupposes the same space presupposed by political geometry: an "available" space that passively waits to be "oriented" by the Subject—only no longer through a contract (as in rationalism) but now through labor and the substance of its contradictions.

Even if Hegelian ethnocentrism and Eurocentrism are absent in Marx, what he describes is not an undifferentiated construction of smooth global space. It is rather the constitution of a world market that is clearly unequal and "striated," even in its universality. The Marxist vision of the world (which would be affirmed by Lenin in his 1916 *Imperialism*) as a universality hierarchized by capitalist power (which is not limited to the internal power of the State but extends to include the State's external colonial power), is neither a moral criticism based on the Ought (as in Kant) nor an acceptance of the *status quo* (where, as in Hegel, "the real is the rational"). It is instead a realistic analysis—inserted into a logic of determinate negation—of revolution born from the very interior of modern political space. Marx's approach to overturning this state of affairs, which would realize humanity's universality, is not at all liberal or Kantian. The "*vereinigt euch*" ("Unite!") in Marx's famous "*Proletarier aller Länder, vereinigt euch!*" ("Workers of the World, Unite!") is truly universalistic, but it is not directed at humanity in general as much as it is directed at the worldwide proletariat. In Marx, as in Hegel, the universal is thus contained in a particular that is the determinate negation of a *bad* universal (in Marx's case, politics and bourgeois economics), and that is, as such, destined to open itself to "true" universalism.[13] Which is, in sum, the universalism oriented to class.

The Dialectical Structure of Place

Beyond the contradictions between the space of the Subject, State, and production, and beyond the contradictions, as well, between universals and particulars, there is another dialectic we must consider. This dialectic, which emerges within the paradigm of the *nonnaturalness* of modern political space, is also—as in Hegel and Marx—a structural, specific, and spatial dialectic. But unlike the dialectical thought of Hegel and Marx, it does not resolve itself in any new spatial form. It is a dialectic that amounts only to aporia—to insurmountable contradiction.

Whenever modern political thought attempts to render modern political space usable (and modern political space, remember, is not natural but artificial and represented)—whenever, in other words, modern political thought concerns itself with concrete action—it tries to re-legitimate politics through space. Space is thought to exhibit naturally the qualities and capacities to supply "meaning" to politics and to be its foundation. In truth, in these instances, we should not speak of *space* as much as *place*. Place, in fact, is the concept that actually opposes itself to the undifferentiated universal as a differentiating particular (just as the permanent opposes itself to that which moves or flees, just as the concrete opposes itself to the abstract, the full to the empty, or the vital to the rational).[14] In some way, place is temporalized space; it is the introduction, into space, of the dimension of duration and of the past. Above all, "place" implies the concept of *nature*, which is itself on a collision course with the logics and categories of modernity.[15] Indeed, "place" is the logical root of "natural difference" ideologies, which qualify politics by particularizing it, thereby running the risk of ontologizing and reobjectifying its spatiality, substituting the moderns' "freedom from space" with a politics of ties, rootedness, and "birth" as opposed not only to universalism and cosmopolitanism, but also to the Subject's mobility within the State and, as a consequence, within productive modern economics.

Preceded by the nobility's polemic against the Gauls and the Franks, this tendency to re-naturalize political space is clearly at work and demonstrates its power in a crucial author like Sieyès, who forges the controversial concept of *nation* through a recourse to nature, thanks to which the "bourgeois" revolution definitively surpasses the politics of the *Ancien Régime*.[16] In fact, the equality operative within the nation is the militant objection to the articulated, hierarchical space that has historically survived within the modern State. It is, in other words, an objection to the privileges of "status." To obtain this egalitarian outcome, however, the "particular universal" of the State found itself obliged to take on shape and substance, to become a community of birth, and to remain undamaged by the division of labor (which even Sieyès clearly saw). This substantialization and naturalization of political space brought about a form of social cohesion—national democracy—that was founded not only on citizenship but also on blood relations. National democracy was not, then, just the necessary result of the modern State's smooth spatiality; it defined itself in a novel way, by reinforcing, arming, and battle-training itself against an "internal enemy." Now, the "internal enemy" may be an unusual figure in modern politics (which usually only anticipates the enemy at the exterior), but it is a typical figure for democracy *in statu nascenti* ("in its nascent state"). The modern struggle against the internal enemy is first of all a struggle against the nobility who refuse to give up their differences, their privileges, and their status as a politically organized qualitative difference. As we saw in pseudo-Xenophon's *Athenaion Politeia* (but in a conceptual context that is, to be clear, in no way comparable to the Modern), the smooth space of democracy and equality reveals itself to be potentially "cut" by a conflict that is not dialectical (and therefore surmountable), but structural and constitutive.

Sieyès uses the concept of nation to identify not only the "local" rootedness of modern political space, but also its origin, the *constituent power* that is at once its dynamic foundation and its mobilizing breakthrough. The will of the nation (like Spinoza's God, in fact) is a perfect substantial immanence, an infinite power that has every constituted political form at its disposal, but that is unable to integrate or represent itself in any of them.[17] The implicit spatiality of constituent power is not, then, limited to "place"; it includes the dimension of nonspace—of an intensity that not only generates but also inflects the spatial extension of politics. As such, the highest expression of political space's rootedness and determination—the nation—is simultaneously also the highest expression of indeterminateness and of potentially revolutionary movement. In Sieyès's only slightly contractarian deduction, in other words, that which was already implicit in the modern theory of the contract emerges much more clearly: that the modern availability of space to political action is the origin of the formation, deformation, and revolutionizing of order. Modern rational mediation therefore entails an originary immediacy: Every smooth space and every closed geometry contains not only the universals that deform it, but also the constituent powers that create, open, and separate it.

This structural and originary contradiction of modern political space—the most radical of them all—will then be taken up implicitly by Weber. It is no accident that Weber juxtaposes a spatial definition of the modern State—"a human community that (successfully) claims the monopoly of the legitimate use of physical force *within a given territory*"[18]—to a genealogical definition. This genealogical definition—in which Weber construes, as the origin of political order, the *politischer Verband* ("political association"), with its intrinsic disposition to conflict and to the introduction of bonds of loyalty that imply the possibility of death[19]—will then be taken up explicitly by Schmitt, who (as we will see in the next chapter) will use it to destroy modern political spatiality and to begin to make a transition to other, post-State spatialities.

In any case, already in Sieyès we see that the logics of "place" produce effects of identitary belonging and of a return to the *jus sanguinis*. Both are intrinsically polemical and capable of striating the smooth space internal to the State as well as the homogeneous space of the system of States at the exterior. Sieyès even requalifies and naturalizes the "external" spatiality of borders marked only *more geometrico* ("in the geometric way") by the politics of the power of the modern sovereign. There is a reason why he forecasts, in a paradoxical and sarcastic manner, that the nobility, boasting of their Frankish descent, will return to the wilds of Franconia.[20] In Sieyès's thought, this region becomes a sort of geographical exteriorization of the ethnically qualified contraposition between Gauls and Germany (which had, until that point, been a polemical formula of internal politics).

In short, when seen from the viewpoint of internal politics, this process—which Sieyès triggers unconsciously, given that his political objective is a constitutional France governed by law and civil equality—means that the State can no longer content itself with being a closed political space devoid of quality, but now wants to be homogeneous and qualified as well, with the unexpected consequence that it becomes internally conflictual. Exclusion—which was, from the beginning, always present in modern politics—now begins to present itself as deportation and loss of place, while political enmity begins to express itself in terms of ethnic difference. From the point of view of external politics, then, international space—which, at least in Europe, did not anticipate qualitative differences between States—begins to appear instead to be marked by radical, natural diversities that even make States different from one another. Far from having a full "geometric" power over space and its differences, States here become the political expression of space.

Enlightenment "nature" here appears not only as the undifferentiated space available to universal human reason, or as the extension and fulfillment of rationalistic modern spatiality; it also constitutes the unconscious anticipation of positivistic scientism's attempts to requalify political spatiality through reterritorializations (to which geopolitics can be ascribed), and ultimately even through nationalisms and theories of "vital space" and "blood and land," that irrationalistic and spurious product of modern rationalism.

The fact that the Enlightenment, that spearhead of the modern project, with all its universalism, also contained these *anti*-modern results (and not just these, obviously), is telling. From this phenomenon, we can understand that modern political space is not constituted *only* by the dynamics we have already outlined (the natural absence of qualified spatiality, geometric politics "without quality"). It is, *in addition*, engaged in a continuous production of place as *compensation for* the absence of qualified spatiality—in short, in a search for security that is not only physical, but also emotional and identitary. In symmetry with this principle, we may also say the following: Every time that anti-modern thought recuperates "natural" political spatiality, either as hierarchy or territoriality (and here, even though we may think of modern ethologists such as Konrad Lorenz and, to a greater degree, Robert Ardrey, we should not forget that Joseph de Maistre *also* denied the existence of Man, and maintained he knew only individual, different and concrete historico-natural nationalities), it does not *break from* the spatial dialectic of modernity, but, to the contrary, *realizes* that dialectic. This dialectic consists of reacting to the experience of smooth and indeterminate space not only with the institution of borders and artificial limits, with a sober and disenchanted awareness of their artificiality, but also with the recovery of a natural qualification of political order.[21]

While nonconstructivist Anglo-American political spatiality was able to accommodate multiple "places" and diverse identities by acting as a sort of plural "freedom," this "localization" of politics in the smooth and unitary space of the continental State has often had disastrous reactionary effects. In fact, in its extreme forms, it was the logical matrix for those ideologies that presented themselves as "natural" political structures, but that actually originated in projects to overcome and deny modern political geometry (but which nonetheless ended up preserving and accentuating its rigorous monism). Because this localization is ideological, it is also paradoxically Utopian, and thus the contrary of what it strives to be. Indeed, in political spaces of this type, "nature" is never present as a given, but always something out of reach and unconquerable; it is not behind us, but is a target moving farther away with every attempt to reach it. There is always some obstacle or enemy between us and the political reconquest of natural "place." Moreover, just as we see in true Utopia, even the ideology of localization interprets space as fully available to its activity of redemption, remoralization and reontologization. Only through the smooth space of modern Utopia, in short, is it possible to gain the determinate concreteness of "place."

However, even when we look beyond ideological extremisms and the contradictions into which they fall, we find that the localization of politics is actually present throughout the Modern. Indeed, we could say that from a historico-empirical point of view, there is no modern political experience that is simply and purely "modern." Modernity is everywhere double; it everywhere contains *not only* the empty space crossed by the artificial geometrico-political figures of the individual and the State, *but also* the compensatory force to produce a "filling" effect on this spatiality with some form of "naturalness" (or, to be precise, with the cultural and mythical construction of some form of nature).[22] Even if, logically speaking, "place" is the opposite of modern spatiality, it is nevertheless the case that "place" substantially reinforced modern spatiality from the beginning of the nineteenth century to the first years of the twentieth. The modern State, for instance, fully validates its own sovereignty as a "nation" or *patria*; modern citizenship is not just the attribution of rights according to the *jus soli*, but also national "belonging"; modern borders are not simple geometry, but also "natural borders." Wherever the encounter between Nation and State has not stabilized itself in this way—as, for example, in the Balkans—it has manifested itself in extremely negative forms.

In this oscillation between, on the one hand, the experience of emptiness, limitlessness, artificial borders and, on the other, the search (itself unknowingly "artificial") for the "natural," the "full" and the limited, there is one figure in particular that is worthy of our attention: the pairing of society and community. Ferdinand Tönnies addressed this pairing by formalizing and drawing on the romanticism of Adam Müller's *Lehre von Gegensatz* ("*Theory of Contrast*"). This ideological "series" consists of two principal currents: on the one hand, state, function, role, quantitative space, service, legality, mechanicalness, extension; and, on the other, history, memory, identity, connotation, organicity, nation—a qualified, dense, and essential space. Schmitt, we should note, would ascribe this series to the "compensatory" needs of the Modern.[23] For Tönnies, the spatial characteristics of community and society are that community is centered on "place"—on proximity and cohabitation in the communal "house"—while society is "thought as though it really consisted of separate individuals." Community is here both the result of, and the transcendental horizon for, the individual interactions of exchange that "take place in" a smooth, dequalified space (which is, on its own terms, characterized by a centrifugal action opposed to the centripetal action of community). This centripetal action, which in the individuation of a "center" of authority exhibits an explicit hierarchization of "place," is inevitably open to a worldwide dimension.[24] Furthermore, Tönnies is aware that even though the modern dynamic toward society entails the devaluation of community in the name of progress, the dimensions of will and human existence are actually both present and, if the corporate element becomes predominant, will both need re-equilibration (this is Tönnies's "socialism").[25]

It is almost useless to recall here how much the community dimension has been used for ideological purposes in irrationalistic and reactionary circles, in order to thematize, in a infinite series of variations, the qualitative difference between those rooted to the ground and those—the liberal, the capitalist, the Jew, the Bolshevik—who wander, carrying the seeds of instability and uprooting.[26] These discourses incorporate anti-modern mythologies into modernity once it is already in crisis, negating the Subject's freedom from space as well as his capacity to overcome it in the universal, replacing both with a politics of rootedness.

A Historical Phase of Equilibrium

Despite these dialectics and their more or less conceptualizable and "surmountable" contradictions, in the nineteenth century we observe a stabilization of the relations not only among space, place, and production, but also among the rule of law, the principle of the nation, and capitalist society. This double stabilization, as we know, would then project itself outward on a world scale, while also remaining centered in the European nation-states. The "bourgeois" activation of the *constituting* power of the people-nation through revolution, which introduced intolerable lacerations into internal political space, was exorcised by juridical theories and individualistic liberal politics that, beginning with Benjamin Constant, concentrated instead on the dimension of *constituted* powers.[27] The profound lacerations that Marx's class perspective detected in internal political space, meanwhile, were resolved in the ambit of State and Nationality in a manner that was, at best, precarious, setting into motion political apparatuses that shortened the distance between center and periphery, and initiating reformist processes that advanced the working class toward citizenship.

However, this relationship contained very strong contradictions, both logical and concrete. At the exterior, we must consider colonialism, which, just as it had at the dawning of modernity, preserved the discordant spatiality of the *jus publicum europæum*—a spatiality borrowed from discovery and conquest, and reinforced by the power of production and commerce, which would instead imply a homogeneous spatiality. With a partial exception on the part of the English, this colonialism would further unite the imperialistic drive and autarchic closure, thus losing the internal pluralism that characterizes Empire. We must also consider the progressive contraction of space (and of time) that the same mobilizing principle of production gradually realized as it extended itself throughout the world, making it increasingly small and uniform.[28] Meanwhile, technology rendered the natural landscape useful as a panorama, while far-off countries started becoming the object of Western consumption of exoticism.[29]

Concurrently, a precarious equilibrium was realized between statual order, on one hand, and universalist efforts to force and exceed borders, on the other. At the Hague, the first constructions of international juridical unity for Europe and the world were born, extending the smooth and juridically controllable spatiality typical of internal political space. These constructions were born, however, from the State's persistent capacity to present itself as *dominus* ("master") of political spatiality; they were the fruit of a conscious, partial abandonment of the spatial and political principle implicit in the State's sovereign exclusivity. But the State also had to confront another offensive of universalism, this time political and not juridical: socialist internationalism, the external projection of the social mobilization laid out in Marxism, which on the internal side promised once more to draw out political mobilization and revolution. In resisting this universalism—which, remember, is logically homogeneous with statual spatiality, even though it is, politically, its enemy—the State was forced to ally itself more and more with nationalism, and make its own space progressively more like a "place" (that is to say, a nation or *patria*), until finally it constructed an ethnicity and after that, by further twisting nature as metaphor into nature as biology, a race. This passage from space to "place" is a possible spatial interpretation of the so-called irrationalism that emerged in the passage between the nineteenth and twentieth centuries.

As we know, the alliance between State and Nation contained deadly seeds that quickly demonstrated their virulence. In fact, after having allied itself with the State against internationalism in the nineteenth century, nationalism carried both of them away in the first half of the twentieth. The State and internationalism gravitate on the same logic of "space," either closed or open, while nationalism is the expression of the logic of "place," which, even though it is necessarily born within the logic of space, opposes it and is one of the factors responsible for its dissolution.

Naturally, this dissolution also involves the other great protagonist of modern political spatiality: the Subject, about whom the twentieth century soon revealed how much Foucault—a reader of Nietzsche and an interpreter of his criticism on rational mediation—had gathered from the originary logics of the Modern. What Foucault understood was that the Subject, rather than being that figure which defines itself within the State's political geometries, was nothing more than a "face" drawn on the "sand"[30]—drawn, in other words, in the disordered space of a state of nature that does not allow itself to be represented or fully geometrized.

6

The Twentieth Century: Crisis and Restoration

The twentieth century was essentially divided by the catastrophe of the Second World War, which acted as a watershed separating the radical and totalitarian first half, and the second half, defined by democracy and compromise.

Total Mobilization

The emblem of this first half of the twentieth century, according to the literary intuition expressed by Franz Kafka in *The Castle*, is the anguished figure of a land surveyor, the professional measurer of space—who is no longer truly capable of realizing any measure—whose very person demonstrates an incurable disorientation. The same crisis of modern spatiality also inspired Kafka's "In the Penal Colony," or, rather, his description of the experience of deportation and death as a norm—as the condition for the uprooting of the geometries and "places" of modern politics that was, by then, completed.[1]

In historico-political reality, the First World War and its consequences (which generated the Second World War) threw into irreversible crisis the unstable equilibriums reached in the nineteenth century. Statual political space disappeared, swept away by the "movement" that had originally belonged to it, the "place" with which it had made a fatal alliance, and the technology that constituted it and from which it was born. We here see the collapse of modern geometrico-political space, whose mobile, artificial borders between State, individual, and Society no longer appear capable of describing, containing, or organizing political order. We also see the collapse of those "places" of natural belonging, the Nations, whose effects of inter-State differentiation came to contradict openly modern political spatiality, generating hypernationalistic incommunicability among the members of

European political space. During the first half of the twentieth century, then, we witness the *jus publicum europæum* in the process of undoing its own political spaces—not only does the *jus publicum europæum* here lose the fundamental spatial distinctions among public, private, and social, and between universal and particular; it also begins to lose the distinctions between internal and external, on the one hand, and enemy and criminal, on the other.

The framework of the two World Wars was undoubtedly geopolitical, as we can observe through several phenomena. In Europe, we find the opposition of Land against Sea, which is to say, the confrontation between, on the one hand, the American, Wilsonian, and Rooseveltian interventionist logics of "democratic" war (universalisms of a utopian–Protestant origin) and, on the other, the German logic of continental hegemony and its *Drang nach Osten* ("Drive to the East") toward Slavic areas. In the Pacific, meanwhile, we witness the Japanese effort to organize a "sphere of co-prosperity that is the greatest in Asia," a closed *Grossraum* antagonistic to the American naval principle of "open sea" (which, do not forget, included the naval blockage of Japan). However, the spatial crisis of the first half of the twentieth century is not the victory of the bourgeois over the soldier, the merchant over the hero,[2] smooth over striated space, or uprooting over rootedness. The crisis is born not so much from the clash of foreign principles that are opposed to one another as from *the collapse, from within, of the entire modern spatial and political architecture*, which, in realizing itself, pushed its contradictions to the limit and brought about its own downfall.

This collapse, which occurs at the exterior of modern political spatiality, goes hand in hand with the advance of ideologies, both left and right, at its interior.[3] The ideologies of the left derive from a simplified reading of Marxian dialectics, the complex spatiality of which was reduced to an aggressive and Utopian spatiality, a humanist Utopia to come, one that sacrifices the present in favor of the future. The ideologies of the right, meanwhile, which derive from the dialectics of localization, transform themselves into regressive Utopias of nature. They are regressive because they sacrifice the present to the past, but they are also aggressive, for they are constantly projected toward the future realization of this regressive return to the past. Leaving aside the differences between these ideologies—the former universalistic and the latter particularistic—we recognize that what is important here is that all of them, with their Utopian, substantive drive and their claim to realize truth instead of criticism, deform political space and project politics toward the extreme. This extremism destroys the very State spatiality that also hosts it, resulting in the laceration of the State's geometry from within, not only by the opening of warfronts internal to the State but also by the emergence of an absolute and moralistic dimension within its finite horizon. Put simply, we are dealing here with the polemical and militant universalism typical of Utopian logics and spatialities—the "totalitarian" revolutions of the twentieth century: fascism and communism.

Totalitarianism

In order to find the causes of the twentieth-century crisis, we must look beyond the struggle of ideologies and revolutions against the borders and limits inherent in the State. Their course is, certainly, a mobilization (which, however, turned out to be devoid of modern mobilization's elements of progressivity) that not only placed stress on modern political geometry, but also swept it away completely. Undoubtedly, modern political geometry here experienced a collapse, an implosion of political space stemming from its dilated extreme, its ideological Utopia, its extreme contract, the weight of "place" that breaks through space, universalistic communism (though in reality only "in one country"), and particularistic nationalism. Above all, we must stress that in totalitarianism, the structural contradictions of the Modern came to light in aporetical form, that the crisis manifested itself *from within* modern political spaces.

As such, we may seek the etiology and the phenomenology of this new spatial revolution in the phenomena and processes elaborated by Ernst Jünger in "Total Mobilization."[4] Total mobilization is a question of total war (for it is the culmination of the principle of nationality, difference, and "localization"); it is a question of technology (which, as we have seen, is equally essential to the principle of empty spatiality, the modern assumption of the world's infinite availability and artificial malleability); and it is a question of progress (which, for Jünger, is not only progressive ideology, but also the world's uniformity, made into one universal space by the power of production).

In total mobilization, in short, *modern political space destroys itself.* Because these factors—place, the universal, technology—are all *internal to* modernity, they all contribute to the originary difficulty it experiences in its attempt to spatialize politics in a stable way. Technology, in particular, is an originary factor of modern politics; it is the constitutive horizon of the smooth, closed spatiality of the State. However, it becomes clear in the twentieth century that technology is also a universal power that breaks through the closed space of the State, opposing its own smooth and infinitely open spatiality to the space of the State—which is smooth but closed. As a principle of the world's limitless availability to human work, and as a criteria of neutralization closed within the State's borders, technology by itself brings about modernity's final spatial neutralization, extending its own internal compulsions worldwide like automatons, supplanting every delimitation and every particular sphere, and taking the place of politics as the space of relations between universals and particulars.[5]

Total mobilization realizes in itself the catastrophe that puts the whole of the political architecture of the Modern into play, along with the contraction or destruction of all of its spaces and borders, its "stability," and its figures. These figures (peace and war, internal and external, State and Society, political power and economic power, civil production and military destruction) all become confused in one and the same "volcanic magma," in a new dimension that is neither smooth nor striated, but instead mobilized by an energy at once substantial and nihilistic,[6] an energy that could no longer be ascribed to human logics. This energy was destined to transform itself into the geometries and the *Gestalt* of a superhuman order, which maintains that all of modernity's political geometries ("individual mobilization," "social mobilization," and "political mobilization") were now surpassed. "Total mobilization" is, consequently, neither dynamic nor re-regulating. It is destructive; it joins technology to danger. Although, of course, we can only say this from the perspective of modern spatiality, since from the standpoint of the postmodern Titans, this same process is not so much a destruction as the construction of a new, iron order and a new, uniform *Gestalt.*[7]

In this new reality—which is neither "space" nor "place," but a movement that whips away everything—the first thing to be swallowed up is *the Subject.* In total mobilization, there is, quite literally, *no room* for the Subject, who instead experiences a universal loss of orientation, be it "natural" or artificial. Furthermore, according to Eric Leed,[8] in the disquieting labyrinth of the trench that was so characteristic of World War I, twentieth-century man lived the collapse and confusion of spaces and their borders, public and private, and intimacy and the social sphere, and left with his identity in tatters. Put simply, the State, which had unleashed the conflict and was then carried away by it, fails along with the Subject.

Totalitarianism, the child of World War I and the parent of World War II, does indeed destroy the clear distinctions of the State's political spatiality. As Arendt has noted, totalitarianism is ideology rendered effective and self-destructive.[9] In it, the extreme—the ideological Utopia—no longer has the role of criticism, laceration, or the critico-progressive mobilization of the closed space of politics. Rather, it is reabsorbed into the new political totality, which it in turn propels and saturates. By putting the masses produced by totalitarian democracy in place of a society of individuals, by substituting the charisma of the leader for sovereignty, and by replacing citizenship and its inclusive, rational logics with terror and total exclusion, totalitarianism attempts to "fill" the "empty" space of the State with truth and substance.

This search for "full" space through ideologized substance radically differentiates totalitarian totality from Hegel's dialectical totality. Totality in Hegel includes all of the logical categories of real experiences that together allow for a plurivocal comprehension of the complexity of political space. Totalitarian totality, by contrast, is an essentially nihilistic substance that functions to annihilate every spatial differentiation between internal and external, between public and private, and between enemy and criminal. The supposed "fullness" of totalitarianism is therefore, in reality, a most disquieting emptiness. The ideological logic of the Whole, in fact, culminates where it is annulled, in the *Lager*. In this extreme realization of Utopia, both belonging and citizenship fail—as do closeness between community members and the distance between citizens, as do place and space. The destruction of political space that manifested itself in the crisis of stateless and displaced persons here achieves utter paroxysm.

Along with the *Lager*, the age of total mobilization produces World War II—which is, from the perspective of political spatiality, *chaos*. In fact, it is not just air weaponry that renders space completely smooth by canceling out the difference between military and civilian. It is also, and above all, the totalitarian ideology of enemy extermination, in combination with the Western, interventionist logic of the "Crusade," that turn this conflict into a worldwide civil war and erase modern spaces, paving the way for figures like the external criminal and the internal enemy. And, of course, nowhere is the "miracle" of the annihilation of space and place accomplished more fully than in the introduction of atomic war.

The convulsions of the 1914–1945 worldwide civil war claim Europe as its first victim, destroying the spatial centrality—the international differentiation between center and periphery and between Europe and the rest of the world—that was the mainstay of the *jus publicum europæum*. With this destruction, we also observe the disappearance, or at least the eclipse, of the very existence of a European political space endowed with historico-political meaning.

Schmitt

Even Schmitt's famous identification of the criterion of the "political" in the relationship of friend and enemy[10] is colored by the collapse of the spatiality that allowed the distinction of clear borders between the external enemy and the internal criminal, and indeed presents itself as a conceptualization adapted to politics in the age of total mobilization (while at the same time amounting to a genealogy of modern politics). The age of total mobilization is thus an age of disorder, of repoliticization of the social, of the escape of the political out of the statual space in which the Modern had hoped to confine and neutralize it. Properly speaking, the "political" has neither space nor place. It is "free" power, which, even if it can be ordered, cannot constitute a space that is either "closed" or "stable." The "political," in other words, cannot be a "State." Instead, it is crossed by conflict in an originary and constitutive way, or better, crossed by the sovereignty that assumes the task of deciding and "cutting" it.[11] This is all the result of the crisis of the twentieth century, but it is also the origin of political modernity; beginning from the conceptual recovery of constituent power and its dialectic between immediateness and mediation, between intensity and extension,[12] modern political space appears to Schmitt as originarily disconnected. If it is to be effective, politics cannot institute the smooth space of law within itself, nor can it neutralize itself in complete political geometries.

In this concept of the "political," Schmitt's opposition to the "constructive" modality of rationalism's political geometry, as well as to the modality of "accompaniment" (even if with revolutionary intent) of the contradictions of dialectical thought, is quite evident. The fact that the disconnected political space must necessarily be "cut" by sovereign decision (and never simply closed or ordered) is a sign that Schmitt takes very seriously the non-spatiality of the Modern. The "political" and the decision (which is always the decision of a Subject, though certainly not that of the modern liberal Subject) are thus the truth and at the same time the negation of every modern, rational political figure. In fact, the "political" implies an *Entortung*, a disorientation that signals the end of modern political geometries as well as the end of subjectivities. Even the State is here in crisis. It is in crisis *internally* because in order to control all of Society through its dynamics, the State extends itself as a "Total State" and loses the borders (which, as we have seen, have revealed themselves to be fleeting and transient) between individual, Society, and politics, losing every capacity to give form to the "political." At the same time, however, the State is also in crisis *externally*, for the statualization of the world—the process that will eliminate the colonial system after the two World Wars and will bring formal equality among all the States of the planet—does not produce any order in and of itself, given that it is a simple juxtaposition of multiple sovereignties (unlike the situation in the *jus publicum europæum*).[13] That the State's sovereignty, extended universally, is no longer able to determine a regulating order for world spaces and hence becomes mere "technology" is demonstrated, for Schmitt, by the fact that the universalistic and "naval" forces—liberalism, capitalist economy, and technology—here take the upper hand and sweep away the distinctions between internal and external, enemy and criminal, giving life to various forms of interventionism and discriminatory wars or crusades. As such, a *unity of the world* is realized which, in its status as "universe," profoundly contradicts the defining feature of politics, which for Schmitt can only be a "pluriverse"[14] that is by definition unequal.

Schmitt's polemic against universalisms shows us that he identified the nucleus of the spatial problem of modern politics in the link between the particular and the universal. For Schmitt, this link never amounts to a stable relationship or a truly rational mediation. Rather, it resolves itself in either the bad particularity of the Subject or the bad universality of technology. International space must therefore find a new, post-subjective, post-statual, and post-technological principle of organization, capable of responding to the challenge of unrestrained technology by giving it a new form,[15] and thereby of redesigning the relationships between universal and particular in a "concrete" way.

Schmitt first elaborated his theory of the *Großraum* to overcome the crisis of modern political spatiality. This theory supported totalitarian war in Germany, even if it did not exactly coincide with it, being more tied to the theoretical tradition of hegemony than it was to the new reality of annihilating the racial enemy. Despite its propagandist nature, Schmitt's theory of *Großraume* is an attempt to think a continental organization that is neither statual nor universalistic-liberal, but imperial (the term *Reich* is central to this concept, though not at all "pluralistic" in meaning) and "concrete," based on the hegemonic and territorially exclusive capacity of "terrestrial" powers. Among these continental organizations, Schmitt would also have numbered the United States, by virtue of the Monroe Doctrine (had Roosevelt not, according to Schmitt, twisted its meaning from defensive-continental to naval-aggressive).[16] In the postwar period, Schmitt would re-propose his theory of *Großraume* (practically unchanged but now ideologically "clean") in the form of his doctrine of the *nomos*.

Schmitt's concept of the *nomos* does not envision an intrinsic politicity for space (in either mythic or geopolitical form), but it certainly does challenge the modern thesis that assumes political action on space will take place in a way that is indifferent to that space, for Schmitt affirms that politics must recognize its own originary rootedness in space and its own originary right, well before the emergence of law (which Schmitt does not define ontologically but rather through the *Ur-Akt* of *Nehmen/Teilen/Weiden* ["Appropriation/Distribution/Production"][17]). In short, politics must be spatial before it can be anything else, but this does not exactly mean that politics draws its measure from space, or that it actually takes root in it. Rather, it means that politics must engage with space through *the cut*, which is to say, the violence of uprooting, distribution, and the creation of "sides." Indeed, for Schmitt, the violence of "taking sides" is even the originary condition of every political space that claims to be "universal."

Though it is no doubt present in Schmitt's thought, the opposition of rootedness and modern uprooting is nevertheless not central to Schmitt's thought. Rather, what emerges from his spatial theory is the idea that, whereas modern politics is always unbalanced and aporetically oscillating between particular and universal, the politics of *nomos* renders itself concrete from the very beginning, in and through its adherence to the "partial" act of the cut, and by its own nonneutrality. This is the predominance that spatiality takes over individuality in Schmitt's postwar theory,[18] in opposition to the dominance of technology over space, truth, and the overturning of every claim to rational and subjective domination of space. As in his writings on technology, and for the same reasons, Schmitt polemicizes bitterly against the two opposed and victorious universalisms: the liberal-democratic and the communist. Since they are not explicitly founded on a *nomos* and instead base themselves merely on an "armistice," their division of the world into East and West expresses neither the line or passage of the history of the Spirit, nor a stable post-State order, but only the disorder of an amorphous space and a subjectivity that has been overturned and transformed into its own opposite.[19] The principle of *cujus regio, ejus œconomica*[20]—the new code of the relationship between space and politics and the distinction between capitalism and communism—is not then capable, in Schmitt's opinion, of organizing the world in a stable way, or of realizing the objective of avoiding the "bad" unity of the world that was then coming into profile, in order to find a different equilibrium between particular and universal.

Even when he lapses into ontology and ideology, Schmitt is nonetheless aware that politics now finds itself in a situation where it must address the task of redesigning all of its own spatiality, no longer from a techno-individualistic-rationalist viewpoint, but not from a statualistic viewpoint, either. It is the exigency of rethinking the relationship between politics and space that really distances Schmitt from Kelsen. Indeed, the Austrian jurist, drawing on his neo-Kantian background, interprets the crisis of sovereignty, which he, like Schmitt, views as the irreversible dissociation between modern (statual) politics and spatiality, as a scientific and political evolution that can only culminate in a post-statual juridical universalism that is indifferent to empirical space, and that expressly recalls the ideal (which Kelsen considers "scientific") of Kant's *civitas maxima*.[21]

Negative Thought and the Space of the Nothing

Within the circle of "negative thought" (in which Schmitt may be included, but with many precautions due to his concreteness as a jurist), the loss of political space is not an evolution, but rather a catastrophe, a nihilistic loss of space and place for modern and contemporary politics that is realized not only in totalitarian realities, but also in the liberal-democratic forms of triumphant capitalism. Here, the West is truly the space of decline, because its triumph—apparently economic and political, but really "technological"—reveals the fulfillment of modern spatiality, which has always actually been absent, because natural space has always been annihilated by the geometric gaze of the modern man, who interpreted it as infinitely available to his configurations. In this context, all modern history is only superficially the history of the conflict between the State and the Subject's "freedom from." From a substantial viewpoint, it is instead the history of the construction of a space that is first the State and the constraint of the Subject, and second, though without any break, the dissolution of both the State and the Subject, the global triumph of technology, which—in overcoming the State and the Subject—liberates itself from its primitive, obsolete forms and its limited spaces, adapting to its own nihilistic concept. It is no accident, then, that in the Heidegger-Jünger confrontation, the West is defined as a "space of nothing," and is thus not an extension but a "line," a line of nihilism that substitutes itself for the surface of the sphere.[22] Negative thought advances in the impossible equilibrium marked by this line, and in superhuman itineraries through the space of nothing, and some of its results prefigure, though only on a theoretical level, the attempts at a new setting for the relationship between universal and particular that would be advanced in the global age, following the crisis of both categories.

Jünger's critiques, which he elaborated in the first half of the twentieth century and proposed at least until the 1950s, juxtapose striking spatial oppositions with a diagnostic, metapolitical element. Consider Jünger's rereading of the ancient opposition of Land and Sea, between house (or State) and ship; in late modernity, this polarity no longer seems significant to him, since at that point the world is, for him, as much a Leviathan as a Titanic. Mobilization and political form, in short, coexist even in the space of post-totalitarian democracies, with destructive effects on subjectivity. However, Jünger now concentrates his efforts on reinterpreting mobilization and political form as manifestations of another, more originary space, which contains and gives meaning to both of them. This space is the *forest*, a new figure for substance, and a name for an origin that can endure and overcome even the age of technology. Land has an analogous meaning for Jünger, with a depth that is not only chronological but geological and ontological, as seen in his 1959 book *An der Zeitmauer* ("At the Wall of Time").[23]

But this is not a question of escaping a space rendered uninhabitable, or a necessity of thinking a new *nomos* of the Earth. With a kind of faith in automatons—and also in the automatic surpassing of the automaton world, characteristic of the early 1930s faith in technology's morphogenetic power—which Schmitt would never have shared—Jünger intuited that if the modern Subject was no longer at home in his technological world, it was not the end of the world, but only the end of modernity. Indeed, for Jünger, the end of modernity is not an end, but an evolution; the titanic forces of technology, of planning, and of uniformity are now interpreted by Jünger as midwives at a birth. The organization of a world-wide State produces a unity that is not just superficial or technical, but also substantial and organic. A new "chaotic fertility" is forming on the horizon, and from within global domination and unified space, a new natural substance emerges: a new, ancient reign of organic differences, in line with a logic of unity in variety, which, for Jünger, derives from the Goethian philosophy of nature, in a sort of mythical-poetical anticipation of the ideologically opposed theses of those who see the multiple and alternative power of the multitude self-producing and growing within the net of imperial global power (just as the Anarch's singular viewpoint is opposed to the plural and collective viewpoint of the revolutionaries).[24] It is clear that this is an anticipation for both sides, which is not only involuntary, but also very approximate; and if nothing else, it is indicative of an "optimism," be it scientific or mythological, which is rare in the most radical theoretical positions.

In fact, hopeful tones are almost completely absent in the diametrically opposed context of Theodor Adorno and Max Horkheimer's *Dialectic of Enlightenment*, the neo-Marxism of which shrinks from Jüngerian ontologizations. Here it becomes clear that modern space has lost all its complexity, and that neither State nor Subject has importance anymore, leaving only the undifferentiated spatiality of technological reason, which renders the "wholly enlightened earth"[25] an undifferentiated unity, subjected to a single rule.

In *Being and Time*, Heidegger had already indentified space not as a pure *a priori* category of the world but, on the contrary, as a dimension made possible by its being-in-the-world, the care for Being that delineates the "wherein" as the "ready-at-hand," that is to say, as usability.[26] In these years, Heidegger too was concentrating his efforts on thinking a spatiality different from the modern one, "given in anticipation by the techno-scientific project," in order to think a space that would be a "free granting of places," even in the form of deforestation and "clearing."

Heidegger's "opening of space" is not Schmitt's *nomos*. Though, like Schmitt's, it is internal to a thought that does not attribute the capacity to operate sensibly on space to the individual Subject, Heidegger's "opening" is not an action in the sense of partition and distribution; it has neither the intent nor the political and formative character that inheres to Schmittian thought, though it does so in a form that is not individualist, rationalist, or universalist. More importantly, the pluralities that Heidegger notes are not "cut" by difference or by the originary violence of *nomos*; their coexistence is free, because everyone discounts the Nothing within themselves.[27]

Heidegger's thought of space is also different from Jünger's theory of the "forest," though this difference is less an opposition than a radicalization. Of course, the *Verwindung* ("recovery" or "retrieval") Heidegger sets against Jünger's *Überwindung* ("overcoming") shows that the philosopher is more aware than the writer of the impossibility of accelerating modern nihilism's age of consumption. Heidegger is unable to guarantee philosophically the mythical institution of the self-revealing of substance through the nihilism of technology. Rather than prefiguring the surpassing of technology in any positive sense, Heidegger allows us to say only that technology must be left to run its own course.[28]

However, Heidegger's "deforestation" does not occur for technological reasons, but rather to gather the event that makes things rise and rest in themselves in the *Lichtung*, the "clearing." It is an "opening" that is not, therefore, a geometric domination, but a securing, a space made up of places, or better, of finite "things"—things that do not *belong* to a place, but *are* places.[29] Heidegger's recovery of places in a pluralistic sense is no longer monistic, as was space in modern thought. In its opposition to the unitary uniformity of modern space, in its need for fidelity to the originary spatial rootedness of Being—which is, however, an instance of "taking root in the open," and therefore seeks to remove itself from the modern dialectic between community rootedness and social uprooting—man's perception of the uninhabitability of modern space (despite its having been designed precisely for habitation) manifests itself. Likewise, we see that technology, which follows and realizes the universal domination of smooth space, condemns to insignificance that political geometry that smooth space claims to institute (for the purposes of ordering it). Heidegger's many *Wege* are not "paths" through space, or human works (*Werke*). They are traces that, because they interrupt themselves—because they unfold as a "wandering" and a "displacing"—go from metaphysics and rationalism to Nothing, and then from Nothing to Being, opening themselves along the way to the plural finiteness of things.[30]

The Cold War and the Social State

Between approximately 1945 and 1989, a new respatialization of politics was realized which, to say the least, slowed down the historico-institutional collapse of modern political geometries. This restoration (in the true sense of the word) of political space defined itself, beginning from the war years, as a return to "open society,"[31] and entailed a strong and polemical employment of the pluralistic, Anglo-Saxon social and political model. The employment of this model spoke to the need for an antidote to the mistaken but understandable view that there was a continuity between the State and Nazism, or better, between the ontology of "place" and the formal monism of closed "space" on the one hand, and of totalitarianism's destructive dynamism, on the other. In reality, at least in countries with a statualistic tradition, this open society was realized in the years following the Second World War thanks to a new "closing" of political space and a redefinition of borders.

The "political," in fact, was re-confined in new forms and figures, and the nihilistic paroxysm of total mobilization and totalitarian utopias was surpassed and nearly frozen, in these years, by a new political spatiality. From an external viewpoint, this spatiality consists of the world unity of international institutions like the United Nations, which at this moment still organizes the various particular sovereignties of the States, which were weakened but not eliminated, since with decolonization they are extended all over the planet, unanimously accepting and recognizing strong limitations of the *jus ad bellum*. Also, though admittedly only partially, this spatiality consists of the unity of capital's *mondialization*, a process already underway with effects of unequal development and even underdevelopment in the periphery of the Third World—effects which, do not forget, are critical for the development of the First World's metropolises.[32] The unity of human rights, universally proclaimed in 1948, exists in the background, emerging only in the global age.

Nevertheless, the most authentic spatial code of politics in the second half of the century is not the relationship between the capitalistic North and the exploited South, but that of ideological, economical, and political barriers between East and West. In fact, the "One" that international institutions hope to establish on the planet during the Cold War years is, in reality, a "Two." In the system of the Cold War, every particular political entity and every universal affirmation of rights is involved in the economic and civilizational conflicts between East and West (the power of the Third World remains latent, despite Mao's efforts to respatialize politics by centering it on the global conflict between City and Country, as it does not have the strength, in the context of the Cold War, to reshape the international political space).[33] Just as the Modern was marked by the simplification of internal space, now the simplification of external space is central. The differences between continental Europe and the Atlantic world disappear, and when confronted with the huge weight of communist Asia, these two entities base themselves in the "amphibious" space of the West, which is to say, within American hegemony. In this Western space, Europe—cut as it is by the Iron Curtain after the fatal succession of the decisions of Moscow, Tehran, Yalta, and Potsdam—is no longer central, nor torn apart by civil conflict. Instead, the Cold War freezes it into a frontier land, put into play by the confrontation between superpowers. However precarious and painful it might have been, this was truly a new political articulation of world space.

However, from an internal viewpoint, modern political spatiality showed itself to be less subject to revolutionizing. In fact, the West was capable of differentiating itself from the communist East precisely because it was able to organize its own political spatiality according to an architecture capable of giving new life to the modern game of the spatialities of the Subject and the State, and to make them play that game in a way that was still productive. This internal revitalization of modern political spatiality passes through social rights, a concept elaborated by Thomas Marshall.[34] It was also endorsed in different ways by the social-democratic or liberal-democratic models of governance that became hegemonic in the second half of the century in the West, and, in terms of economico-political efficiency, even defeated Soviet communism. Soviet communism was disproven in its claim that the internal division of class in the "bourgeois" State was an unbridgeable gap, and thus a potentially revolutionary conflict. Instead, thanks to the competitive collaboration among unions, mass parties, big business, and public-political institutions, that State was once again able to manage the borders between private, social, and public, and to widen the spaces of its action. In fact, the State discovered in social right a new legitimation; it charged itself with the promotion of these new social rights and with the regulation of production, or at least the redistribution of wealth, through the fiscal lever. The potential and tendential limitlessness of production (organized according to the modalities of "Fordism") was maintained as a social market economy internal to political form, in order to avoid market spaces becoming exclusive and monopolistic. As a result of the Social State, the market economy did not end up creating a market society, and at the same time, it showed itself to be far superior, in terms of efficiency, to the economy of communist control. On the whole, we find in the realization of social democracy a form of politics that presents itself as an autonomous model as compared to individual democracy, national democracy, and totalitarian democracy.

The State, the Subject, and their spaces were all changed by this experience. The State's political objective—profoundly modified compared to the liberal form, which wanted to separate and distinguish State from Society—came to coincide with Society in its effort to include, in its own space, as much social and individual space as possible. This produced a growth of bureaucracy, reducing (and according to the more radical critics, erasing) the space of the Subject while affirming new rights. Thus, that strict interdependence between Subjective rights and State rights that characterizes modern political logic was realized once again.

Though the space of the Social State remains artificial (as is obvious in modernity), it ceases to be "empty" and smooth. The need to "fill" State space was, of course, also present in totalitarianism, though in that case, remember, it was pursued through recourse to "nature" and "ideology" in destructive ways. The Social State also parted ways with the notion that political space is nothing more than a space surrounded by a State, and thereby allowed citizens' economic and juridical interactions. It now became the space of mass democracy, which not only guarantees everyone's rights, but also cares for citizens, treating them differently in certain domains, as in fiscal matters, in order to encourage the disadvantaged. At the same time, the verticality of sovereignty dramatically diminished. It found itself supported by a group of institutions capable of containing political pluralism like an arena and, as such, capable, too, of avoiding being overwhelmed by social waves that pushed toward the center from the periphery of the system, toward the conquest of full citizenship.

The Social State, along with the Cold War, acted as a *katechon* (or "brake") with regard to the potential obliteration of the spatial dimension of politics that was contained in total mobilization—in the encounter of production, technology, and conflictuality that had already manifested in the first half of the twentieth century—and that would be taken up again in new forms by globalization. The Social State also contributed to the making of democracy, understood now as respect for human rights and as political pluralism, as the normative horizon of much of political thought, and as the political space that must be kept open against authoritarian closures and against totalitarian destructiveness. Globalization, as we will see, has displaced the problem, imposing the goal of bringing back the political space of democracy, in a purely new mode, namely, in a position of "closure." That is, globalization attempted to use certain rules, which limited power, to form and structure the political space of democracy, which found itself threatened by the global opening of the economy and technology whose universal power tends to sweep away every limit and every border, every certainty and every rule.

7

Globalization

In the last ten years of the twentieth century, three incendiary events—economic, political, and technological—triggered an explosion in the quality of capital's *mondialization* (which had already been underway with growing intensity since the origin of the modern age). These events were the deregulation of the circulation of capital, the fall of communism, and the electronic boom—an ensemble of phenomena that resulted not only from the development of certain preexisting tendencies but also from a profound modification of the relationships between economics and politics. Indeed, globalization—the name that is given to these processes, which are of course very much still in process—is so new and radical that it may indeed be taken up as the emblematic watchword that qualifies the end of the century (and, probably, the coming decades) as an *epoch*: a modality of action, production, and cultural elaboration that involves and determines all levels of existence.

Marxist criticism tends to give a monocausal reading of globalization, seeing it as a complication in, and renewal of, the dynamics of capitalism—or, in short, as a particular phase in the development of the system of capital.[1] Others, predominantly in sociological circles, interpret the elements of discontinuity or differentiation in globalization with varying degrees of exaggeration, and as such reinterpret globalization in a multicausal way, as an ensemble of processes that derive from modernization, but that carry its dynamisms, to some extent, beyond themselves.[2]

Here, by contrast, are some of the assumptions that shall guide our reflections. First, our analysis of globalization will pay greater attention to its factors of *internal contradiction* than to its elements of integration and inclusion (although the latter are, of course, also present). Second, we will argue that, from the viewpoint of political spatiality, globalization marks a *new epochality*. Third, we will assume that the logics of the "modern project," and the drive to the technological neutralization of the political that governs the modern age, indeed bring about the failure of the temporal vectors and spatial architectures of modern politics that confronts us today (and in globalization, there is, of course, a crisis in the idea of progress, in the internal space of the Social State, in the difference between States and, most important, in the external space between East and West).[3] However, this fulfillment of modernity is also its overturning and surpassing, and as such, our challenge is to understand how it might be possible to reconceptualize the current dynamics of politics, and how, in the age of the *Displacement of Politics*,[4] we might eventually be able to redefine the very meaning of spaces and places themselves.

On the whole, we believe we can assert that globalization is *that ensemble of processes in which all the tensions of modernity explode*, resulting in configurations that are completely postmodern. In globalization, in other words, all of the spatial contradictions inherent in the relation of universal and particular—all the difficulties involved in the coexistence of closed space and limitless space—now manifest themselves as explicit aporias, impasses that produce neither political form nor freedom. Freedom in particular, which in the Modern charged itself with the task of "opening" the closed geometry of the State, today seems to require of us, if not a respatialization of politics, then at the very least a redefinition, even if only dialectical, of new borders. For, paradoxically, the completely open space of globality (or at least the space which, in globalization, tends to present itself as such) can be as suffocating as the narrow space of statuality (even though the latter tends to present itself as closed).

Phenomenology: Border Crossing

The task of outlining a phenomenology of globalization is not easy. Not, of course, because there is a lack of material evidence for us to consider, but rather because this task amounts to an attempt to compose a map without using the geometrico-political coordinates provided to us by modernity. Globalization is indeed essentially *border-crossing*, the breach of boundaries and the deformation of political geometry. The difficulty we encounter when trying to put a name to our experience of border-crossing is responsible for that fact that many of the emerging definitions of the spatiality implicit in globalization are first of all "negative," and cannot always be formulated positively.

Economics

Among the principal signs of globalization,[5] revealing its novelty and discontinuity (well beyond the deregulation of international money markets) is first of all that new form of capitalism—so accelerated and developed that some have proposed calling it "turbo-capitalism"—that is marked by the passage from Fordism to "Toyotism." This term describes a series of phenomena inherent, at first, to the internal organization of the factory; the production that, in the Fordist age, was essentially limitless but confined to a limited territory (involving, for example, large national factories), is now effected by the presence of new obstacles in the market (saturation, competition, ecological limits) and becomes flexible with regard to its workers' recruitment, training, and job description. This flexibility extends to the mode of production, which turns into a "just-in-time" reaction to the demands of the market. In a later phase, production will decentralize itself, moving toward some areas of the Third World (thanks also to new forms of communication) whose "emerging countries" reveal themselves to be ready and willing to move into a new economic phase. Ultimately, the new economy deterritorializes and dematerializes itself to a point where, paradoxically, the moment of production occurs in the background of consumption. This is what comes to be somewhat hastily defined as "the end of work," but which is really only labor's disarticulation and integral acceptance in the logics of new capitalism.[6]

The birth of transnational business signals, in every way, the eventual end of the Fordist factory and its multinational projection, as well as the social and political centrality of workers' organizations and the Social State.[7] It is also, however, the end of the containment of the limitless within the limited—the end, in other words, of one of the key spatial assumptions of modern politics, of the space that enabled politics to command economics (or, at the very least, enabled it to give economy and society a political figure and form). The politics that, in modernity, used to give meaning to space, is here replaced by an economics, as financial as it is productive, that crosses the space of borders and vital forms, giving rise to what some have already called "geo-economics," which sees the State as only one among many variables of the economic process.[8] In short, with globalization, particular interests fully affirm their own universal reach—one that, in the modern age, had been regulated and formed by the "universal particular," the State.

As such, let us emphasize, the new economics is not indifferent to space in general, but only to the modern space of politics. In fact, it organizes new spaces for itself in a new way. As far as economic power is concerned, we see it removing itself more and more from political power and organizing itself cybernetically with a network spatiality,[9] where systemic logic determines far more than do the intentional actions of individual subjective actors, primarily with regard to labor but also to capitalists as single individuals. The "nodes" of this network, then, are really new spaces. The "regional economies" and "global cities" that constitute global economics are, in effect, spaces that are *immediately* exposed to the flows and dynamics of the global economy, heedless of the State borders demanded by the "region," where the "city" no longer needs to rely on the mediation of a State and its spatial hierarchies between center and periphery.[10] Predictably, the planet's large economic areas and global cities now witness, just as did States, the opening of unequal spaces at their interiors: spaces of poverty and wealth, of workforce immigrations, of the concentration of intellect and innovative technologies, and of dominance and dependence.[11] Economics is not neutral, even if it presents itself as such. The network coexists with the most profound differences, which are now no longer determined by politics, but rather by economics, which today tends to exercise a direct and politically unmediated command.

Politics

In the age of globalization, we see the supersession of two defining modern political spaces: the sovereign confinement of conflict within the closed space of politics, and the etching of lines of class conflict (which are not only internal, but international, between the North and South of the world and between the First and Third Worlds).[12] The Second World has disappeared, swept away by its defeat in the conflict—by now archived, spatially represented in the fall of the Berlin Wall—between East and West. The Third World, meanwhile, enters the First, and *vice versa*, in an exchange that is unequal not only in terms of capital investments but also in the "migration of peoples." Those who enter the State's space in an irregular way present the State with a nearly insurmountable challenge. While they are not enemies or criminals, these people are still not citizens or documented foreigners. In order to bring them "into focus," the State can only reason on a case-by-case basis, offering or refusing citizenship with varying degrees of liberality.[13] The State continues to operate, in other words, in terms of exclusion and inclusion. However, the migrants' true challenge is that of freeing subjective rights from the spatial embrace of modern statual geometry. This is, moreover, just what juridical globalism attempts to do by stabilizing a set of international civil rights laws as *jus cogens*,[14] which is valid regardless of State territory (as we will discuss later).

Of course, it is not only these very concrete, material flows of people or the economic flows of goods and capital that today challenge and perforate the political space of the State. The State must now also reckon with the virtual space of the Web, which, in principle, can allow it to be encircled and short-circuited. Compared with the political space of the State, the Web offers a kind of contemporary edition of the Sea's modern spatial alterity, and it is not by chance that new "pirates" operate within it (though it is nevertheless premature, at the very least, to see them as new figures of individual liberty). On the whole, however much the virtual world seems capable of undermining the State's political space, for the moment it seems to be a function of technology's planetary domination, and not of liberty (and this, too, we will discuss in a moment).

Now, it is through these exchanges and these penetrations of spaces that the unification of the world, for the first time in human history, is realized. This is a world without a center but with many peripheries, unified but not unitary, technicized and economized, but not neutralized.

The political consequences are evident. The modern centrality of the State's space is seriously shaken not only by the phenomenon of migration (in the ways we have already mentioned), but also by the "dispersion" of the economic (which, as we have also seen, is now no longer shaped by politics). The first and most evident effect is the characteristic narrowing of the space of the Social State (against which, clearly, the forces and interests connected to it react), the slowing of the State's redistributive hold on society, and the consequent liberation of "mobility" belonging to the individual Subject and his social production. This "liberation" of the subjective takes a collective form; in it, subjectivities old (e.g., churches) and new (the most different "groups" and "communities") struggle for recognition of their identities at a political level, with the result that social, economic, and private law becomes autonomous from the politico-statual, and public law. In this process, we can see one of the most evident characteristics of globalization.[15] It is as though politics is weakening, as though its space is becoming scarcer and more slender, as though the duties of the government are decreasing in number and intensity, delegated instead to the market, to society, and to middlemen, in a trend that is progressively demolishing the "big government" of the postwar period. Nonetheless, this tendency is not without its opposite, for the obsolescence of politico-statual spatiality provokes a reaction in the same State powers, who, along with the new social powers, respond by operating "out of order" and by entering into "extraordinary" conflicts, in renegotiations outside of every rule, with the new and old subjectivities who demand, for their part, the formulation of new statutes of belonging and new rules for the exercise of rights. The presence of these political spatialities produces an effect of a new, postmodern *medievalism*, the full spatial implications of which have yet to be conceptualized.[16]

In short, every political space that was initially relatively closed and homogeneous is now potentially an ethnic mixture destined to multiculturalism and to the struggles for recognition manifesting themselves in States that are no longer monocultural political spaces. Instead, in these States, the new criteria, the modalities, and the meanings of citizenship are still unwritten, while the "old" ones of modernity and the National State are put under increasing amounts of stress.[17]

However, the openings of modern political space realized by economic and population flows also generate phenomena of agoraphobia,[18] which lead to resistances that define themselves as "traditional," to local insurgencies, and to new communitarianisms. We see, in short, a reaction on the part of those who reject a hybridized destiny or even just multiethnic cohabitation, and who invent an identity for themselves, resulting in conflict that can become so strong that it sometimes entails secession from the State,[19] and almost always entails new forms of exclusion toward newcomers. Thanks to this construction—which is really completely "postmodern"—of ethnicities and cultures, the modern link between State and Nation is dissolved,[20] and we may say that the political space of the National State is challenged and split open not just from above, but also from below.

But even this plurality of cultures is problematic. The thesis of multiculturalism is that the conflict between cultures is the new figure of the present, capable of substituting Marxist class struggle and the liberal contract as the genetic moment for the order of political space, and that the true political problem today consists in allowing for the coexistence of a plurality of culturally determined and spatially qualified identities within a political space that is free from the effects of monopolization and exclusion. However, this thesis does not place enough importance on the fact that these "cultures" are not at all "natural" in and of themselves, but are heavily modified by the social contradictions that run through them. Nor does this thesis pay enough attention to the quite frequent occurrence that individuals determine their identities against these contradictions rather than through them.[21] This phenomenon—in antithesis to the other definitive processes of globalization—would make it indispensable for the individual to rely on a set of norms that can only derive from the State (unless we imagine a "nomad" subjectivity, indifferent to space and capable of affirming itself against both communities and Statehoods; but we will address this later).

Another indicator of globalization is the loss of the borders of daily action,[22] or rather, the evident exposure of everyone's vital sphere to the highest level of interdependence—aggravated by worldwide electronic communication—with regard to the social and cultural processes taking place in the world universe. The evanescence of every possible representation of closed spaces causes a common world destiny to emerge, thereby forming a *transnational* or *world society*.[23] This would not necessarily be homogeneous, but unitary, at least in the sense that it no longer allows any culture to resist in its own traditional "purity" or "autochthony." The result is a *global culture* that is sometimes seen as Westernizing banality, sometimes as original novelty, sometimes as a cultural universe subject to internal self-differentiation into "cultures," sometimes as a homogenization that, because of the way it shuts down or contaminates histories, memories, identities, and hopes, actually becomes the real enemy to subdue.²⁴

International Relations

From the viewpoint of international relations, globalization consists in the fact that politics is now much more "global" than it is "international," and that it therefore occurs in a different space—a space that is neither the dual space of the Cold War nor the plural space of the sovereign States' multiplicity in the *jus publicum europæum*. This is a space of turbulence; in it, lines of conflict multiply themselves and manifest themselves in con- tradictory phenomena. On the one hand, the polycentrism of this space results from the residual but tenacious persistence of the State-Form. On the other hand, it is the result of the growth of international organiza- tions (of a political and juridical type, such as the United Nations and world courts), transnational organizations (of an economic sort, such as the World Bank, the International Monetary Fund, and the World Trade Organization), and the birth of a plurality of "regional regimes" (includ- ing Europe) that are capable of reconfiguring the distribution of global power.²⁵ From still another perspective, it emerges from the absence of a center, due—paradoxically—to the projection on a global scale of the very superpower whose victory in the Cold War brought about the birth of globalization. For despite this superpower's unilateral reliance on wars it legitimizes as police or humanitarian interventions (in keeping with neo-Wilsonian logics), it is nevertheless unable to "keep order" in a world where conflicts arise from interstices that are increasingly ethnic and sub- statual (or, some would say, suprastatual, taking place at the level of "clash of civilizations," or what we might define as "cultural *Großraume*").²⁶

Of all the spatial revolutions that modern political geometry has undergone in the global age, the most spectacular is undoubtedly this crisis of borders, this trend toward the obsolescence of the distinction between internal and external. This obsolescence (which is, obviously, violently opposed by the new and old defenders of sovereignty, but affirmed by those who see world space as One) has an important corollary: Where the distinction between internal and external has become obsolete, war acquires the form of police action against criminal actions. The new form of universality that results from this trend unites within itself the various forms of universalism that were at work in modern political space (the Utopian spatiality that sees the Good concentrated on the Island spreading toward external space in order to impose itself; the spatiality qualified by opposition typical of "just war"; and, once again, a universal spatiality qualified in a moral sense, of the Kantian type). What we must remember, however, is that, much like the "particular universals" of modernity, this new universality is less a true universalism than an ideological interpretation of international anarchy—a useful tool for the United States (both with and without the United Nations' protection) to use for humanitarian intervention, but ultimately in the name of securing "American primacy" within that absence of clear political spatiality that is globalization.[27]

Contradiction without System

Globalization is therefore real but contradictory, and cannot be read as a unidirectional process; the victory of Society and the market over the State, assuming that it has already occurred, is the victory of economics over a modality of politics (in addition to being a victory over the cultural and critical sphere). It is evident that politics clearly persists in the new phenomenologies of power and in the still open, though problematic, exigencies of justice.[28] The end of international duality is neither unity nor peace; the end of spaces striated by politics does not imply the unification of space but the creation of multiple, overlapping spaces, a plurality of networks that rearticulate space in new hierarchies of domination. Global culture is constantly intersected by new inventions of particular cultures, which are able to open into numerous enclaves in its unitary space; the victory of the West over communism is not, then, in and of itself the victory of the individual and liberal democracy.

In fact, the so-called "age of individualism" sees the triumph of an economics whose power so transcends individual calculations (or, at least, rational calculations) that it even becomes difficult to recognize in it the modern universalism of profit. It sees the "free" Subject assert his own identity as "sovereignty of the consumer" with no regard for the State, Nation, or Society (and thus, the market and not the State becomes the space of indispensable identification for the formation of the identities of individuals), but at the same time, it also sees him detached, not only from what he produces (the paradigmatic form of modern alienation) but also from his own culture (the new form of contemporary alienation). It sees him "wandering" freely, but also insecurely and in a disoriented way. It sees him crossing all borders, but also crossed by the thousands of exclusions presented by multiethnic society. And it sees him lost—for there are no longer any places in which to build a home nor spaces in which to be represented.[29] The age of world unity is neither truly unitary (which is the mark of the Sea), as Schmitt feared, nor truly humanist, as Alfonse Dupront hoped.[30]

The global age's various settings—the *globalscapes* that Arjun Appadurai[31] describes—amount to a multiplicity of spaces devoid of logic or orientation; the intrinsic law of globalization seems to be that there are no longer the usual spaces or places of politics, and that indeterminate risk is the central category of the present (and not, as in the Modern, security from "danger," which was clearly determinable and identifiable at an anthropological and political level). This is a risk that ricochets immediately off the complexity of the world and onto the individual Subject.[32] The State, constructed in order "not to be afraid," is run through with factors of uneasiness; the unwanted effects and the contradictions of the modern project take the upper hand over its geometric rationality, and together constitute what Ulrich Beck has defined "second modernity."

In the most optimistic interpretation of this process, this process renders modernity fully *reflexive*: It confers upon modernity the capacity to create uninterrupted interaction between the level of action and the level of culture. In this reading, modernity then becomes able to reincorporate into its newly "elastic" order the very "political" (in the Schmittian sense of the word) that modern "geometric reason" did not know how to "confine" fully within the State and which, in a negation of the hypotheses of the decline of politics, has repoliticized society.[33] This offers new opportunities to political action, but also deprives it of any certainty; we can no longer hypothesize a modality of thought that would be able to capture reality in the certain and secure modes that were evident in rationalistic constructivism (with its geometric capacity) or dialectics (with its capacity to adapt to the "shifting" profile of the real).

The fact is that what was once the pluralism of interests and ideologies in the political space of the Social State and the space of democracy becomes in globalized space an inextricable complexity. This ensemble—which is comprised of universalization and particularization, homogenization and differentiation, integration and fragmentation, dislocations and new spatializations, chaos and new opportunities, apertures and closures—does not take the shape of a contradiction, either in a structural sense or a dialectical sense. It does not, in short, amount to a *system*.

But neither does it assume the form of a simple, immediate contradiction. That modern political geometries are obsolete, that the spatial categories of the Modern are no longer sufficient to describe the complexity of contemporary globalization, that its space is neither a representation of the Subject's need for order nor a manifestation of his mobilizing liberty—none of this means that the artificial spatiality of modernity has been substituted by a return to the "state of nature." In the global age, in fact, artifice has been supplanted by the *virtual*, which is to say, the new mode of being brought about by globalization. Although virtuality can be a space for new forms of extraterritorial freedom, at the moment it is really the last and most sophisticated face of technology, which today seems not to want to leave visible traces of itself or to dominate the world from the exterior. Rather, it seems completely engaged and directed toward excluding and making its "users" forget the existence of anything like a material world, removed from manipulation and formed by a mediation that is still, at least partially, controlled by some subjectivity. Naturally, the immaterial element of communication, the "cultural" and "representative" level transformed by electronics, is, now more than ever, a real and concrete factor of power, in its new form of *soft power*.[34] The *Panopticon* order of the modern age—which rendered space visible from the viewpoint of the State—has today morphed into something different but nonetheless quite real: a *Synopticon*, an order of global media visibility that seems to be the visibility of all on behalf of all, but is actually the visibility of the few, bearing symbolic power, on behalf of many seduced "spectators."[35] The image of the world, or better, the world reduced to image, is not itself removed from the reality of power.

Global Mobilization and "Glocalism"

If, at this point, we wish to define the typical spatiality of globalization in order to analyze various proposals for modes of political intervention that are adequate to this space, we first need to proceed in the negative—to recognize that, although global space deals with the universalism of profit, it does not coincide with it. This is because the dominating force in the so-called privatization of the world[36] is actually an economics whose logics are hardly ever attributable to private individuals, who are, if anything, the personal figure for impersonal (which is not to say neuter or neutral) techno-economic forces. Global space is a space of universality that is not exactly the paradoxical universality implicit in Utopia. Globalization is not a Utopia hoping to make itself into a reality; it is, in essence, always devoid of spatiality and assumes the form of a virtuality that is always already realized and sure of itself.

With this, we see the modern dialectic of the universal present itself in a new form; globalization is an amorphous and immediate space, in that it lacks its own "counterpart" of closed, statual spatiality. This immediacy means that political mediation no longer has an important role in determining the forms of spatiality. It does not mean, however, that the universal in existence today is "natural"; although the logic of an opposition between nature and mediation may today be obsolete, the universal and amorphous spatiality of globalization nevertheless cannot be understood as a simple, natural immediacy. If anything, global space forms itself through a *universal immediacy of mediations*—or, more precisely, a mediation that is at once dequalified and accidental. Global space may, in other words, be universal, but this does not mean that it is unitary; it is, so to speak, riddled with fractures.

At this point, to define the spatiality of globalization in the positive, we must remember that the defining feature of a world constituted by an unequal flow of movements—capital, raw materials, goods, people fleeing from poverty or war—is, fundamentally, *mobility*. This is precisely what Zygmunt Bauman grasps in his book analyzing the effects of globalization on people:[37] The comprehensive meaning of globalization is that, in the unstable world of economic globalization, *everyone is in movement,* whether they want to be or do not want to be, whether they are physically immobile or mobile. This perpetual motion creates a polarization between, on the one hand, the "globalized wealthy" (the tourists who, after the nineteenth-century transformation of the distant into the exotic, now experience the transformation of the exotic into the everyday, and for whom space tends to disappear) and, on the other hand, the "localized poor" (who are trapped in dequalified spaces or forced to move and be "vagabonds" because their local world has become inhospitable or has disappeared). This is a polarity between those who are at home everywhere and those who see the entire world fleeing from them, and are unwanted and rejected everywhere they go. Moreover, despite the asymmetry between these figures, they share a single destiny, a common lack of directionality and orientation; while the capitalism of the last century stimulated desire and consumption for the wealthy and triggered more immigration for the poor, in today's world, everyone moves without a conscious target, immersed in the uncertainty and anxiety that characterize the global world.

Particularly when we extend our argument from persons to include politics and economics, we may propose that the most fitting name for the entire process of globalization is *global mobilization*. What this means, however, is that globalization is—to the extent that we view it from the standpoint of modern spatiality—bound to appear "elusive." Indeed, after "individual" spatiality revealed itself to have the potential to throw modern political geometries into crisis (because it had that capacity to translate itself into both social and political forms), and after "total" spatiality expressed the convulsive fury used by totalitarianism to implode modern space, "global" mobilization actually erases every modern spatial determination, for it knows only energies of movement and not factors of stability. Nonetheless, this defining feature does not mean that globalization is thereby similar to total mobilization (and, indeed, the concept of "globalitarianism" is off the mark).[38] Totalitarianism, after all, emerges from a degeneration of modern political spaces and their internal dynamics that is based on a destructive energy with a strong political priority, while the mobilization produced by globalization, by contrast, is primarily economic. Furthermore, the former is an end—an implosion—while the latter is, on the contrary, a beginning—an explosion.

Now, of all the spatial oppositions typical of the Modern—between Land and Sea, Europe and the rest of the world, Empire and State, market and *patria*, rights and sovereignty, particular and universal—there is not any one that is typical of global mobilization. Rather, global mobilization tends to evacuate all of these oppositions of their meaning. It even plays down the oppositions between left and right and between democracy and authoritarianism. All this poses the question of how to give voice and standing to the contradictions that *do* remain in globalization and are immanent to it (and we shall address this question in a moment). For now, it is enough to say that global mobilization pushes its ideologies to reinterpret and redefine the oppositions above as a conflict between advanced civilization and residual areas. In the supposedly smooth space of globality, these "residual areas" are nothing other than enclaves of backwardness—from a chronological viewpoint, they are anachronistic exceptions from the "progressive" processes underway—where authoritarian regimes may continue to nest, until the advance of the free world sweeps them away according to the "Utopian" spatial logics we have already discussed.[39]

Meanwhile, traditional political oppositions seem to vanish in a trend toward their reciprocal homogenization in a *virtual democracy*. This is the most apt definition for the mode of politics that emerges in the absence of political space that is typical of global mobilization. Virtual democracy transforms representation and militancy—the rational forms of the plan for the construction of modern political space—into the irrelevant accompaniment of the processes underway through the media method of opinion polls. This method realizes the exact opposite of public opinion, and in general, also of the system of modern rational mediation. In fact, it gives life to the eternal present of private opinions that react passively, in direct contact and in real time, believing themselves content to "participate" in events as they happen. It is a kind of "political romanticism"[40] in grand style; it takes away from the intellectual the illusory presumption of being at the center of the world, in order to give it to the mass of individuals instead. But of course, the globalized world has no rationally identifiable or controllable center. In its politics, as in its economics, globalization implies that the center of gravity is moving from production (the project) to consumption (passivity).

This absence of modern political spatiality is supported by the fact that, having openly discounted the link between particular and universal, global mobilization knows only (to phrase it in the positive), a spatiality that defines itself with reference to the relationship between *local* and *global*. But under conditions of global mobilization, this relationship is so indeterminate that it no longer means anything if not the supreme *dequalification* of space, which by now is neither center nor periphery, without *Ortung* ("location") or *Ordnung* ("order"). Second, this is not a true opposition, given that no "place" still has the strength and authenticity to oppose itself to global logics.

There are, as we know, many interpretations of the "local." For Zygmunt Bauman, it is completely negative, in that it is marked by defeat, inferiority, emptying, and marginalization. Clifford Geertz sees more possibility; for him, the "local" grasps the possible vitality of identity conflicts, whereas the "global" is, for him, a heterogeneous totality of "locals." But beyond these differences, the opposition of the global and the local signifies that, under conditions of global mobilization, *every point can be immediately exposed to the totality of immediate mediations*. It is not by chance, therefore, that some today speak about *glocalization*.[41] This property of global space does not, of course, mean that all points are equal—as we have said, hierarchy as a difference in power continues to exist in the global age—but rather, that *the loss of every organizational reference to space is now complete*, that the world is "in fragments."[42] In short, global mobilization means that anything can happen anywhere, even if this is less true in certain places: The "West" today (as distinct from the geographical and historical West) has become that Northern strip of the European and American world (to which we can also add the exceptions of Australia and New Zealand, those remains of the British Empire) that, even though infiltrated by what was once the Third World, has a lower probability of hosting the war and dictatorship that that region was once susceptible to within itself.

Thus, having defined globalization in terms of crisis, contradiction, global mobilization, and glocality, a truly new challenge emerges: Will the future of politics, perhaps, be devoid of spatiality? If this is the case, what are its characteristics? If this is not the case, what spaces of politics, if not political geometries, can we today identify and realize?

To put the question in greater detail, from a viewpoint that once could have been called "internal": How can political spaces be organized if we are no longer able to draw borders? Or, rather, what could the political space of a State be today, if it can no longer be the "particular universal" whose end is the salvation of individual lives and the confinement of conflict, while at the same time remaining unitary and plural with the end of "containing" different identities? If, in other words, the State cannot strive to be the producer of single identities for its citizens and of the homogeneous identity of the people? How can individual and collective subjective identities coexist when they deny, or precede, identification in a common political space, and demand something much more challenging than a safe life, given that they require recognition?

And finally, in the "international" context: Can global space take up (or really, already have within itself) a new configuration in which the relationship between particular and universal is able to restabilize itself? Or will it continue to oscillate, as it is does now, between the fiction of sovereignties and their worldwide "concert," and the reality of anarchy and "moral" pan-interventionism?

The issues raised by globalization can be summarized in a single question: What is left of the space of politics (which, from the mid-twentieth century, coincides with democracy) after the collapse of the figures and borders that constituted it in the various phases of the modern age (namely, Subject, Society, State, international state system, and conflict between East and West)?

Responses to the Challenge

Today, there are many answers to this question that are organized on the basis of a growing propensity to interpret globalization as a space that is not as smooth as its apologists believe, and to see in it not only a trend in need of restraint, but also an opportunity to be seized. Among the responses that we here analyze, what is initially evident (in those responses organized around the theme of democracy), is the common conviction that, under globalization, particulars and individuals are immediately exposed to global universality. According to some (but not all) of the authors we are about to read, these particulars are bearers of rights in a direct and immediate way—which is to say, they can be universally guaranteed without the need to rely upon political mediations. In the passages below that are dedicated to the problem of freedom, we will problematize this idea of "exposure," demonstrating that it can be interpreted as the opening of the particular space of the individual, not to the generic universal, but to another particular, the movement of which realizes itself in a *determinate in-finiteness (in-finità determinata)*. In this movement, we will suggest, the particular enters into a "virtuous" short-circuit with itself. Last but not least, we will consider the concept of the *new Empire*, which is to say, the theoretical position of those who think that global space is already completely political in and of itself, and that the particular and the universal, taken up like the subjectivities which are produced within the global megamachine, exist in a relationship of determinate negation and material dialectics.

Democracy between Globality and Respatialization

When we examine the relationship between particular and universal, and between difference and uniformity, we can see that it is possible to rethink this relation as a question of "new democracy."

Let us begin by considering those positions that understand globalization's defining feature to be the fact that it is a smooth space that threatens the very existence of modern politics. In this circle, we have the representatives of the editorial board of the journal *Le Monde Diplomatique*, who see globalization essentially as the triumph of liberalism, supported by an ideology—defined as *one-dimensional thought*[43]—that preaches its "naturalness" and therefore its desirability. From the board's viewpoint, the ideology of smooth space is central to globalization. Clearly, for these extremely polemical and antagonistic authors who align themselves with Catholic, Third World, and Marxist discourses, globalization is, in concrete reality, not at all devoid of contradictions. Even though they identify the novelty of globalization in the extremely powerful "recoil" effect of the economy upon politics and culture, these authors generally emphasize globalization's essentially capitalist nature and its status as a manifestation of Anglo-American political and economic imperialism, and as the enemy of closed spaces, national cultures, and state sovereignty. The relationship between particular and universal is here completely unbalanced in favor of the particular.

Others read the same (and all too easily asserted) world unity and the same smooth space of globalization with different eyes, more oriented toward discovering, in these conditions and situations, the opportunity to increase the universalisms born in modern political spaces and always prisoners of the political geometries of modernity. For these thinkers, the rational, progressive, and morally cogent universalisms of human rights, which today are finally autonomous and removed from the State's tutelage, can and must become the foundation of a new cosmopolis. If, as an empirical fact, globalization is the triumph of economics over politics, we may think that the entire process can still be placed under the control of a politics that is, in reality, the combination of law and ethics. Indeed, this *mondialization* of human rights occurs primarily through the assumption that their universal juridical tutelage is entrusted not to national States, but to international courts, whose work would represent the first step toward a new *global democracy*.[44] An example of this position would be Otfried Höffe's theory,[45] which outlines a global political order characterized by the weakening of the State and by the effective presence of subsidiary, federal, democratic institutions. This global political order is not a worldwide super-State, but a *Weltrepublik* ("World Republic") (similar to the Kantian *civitas maxima*), founded on the hypothesis that politics is not completely interchangeable with economics.

However, this hypothesis of an effective positive law, freed from the *jus soli*, really conceals another hypothesis: namely, that it is thanks to globalization that something like a *worldwide civil society* exists, and that smooth planetary space is juridifiable. In reality, precisely here where the State short-circuits itself and seems to be dead, it at the same time engages with what (as we have discovered) is in fact one of its principal effects: the existence of a society, now more or less on a worldwide scale, where the *jus cogens* can be applied through the work of the courts. It is clear that the agreement between politics, law, and ethics (the principal effect of juridical globalism), is founded on a "domestic analogy," or the assumption that the *Weltpolitik* can be transformed into *Weltinnenpolitik*, or "internal world politics." As such, these forms of thought are characterized by the somewhat ingenuous desire to apply a conceptuality to globalization that is modern, but also halved, dehistoricized, and despatialized, thereby reduced only to "universals" (and, moreover, only to *some* of these universals—reason, law, and ethics—and not others) that are then immediately adopted. But in this way, the space of globalization becomes an interior without exterior, a universal without a particular. Put simply, it becomes a bad universality, a well-meaning ideology.[46]

Jürgen Habermas's position on these matters is different and much more complex, though he too orients his thinking around the notion that modern Western democracy must continue to constitute a horizon to contain the processes of globalization. For him, the main question is how to bring democracy to safety after the crisis of the State and the triumph of the market (which Habermas understands to be incapable of self-regulating). The problem of how to exit from the national constellation—from the State link between space and politics, space and economics—and how to think democracy within a postnational constellation is therefore, for him, the challenge.[47] From this foundation, we see the clear emergence, in Habermas, of an awareness of the spatial dimension of the problems and the novelty that globalization represents (despite all of its continuities with the Modern). Of course, this awareness does not follow the movements of juridical globalism, but is more traditionally inclined toward a *respatialization* of politics, in a two-pronged attempt to "close" the threatening universal of the market. On the one hand, we have the European federation, capable of effecting, once again, the redistributive politics of the Social State on a supra-State scale. On the other hand—from the viewpoint of deliberative democracy, of a sort of "universalism of differences"—we have telecommunication networks of discussion, managed by the many autonomous subjectivities freed by globalization. It goes without saying that Habermas's respatialization does not entrust closed space (whatever that might be) with the task of securing the political identities of Subjects, but only with that of guaranteeing them. Habermas's thought does not then propose a new political geometry, but if anything, only a new and unrevised constitutionalism.

David Held also posits a strategy for respatializing politics.[48] Like Habermas, he assumes that the traditional positions, be they liberal or Marxist, are ill-suited to the global age, whose characteristic is that of the "dispersion" of unitary political forms—and univocal political logics—that characterized modernity. Held, like Habermas, is oriented toward ensuring that globalization's "rupture of borders" does not entail a defeat of democracy. He had previously outlined the "cosmopolitical" characteristics of democracy in the creation of regional parliaments and, eventually, the creation of a world parliament, as well as in the formation of an increasingly cogent international law, which anticipated the creation of a new bill of rights and duties, related to new "domains of power."[49] But as far as saving democracy is concerned, for Held, neither constitutional engineering nor dreams of community will suffice. Instead, it is possible to exploit the plurality of vital worlds and experiences, and to think of them as respatialized, removed from global dispersion. Here, it is also a question of a respatialization that is no longer tied to a State territory, but now to "common structures of political action," interactive spaces where individuals can come together in common interests, where "sites of power" and localizations of power come into play (for example, the human body, the Social State, culture, economics, juridical institutions, and so on).

Therefore, in Held, we are dealing with thematic spaces, where forms of power are localized not in "places" but in domains and functions of existence. In these spaces, it is possible to think of instituting a form that is not closed, but only "a stable and durable framework" within which the always-open and variable relationship between obedience to power and participation in decisional processes could be democratically managed (as in deliberative democracy, through the encounter between different arguments) with the objective of smoothing out at least the most unacceptable differences. Even from the democratic viewpoint of the respatialization of politics, then, globalization noticeably weakens the modern project of rational planning that recently has been re-proposed, in neo-Kantian terms, by John Rawls in his 1999 book *The Law of Peoples*.

In essence, the common thread linking these "respatializing" theoretical positions is that they respond to economic universals that are out of control (the triumph of capitalism, and of technology in its service) with proposals of ethico-political universals. The allure of these proposals is their supposed capacity to restore form and spatiality in a way that would be *both* universal *and* determinate—in short, in a manner that is global, but that does not also abandon a human, rational project to the dynamics of globalization. These thinkers, in other words, treat the global degeneration of modernity with remedies that remain, in essence, Modern.

These remedies re-propose the traditional aporia of modern political spatiality, which is emphasized but not surpassed in the age of globalization. That aporia is the following: On the one hand, there is no universal that exists objectively as such, but always remains a particular, while on the other hand, there is no particular that is truly a closed space, and that is not deformed by the power of the universal. In fact, even if the State has lost its ability to contain and give form to those universals that are born at its interior or to human rights, and even if these universals are presented as being valid for the entire planet, they always remain within a particular sphere, a specific culture or civilization: the West. Furthermore, it is no accident that they are refused by many cultures as manifestations of Western imperialism. Globalization is the Westernization of the world, which today seems to have only one cardinal point: the West.

That there is open and explicit awareness of this fact where internal political space is concerned is clear enough from the recent debate between liberalism and communitarianism.[50] The smooth and planar space implicit in John Rawls's *A Theory of Justice*, which is inhabited by "theoretical," monocultural subjects who are politically equal and equivalent in terms of planning, sets itself against a complex political space organized in multiple "spheres" and inhabited by selves rooted in history and in different ideas of belonging, conceptions of good, and life plans. Some scholars have objected to such a neutral, procedural politics, claiming that such neutrality is always oriented toward accommodating, if anything, a precise category of person: the modern Westerner. Still other objectors argue that political philosophy must, if anything, think the conditions of cohabitation for a plurality of "political lives" and not the simple unity of rationalistic projections of the modern man and his plan. After all, this same political liberalism was forced to reduce, at least in part, its own pretexts, and to imagine political space as an arena to be furnished with liberal institutions, which now are no longer designed geometrically by a contract, but by the overlapping of different beliefs and values.[51]

On a global scale, meanwhile, Martha Nussbaum's response to the challenges of globalization is particularly sophisticated.[52] In the context of globalization, her underlying neo-Aristotelianism,[53] which leads her to distrust exclusively rationalistic political strategies, becomes a liberal position. That is, it becomes a specific form of universalism, a principled and challenging feminism. For Nussbaum, to respond to the question of the global extendibility of Rawls's theory of rights and justice—the problem of making universals truly universal—would require us to resolve the problem of the relationship between universal values, on the one hand, and the local, traditional cultures that frequently oppress women, on the other. In order to affirm a universalism that has parted ways with Western imperialism, Nussbaum knows that she must go beyond the logic of rights (namely, their immediate universalism and their tendency to demand the support of State-based sovereignty, which is to say, the support of Western culture). Indeed, Nussbaum prefers to talk about "capabilities" rather than rights, of the innate possibilities in every human being to conduct a "good life." More than simple utilitarian "preferences," but less than a monistic idea of the "good," Nussbaum's capabilities are also more than "freedom from" because they involve the possibility that a human being can "flourish" and conduct a full life, free from need, fear and oppression, while still being active and realizing personal objectives. Public intervention is only necessary in the few cases where its aim is to remove obstacles that impede the formation of "flourishing" personalities. Even in the case of apparently private questions like religious beliefs, family roles, sexual lives, and so on, the objective of Nussbaum's thought is an equality of possibilities to "flourish," for women and for men.

For Nussbaum, in other words, universals are not abstract and do not end up being the imposition of specific Western values. Instead, they are transformed into respect for human beings as a goal in and of itself: an objective that is universal, but concrete, compatible with local specificities, or, rather, with those traditional values of different cultures that people have freely chosen.

Liberty

Instead of attempting to close the supposedly smooth space of globalization in order to "control the damage" that the economy inflicts on politics, or attempting to come out of the aporiae which emerge here through use of Aristotelian categories, other thinkers take up globalization as a challenge that carries a still more radical demand. For these thinkers, the challenge is to think and enact politics while also leaving all closures aside, be they spatial, global, statual, or even thematic.

To avoid falling into the "trap" of respatialization, let us now attempt to theorize rights without spatial fixation and identities that do not need the

State (or at least distrust it and seek to establish contractual relationships of private law and exchange with it, rather than relationships of public law and political representation). We will consider nomad subjectivities that are opposed to space, that carry an identity that does not coincide with stability or identification within the State (or with being identified by the State)—subjectivities that, in short, do not accept the static logic of citizenship, and, if anything, turn it into a polemical concept. These subjectivities model themselves after migrants, but unlike migrants, they do not seek inclusion and integration. Rather, they seek mobility, possibilities of not adhering, of seceding, of struggle (a term much more appropriate than "revolution"), of plural, temporary, or partial citizenship. For these subjectivities, the geometrico-political effectiveness of static and statual borders is lost, and borders could be anywhere—wherever space is a "space of transition," wherever it is more conflictual than definable on the basis of logics of security.[54]

In short, in the world that globalization has put into motion, these subjectivities would exercise their "right to escape."[55] When confronted with global mobilization, they would respond with subjective mobilization, which, unlike liberal, protomodern mobilization, would demand to exist outside of any political geometry. It is necessary here, therefore, to go beyond the modern destiny that sees the universal liberty of the particular—the "freedom from," hostile to fixations in space—giving itself over to the particular universal's political spatiality, to the State, and fixing itself within the political dominion that should be protecting it and making it concretely usable. The result is an agonal freedom. This agonal freedom may seem assonant with Machiavellian freedom, which also understands political space to be shot through by multiple vectors of conflict. However, the conflict here is triggered not by the goal of "glory," but only by the affirmation of subjectivity.

Jean-Luc Nancy's position is even more radical, though less concerned with the concrete dimension of power and conflict.[56] He correctly reconstructs the ways in which Europe has established its internal and external frontiers in the course of modern history (borders that are closed limits and not the open, American variety, and which affirm identity or, rather, constitute the space in which many different identities coexist). He continues to describe how Europe then reinforced this concept of space when, with the emergence of the concept of the "nation," political domination became homothetical to the "ground" (by which we here mean the "place" that presumes itself to be qualified in some special way, and not simply the "territory" over which the State exercises its spatial sovereignty). Nancy's intent is not to "fix" the frontier as though it were a border, but rather to "mobilize it," not toward the aforementioned struggle, but toward freedom. Nancy's concept of "freedom" is, however, neither a "freedom from" nor a "freedom of"; it is not an internal opposition to the geometric figure of political order that refuses the logic of particular and universal. Rather, it is a fact that regulates itself (as in Kant), and, moreover, a concrete experience (which is where we see Heidegger's legacy).[57]

Nancy interprets the frontier as an expression of subjective identity whose limit is not a limitation. The Subject that experiences this limit without limitation not only reaches its own end—not only ceases—but *by* ceasing (or, better, by entering in contact with the Other without losing itself or resisting absolutely) *begins*. For Nancy, the frontier is thus an expression of an identity that asserts itself only by exposing itself, only by presenting itself as a singularity confronting its own alteration.

This interpretation of the frontier as limit in a dialectical-Hegelian sense (though without accepting the dialectical "surpassing" of the limit) thereby excludes the idea of the frontier as a line where closed communities face one another. It even goes far beyond traditional modern universalism. In fact, as a result of this, Nancy thinks a politics in which space is formed by Subjects who do not hold their universals in common—in the case of universalistic politics, reason; in statual politics, citizenship—but instead share a common, irreducible singularity. From this point of view, the frontier ceases to be the rigid establishment of the political figure in space, an outline of a previously supplied identity, and comes to be responsible for contiguity and proximity. It is not a separating force, but a uniting one, though in reality it does not unite and instead allows these singularities to subsist in a fractal, uncertain, irregular existence, in which they constitute a kind of universal polychrome, an "exposure" of "colors," single identities, which then goes beyond the logic of universal and particular. This "exposure" is contingency as freedom. It was the need for containment that gave rise to modern political geometries, and that transformed itself into "freedom from" within them. This same need is now clearing a path through the rubble of spatial representations, without conflictually breaking them apart, in order to expose them to their "unpolitical" reversal.[58]

This "unpolitical" frontier is the condition for the thinkability of a spatial configuration that is neither figure nor form, and that realizes itself—or at least, is able to realize itself—in what Nancy calls *mondialisation* (which, from his viewpoint, is equivalent to globalization).[59] This is, of course, a blind process generated by techno-economic logics, but it can also be the condition for a "becoming-human" that is without limits (*un divenire umano senza limiti*), a becoming that invents man's *humanitas* by emancipating him from the modern compulsion to make truth coincide with the "meaning of the world." For Nancy, this compulsion manifested itself in "political theology," both in the theologization of the "political" and in what we have defined as "political geometry." In other words, it manifested in the action taken by modern political identities to construct themselves as closed representations, which derive a "meaning," a value, or a truth either from the exterior (if not from God, from a functional substitute like history, progress, and so on) or from their own closed immanence (from the State as the universal identity of individual, particular identities). In any case, the end result, as the twentieth century has shown, is nihilistic senselessness.

This modern compulsion to represent and valorize is overcome in globalization, when a "being-in-common" that claimed no global significance was (or, rather, could be) realized. The sense of the world today consists not in the political production of identity, similar in grand style and grand scale to the closed spaces of the Modern. It is precisely this world, this sharing of things. The political space of globalization is a community that realizes the appropriation of its own negativity, which puts no positive in common, which is not a community of One. This political space is not theatrical, not represented, but is constituted by the simple fact of interdependency among entities, by the simple humanity of mankind, by human beings' immediate realization of a network of relationships that is executed without intentional weaving—by the reciprocal interaction that sets them free.

Globalization—the end of political theology and modern political geometries—is also the moment in which the "meaning of the world" ceases to come from the pontifical mediation between Heaven and Earth, or from the rational mediation of the Subject who has the world at his disposal and arranges objects within that world. Immediate mediation—which is to say, the immediate relationship between beings—is the occasion that makes possible a space in which being together is not reabsorbed into truth, but simply coincides with the local, particular meaning that resides in each "node" of the "network," without referring back to itself or to a theological Other. The space, therefore, is not one of hierarchy, but neither is it one of equality (which would be a superficial thesis) or of fraternity (which would be excessive). Rather, it is a space of contingency, or better, of proximity and distance, detachment and entanglement. For Nancy, globalization is not, then, a geometry of borders or a universal design constituted by confined identities. It is a systemic network space with the potential to realize a radical transformation of political spatiality. With a clear debt to Heidegger, Nancy reformulates political spatiality as the totality of relationships between "things" and "places," though it is not possible, ultimately, to hypothesize that Being supports them, not even in postmetaphysical forms.

The New Empire

Hardt and Negri's model for interpreting globalization in terms of Empire[60] is equally radical, in that it takes up globalization as a epochal threshold opening toward new spatialities, rather than a challenge that needs to be confronted in order to "control the damage." Their model, however, is much more concerned with understanding the dimension of power in globalization, an ambitious attempt to redefine the entire conceptual and spatial apparatus of global politics.

Hardt and Negri's is a new kind of Empire, one that is not defined in space or in time. To be precise, it does not have a territorial center of power but only a decentered and deterritorialized apparatus; it does not propose the realization of any progressive "universal," but only the fulfillment and maintenance of systemic equilibrium within the world's productive machine, the freezing of time into an eternal necessity. Beyond its ideological self-promotion, Empire is actually evoked by the productive machine because of its capacity to solve conflicts. It is neither founded nor created, but instead is made systemically necessary by the need for peace and for the continuing removal of the crises that are born within the world's productive machine. Thus, it is economics that demands politics; it is economics that appeals to authority. This authority legitimizes itself as a permanent and indispensable necessity; founded on universal ethical values, it projects itself into juridical values that, in turn, validate just war and international police in areas of crisis.[61]

In short, the very existence of this imperial power and military apparatus is ethically legitimated and justified by the goal of peace and order, demonstrating that globalization is a contradiction that reproduces itself in the mode of an "exception." Kelsen's domestic analogy, which sees the world external to the State as a smooth space similar to the State's interior, is therefore incorrect. If anything, the opposite is true, and the internal events of Empire are governed by the same logics of crisis that govern supranational events. Indeed, Empire has no borders; it is a space without edges that suspends the relationship between internal and external, or, better, it is a space in which everything is simultaneously internal and external. In any case, the exception is the key, both to internal and international law. The exception must continually be removed in the name of superior or universal ethical values.[62]

With its systemic needs, decisionist logics, and universalistic legitimation, Empire is truly novel. It is a "monster" that brings about unheard of and much more audacious syntheses than the "mixed constitution" of the Roman Empire.[63] The Empire is both pluralistic and unitary, the synergy and the contradiction between the residual powers of national sovereignties, supranational organizations, and the imperatives of systemic logics. Moreover, it is different from classical imperialism because it cannot be brought back to the initiative of a single First World State constructing spheres of domination that are impermeable to other States. Rather, the Three Worlds are now exchangeable, connected one within the other in a unitary space that is, at the same time, divided, and operating through its internalization of the external.[64] Its normality is exceptionality.

Hardt and Negri assume that these are juridical, political, and military expressions of the global economic machine, and that the machine operates by passing from the traditional, *formal* subsumption of labor to capital to its *real* subsumption. Empire produces social reality through law and force, but it is essentially *biopower*, a biopolitical power that completely seizes the social body without needing to establish a totalitarian dictatorship. At its deepest and most essential level, Empire organizes live, immaterial labor in an immediately social and communicative dimension; it disciplines singularities, making them compatible with the productive fluxes that constitute its existence. In short, industrial and financial power not only produce goods, but also subjectivities; life in Empire is structured around work for production, and production is made to work for life. Transnational "corporations" are the fundamental connective structures in the biopolitical world, and far from being simple continuations of European imperialism, these directly structure territories and populations, distributing labor and organizing the hierarchies of production. Empire's profound rationality is not described by traditional juridical categories, but by the history of management, by the political use of technologies, and by theories of communication. In fact, while Empire is producing goods, it is also producing its own image of authority through large-scale self-legitimating narratives that are fundamental for producing equilibriums or reducing complexity before imperial authority can militarily manage the exception.[65]

For Hardt and Negri, Empire is not invincible. Indeed, even as it is being born, it experiences its own decline and its own fall; its global organization of power is challenged by new, internal barbarians. The creative opposition forces growing within the vortex of Empire—like a counter-Empire or the other face of the spiral—Hardt and Negri call *multitude*: a "reversal" of imperial political space that does not want to be "unpolitical," and a politics of freedom opposed to the politics of domination. In fact, just as the modern struggles against expropriation, nationalism, colonialism, and imperialism produced an early form of human unity, today it is the multitude itself that has the strength to constitute itself as the concrete, material viewpoint that reveals Empire as a *non-place*, a vortex, and a "black hole" of expropriation that attracts and annihilates humanity. However, this non-place is also "living"; it has bodies and brains, it is the universality of human creativity, the synthesis of freedom, desire, and live labor that Hardt and Negri define as "republicanism," a phenomenon significantly different from juridical globalism's "democracy of rights." While in Jünger's world-State the organism emerged from the organization's interior, the multitude that is at once *within* Empire and *against* Empire constitutes itself as innumerable nomadic and "barbarian" living experiences, not mythically as in Jünger, but dialectically, with a decided shift from ontology to the antagonistic plurality of concrete subjectivities and living "particulars." Despite Empire's corrupt operating practices (segmentation, division), these living experiences can unite in the new, materialistic generation, and also in the new power appropriated from the new rights of global citizenship and from one's own body through the guaranteed social wage.[66]

In short, globalization is a political space, even if big government has been replaced by systemic intelligence. Indeed, globalization is Empire precisely because it is a system of contradictions, despite the fact that this systematic nature does not confer suprapersonal subjectivity on it, as occurred in the Hegelian notion of the Spirit. It is a system of the non-Subject, the non-State, and the non-place, and of "negative" and "corrupting" production. Within the virtual but highly effective body of this system of immediate mediation, the ontological bases of antagonism form themselves out of a sort of materialistic necessity, and the mediated immediacy of the creative oppositional forces are generated—just as within the Roman Empire we observe the formation of the enormous subjectivity and absolute alternative of Christianity. In this vision, optimistic after all, where the materialism of Lucretius and Spinoza joins with that of Marx, globalization becomes the transformation of space, production, politics, and subjectivity. It is characterized by a space that is simultaneously smooth and striated, collapsing in its alienation and noted for its revolutionary power. As such, the global age is that new epoch that, in a manner of speaking, unlocks the possibility of new Heavens and a new Earth.

"Necessary" Europe

If, as we have said, what is at stake in our inquiry is the redefinition of the relationships between universals and particulars, no obvious conclusions are possible at this point. Globalization is *in fieri*, and we are confronting, or suffering, its processes in real time. If a cartography is possible, even with the difficulties which we have addressed, it is still impossible to put it into perspective.

Moreover, the responses we have discussed are certainly not the only responses to the "spatial" challenge of the global age. We should also remember David Harvey's dialectical Utopianism,[67] as well as Daniel Elazar's neofederalism,[68] oriented toward creating political unities larger and smaller than the States, with different goals and on different scales. Similarly, we should not forget the proposals for "global regions" for sustainable economic development as a political response to globalization's redesign of the world's political landscape.[69]

The fact remains that even globalization requires a suitable political space—one that is not, paradoxically, a global space—in order to enable the development of the dynamics it carries within itself. In short, avoiding the reactive (or reactionary) responses to globalization that re-propose large or small communities, while not giving in to the other, tragic senselessness of universal alienation or the vortexes of the "hellish squall, which never rests"[70]—to which a believer's conscience could only oppose the motto "*stat crux dum volvitur orbis*" ("the Cross stands while the world turns")—it is not necessarily true that we must comply with cosmopolitical democratic dreams, which are destined to shatter against the reality of new hierarchies and new particularistic striations of space that define the new "fortresses" of wealth.

In fact, since it is politics that renders the unpolitical possible, a determinate political space is the condition of every thinkable "exposure" of the self to other, and also of every dialectical encounter with the global vortex of the New Empire. Whatever new politics is able to take life from globalization will be a politics that does not emerge by chance, but in a space that—though not qualified or geometrized—will at least have been prepared to recognize the possibility of the New. Without a concrete politico-spatial determination, there is only formless virtuality and dominated inauthenticity. There is not even plurality—only dispersal.

At the threshold of this transitional time and space, the outline of a European alternative begins to define itself. This is the alternative of a Europe that would return to being the land of difference. But the difference in question would now itself be different. The European alternative we have in mind would no longer receive its sense from the oppositions of ancient political geographies. Nor would it require Europe to return to being the center of the world, as it was in the time of the *jus publicum europæum*. Nor, finally, would it position Europe as the land of self-conscious Spirit, as the bleeding wound of the frontier land during the Cold War. We are thinking of a Europe that has completely carried out its nihilistic decline, and has therefore left behind its alleged destiny of being an appendix to the West, a Europe that does not claim to be, in the words of Edmund Husserl, "the historical teleology of the infinite goals of reason,"[71] and which consequently has no desire to save the world from itself. We are thinking only of a Europe that presents itself as a political space endowed with sense.

To be precise, we are proposing a Europe that will be able to *reactualize politics*: not by resuscitating big government, but by leaving behind the belief in the market's supposed automatisms. This Europe would not seek to extend the space of politics, but to increase its intensity—to engage in "visionary" planning—so that politics can still create space for itself. From this viewpoint, Europe's difference would consist of its status as a space that is not just one more random, "glocal" function of the automatisms of domination. It would become a different kind of space, a space that has no need to pose pathetically as the *katechon* of globalization, as the political Idea that opposes globalization head-on, or as a "place" that is grounded in its "roots"—a "small *patria*" in the regressive and agoraphobic sense. Rather, it would be a space that presents an alternative to the global horizon, even while existing within that same horizon, because it would be the space in which the closures and openings (cosmopolitical, unpolitical, or revolutionary) that globalization strives to imagine could become effective. It would be the space—which neither proudly closes nor passively opens—in which the challenges and opportunities of globalization are neither refused nor submissively accepted, but are instead collected and put to use.

We are thus proposing a Europe that would be the fruit of practical reason, the result of a prosaic but passionate effort to outline new borders that would be capable of once again establishing that there is a space in which not everything is possible, a space in which global powers must bend and take on determinate figures, in which mobility and the cosmopolitical encounter are also a human wealth and not simply a compulsion dictated by economic imperatives. Concretely, this Europe would exist as a sovereign space of rights that are not generically human but constitutionally and institutionally guaranteed in a continental *political constitution*. This would be similar to the real space of constitutionalism, where—placing increasingly less importance on the question of citizenship and allowing the possibility of plural, even provisional, citizens—an equilibrium between particular and universal would be realized, similar in some ways to Montesquieu's "coordinated diversity."

The actual reality of this Europe can certainly not be deduced from its necessity. But at the very least, we can draw an engagement from it—an infinitely long engagement, one that is difficult to realize—to imagine a constituent process in federal terms, capable of organizing a constitution whose "constituted" institutions do not claim to exhaust or close the "constituent" energies; to imagine a political process that does not fall back into the unitary mysticism of constituent power.[72] This will be a process that goes far beyond common banknotes, but it is not yet possible to see either the Subjects (State and peoples must coexist for a long while, though they hold different interests) or the outcome, which can be neither the restoration of the Westphalian system, a single mega-State, nor a reenactment of the Holy Roman Empire. This will be a process capable of "representing"—but it certainly will not represent the borders of a new fortress-Europe. Perhaps it will represent a new political space, one that allows us to think the Earth as something more than a void, a vacuum waiting to be filled by the oil pipelines designed by the cartographies of global power.

II

Global War

Global War

The presupposition of this work is that the events of September 11, 2001, did not constitute a "normal" terrorist attack, and that the military actions that followed were not a "normal" reprisal or a "normal" war. The attack had the effect of exposing the dense tangle of confused categories, spheres, and spaces that are at work in globalization, from the horizon of which the attacks derive their sense. Our claim in this work is that America's catastrophe threatens to become chronic, marking, if not the beginning, then at least the first large-scale manifestation of a new type of war: *Global War*, which we must learn to recognize as a *modality of globalization*.

In order to bring to light however many or few concepts political thought is able to decipher from our experience of Global War, we feel it is premature, and perhaps excessive or even impossible, to insist that our concepts assume the form of a system. The concept of "Global War" will require us to make an exit from not only liberal conceptuality, but also Marxism and the "negative thought" of Carl Schmitt. As such, it will be enough for now to sketch this phenomenon with broad brushstrokes, using a strong chiaroscuro, in order to highlight, differentiate, and define what, in reality, are only ambiguous shades of gray on gray.

Two Empires, One Question

In 400 A.D., an anonymous author, perhaps a bureaucrat who was exasperated but not yet desperate about the Roman Empire's fiscal and military situation, wrote a treatise called *De rebus bellicis*.[1] This work imagined, among other things, a whole range of devices and machines of war that could get the better of Rome's enemies. Besides the fanciful images contained in its pages—the *ballista* (four-wheeled or *fulminalis*), the *tichodifrus*, the spiked shield, the *plumbata* (*tribolata* or *mamillata*), the *currodrepanus*, the armored scythed chariot, the *thoracomachi*, the *liburna*—which are spectacular despite their dubious effectiveness, *De rebus bellicis* offers an extraordinary perspective on the strategic situation at the time. It represents the *Imperium romanum* as a space that finds itself surrounded by treacherous savagery (*dolosa*) and "frenzied native tribes, yelping everywhere around," who "hem the Roman empire in" (*insania nationum ubique cirumlatrantium*).[2]

In this rapid and powerful sketch, we see humankind besieged by animal nature, a City surrounded by the Country, a Civilization exposed to hostile Nature, an internal Good assailed by an external Evil. We see the author's disdain, anxiety, rage, and racial contempt, as well as his awareness of the burden that is shouldered by the Eternal City, and the disenchanted conviction that it is her duty to withstand it. This mix of emotions is similar, though not identical, to the underlying motivations that, nearly seventeen centuries later, would help construct the ideological understanding of the relationship between "the West" and "the rest of the world." And it was precisely this same understanding that was elaborated politically and intellectually, then spread by the media under the guise of "common sense," in the aftermath of the terrorist crimes of September 11, 2001.

Now, as then, the understanding of "external aggression" passes through the optic of a conflictual relation between Us and Them, even if today the opposing identities are less frequently defined in racial terms, and more often in terms of religion or ideology (Islam versus Christianity, anti-Americanism versus the free world and its values). Now, as then, the attacked parties' self-awareness of their role as world leaders stems from a faith in technology as a remedy against Evil—as if the mere fact of technology were evidence of a more fundamental intellectual superiority, one that will always somehow manage to be able to get the better of barbarian fury and animalistic cunning.

However, at least one very important difference exists between these two representations of aggression. The late Roman image is, above all, *reassuring*, for it is based on a spatial simplification, on a clear opposition between internal and external space. Our contemporary perception, on the other hand, feeds on (and, indeed, feeds into) fantasies of penetration and specters of contamination. The notion of a clear distinction between Us and Them, which certainly continues to exist in contemporary discourse, is now intensified by the disquieting experience of vanishing boundaries and uncertain borders. Spaces today are, more and more, becoming complicated, distorted, and confused. Barbarians are not only baying at the gates of the Empire, but are rabidly biting right at its heart, demonstrating that they know very well how it functions and that they possess the "know how" [English in original] to strike a crushing blow. The external seems to have become internal, and to have opened up a second front. The West feels forced to respond, and so unleashes technological power against its outside, while deploying institutional cunning (also in the form of technology) within its interior. Thus it is that while the machines of imperial technology—spy satellites, Echelon ears, B-2 Stealth bombers, B-52s, Predator planes, cruise missiles, F-16 Falcons, smart bombs, cluster bombs, daisy-cutters, thermobaric bombs—hunt down and strike enemies in the deserts and the caves of central Asia, the Horn of Africa and Mesopotamia, the apparatuses of security simultaneously use detectors and interceptions, video cameras and tabulations, as well as an infinite number of checkpoints, seeking to ferret out the infiltrators and the Fifth Columns.

The confusion of internal and external spaces is further complicated by the confusion of identities. Edward Luttwak reads September 11 as a phase in the struggle between the "new" warrior barbarians against the "old" Western bourgeoisie who are at this point incapable of heroism (Michael Howard also speaks of "post-heroic" war). Pierre Hasner, meanwhile, voices the suspicion that even as the barbarians are becoming far too technological, the civilized bourgeoisie are becoming barbarous in their attempts to respond to the attacks against them. This theory is supported by al Qaeda's unsettling military and financial abilities, as well as certain clauses of the Patriot Act that deal with the judicial treatment of foreigners accused of terrorism, not to mention the American media's discussion of the legality of torture in preventing terrorist attacks.

What is responsible for generating this path of analysis in the new Western discourse on war? We believe that it is a complication internal to the perceptibility and intelligibility of *political space*. As we have seen, the West's new discourse on war is quite effective; its primary objective is to win concessions regarding a series of antiterrorist measures, both military and nonmilitary, which it hopes to guide and legitimate. For precisely this reason, however, it is a discourse that must be deconstructed—not, to be clear, because of the sophistic idea that objectivity is not attainable in any form and that the world is nothing but an interpretation, but instead because our critical discourse *on* war must adhere as much as possible to the official discourse *of* war, so that in our words we remain capable of speaking *iuxta rerum principia*, in a manner that is adequate to the course of the world.

In order to dissipate the suspicions that have grown over time, we must reaffirm that our deconstruction will not invert the relationship between aggressor and victim, or justify today's "barbaric" violence as a response to the "civilizing" violence of yesterday's colonialism, or back-date September 11's causes by ascribing them to the original sin of Western claims of superiority—claims that would only cloud our precise responsibility. Similarly, our deconstruction will not seek to neutralize the horror by explaining the principles at stake in the conflict with reference to fine distinctions and much-abused oppositions (like nomad/sedentary, Land/Sea, Empire/multitude, etc.). Our aim is not to reaffirm a comforting system of historical, sociological, and metaphysical dualisms. It is to eliminate those dualisms, to reveal that *behind this supposed conflict of Two stands a One—globality—which involves us all because it upsets our interpretive paradigms of politics and its dark side: war.* In short, our deconstruction will attempt to decipher the experience of "modern things" in order, by contrast, to begin the process of finding suitable categories for illuminating the "new things" that are happening today. Finally, we will seek to compare our experience to the lesson of the ancients, with the conviction that today, despite every empirical continuity (and most unlike Machiavelli's reflections on his own time), we today find ourselves faced with an event, Global War, that in fact marks a strong conceptual discontinuity—a *caesura* for which the definition "epochal," is, for once, apt.

The question that the anonymous author of *De rebus bellicis* was unable to pose—and that poses itself today with a finality so inescapable that it almost seems new compared to what was happening ten years ago—is: What do "internal" and "external" mean? The very fact that we can (and even must) ask this question is *itself* a sign of the radical transformation of political space—not only compared to the Roman Empire of the fourth century but also compared to the Cold War of the twentieth—that is globalization's most obvious, and most loaded, characteristic. This complication of the relationship between external and internal space also opens up a set of questions about identity. More than any simple opposition between well-defined identities (e.g. Us and Them), these questions of identity become a play of mirrors in which identities run the risk of confusing and losing themselves. The Enemy is not here (as it was for Schmitt[3]) an Other in relation to whom we can dialectically figure our own question. Rather, the Enemy is an alterity that is at the same time infinitely distant and monstrous, on the one hand, and internal and disquieting, on the other. However much we might want to distance him or place him at the exterior, the Enemy today presents himself as the Disturber, the specter of all that is internal and domestic—as our own wicked caricature, our Double, our Shadow.

The spaces, categories, and identities that were put into play on September 11 all have meanings and values that are superficially similar to those of modernity, and that seem like they could be used in analogy and continuity with modernity's meanings and values. In fact, however, modern concepts lead to nothing but disorientation; if we attempt to interpret September 11 and the events that followed according to these concepts, we will find that nothing is as it seems.

We make this point not to muddy the waters, but simply to cast our gaze into the gloom in order to pick out an image that is more adequate to the totality of military and political events which, from September 11 onward, gave life to what we must, for lack of a better term, call the "First Global War"—the other side of the "new politics" of globalization. As such, we shall first attempt an analysis of what has been said about Global War. After that, we shall attempt to say what Global War is—what it says to us and about us.

To correctly hear the word—the *logos*—of Global War is also to know how to adequately perceive the Idea that configures it and gives it form. Even the root of the word "Idea" (*vid*) belongs to the same lexical family as "see" (*"vedere"*). To grasp the basic Idea of Global War, we must therefore create a sketch, through the philosophico-diagnostic gesture of looking without prejudice, of its essential image.

To See the War

"I saw the Emperor—this world-soul—riding out of the city on reconnaissance. It is indeed a wonderful sensation to see such an individual, who, concentrated here at a single point, astride a horse, reaches out over the world and masters it."[4] Thus wrote Hegel to Friedrich Immanuel Niethammer from Jena on October 13, 1806, after a battle in which the Prussians had been defeated. For Hegel, however, this battle was a crucial point in the evolution of the Spirit, a secularized and revolutionary version of the *gesta Dei per Francos*, God's providential action manifested though the French people.[5]

"I have seen the world spirit, not on horseback, but on wings and without a head,"[6] wrote Theodor Adorno in *Minima Moralia* in 1944 on the subject of Hitler's V2 rockets, which "like Fascism . . . arouse mortal terror and are wholly futile," a fact that, for him "refutes . . . Hegel's philosophy of history."[7]

Two wars, one quite different from the other. The first is an Idea that found its bayonets and, through Napoleon's political and military genius, its projection of power in European space. This is an Idea of the State of Peoples, of the Nation's armed sovereignty upsetting not only the *ancien régime* but also its dynastic logics and its "war-in-form," which is to say, its notion that war is an exercise of instrumental, well-calculated, and limited violence that is fully controlled by politics and according to a geometric logic.[8] Now, however, Napoleon's cannons act like Beethoven's drums, keeping the time of a new figure of destiny: the triad of state, people, and leader, which Clausewitz, in *On War*, defines as the spine of "real absolute war."[9]

The second war is a "total war." Technology has here found the political theology it can use to validate all the violence that loaded the spring of contemporary history, namely, the will to conquer world space with goals of racial hygiene. This brought about the realization of technology's anti-human potential, crystallized in a machine of war and extermination—the most radical ever conceived—that was simultaneously powerful and nihilistic. This terrifying yet unstable machine was destined to collapse from the start, because its unstoppable qualities gave rise to logics of a power that called up other, even more powerful forces against it.

On the one hand, then, we have terrestrial space and the politico-military leader guiding his people to victory. On the other, we have air space and the automatic blindness of politico-technological death. This, at least, is what the philosophers have seen in these two acts of war. These differences do not, however, change the fact that in both cases the philosopher sees war as a radical experience that *destroys old politico-spatial orders*—in the one case, the *ancien régime*; in the other, the civilization of National States—*and generates new ones.* The abolition of the protagonists, Napoleon and Hitler, brought forth a legacy (though very different in the context of the development of civilizations) in the political order that formed to oppose them. On one side we see the emergence of nineteenth-century Europe, which consisted of National States, and certainly not the French Empire. On the other side, we certainly do not see a German *Grossraum*. Rather, what emerges is the worldwide bipolarity between the United States and the U.S.S.R., which became the *nomos* of the Earth for the latter part of the twentieth century.

If we want to understand what a perceptive philosopher can discern from war, we could do worse than to recall Alexandre Kojève's witty observation that the Battle of Stalingrad in effect amounted to a conflict between the left wing and the right wing of Hegel's school. Nevertheless, it was not a philosopher but a writer, Ernst Jünger, who demonstrated the keenest perception when, in 1930, he was able to see through the fire, blood, and mud of the First World War—in which he had heroically participated—and to make out the anti-heroic, cold, mechanical geometric power of *Total Mobilization*. With his diagnostician's eyes, Jünger recognizes all the features of the future total war, and all its consequences:

> We have touched on the technical aspects of Total Mobilization;
> their perfection can be traced from the first conscriptions of
> the Convention government during the French Revolution and
> Scharnhorst's army reorganization to the dynamic armament
> program of the World War's last years—when states transformed
> themselves into giant factories, producing armies on the assembly
> lines that they sent to the battlefield both day and night, where
> an equally mechanical bloody maw took over the role of con-
> sumer. The monotony of such a spectacle—evoking the precise
> labor of turbine fueled by blood—is indeed painful to the heroic
> temperament; still, there can be no doubt regarding its symbolic
> meaning. Here a severe necessity reveals itself: the hard stamp of
> an age in a martial medium.[10]

Furthermore:

> ... [T]he image of war as armed combat merges into the more
> extended images of a gigantic labor process (*Arbeitsprozesses*).
> In addition to the armies that meet on battlefields, originate
> the modern armies of commerce and transport, foodstuffs, the
> manufacture of armaments—the army of labor in general. In the
> final phase, which was already hinted at toward the end of the last
> war, there is no longer any movement whatsoever—be it that of
> a homemaker at her sewing machine—without at least indirect
> use for the battlefield. In this unlimited marshaling of potential
> energies, which transforms the warring industrial countries into
> volcanic forges, we perhaps find the most striking sign of the dawn
> of the age of labor (*Arbeitszeitalter*). It makes the World War a
> historical event superior in significance to the French Revolution.[11]

Therefore:

> It suffices simply to consider our daily life, with its inexorability
> and merciless discipline, its smoking, glowing districts, the
> physics and metaphysics of its commerce, its motors, airplanes,
> and burgeoning cities. With a pleasure-tinged horror, we sense
> that here, not a single atom is not in motion—that we are pro-
> foundly inscribed in this raging process. Total Mobilization is far
> less consummated than it consummates itself; in war and peace,
> it expresses the secret and inexorable claim to which our life in
> the age of masses and machines subjects us. It thus turns out that
> each individual life becomes, ever more unambiguously, the life of
> a worker; and that, following the wars of knights, kings, and citi-
> zens, we now have wars of workers. The first great twentieth-cen-
> tury conflict has offered us a pre-sentiment of both their rational
> structure and their mercilessness.[12]

Here is a case where the *Kampferlebnis*—the lived experience of combat—
has become much more than the memory of the trench, or revanchist,
hypernationalistic policy. For Jünger, knowledge arrives through sight, the

concept through the image. Jünger looks at war, restoring his own sight in essential images, and sees, in reality, from a sociological viewpoint, the subsumption of labor within violence. Politically, he sees society becoming militarized and war becoming "total," as it loses its specificity and limitedness in order to intensify and extend itself into every sphere of social life. In short, Jünger sees the borders vanishing between public and private, state and social, peace and war. He sees the inversion and reciprocal penetration of their spaces under the push of the uncontainable energy of progress, technology and the masses. He sees a new form of collective existence—the form of *Arbeiter*, the Worker—a new order founded not on the search for stability but on mobility and risk, which make the legitimating categories and the self-interpretation of old obsolete.

Extreme Theology

What, then, did we see on September 11? What are we able to conceptualize from "9/11," from the moment of the terrorist act that toppled the Twin Towers and one wing of the Pentagon? What phenomena, what spaces and political orders, are involved in what took place—and in what is still taking place?

The obvious response would be that we saw everything. It is, after all, one of the dubious privileges of our age that we are able to witness great historical events on live television and in real time. Indeed, the centrality of communication in today's system of war is, by this point, a commonplace; making an attack visible, or being able to censure or manipulate that attack, is more important than the military act itself.

However, complications and doubts on this point are already emerging. In the first place, because even if the act, the collapse of the Twin Towers (the primary scene of the rape, or perhaps the castration, that opened the way to Global War) was seen many times, the result, the wound at Ground Zero, was shown by the media with unusual modesty and a strange reticence that gave the site itself even more symbolic meaning, making it an unseeable violation, a scar sustained by the new cathedrals of power that is hidden and cannot be talked about. Even the light show commemorating the six-month anniversary of the attacks reconstructed the image of the fallen towers, which we were made to see as a mystical body in the splendor of glory—evidence of the need to restore the visibility of power with the maximum exterior representation.

Furthermore, what seems to be the absolute icon of the Twin Towers is actually "sullied": the airplanes that raze skyscrapers and the towers that collapse on themselves in clouds of smoke have, for quite some time, belonged to Western cinematographic and television imagery. From *King Kong* to *Godzilla*, from catastrophe films to science fiction and futuristic political novels (with the Japanese playing aliens, as in Tom Clancy's *Debt of Honor*), the Great Disaster is always a recurring fantasy, or nightmare. The rule of reason—or, better, of Western rationalism—has been generating monsters for a long time, monsters amply represented and described by cinema and other popular arts. This creates a sense of *déjà vu* that does not necessarily mean, as Jean Baudrillard would have it, that the monstrous excessiveness of Evil is in some way expected because it rises from within the supposed excessiveness of Good, making terrorism the whole world's protest against *globalization*, turning the collapse of the Twin Towers into a suicide as well.[13] If September 11 was not completely unexpected at a symbolic level (while at a military level it was a well-executed surprise, even if it was "announced"), it is because the West had long been brooding over the possibility that the great construction—its artificial civilization, whose splendors are embodied in New York—was constitutively exposed to great destruction. The West's greatest fear, never articulated as such but expressed only as a fantasy, is a modern *phthonos ton theon* ("envy of the gods"), an updated version of the gods' anger at us for our hubris.

In any case, the theoretical difficulty that confronts us now is to eliminate from our minds whatever content we feel we have "already seen" in all of these images, and to understand what new elements actually *were* contained therein. The challenge thus lies in liberating the imagery of the attacks from the stereotypes that preexisted them, in order to allow our imagination to go off its preestablished tracks. Indeed, there is a real need for imagination and for the production of new concepts; today, we need *to relearn how to look*—seeing, the Idea, is a problem once more.

In the first place, we must see the theological quality to September 11; that day, in fact, God's wrath against the capital of Evil came into play. This reference to the divine is immanent in what we have seen again and again.

Furthermore, it was the clearly stated message of the attack, according to Bin Laden, who, in one of the recordings he periodically made in order to reach an Islamic and international audience, mentioned the "blessed strikes against global unbelief and its leader America."[14] Even the victims should have been able to find the key to understanding the attacks within their own Christian culture. When faced with Manhattan in flames, they should have turned to Revelation 18:

> Fallen, fallen is Babylon the great! It has become a dwelling place of demons, a haunt of every foul spirit . . . For all the nations have drunk of the wine of the wrath of her fornication, and the kings of the earth have committed fornication with her, and the merchants of the earth have grown rich from the power of her luxury . . .
>
> Render to her as she herself has rendered, and repay her double for her deeds . . . as she glorified herself and lived luxuriously, so give her a like measure of torment and grief . . . therefore her plagues will come in a single day . . . and she will be burned with fire; for mighty is the Lord God who judges her . . .
>
> The merchants of these wares, who gained wealth from her, will stand far off, in fear of her torment, weeping and mourning aloud, "Alas, alas, the great city, clothed in fine linen, in purple and scarlet, adorned with gold, with jewels, and with pearls! For in one hour all this wealth has been laid waste! . . .
>
> With such violence Babylon the great city will be thrown down . . . and the sound of harpists and minstrels and of flutists and trumpeters will be heard in you no more; and an artisan of any trade will be found in you no more; and the sound of the millstone will be heard in you no more; and the light of a lamp will shine in you no more; for your merchants were the magnates of the earth, and all nations were deceived by your sorcery."[15]

The similarities in imagery and state of mind between John's prophecy of the fall of Rome and Manhattan's collapse derive from the imperfect "imperial analogy" that exists between these two geopolitical situations, these two cities, and these two ideologies. The ideologies, without necessarily being true or even verisimilar, nonetheless feed the resentments and anxieties about justice (or revenge) that the Empire generates in the masses who inhabit it, especially at the margins.

Above all, there is the similarity in the fact that—now as before, in the first century as in the twenty-first—the theology that has entered in play has a definite political significance. Today, however, it is no longer "political theology," but instead "extreme theology." The Book of Revelation reveals the plot of historico-political events in the light of transcendence, which annihilates them. In the apocalyptic theology implicit in the events of September 11 we clearly see the absolute immanence of transcendence, the radical destructiveness of divine exception. But these theologies are completely lacking the ordinative vectors that were present in the political theology of the modern age, which prepared the conceptual drama of rational political mediation, of the construction of political form, beginning from the sovereign neutralization of religious conflicts.

In the modern age, the sovereigns of Westphalian Europe brought an end to civil wars by neutralizing them in the political order of the State, which secularized religion in the name of God, using religion as a formal exteriority or an ordinative tool. Miracle and exception thus became sovereign decision; God's theological centrality became the State's juridical centrality; divine reason was transformed into worldly reason, and theology became politology—rational political theory. These transformations created political space and concrete order. In the hands of the sovereign, religion produced the spatialization of politics and came to constitute uniformity within a region: the principle of *cuius regio, eius religio*.[16]

With September 11, religion once again become the tool of an ultimate will to conflict: the anxiety over justice and counterjustice, which religion now conveys, is incapable of enclosing any region. Instead, they turn religion into a force that manifests itself in and crosses every space. Where attack takes on the status of "holy war" and the response assumes the form of "just war," Asia will penetrate America, and America Asia; Islam will penetrate Christianity, and Christianity Islam. And so on. These exchanges take place without any recognizable border, in a way which is at once punctual, episodic, and random. An exception reveals itself in September 11 and its manifestations of extreme theology—a tragic immediacy that cannot be mediated structurally in any order or any construction of civilization. This is a theology that does not permit itself to be neutralized, that presents itself as the fury of an interminable conflict, and that is part of the problem rather than the solution.

Within the space of modern political theology, religion becomes *logos*, reason, the principle of order that makes the word and discursive communication possible. Extreme theology, by contrast, does not recognize the *logos* element; it does not communicate; it has nothing to say. With the mute evidence of his terroristic message, the extremist does not want to tolerate anyone, convert anyone, or negotiate in any way. He wants only to assert his own existence and the inexistence of others. The word and communicative ability were the first victims of terroristic violence, generating two adversarial groups, two identities that are unable even to speak to each other. Bin Laden communicated with his Islamic public opinion primarily through Al Jazeera, while America communicated through its own networks to its own public opinion. The crossover effects on the adversary's public opinion were rudimentary, uncontrolled, and often counterproductive. In this way, the intense and mortal enmity of the large-scale terrorist act perpetrated on September 11 contains a theologizing politicity that does not possess the force to organize space, that "means" nothing, and that does not determine regions of the Spirit or the Earth, but only two projectional specters: a generic West on one hand, and a generic Islamic danger, on the other.

Identity and Specters

This lack of *logos*, this opacity that obscures our vision, join together with something that, despite appearances, amounts to a defect of political identity for both contenders. It is true that in the postmodern (or "global") age, identity conflict, usually ethnic or cultural in nature, has replaced class conflict—at least in theory. It is also true that September 11 introduced a new element onto the political stage: that symbolic and concrete epitome of identity, the body. These are often the real bodies of Islamic "martyrs," thrown against the steel and crystal machine of Western power, and also against the innocent bodies that live within it. However, it is true that this is a question of identities that are loaded but at the same time indeterminate, of symbols that do not correspond to any precise content and consequently exhaust themselves in ideological representations. In the global age, identity conflict, though it often involves flesh and bone, is a conflict fought by specters.

We must remember that Western identity has never been more in doubt than in recent months, when it has been emphasized by warlike trumpet blasts. This alone points to a historically complex and contradictory identity marked by a karstic cycle, oscillating between "declines" and "splendid dawns," between crises and reawakenings, decadence and rebirth. This identity, which initially connoted Europe and was formed in opposition to Asia (beginning from Herodotus and the Greek tragedians), went on to designate Europe in opposition to the rest of the world (even to the New World, though it was even further West), then to place America in opposition to Europe (the Monroe doctrine of the Western hemisphere, composed in the 1930s), and finally, after the 1940s, to absorb Europe into the political and economic sphere of America's opposition to communism. In this last configuration, certainly, a world order was constructed, but not a precise spatial determination, since the West presented itself as an world complete unto itself—as the "free world," set against the East, the "world of despotism." In any case, Euro-American identity today contains everything: the primacy of politics and of economics, the State and its sovereignty, but also the market and its Society, the "continental" civilization model and also the "naval" model. It contains everything; it is one part claiming to make the entire planet conform to itself.

Even the military response to September 11 preserved something of the imprecision of Western identity. In fact, from the outset, it was difficult to understand if it was a response legitimated by the United Nations or only by the United States, or instead, by NATO as a whole, or perhaps by the United States together with the European Union, or simply with some European countries and not others (without getting into an analysis of the real motivations for the attempted co-belligerence in Afghanistan among American allies, which was dictated less by Western solidarity than by a desire to balance the United States' excessive power).

Drawing attention to the contradictions of Western identity certainly does not imply a cynical cultural relativism. In this case, the choice of the field and the judgment of value are obvious and unavoidable: Western societies and political forms contain contradictions that are often serious, even aporetical, but they also contain the promise of collective and individual liberty, both in theory and in practice. Some of the least fortunate and least "seen" images (the latter out of intrinsic necessity, because the witnesses and protagonists were killed in the action) are, at the same time, the most deserving of becoming mental icons: those of the passengers of one of the hijacked planes who orchestrated their own crash in Pennsylvania in order to avoid a greater disaster, namely, their plane's intended target of the White House. In order to decide their own desperate course of action against the hijackers, the passengers put it to a vote. This vote acted as a normally democratic procedure within a dramatic case of exception, and shows us that despite all the denials in daily political and social practice, respect for personal dignity and subjective will, at least on a theoretical level, is actually second nature for our society, especially the Anglo-Saxon variant. The value of the individual's autonomy so profoundly defines the Western/American identity that it is able to generate "decision," to push nonfanatical people to give up their own bodies. This is a democratic and patriotic heroism, as authentic as it is devoid of any satisfaction; it is quick and concrete in the slangy, conclusive formulation transmitted to us via radio: "Let's roll."[17]

Instead, the "Taliban model" or the "al Qaeda model" are not contradictory, but completely unacceptable, not susceptible to any development, and closed into a base fanaticism and a blind will to power. The objective of these models, at least the declared one, is punishing the Western infidels' aggression toward the Islamic world with death. Of course, even Taliban members are capable of "heroism," of radically putting their own bodies into play. Even the Pentagon acknowledged this in their account of Operation Anaconda, the high-altitude battle in Gardez, Eastern Afghanistan, in March of 2002. Here, however, we are not interested in comparing individual acts of valor, which can be generated even by terrible causes. Rather, we would like to focus on the motivating ethical and civil models behind these combatants.

We are not, then, discussing a comparison of values (which would be completely pointless). We are instead examining the fact that a comparison of this nature does not produce political identities understood as factors of political order, but only fantastical images in immediate, reciprocal negation. What we would like to argue here, in short, is that these identities are incapable of creating their own political space precisely because they are the result of a solely polemical process, or better, because they are a product (and constitute the primary form of accompaniment) of that tumultuous despatialization of politics: globalization. The "clash of civilizations" is a projective effect of globalization; in reality, civilizations do not arm themselves. Instead, in a manner of speaking, it is the arms, and the armed interests, that rely on "cultural" and "civilization-based" justifications in order to ideologically legitimate the conflict.

This insufficiency of political identities that presented itself in the wake of September 11, at least as far as Western identity is concerned, emerges in two distinct lines, one emotional and one moralistic. The first occurs when admiration for the West's grand history and heritage stops being a private emotion and becomes a claim to give form to public space (a good example would be the case of Oriana Fallaci[18]). The result, even when we consider mitigating factors in good faith, is a kind of regression where identitary belonging, instead of being entrusted to citizenship and the law, to "forms," rules, and procedures, is sought in the "natural" (by birth or faith) sharing of "substances" and foundations—in other words, to belonging within a culture, a religion, a political credo, or an economic system. Here, emotional intensity wins out over political rationality; the symbolic becomes abstract or ideological, and generates an even greater potential for conflict.

A political identity founded on ultimate values, for which we die and kill, would be a fundamentalism like the Taliban's, a by-product of globalization and its contradictions, as well as the security needs generated by widespread insecurity, the lack of defined political spatiality and secure borders. A political identity of this nature does not express a need for rationally mediated order—like the nineteenth-century National State, or the Social State of the late twentieth century—but is an immediate defensive reflex to the threat of global dynamics.

Even if it is only formal and official, the impossibility of legitimating war with ultimate values reveals itself in the fact that America presented its reaction against Afghanistan as an exercise of the right to self-defense (as it claimed when it notified the United Nations as it began bombing). Self-defense is, perhaps, an elementary and insufficient position, but it is certainly a more acceptable optic than the clash between humanity and barbarism (which could serve as an appropriate definition of the situation only in a moral sense, remaining, in any case, too generic to decipher this situation, and, more importantly, not containing any determination of politico-spatial order, in that such a definition would necessarily place itself above or below such order).

The second, moralistic line is outlined in *What We're Fighting For*,[19] a text composed by around sixty American intellectuals, Michael Walzer among them, with a solemnity indicated by frequent stylistic and lexical nods to the Declaration of Independence and the Constitution. This work elaborates a theory of just war, but also seeks to express an American identity at once political, religious, and cultural. This identity is found in the affirmation that all men are created equal, in their dignity and in their rights, one of which is the free pursuit of the ultimate meanings of existence. Consequently, freedom of conscience and of religion are also inalienable rights. These principles are presented as "absolute" positions that, nonetheless, want to be inclusive and not hostile, universal and not particular, and thus, without lapses into relativism, imply that politics must respect every religion, every search for Truth, and must base itself on the moral rules of nature, which are also divine laws. The result is a sort of constitutionalization of religious liberty on a world scale, similar to the founding principles of the United States both as a secular state and a society of believers, free to have faith in every possible divinity and to exhibit that faith. The resulting society would be a religious Pantheon, a social pluralism of faiths guaranteed by political freedom rather than by a Prince's tolerance.

The authors who signed their names to this document understand the essence of American values to consist in this model of the relationship between politics, religion, and nature, this relationship between public space and individual freedom. They then universalize this model (not the concrete political conduct of the United States, which they admit is open to criticism) as a set of values valid for all humanity. It is therefore this *consensus gentium*, and not the West's cultural imperialism, that enables and legitimates the "essential agreement" between American values and human values.

Now, it is obvious that this position—which tends to make the United States the epitome of the human race—is inevitably moralistic and peda-gogic, and can only place the enemy outside of humanity. As such, it designs an identity that is immediately conflictual but not dialectical, and thus is quite different from the identity facing the struggle for recognition in Hegel's *Phenomenology of Spirit*. The Western *logos* exhibits an identity that, though it is seeking to supply an articulated response to the terrorist act's mute evidence, ends up reaffirming itself as Good and the adversary as Evil. It makes them into generic, indeterminate symbols. This is an identity that, even in asserting the all-inclusive reasons for a Self opened to a Uniqueness of the human race, at the same time, opens to a "bad" duality: Us and Them, humanity and inhumanity. Even here, in short, two identities produce themselves in a war without end, incommunicative but mirroring each other, each the other's specter. Once more, we see two forms of immediate accompaniment, two reflections of globalization.

Global War and Globalization

In the end, September 11 cannot be adequately explained either with theological references or with assertions about opposed symbolic and cultural identities (though both these factors are certainly involved in the attacks). In order for our analysis to be *truly* comprehensive, we now need to shift our focus from phenomena to context. We need to learn how to see not just the events but also the background that gives them form and meaning; we need to be able to look at September 11 and to see, in it, *the first significant manifestation of Global War*. We need to learn, in other words, how to reconsider the problem of war, along with the problem of struggle between identities, in the light of globalization—understood as a new mode of being in the world.

Global Time and Space

In short, we must learn how to see globalization—global politics and Global War—as the explanatory horizon of September 11. This is a horizon that opens itself in discontinuity with the Modern, allowing us to talk about a real and true "global age," the first form of postmodernity. Indeed, the global age has many of the characteristics of the destructuration—but none of the "levity"—foreseen by the theories of the Postmodern formulated in the 1980s.

Rather than explain globalization as the realization of "modern" logics, or as a quantitative extension of capitalist economics at a world level, or as the affirmation of technology's dominance of the planet, our interpretation will emphasize its *discontinuity*. This is no doubt connected to technology and capitalism, but it also reveals new dynamics that develop the instability—or, if you prefer, *structural nihilism*—of the modern order, pushing it in new directions.

Globalization is an ensemble of many irreversible, yet open and contradictory, processes that began in the 1980s. From an economic viewpoint, these processes are the deregulation of the movement of capital, the displacement and acceleration of production, and orientation of production to the momentary needs of the market (in a sharp reversal of the Fordist age, when big business strategically created market space). It is the rewriting of the world and of life in a new code, which Edward Luttwak would define as "turbo-capitalism," the global triumph of goods.[20] As Marx and Engels had already noted in *The Communist Manifesto*, "all that is solid" in the world of goods "melts into air."[21] In the global world—this world of "liquid modernity," as Bauman puts it[22]—even that which remains concrete loses its reality, and becomes decontextualized and disoriented. The most radical figure of the global world is this incessant rewriting of social and political phenomena in codes that are external to them, that transform any event into a postponement, a function of processes that can never be determined or circumscribed. Just as, in the global age, every event is deprived of essence (which is not to say efficacy), and lives only in relation to and in mediation with other events (the principle of "virtuality"), so too does every local point become an immediate function of a single global Totality (the principle of "glocality").

This global inclusion of every life in the totality of economic relationships is not, of course, homogeneous. Rather, it is unequal, and occurs according to "regional" lines of exclusion. These inequalities are not stable; nor are they the expression of any sort of order. On the contrary, they are mobile and spin like vortices in the open waters of globalization—making, as it were, for stormy seas.

From a political viewpoint, the anarchy that characterizes globalization is born of processes that, from the external viewpoint of international politics, signal the end of communism in Europe and the beginning of powerful westward migratory flows. From the viewpoint of internal politics, these processes mark the crisis of the Social State, or at least the weakening of the principal protagonists of its political space (i.e., parties, labor unions, democratic and representative institutions). But these processes are neither peaceful nor linear. To the contrary, they reintroduce the internal conflict, social turbulence, and ethnic claims that the State (especially the Social State) had tranquilized. From the viewpoint of external politics, September 11—the devastating attack on America's heart ten years after the fall of the Soviet Union—demonstrates dramatically that the end of the Cold War did not produce the peace—the juridification of international relationships—for which so many had hoped. It also reveals that the global world is much more violent and dynamic than was the "glacial" world dominated by the superpowers.

In *Political Spaces*, we defined this ensemble of political and economic processes as the "universal immediacy of mediations," which is to say, a "global mobilization" of the categories and orders of modernity that culminates both in their exhaustion and annulment, and in their realization and complete fulfillment.[23] This is true for the political category of time—which, in the modern age, was understood as progress, and which has been seriously involved in the destructuration of modernity effected by globalization. In fact, beginning with its economic matrix—the "just-in-time" production of goods—globalization is so characterized by velocity that its convulsive processes no longer have any time to settle down or to become tradition. Nor, therefore, can they establish any sort of progressive temporality.

Globalization does not constitute any kind of *traditum*, nor does it pass on anything to history. To the contrary, it consumes the future by turning it into nothing more than one among many perspectives—a "future past"—in a manner reminiscent of similar processes in the Modern, but which is actually much more accelerated. Indeed, it is so fast that the global age no longer arranges its own events in chronological order, into a "before" and "after" that would be capable of orienting politics in either a reactionary or advanced way. Rather, events today are grouped into simultaneities, with a co-presence of past and future, in a multiple entirety of contexts where the old lives alongside the new (and, really, both of these terms have today lost their political significance and their regulating capacity). To the extent that the categories of the old and the new survive at all today, they manifest themselves in the mode of postponements or "citations"—plural times that become stratified and refer back to one another. For example, in a land war like that in Palestine, which is not without its archaic dimension, conflict is nonetheless conducted with the new postmodern method of detaching value from arms in order to attach it immediately to the body of martyrs, who transform themselves into human bombs. Land war here thus coexists with the deterritorialized wars of international terrorism, interacting with those wars and, at least in part, determining them.

This irrelevance of the dimension of time joins itself to, and indeed superimposes itself on, an irrelevance of the dimension of space. In the global age, modern political spatiality—the State, with its right and its ability to enclose an internal sphere with order and security, creating a space where "not everything can happen"—has ceased to be fully in effect, challenged as it is by the power of economic flows and the needs of capital, which demand a new politics and which no longer allow the State to be the operative center of political reality and its interpretation. Globalization consists in the mobilization of modern rational mediation and in the progressive evanescence of the State's "stable" order—which is to say, of representative political institutions' ability to guarantee the distinction between individual, social, economic, and political spheres. Of course, in certain areas of the West, whatever remains of the Social State still exercises important functions, but it is now no longer the center of politics, nor does it hold a monopoly. Today, all the important spatial axes on the basis of which the State constructed itself—internal/external, public/social/private, particular/universal, center/periphery, order/disorder—have become obsolete.

As such, the vertical organization of power—sovereignty, which created a pacified and juridified internal political space—tends to weaken, while power begins to present itself in trans-statal flows (of both the sub-State and supra-State sort), which, in turn, act as a horizontal network supporting economic dynamics. Indeed, in those areas where the burden of institutions is less evident, namely, outside the West, a new power of the global age manifests itself. This new power (which is not a single global power, but a segmentation into regional powers) manifests itself in and through its own mode of efficacy, namely, the production of a disorder (with terrorism, deportation, and the violent domination of populations) that then seeks to legitimize itself through offers of order. Politics, in the global age, is the coincidence of real insecurity and illusory security; it is the concurrence of real conflict and the specter of peace. In general, the State-operated distinction between secure internal space and dangerous external space has vanished, leaving us with our current "risk society." Globalization is the epoch in which the State no longer protects its citizens from external turbulence. The principle of *protego ergo obligo* ("protection, therefore obedience") was the load-bearing column of modern politics,[24] but in the global age, anything can happen anywhere, at any moment, precisely because the State no longer filters disorder from the external environment (terrorist acts, migratory flows, the movement of capital) and is no longer capable of transforming it into internal peace. In this context, the "public" no longer assumes the traditional institutionalized form of politics, the State; it is now that event that, for better or for worse, immediately touches the lives of many "private" individuals with particular importance and intensity.

Globalization's lack of political spatiality does not, of course, mark the triumph of some universalism—the result of some process of world standardization or homogenization. Historically, universalisms have represented the projection, on a grand scale, of demands for political and social rationality. These demands, which originated from within the rational space of the State, gradually came to find the State's borders too narrow, and to discover contradictions in the State's closed and self-referential rationality. Universalisms emerged out of the desire both to adjust to and to overcome the limits of the State's particularistic, egotistical rationality. With the disappearance of the State's political centrality, universality thus also failed—being, as they were, dialectically immanent to the very State space in opposition to which they had defined themselves.

This does not mean that the Particular, the Concrete, and Difference are able to reconquer political space today, for they are also involved in the collapse of the universal. As far as the State's modern correlate, the Subject, is concerned, it seems clear that even where it retains some validity (the West), it is no longer the hub of society or its even interpretative key. In today's society, which is increasingly constituted by subjects who are "escaping,"[25] the Subject is no longer operative as the center for the imputation of modern political spatiality. It is displaced by subjects who give up their citizenship and remove themselves from the State, who implode into a privacy that amounts to a total opacity, who embrace a singular and immediate life that is radically lacking any relationship with the mediations of institutional politics, or who seek to remove themselves from the space of the State by way of diaspora and migration, by escaping from global powers. As a result, the Subject can no longer be rendered intelligible with recourse to modern political anthropology; he can no longer be considered a "naturally unstable" being who creates stabilizing political institutions for himself; he no longer exists for the State, and indeed no longer needs the State in order to exist politically and socially. The Subject today is a particular who no longer needs the universal, not even in a dialectical way. Today, not only is the individual without the State, he is also without home and without a solid and stable identity; never residing with himself, the Subject is, for better or for worse, by this point only and immediately a body—as much from desperation and reification as from a search for freedom of movement and action.

Because the time of globalization is not linear but plural, and because both the concrete and universal are vanishing in its processes, we may say that globalization is a space constituted not by order, but by a disorder that springs from the juxtaposition, within it, of many different "regional" orders. These orders, which are not governed by any hierarchy or composition of scale or proportion—which exist in the absence of the internal space designed by the State and the external space designed by States—enter in immediate contact and immediate conflict with each other. Of course, political power in the global age manifests itself in space in a differentiated and articulated way, but it is not determined by space, nor is it interested in determining space in a stable way. In politics—similar in this respect to economics—globalization adds to and subtracts from mobile differences according to patterns that are constantly changing. Under this profile, globalization has neither forms nor figures. Although it is conceptualizable, it removes itself from the Idea; globalization offers nothing to "see" besides shades of gray illuminated by the lightning-images and the sudden flashes that shoot from the discharged energies of its various short-circuits.

Indeed, for better or for worse, every corner of the world is today in direct contact with the world as a whole. Globalization is, at every point, an *immediate short-circuit* between local and global; it is the coincidence of both inclusion and exclusion, assimilation and segregation. It precipitates the collapse of political institutions into a spatiality that is fragmented into an infinite number of points, each immediately exposed—for none of these shards are protected any longer by the State's mediations and interventions—to the totality formed by global powers. In this formless and paradoxical space, the particular ceases to exist (for it relied on the universal, which has also vanished), leaving only the "glocal." Today, every point is in direct contact with the forces of global power flows, with the Whole, and no longer generates (or crosses) border lines or statual surfaces.

This is the secret of the relative differences in the perception of space and identities between, on the one hand, the Roman Empire and, on the other, the contemporary society that stems from it. It is also the secret of the differences, subtle yet decisive, between modern spatiality—even in its imperialistic aspects—and contemporary spatiality. The new Empire—the world-system that is not a new world order and that does not recognize any exteriority—is globalization, which absorbs everything but knows no interiority. Globalization transforms the planet into a space without external edges, but it does not thereby produce a smooth and peaceful "interior." Rather, it is crossed by countless, mobile borders. If there is an Empire today, it is a unique but discontinuous space, functional and relational, nonconstructivist, without a center, capital, or organizationally stable structure. Today's Empire cannot be described through categories of internal and external; it is a space that is not the West (or the American Empire) locked in a struggle against external barbarians. Instead, it is a global Empire locked in a struggle against itself, against anomalous functions that exist within it. In short, it is an Empire whose inner discontinuity produces conflicts that, no matter where or how they are generated, all have a local status, and all of which also fall immediately—with unforeseeable effects—into the Whole.

In sum, we can say that the completion of the State's decline as the exclusive center for the imputation of politics, and as the actor who is capable of distinguishing peace from war—a feat that totalitarianism, remember, could not successfully achieve—is brought to term by globalization.

War and Space

The absence of modern political spatiality does not mean that the global age is without politics and war. In the global age—with a crescendo beginning with the Gulf War, through the Balkan Wars of the 1990s, and culminating with September 11—a new figure of war and a new relationship between war and politics emerges. This figure no longer passes through institutions, or through the construction of geometric State spaces. In the global age, war and politics neither have space nor make space in the modern, Westphalian political sense. According to this understanding, it was possible to see war contained in politics—but only to the extent that *war* remained a public military instrument used by the State in *external* space against other sovereign States, while the *police* remained an administrative instrument *internal* to the space of the State, a means to the end of securing order and peace. In this way, the States and their modern political geometries used the distinction between inside and outside to articulate a logical and political distance between enemy and criminal, peace and war.

Global War, by contrast, manifests itself in the nonspace of globalization (where, to be clear, "space" is understood in a specifically modern sense). It fulfills, with a leap in quality, the spatially nihilistic dynamics of Total Mobilization and of the totalitarianisms of total war, already underway in the first half of the twentieth century, and temporarily halted during the Cold War. The (then) much-condemned bipolarity between the United States and the U.S.S.R. was truly, as we now know, the last *katechon*—the last "restraining force" holding back the coming of a new age.

In the wars and politics of the twentieth century, of course, modern political space also underwent a reversal. The World Wars of the twentieth century, particularly the Second World War—in which the Total Mobilization and the total war that had been outlined during World War I were fully realized—produced the figures of the internal enemy and the external criminal, examples of which can be seen in the classification of Jews as "enemies" of the Third Reich and the Republic of Salò, on the one hand, and the trials of vanquished "criminals" in Nuremberg and Yokohama, on the other. Nonetheless, even though world war destroyed modern political order and its space, total world war preserved its morphogenetic power, and retained its capacity for the creation of political form. The enemy, even when criminalized, had an image and a face; physical and ideological fronts existed, and war strategies and tactics were visible. Above all, total world war was brought to a conclusion: It created peace and political space (in particular, the external space of bipolar international order, and the internal space of the Social State). Even if the second half of the twentieth century cannot then be understood on the basis of a classical Westphalian scenario (characterized by a plurality of joint sovereignties), and instead existed in a new horizon constituted by two superpowers whose military, economic, and ideological sovereignty cut planetary space in two and deprived "normal" States of their external sovereignty, it still recognized a spatial order, however unstable. This was, of course, the late-modern order of the Cold War, which ended with the collapse of the Soviet Union—the event that, from a political viewpoint, marked the beginning of the global age and its modality of international relations, of the new relationships between war and peace from which Global War springs.

Global War is a new, postmodern kind of war. It is a war without frontiers, without advances or retreats, consisting only of acts that concentrate into "precise" spaces, and in real time, the logics of war, economics and technology. Global War may therefore be characterized as "glocal" war, in which a single point is in immediate contact with the Whole—the world-system. It is a very different kind of war both from world war and from limited local war (such as the Vietnam War, which placed that country in a point of friction between two different imperialisms and two universal ideologies). This, then, is the essence of Global War. It is not World War III (for it lacks the requisite ideological and economic suppositions). Nor is it a war of the worlds (the Islamic world versus the Christian world). It is instead the manifestation of the fact that *globalization is itself a world of war*.

The qualifying element of Global War is that it has no distinct origin and no clear *telos*. Nor is it really possible to find in Global War a strategic contradiction, or to say that Global War is "determined" by globalization in any direct sense (as though globalization were somehow the primary cause of every conflict, transmitting itself to secondary causes and acting as an empirical detonator). Indeed, there really is not any single chain of causes at work in Global War. Even though it is always "overdetermined" by political and economic globalization, Global War's various concrete forms each have their own, quite different geneses (from minority claims to identitary issues that present themselves in religious forms, to the need to control resources like water, oil, and precious-metal mines). If we nevertheless maintain that, in the age of Global War, every conflict that arises in global political space is potentially a global conflict, this is because global political space arranges itself as a durable disorder—a space that is not made for *containing* conflict, but, to the contrary, for *allowing it to be*, or even for *producing* it. In Global War, in other words, we find all of the hallmarks of globalization, *only now reproduced in a military form.* As such, we may say that *Global War is one of globalization's modes of being.* It is further evidence of the fact that globalization is a "contradiction without system."[26] This means that global politics contains war not as a tool that can be used for the production of political form (as did modern politics), but as an immediate manifestation of its own contradictions. This new, immediate relationship between war and politics means that war is no longer decided with a sovereign act on the part of political institutions or the State, as happened in the modern age. Instead, it presents itself as a "natural" phenomenon, no longer circumscribed by the limits, borders, or conceptual and spatial axes (between internal and external, public and private, civil and military) that were forged by the modern era, and that the modern State used to reintroduce politics and war within itself as a normal and regular phenomenon. Today, it is precisely the relationship between regular and irregular, norm and exception, that have been subtly but radically modified in Global War.

The difficulties that arise when we try to comprehend this new a-geometrical and a-spatial war are clearly demonstrated by the fact that, despite a decade of terrorist attacks, from the World Trade Center in 1993 to Dar es Salaam in Somalia, despite the widespread conviction that the Cold War and the bilateral world were in the past, despite the fact that the Gulf War and the Balkan Wars exhibited an increasingly pronounced failure of strategic land maneuvers (of spatiality) in the practice of war—despite all of these factors, the United States was still caught with its guns pointed in the wrong direction. They were looking for missiles from rogue states, and were hit by their own civilian airplanes, hijacked by terrorists. Global War is exactly this: new types of weapons, enemies, times, and spaces—all within a new politics.

Indistinctness and Asymmetry

The decline of modern and late-modern spatial axes has been accompanied by the decline of the conceptual distinctions they generated, which today have evaporated into a gray area with no recognizable borders. If, in the global age, social, political, and military phenomena occur without any mediation, structure, borders, or any conceptual distinction between regularity and irregularity, and are, as such, directly exposed to global mobilization, then the distinction between peace and war—which, do not forget, is *grounded on* the distinction between inside and outside—will be the first victim. This indistinction makes Global War a "chameleon" in more ways than Clausewitz could have imagined when he used that word to describe "traditional" war in his great work.[27] But if, for Clausewitz, war's lack of form was traceable back to statualized politics, which was more than capable of guiding war, today, the chaos of Global War is not backed by any political order that controls or explains it. Modern political form is today in crisis, and the manifestation of this crisis is Global War. For Clausewitz, the tendency for warfare to "ascend to extremes"—to overflow and overwhelm political form from within—was the exception.[28] For us, however, it is the norm. This is not because Global War often exhibits the same heights of violence seen in the "great war," but rather, because in Global War the crisis of the modern relationship between war and politics becomes chronic. The result is an immediate mixture of war and politics that, today more than ever, makes the maxim *inter pacem et bellum nihil medium* ("between peace and war there is no middle") outdated (and it was to this same maxim, remember, that Carl Schmitt appealed to express his perplexity about the gray zones which, beginning from the 1930s, began to erase every clear demarcation line between light and shadow, peace and war.[29])

In order to decipher this gray zone of indistinction between peace and war—this gray zone that is, in effect, the "proper" space of Global War—we need to conduct a closer analysis of several categories: public and private, civilian and military, criminal and enemy, internal and external, peaceful economics and armed violence.

(a) The conceptual and spatial crisis experienced by modern politics in the global age can explain several of the phenomena that are most striking to military theorists and scholars of international relations. While some of them propose an analysis of Global War within traditional categories of political realism (or of an anarchic international scenario populated by actors interested in guaranteeing security and power), thus negating every new, qualitative novelty, others recognize that this new war exhibits strange, "anomalous" traits. These scholars define Global War as a chronic development, with acute crisis points, of the so-called "low-intensity wars" that multiplied in frequency after the fall of the Soviet Union, wars that were different still from the territorial wars and anti-imperialist guerilla warfare of the Cold War.

Even a temporal concept like Global War's "chronicity," the "normality" of its permanent exception, is actually determined by the peculiar spatiality (or rather, the a-spatiality) of the global age. It is the political insignificance of the spatiality of the States, the inexistence of borders which prevent the neutralization of conflict and make it "cross borders," making sure that Global War has a near-infinite length, that whatever ends it proposes, it has no end. Of course, gangrenous crisis situations and widespread areas of injustice and misery furnish countless desperate troops with existential motivations, but the chronicity of the war that these troops unleash is generated by the collapse of modern political space. Global War's contenders are well aware of this, attributing an infinite duration to their engagements. This characterizes Bin Laden's countercrusade, as well as the American counter-countercrusade, *Enduring Freedom*, which is not enduring peace, but a continuous struggle for freedom. This is only slightly weaker, semantically, than the first appellation of the American response to the September 11 attacks, *Infinite Justice*. In this way, if it is true that, as Hugo Grotius asserted at the start of the modern age, *pax finis belli*, that "war itself will lead us to peace, as to its proper end,"[30] if it is true that even the World Wars had peace as their objective, then it becomes clear that one of the novelties of this new war is that it never ends. Indeed, setting aside for now the question of when and how this first phase of

Global War might conclude, we may say that Global War, in general, tends to transform itself into a conflict-world.

The despatialization and the deinstitutionalization of politics also explains another anomalous trait of Global War: Within it, we lose the difference between sky, land, and sea. All the traditional theaters overlap and intersect in a war without strategy or frontier—similar, more than anything, to a dogfight—in which we attempt to do things from the sky that were once done on land (for example, manhunts). In its most advanced and typical manifestations, it is not a war between different historical times; the Taliban is certainly reactionary, but it is also an aspect of the Postmodern that is not playful but somber, not liberating but surreal (and what could be more surreal than Mullah Omar fleeing Kandahar on a motorcycle, or the president of the United States having Bin Laden followed with B-52 strategic bombers, two iconic images that, until recently, would have been possible only in a fiction like *Dr. Strangelove*)? Rather, Global War combines local wars in which quite disparate conflicts of origin are embedded. The crises from which these conflicts emerge follow an arc that has both conti-nental and transcontinental dimensions—from the Balkans to the Palestinian Near East, from the Kurdish and Iraqi Middle East to Kashmir and Afghanistan's Central Asia and the Caspian's pipelines, from the Philippines to Indonesia. Many of these conflicts are still "modern" in that they can be ascribed to issues of territoriality and national identity (India-Pakistan, Ethiopia-Eritrea), but they take place in a borderless and limitless global context. As such, they are translated into the metalanguage of global mobilization, which decontextualizes whatever traditional and local languages serve its needs. In the end, Global War knows no fronts and cannot be seen on a map. It knows only expeditions and incursions, attacks and reprisals—essentially, reciprocal systematic violations of each adversary's territorial integrity, though in reality, this integrity (of spatiality) is missing. This makes Global War not only infinite, but ubiquitous.

(b) If the spatial axis of inside and outside cannot explain Global War, neither can the link between the public and the private, the distinction between military and civilian, or its wartime specification, the distinction between enemy and criminal. Understanding this specific indistinction is extremely important if we want to understand the so-called "asymmetry" of Global War.

Though it constitutes a true novelty, Global War is situated in the terminal point of the process, which had already been underway since the First World War and witnessed the end of the distinction between military and civilian. The proportion of civilian to military deaths, which was one to eight at the beginning of the century, became equal during the Second World War, and today is reversed, at eight to one. Civilians are not just suffering the new war; they are also waging it, destroying the State's monopoly on legitimate violence by privatizing war. The "new wars" of the 1990s—in the Balkans, Chechnya, Africa, South America, and the South Pacific—all involved armed gangs as protagonists. However, the West also contributed to the privatization of violence, both through the traditional commercial liaison between the private arms industry and the State (the military-industrial complex) and through mercenary companies. For at least twenty-five years, sovereign States and international organizations who cannot act (or will not act) have entrusted the administration of political acts to these mercenaries, especially in the global South. They control elections, maintain public order, combat guerrillas, and create enclaves removed from the sovereignty of the host country; they also perform ethnic cleansing and *coups d'état*. The range of political activities that these sub-State companies perform is truly vast, in that "durable disorder" of the deinstitutionalized politics of the global age.

In this scenario, we can also observe private groups taking on "public" duties, to the point where we also witness the creation of "Criminal States"—paracriminal gangs that take on semipublic status. We have already seen this—in the Balkans, in Africa, in Oceania, in Bosnia and Kosovo, in Sierra Leone, in Congo-Brazzaville, in Bougainville—and we will probably continue to see it elsewhere. This is how the circle of deinstitutionalized politics and "private" postmodern war closes, going from the privatization of war entrusted to companies, to the precarious statualization of armed gangs, to the encounter, in many parts of the world which Mary Kaldor describes, between the traditional, de-legitimated political elite and new, essentially criminal elite.[31] In these cases, global politics reveals itself as a mixture with many intersecting levels, which are always changeable: the public and private, the reality of war and the illusion of peace. Faced with the indistinction between peace and war, all other conceptual distinctions collapse.

Nonetheless, Global War seems to contain a peculiar asymmetry, a qualifying distinction between terrorism, on the one hand, and police action, on the other. In fact, we may say that Global War is certainly not waged against identified enemies, but against "nebulas," adversaries who have no face, but instead are specters onto which we can project our own specters. We must, however, underline that there are two very different specters at issue here: one of the contenders (the "fanatic" or the informal power) disdains human life, including its own, and sacrifices its body; the other (the "policeman," structured, institutionalized, and legitimated power) seeks to avoid hand-to-hand combat and direct physical involvement by waging a post-heroic war which—thanks to technology—no longer demands a tribute of Western blood.

If we are using "asymmetry" to mean a deformity of the values, armaments, and statuses that characterize the two adversaries (the United States and the terrorists, Taliban, or any other paraterrorist power), we are correct to use the concept here. September 11 is not Pearl Harbor, because al Qaeda is not the Japanese Empire; it is not an entity of international public law. If, however, by "asymmetry" we want to reconstruct a differentiation of identity and to reestablish a clear distinction between Us and Them, beginning from the assumption that the public–private axis can be used as a key for legitimation, we must submit the concept to deconstruction. For in this second definition, we see the residual idea that the State—that quintessentially modern form of institutionalized politics—is still an entity capable of constituting the qualitative differences of politics.

Terrorism is the culminating moment of the indistinctness between civilians and military that progressively characterized the twentieth century. To all appearances, the concept of terrorism is clear and intuitive: It suggests armed action against innocent civilians or soldiers by armed gangs or political groups, with the objective of generating a collapse of morale within a population, and hence acquisition of political and military advantages. Precisely because terrorism does not distinguish between civilians and military, neither for the victims of its violence nor for the perpetrators of the violent act, States tend to institute the maximum possible distance between themselves and the terrorists. States assert that they respect the distinctions that the terrorists ignore, that they do not wage war against helpless populations, and that it is precisely this difference that qualifies them and allows them to distinguish between legitimate public powers and criminal gangs. Thus, when terrorism is supported by a State (as in Afghanistan, Iraq, and other States accused by the United States of housing terrorists and therefore being, inasmuch as they are States, responsible for the terrorists' actions), a terrorist act can be interpreted as a traditional act of war on the part of the host State. Against gangs and groups, by contrast, one can only fight an asymmetrical war—a war that is also an act of justice, a just war.

And that, in the end, is the thesis of *What We're Fighting For*: Asymmetry—in this second sense—is the defining feature of Global War. The authors thus present the United States' military action against Afghanistan as a "just war" as distinct from a terroristic "holy war." It is no accident, however, that the first name the Pentagon gave to this war was *Infinite Justice*; from their view, this operation is a endless reparative action against extremist movements that deny the modern world and the United Nations' Declaration of Rights that founded that world. Above all, the authors of *What We're Fighting For* understand the American war to be conducted by a legitimate, public, and democratic authority against illegitimate, freelance violence carried out by semiprivate terrorist groups. This type of war can then take on the guise of a "good war" (the exact opposite of Henry de Montherlant's "*bonne guerre*,"[32] which was actually civil war), in which bombs are accompanied by aid to the population (as is happening in Afghanistan, where the humanitarian efforts go hand in hand with police efforts).

In reality, the concept of terrorism is not easily recognizable, and requires many specifications. In the first place, perpetrators of terrorism can be formal public entities—States (during the Second World War, for example, deliberate "terrorist" bombings were carried out by all parties on civilian populations in order to destroy morale). Second, the term has been so strongly devalued and polemical that today it simply ricochets around between one contender and another. It has, for a long time, been standard practice for States to define all nonconventional wars as terrorism (for example, wars of liberation from the European antifascist resistance to the wars of decolonization). These wars, waged by populations with forces far inferior to their statual enemy, also employ "treacherous" aggression against a uniformed military, sometimes resulting in civilian victims. Similarly, the reprisals taken against civilians by military personnel are also "terroristic," in that their aim is to produce terror.

In our search for clarity, we can certainly attempt to make terrorism a specific crime that is distinct from homicide, massacre, or sabotage because of its political objective or the associative nature of the perpetrator. This juridification of terrorism would certainly seem to resolve every problem—and it would also, at the same time, demonstrate the State's permanent political centrality, showing that it remains capable of criminalizing every nonstatual adversary. It would, moreover, demonstrate the existence of solid international juridical institutions that remain able, if necessary, to judge States as well as private citizens. But this is precisely the point: This juridification is not successful, and is nowhere near success, as was clearly shown by the aftermath of September 11, when America responded to terrorism with a war, instead of a trial. This same failure of juridification is evident from the fact that not only regular military forces (the United States and other States) but also irregular pro-Western groups (the *mujahidin* of the Northern Alliance) are participating in the fight against terrorism.

This means that even though there is still a difference between, on the one hand, public/State entities that are capable of war and, on the other, private/terrorist entities that are capable of crime—just as there is still a difference between the rationales of the one and the other—this difference is no longer able to create order. These two political realities, which should be radically different from one another, are actually at war (and sometimes even allied, as in the case of the *mujahidin* and the United States), even though, according to modern political logics, a war between a State and terrorists should be impossible. Indeed, modern statuality is familiar with external wars against another State (wars of this sort give the State its only opportunity to face a *iustus hostis* or legitimate enemy), or civil wars (which put the State's unity at risk), or internal police action (which do not put it at risk). On this basis, States treat terrorists not as warriors but as criminals against common law, and they treat prisoners of war not as criminals but as enemies to be sent home after the fighting is over. But the cages at Guantanamo, which contain prisoners of war who are treated like criminals, and/or criminals who are treated like prisoners of war, deny these distinctions.

It is important that we recognize that terrorism is situated within a gray area, extreme and vast though it may be, of behaviors that cover many violent interactions between states and civilians, the public and the private (up to and including, according to some, interactions that are nonmilitary but hostile nonetheless, such as economic speculation). We must recognize that the public–private axis does not define terrorism, but is defined by it, as we see in the dimension of the terrorist act that makes it public (in the sense we have indicated, where "public" means "important" or "intense"). Furthermore, we often observe a difference of quantity turning into a difference of quality; beyond a certain number of victims or a certain amount of damage, what is commonly defined as a "crime" or "infraction" becomes a terrorist act of public importance, an act of Global War.

In the same way, global terrorism is not classic guerrilla warfare that can be met with the tactics of counterinsurgency warfare. The terrorist is not a communist-nationalist from the Third World who fights while hiding among the oppressed population. Rather, he is so decontextualized and uprooted that he feels as comfortable (or as uncomfortable) in Manhattan as he does in Tora Bora, in cities and mountainous deserts. Terrorism is also unrelated to the master-slave dialectic that, for Frantz Fanon, sustains the anti-colonial struggle of "the wretched of the earth."[33] Even where it seeks the liberation of a people, terrorism is characterized by violence that is independent of its declared objectives. Even though these objectives may be local and determined, the global terrorist's area of action is nonetheless the whole planet. In short, even terrorism realizes the glocal short-circuit between the point and the Whole. As such, anti-Western terrorism is less *the enemy* of the West than its *opposite*, its Shadow, the dark face of globalization. Even as terrorism wages war on the West, in other words, it also shares grammars and logics with the West, feeding parasitically on it. Terrorism is, in short, a kind of global insecurity agency, one that is parallel to the many agencies of global security that now exist.

At this stage in our analysis, we have a reached a point where we may define Global War as a "worldwide civil war." The latter is different from a traditional civil war because it does not exist within a State. Nor, however, is it really a war between two States (United States and Afghanistan) or even a war between a State and a non-State actor (United States and al Qaeda). Rather, Global War is a conflict between two global functions, two networks that overlap with one another more than they oppose each other. It is a conflict between an Empire and a counter-Empire that share no borders with one another, but that instead penetrate one another, both deterritorialized and in search of a politically legitimated identity. Unsurprisingly, this identity often turns out to be interchangeable. It is no accident, after all, that the most ferocious attack on the West in sixty years was orchestrated by puppets who were created and armed by the West to fight against the Soviet Union, puppets who turned against their old capitalist supporters, as they were indistinguishable from their old communist invaders.

Despite its superficial manifestations, Global War is not, in essence, the clash between civilization and identity. It is not the war of the *respublica christiana* against the Muslim *Umma* (*patria*). Indeed, if Bin Laden's aim was to purify Saudi Arabia by removing the infidels, this spatial objective was lost within the non-spatiality of the Global War he helped generate and into which he was then sucked. Global War is instead a conflict that opposes capitalistic globality and its armed forces to a terroristic globality, a delocalized and centerless criminal system. The latter is just as effective, but also just as abstract and elusive, as the world economic system. Indeed, it is a fatal caricature of globalization; Global War is a conflict without borders, in which everyone is within everything, where the outside, and the border that determines it, have both vanished.

The fact that, within the space (or nonspace) of Global War, we witness a clash of a "public" function with a "private" function, is thus not a determining difference. More important, it is a difference that does not produce an order, and that does not allow us to identify what is really causing the disorder: the despatialization of politics. We do not, of course, wish to suggest that the United States and al Qaeda are "equal," or that regular power and irregular violence are the same thing. Rather, our proposal is that the global space (the absence of modern political space) in which these two entities exist and fight makes them "analogous" from a functional point of view. In this context, the juridical qualification of Global War as a private terrorist act generating a public counterterrorist act, and a subsequent police punishment of the large crime on an equally large scale, fails to get at the heart of the situation. At best, it is a reassuring way to place order in chaos. But this is only an apparent, superficial order. This is demonstrated by the fact that America's formal declaration of "just" war against Afghanistan on October 7 is in every way less significant than the informal declaration issued on September 11. Publicity and official character are no longer decisive factors for qualifying Global War.

(c) The global mobilization of modern political categories also involves the relationship between economics and war, and more generally between economics and politics. The conflict-world is the other side of the economics-world.

We could describe globalization as the victory of economics over politics, as economics' complete success in crossing borders compared to politics' insistence on barriers and forms. We could call it the triumph of the market over the State (which, remember, had been the market's incubator and caretaker) and all of the logics of the State. Among these logics, we note first of all the logic of war, which belongs sovereignly to the State. In the postmodern One, we could then conclude, the typically liberal dualities—the opposition of "sweet commerce" and the barbarianism of war, of progressive mercantile classes and reactionary warrior classes, of bourgeoisie and soldier, of Society and State—would fail.

In order to deconstruct this pacified, unidirectional, and monodimensional image of globalization, we must emphasize that what is coming into being today at the expense of the confined spatiality of States is not the smooth spatiality of cosmopolitan exchange. Globalization's One is not simply one side, the economic side, of the old modern dualisms. Rather, it is the synthesis, or reciprocal confusion, of those dualisms. In short, even from this viewpoint, in the global age, we instead see a manifestation of a new gray area in which politics and economics immediately belong to each other, where economic command is, in essence, immediately political power (think of the International Monetary Fund [IMF], the World Trade Organization [WTO], the World Bank, and their capacity to manage their global strategy through local political classes), in which production never takes place without war, whether that war be real or potential. Global nonspace is not, in other words, a flat surface. Rather, it is a stormy sea, a jumble from which Global War—the conflictual side of globalization—emerges, realizing the reciprocal penetration of labor and violence with an intensity never reached by Total Mobilization.

Indeed, Jünger's Total Mobilization was the *immediate militarization of society*, while Global War is the *global socialization of violence*. The first declared itself under the banner of war, the second under the banner of economics. The first manifested the crisis of the State before totalitarianism, the second revealed the crisis of the State before globalization. Global War is the fact that in any moment, in any society on Earth, an armed conflict can ignite, motivated by an economic crisis in some other part of the world. As such, Global War, in that it is endemic and ubiquitous, is different from total war, which was the convulsive gathering of all social energies under the banner of violence.

By this same token, however, Global War is therefore also economic war, a military accompaniment to the economic crisis of resources, an armed emphasis of power relationships established (and constantly renewed and overturned) in the economic sphere. It is the ensemble of hostile, but not openly violent, economic acts aimed at subduing the will of an adversary. Global War is also the confrontation of economic powers, the clash of criminal economies among themselves, or against legal economies, as has occurred in Latin America, the Balkans, Central Asia, the Horn of Africa, and the sub-Saharan region. It is the conflict for oil or water, for diamonds or narcotics, that involves States, para-State agencies, private gangs, semi-State mafias, drug lords and arms dealers. However, economic Global War is also the financial speculation that topples national markets, or civil conflicts stemming from the impoverishment of large population segments due to the World Bank's monetarist politics. Economic Global War can also be linked to those forms of economics that sustain themselves with the forced exoduses of populations, with refugee camps used as labor pools, with the control of illegal immigration, with the new slave trade. Even September 11, which did not interrupt globalization, but exposed its conflictual side, has an economic matrix in the conflicts between elite Arabs and Westerners for the control of Saudi oil. It is no accident that the collapse of the Twin Towers at the World Trade Center, and not the attack on the Pentagon, has become the most intense symbol of the attacks. The image that has been remembered the most is not the attack on the military citadel, but the conquest of the economic acropolis.

In Global War, the structural reciprocal penetration between war and modern economics—or better, between economics, conflict, and the power of command—realizes itself in a new and generalized mode. In the institutions of liberal and democratic politics, this penetration was established and clarified only provisionally, and realized itself in an imperfect and transitory division of labor: The State gets politics and war, Society gets economics. This arrangement was described quite aptly by Jan Pieterszoon Coen, an agent of the Dutch East India Company, who in 1614 wrote to his superiors that "commerce cannot be maintained without war, nor can war be maintained without commerce."[34]

From every viewpoint, Global War is not a clash of clear and distinct differences, but a single chaos in which the opposing faces of a single system mix together; it is a One locked in struggle with itself. This places globalization and its war beyond and outside the reach of liberal thought, totalitarian logics, and even Marxist criticism, which never really subscribed to the liberal theory of distinction between political and economic spheres, instead thinking the relationship between the spheres in reciprocal and dialectical terms. Indeed, Marxism always made a point of grasping and exposing the determinate, historical, specific contradiction that links economics and politics: The center of Society and the State, the beating heart of economic alienation and political power, is the form of capitalist production, the conflict between labor and capital. Now, however, it is precisely this incandescent frontier that has become fractured, having lost its own strategic importance in thousands of tactical rivulets. The great class war—the universal Marxist dialectic—is unrecognizable today; it has become an endemic infection, determined by thousands of causes, peddled under thousands of pseudo-identitarian banners that cannot be, and indeed have no desire to be, subsumed under any kind of universal explanation.

The Role of the United States

Of course, even if there is no single focal point or center of gravity to global politics and Global War, there is, at the very least, an epicenter to it: the friction between the United States and the Islamic, or more generally Asiatic, world. Though the United States is a solitary hyperpower, the heart of a hypereconomy for world development, and though it survived the dual conflict between superpowers, it is not the Empire, just as its economy does not coincide with the global economy. And yet, the United States is, more often than not, engaged in Global War.

Having left the Cold War victorious, the United States is, paradoxically, the bearer of the sort of revisionist politics that is more often adopted by defeated powers. The United States wants to change the rules of the game, that old, established, bipolar game that gave order to the second half of the twentieth century. It wants to allow itself something that has never before been allowed in a real and concrete way, to practice the strategy that it has long believed to be more congenial and useful for its own interests: unilateralism, the worldwide advancement of American interests—if necessary against and beyond international organizations and their coordination of actors on the global stage. In the ideological assumption that whatever is good for the United States is good for the rest of the world, or better, that the United States embodies the most precious human values, and thereby merits the leadership that it has so openly claimed since the Clinton presidency, American particularism becomes American universalism.

In truth, the United States is currently unbalanced by their victory over the Soviet Union. Without that enemy, which had also been a forced world partner, the United States now feels alone, exposed and forced to confront the world's disorder and the arc of crises that surrounds the center-south area of the old continent, from Morocco to the Philippines. In this arc of crisis, territorial claims (Kurdistan, Palestine, Chechnya, Kashmir), energy claims (water, oil), and religious claims (Islam, Hinduism, Chinese communism) intertwine, made even more serious by the fact that they are simultaneous and contradictory, and all inscribed in globalization's vortex. September 11 may not have been the end of U.S. power, but it was certainly a radical challenge to it, and America is far from certain that it can win.

To respond to all this, the United States seeks to impose a hierarchical-imperial order on the anarchical-plural disorder of the world, and to this end supplies an impressive military apparatus, easily the most powerful in history. According to the new strategic doctrine recently presented by Secretary of Defense Donald Rumsfeld, this military presence will emphasize "deterrence in four critical theaters."[35] The United States will therefore prepare itself to fight four large conventional wars at the same time, while maintaining its defensive capabilities to protect from a nuclear attack and to deliver a devastating strategic response. This response is ready for China, for rogue States, for terrorist bases, and many more.

This might seem to be the exercise of sovereignty understood in the classical sense: as a "normal" aspiration to power, even if carried out on a much larger scale. It might seem, in other words, that the United States is a political actor that is attempting to execute a reconfiguring design of global space to its own advantage, that it is the institutionalized power seeking to bring order to the conflictual tangle of destructured powers. It might seem that the United States is trying to conquer the Heartland, the heart of the old continent, whose possession has always eluded Anglo-Saxon powers and which has been the major stake for geopolitics throughout history (at least according to geographer Halford Mackinder).[36] The old continent would then allow the United States to become not just a naval and Atlantic power, but also a terrestrial power. The campaign in Afghanistan, seen in this light, would be anything but random; it would be just one piece of the puzzle, the completion of which would allow the insertion of military bases in the steppes of central Asia, in Kyrgyzstan and Uzbekistan, allowing for the control of oil resources in the Caspian region as well as the encirclement of the Islamic world from the North and the South. Indeed, seen in this way, the Shanghai meeting among the leaders of China, Russia, and the United States in October 2001 could be interpreted as a draft of new Yalta, an attempt by the United States to negotiate new areas of influence in Asia with the old terrestrial powers. This was a negotiation sustained by a strategic-spatial design and a military and economic power so impressive that it nearly became an imposition. If this is indeed how everything happened, we could conclude that, underneath the jumble of global politics and Global War, the steady connections of permanent geopolitical interests remain in place (only now interpreted from the American point of view), and that Global War is not inimical to the construction of a precise architecture of world power.

In reality, however, this geopolitical interpretation is not only improbable—politics today is no longer tied to land, as it has been despatialized for quite some time—but also deceptive. It sounds like a retrospective rationalization for a situation that does not in fact follow the creation of a politics or a "great strategy," but instead configures itself as a series of "blows" struck by the United States all over the world in response to local crises, not in order to prevent them, but in an attempt to bring political order to space. In short, American military action does not seem to be a traditional manifestation of sovereignty, but rather a necessity, an operation of continuous substitution (the next villain, when the Afghanistan question has been laid to rest, will be Iraq) of a world order that does not actually exist, the job of a fireman or of a global policeman rather than a politician. The armed struggle against terrorism is one way the United States participates in Global War, and it is a continuation, with new means, of the lack of politics (in the traditional sense) that is so typical of the global age. It is the continuation, in other words, of the new politics of immediacy—of short-circuit—between economic rationality and the manifestation of violence.

Sucked back into the global swamp, the United States does not seem to have a precise strategic design, but rather, many immediate interests to defend and many fears to assuage. Even if the American Empire is not in decline, captured in the vortex of the global Empire, it may truly be the Empire of Chaos, condemned to fight forever and to win, certainly, but never to reach peace or allow peace. Furthermore, were the United States to engage in an attempt to prevent terrorism by reclaiming its sources, it would be obliged to construct or radically reform the internal order of some eighty poor, deinstitutionalized countries, which seems an excessive undertaking, even for a power with military bases in 100 of the 180 countries of the world.

In any case, we can easily say that, even on the American side, there is a fair amount of disorder, and that the United States' self-evident hyperpower is not "sovereignty" in the classical sense. In fact, sovereignty draws its meaning from its plurality and its ability to recognize other sovereign centers, while the United States does not recognize any enemy outside themselves; they have no *iusti hostes*; they see their adversaries only as criminals, rogue states, an "axis of evil." It thus becomes evident that today no "international system" with precisely distinguishable, interdependent actors truly exists. Rather, we see an a-systematic "global system" in which only the "internal" dimension of the "police" exists. More precisely, we see a deterritorialized economics being chased by a deterritorialized politics—which, in turn, brings war along with it like its own Shadow, in an immediate and unthinking way.

On the "Political"

In the global age, we are witnessing several phenomena: a war between adversaries incapable of reciprocal recognition who fatally oppose one another as nondialectical identities; a war that confuses the terrorist and the counterterrorist, and ceases to be explainable by the institutions of politics; and a politics that immediately contains war. All this creates a scenario in which neither liberal categories nor Marxist criticism are valid. It is, therefore, a scenario that seems to be the perfect place to conduct an analysis with the categories of negative thought. Global War would seem, in other words, to validate the Schmittian model of the "political" as the most intense conflict and as the confrontation of friend and enemy. The presence of a theological element in this conflict, along with the collapse of the categories of public law, would seem to confirm this hypothesis.

But this is not the case—at least, not exactly. We have already noted that the politicity of the extreme theology of September 11 is not ascribable to political theology as Schmitt understood it. Indeed, all of Schmitt's politological theses, born as they were at the margins of modernity, tend to lose themselves in the postmodern context of globalization.

If, for Schmitt, the State presupposes the "political," this is not, in and of itself, a trans-epochal constant. Rather, it is that which destructures the State from within. The "political" is the "cut" (the scar) in the political space internal to the State; it is that which is the origin of the State, which allows for the closure of the State—though only partially. It is that disorder which makes order possible—but not completely. It is the obscure trace of politics that crosses, *ab initio*, the statual juridical crystal and constitutes it. In short, the "political" also exhibits a vector of order, even though it is the negation of every closed geometry and every full potential ordering of politics. As such, the "political" is a complication of modern political spatiality, an abyssal inflection of the planarity of the State's political space. In other words, the heart of the Schmittian "political" is not pure enmity, but the fact that politics must assume both the concrete friend and the concrete enemy—not only internal peace and external war, but also the possibility of internal war—as well as someone (the sovereign) who has the political knowledge to decide on them.

The purpose of Schmitt's thought was to distinguish concretely (to decide) between peace and war, drawing the necessary political energy for this purpose from the knowledge of the reality of the "political"—from the indistinctness (the indeterminateness of principle) between war and politics. As extremist as it may be, Schmitt's political theory refers to the State, and though his theory is run through with dismantling drives, it also contains regulating vectors that have lost much of their meaning in today's mutated spatial context. In the global world, the indistinctness between peace and war has become the norm, and knowledge of the "political" no longer gives any sovereign the possibility of creating a space where war and peace are clearly defined.

In the same way, we must be wary of believing that Schmitt's dichotomy between Land and Sea—between statual-territorial political orders and naval-economic-technological orders, between continental Europe with its spatially ordered politics, and the Anglo-Saxon world with its immanent utilitarian individualism, its moralism devoid of measure and its universalistic border-crossing—is fully vital today. The objects of Schmitt's polemics—the homogenizing and standardizing universalism incapable of political form, political liberalism, humanitarianism, and socialism—no longer exist. Of course, we do today have economic liberalism and the power of technology, but they do not produce a "sea," a smooth, uniform space. Instead, the new a-spatial dimension of globalization produces a muddled mix of land and sea, forming chasms as deep as a Maelstrom, insidious shallows, and swampy, treacherous lands. Globalization is the dimension where, as in the Gulf war, Sinbad's sea is run through with the wakes of missiles; where, as in the war between New York and Afghanistan, skyscrapers sink like ships, and strategic bombers are used for manhunts in the same mountainous caves and caravan routes that witnessed the Great Game one hundred years earlier.

In his 1963 work, *Theory of the Partisan*, Schmitt pushed himself as far as his thought would allow. He saw the partisan and his adherence to land from a defensive and regulating viewpoint, and recognized the partisan as "the last sentinel of the earth" in a world possessed by technology's "naval" powers.[37] Schmitt saw the partisan's "irregularity" as a factor of confusion for the continuing regulating capabilities of the State (which at that point were still able to impose laws on war). He also, however, saw an element of concreteness and adherence to the Elementary. In short, he saw a possibility for a new politico-spatial logic. For Schmitt, the partisan is irregular precisely because he opens a new space to war, the space of telluric profundity that challenges the State's traditional space and attempts to crowd it out, prompting the State to react by criminalizing it. But while the State runs the risk of losing concreteness and entrusting its own politics to technology, the partisan is not a simple criminal; he is a political combatant for a concrete cause. He is, in fact, the cosmic-historical figure who announces a new, post-statual order, a new *nomos* of the Earth.

Above all, Schmitt made the distinction between the partisan's real enmity, which was concrete and regulating precisely because it was "telluric," and the absolute (or total) enmity of the Leninist revolutionary, whose ideology's universalistic dimension supplied political energy but also nihilistic indeterminateness and a propensity to destroy the enemy morally. While the partisan has a precise objective (pushing back the invader, chasing the enemy off his land), the revolutionary is fighting for an absolute, universal, and indeterminate *iusta causa* that prefigures a homogeneous and unified world, and thus has no alternative but to seek the enemy's annihilation. As such, the enemy cannot be a *iustis hostis*, a legitimate enemy; it must instead be a monster existing outside humanity. Thus, Schmitt notes that the partisan's concrete political logics run the risk of becoming deformed by the universalistic political context into which they were in danger of being dragged. This is the context of the worldwide revolution and the equally universal context of unrestricted technology, to which Schmitt dedicates a few visionary pages. Schmitt saw the extremely dangerous encounter between the partisan and technology—the "motorized partisan"—against the backdrop of atomic war. After the atomic catastrophe, Schmitt argued, combatants would begin to morph into irregular characters, heralding the advent of terrible "extra-conventional men," militants who would now practice a new type of enmity, one intensified by technology—an *absolute* enmity that comes into being by dissolving the very concept of the enemy, and that sees the adversary as nothing more than a thing to be destroyed.

Today, nearly forty years later, that future has arrived. We are seeing the end of the concrete and spatially determined concept of the enemy, brought about not (or at least not only) by technology, nor by a worldwide revolution, but because of globalization. This is the force that despatializes both politics and war, removing them from the logic of friend and enemy and the categories of the "partisan." According to Schmittian logic, the perpetrators of the massacre in Manhattan are unfamiliar with the concept of enemy. This means that the logical frontier of Schmittian thought, which surpassed itself in the moment it was reached, has become everyday life. The extreme has become normal, and the unthinkable, unplaceable in political space or modern political categories, is today the new figure of politics and war.

Thus, even though we prefer not to say that, with September 11, 2001, the political thought of Schmitt is dead—which would only mimic the way that Schmitt himself declared the death of Hegel's State in January 1933, the moment when the Nazis seized power[38]—we must nonetheless recognize that Global War commences only where Schmittian political theory is exhausted.

Interpretations

In order to summarize what we have discussed until now, we must repeat that Global War is a war without spatiality in the modern sense of the word. Furthermore, it is devoid of a single, determining cause, but has countless incidental causes. It is a systemic war that manifests itself in a dimension, globalization, that clears the categories of modern politics, the liberal distinctions, the Marxian determinate contradiction, and concrete Schmittian enmity. It is a war without center, even though it has a favorite actor: the United States.

Global War is an aspect of global mobilization, or better, a mode of being—an *immediate* mode of being—of global politics, of the disorder that is the postmodern condition. It is not an action but a situation; not an exception but a tragic normality. Its full manifestation on September 11 is not a crisis of globalization, as liberal interpretations would have us believe, but the *globalization of crisis*. It is the end of liberal globalization, and the beginning of armed globalization. If the Cold War was the situation in which "war was improbable and peace impossible," as Raymond Aron has suggested,[39] Global War is the situation of continuous war, both potential and real, fed by an ideology of peace, a mobilizing and ever-elusive specter.

Global War is the circulation of violence within global politics, something similar to the state of nature described in Hobbes's *Leviathan*. However, there is a big difference in the fact that the condition of Global War is not a pre-political sphere, a situation of natural violence from which we can exit through the force of reason. Rather, it is postmodern politics, the unprecedented mix of (or the absence of borders between) violence and normality, peace and war, the immediate identity of politics and war, which seems "natural," but is in reality the last product of historical development. From a theoretical point of view, Global War can be seen as the fulfillment of the conceptual nihilism that, even when it was neutralized and rationalized by the State, has infested modernity and its merely artificial[40] political space devoid of ontological foundation, signaling, from the viewpoint of political analysis, the collapse of the categories of modern political thought.

If the phenomenology of contemporary conflict tells us that nothing we see is what it seems, this does not mean that behind the appearances and the new figures that populate the world stage—the terrorist, the pirate, the migrant, the merchant-adventurer, the just warrior—we can see a hidden essence. Rather, it means that the old categories of politics—theology, identity, war, justice—do not have explicative effectiveness when they are taken from modern space and applied to global nonspace. Nor do these categories allow the establishment of a clear relationship between war and politics, in particular the distinction between war and peace. The effect is that of being lost within a postmodern horizon, and the reconstruction of new regulating configurations has yet to be seen.

Though this war has no morphogenetic ends, and though it does not intend to produce political form and is, in fact, the manifestation of its absence, none of this weakens its intensity. It is obvious that we do not wish to resign ourselves to leaving such an imposing phenomenon as Global War without persuasive explanations, and we must confront the temptation to put traditional, trustworthy interpretative categories back into play. This is the temptation to read Global War as the uprising of the poor against the rich, or as the clash between elite factions for the control of oil, or as a consequence of growing desperation in the Arab world for the lack of a solution in the Israel–Palestine conflict, or as a manifestation of anti-modern resistance movements expressed through Islam, which would legitimate the refusal of political and social logics of secularization. Finally, to illustrate better the intellectual agoraphobia brought about by Global War, we see an affirmation of the thesis that September 11 marked the end of the globalization of the 1990s and a return to the "regional" globalization of the 1980s, suggesting that an era of relatively closed *Großraume* is now beginning.

The point is that none of these causes or trends—past their factual correctness, which should be examined case by case—captures the changes of meaning that were imposed on them by the global age, or the necessity to go beyond the paradigms with which the relationship between war and politics was thought in the modern age.

Pirates

If anything, to make sense of Global War we need to return to previous models of the relationship between regular power and irregular violence in Western cultures. Indeed, to the extent that we may create analogies between our experience and past experiences—to the extent, that is to say, that the imperial analogy between global Empire and historic Empires still holds—we may say that Global War has traits in common with wars against pirates. This is not just because of the metaphor employed by hackers, parasites of the world network, who call themselves "Internet pirates"; the analogy is much more profound and concrete. Like terrorists, pirates are not external enemies, but exist within a system, Mediterranean or Atlantic space. Like terrorists, pirates have been fought everywhere they have been encountered, flushed out of their coves with different weapons and logics than those used in wars of conquest, more to preserve the security of routes and commerce than to mold the Empire's frontiers. Like terrorists, pirates were marauders, not legitimate enemies, but no one hesitated before waging war on them, a more systemic than strategic war, just like Global War. It is no accident that the eponymous hero of the Roman Empire, Caesar, had dealings with Illyrian pirates in his youth.

Having been taken prisoner and waiting for his friends to come up with the money for his ransom, he promised the pirates, half-seriously, that he would bring them all to justice as soon as he was freed, a promise he kept, as Svetonius tells us. Above all, like terrorists, pirates are *hostes humani generis*, enemies of the human race. Cicero insists on this in *De officiis*: "*Nam pirata non est ex perduellium numero, sed communis hostis omnium*"—the pirate cannot be counted among regular enemies, but is a common enemy to all.[41] Like terrorists, finally, pirates were fought with military means, but once captured, they were crucified and hung like bandits.

Beyond their long presence in Western history, pirates hold one direct and explicit place in American historical memory. Even without bringing up the anti-Spanish piracy practiced along the Southern coasts of New England in the colonial age, it is noteworthy that at the dawn of its independent historical existence, U.S. powers found themselves locked in two military campaigns against pirates. The first (1801–1805) was a war against Tripolitan pirates who preyed on the American mercantile fleet in the Mediterranean; this resulted in an American landing at Tripoli, the first extracontinental exercise of the Marines (an event captured in the words of their anthem[42]). The second campaign occurred during the Napoleonic wars and the War of 1812 against the British, during which pirates recommenced their activity. In 1815, a fleet of ten American ships entered the port of Algiers and forced the Bey to sign a treaty that forbade piracy against the United States, with the result that after 1815, the United States no longer paid tribute to barbarian states (Tripolitania, Algeria, Tunisia, and Morocco).

The counterpiracy war—military action against an enemy who is not a *iustus hostis*—is thus part of the historico-political imprinting of the United States. It is not outside the realm of possibility that this has had an effect both on military operations and on the treatment of prisoners, even in the course of the Global War.

War without Limits

The most penetrating interpretation of Global War to date has not come from within Western culture. Instead, two high-ranking officials of the Chinese air force, Liang Qiao and Xiangsui Wang, whose book

Unrestricted Warfare[43] was written at least two years before September 11, but nonetheless demonstrates a clear understanding of the fact that in this new war, the first thing to disappear is the distinction between war and peace.

In the first place, the authors underline that the "non-war actions" are the constitutive factor of the new war's scenario, and that this war is "unrestricted" precisely because all distinctions between war and peace are lost within it. First of all, the new war does not use "weapons of new concepts" but "new concepts of weapons."[44] Ordinary things can become weapons to engage war (a perfect example is the ice picks transformed into deadly weapons and used to highjack the civilian airliners on September 11). Second, the new battlefield is everywhere; this is true not only from the viewpoint of its quantitative expansion, but moreover for its qualitative transformation, for the interlacing and overlapping of natural space and technological space. Third, we must add both new combatants (the Internet pirate, the non-State organizations) and, more importantly, the "nonmilitary war operations" to the lack of distinction between military technology and civilian technology, and between battle space and battle nonspace.[45]

"Nonmilitary war operations" are distinct from "military operations other than war," which are better described as noncombat, support operations foreseen by U.S. military doctrine. "Military operations other than war" are still conventional, while "nonmilitary war operations" entail the extension of war to every aspect of associated life: commercial war, financial war, terrorist war, war on contraband, psychological war, war on drugs, culture war. However, this does not limit itself to the extension of violence in every sphere; in this case, it would be limited to what the authors define as "total dimensional warfare," a total war of the twentieth-century variety.[46] In reality, these two Chinese military officials recognize that this new war can sometimes combine open violence with nonmilitary actions and tools that serve to bend the enemy's will. The flux of global powers is always conflictual, even if it does not always incite open war; many nonwar actions (e.g., speculative interventions on financial markets or on the price of raw materials) are actually comparable to war-like actions when politics is no longer capable of creating spatial order, as occurs in the global age. In other words, when "all principals without national power who employ nonmilitary warfare actions to declare war against the international community use all means that go beyond nations, regions, and measures. Visible national boundaries, invisible internet space, international law, national law, behavioral norms, and ethical principles have absolutely no restraining effects on them."[47] By destroying the spaces and borders of politics, globalization makes life insecure in every sphere: politics, religion, culture, society, custom, energy resources, environmental resources, nutritional resources, water, and communication are all exposed to insecurity and become new spheres of battle, both armed and unarmed. In short, globalization explains how and why this unrestricted warfare unifies both military and nonmilitary fields, forcing them to accept that "the most ideal method of dealing with an enemy who pays no regard to the rules is certainly just being able to break through the rules."[48]

From their polemical viewpoint, these two authors assert the necessity of combining new and old methods in different ways, to allow military methods, transmilitary (irregular) methods, and nonmilitary methods to coexist, and to practice economic war as much as Internet war, to aspire to communication blocks, social crises, political crises, and, of course, military crises. Given that, for these authors, nothing in the global age is what it seems, the principle element of war, the military dimension, can undergo decisive modifications by secondary, nonmilitary elements: "the interactions among all factors have made it difficult for the military sphere to serve as the automatic dominant sphere in every war. War will be conducted in non-war spheres."[49]

This "modified combined war that goes beyond limits"[50] functions as a strategic directive (which the authors recognize has an easy formulation and a difficult concrete application, given the enormous wisdom necessary to actually identify the "secondary" points on which to draw) thanks to which a growing power like China can oppose itself to the U.S. hyperpower without colliding head-on with its immense technological and military superiority.

But beyond the Chinese strategic interest, when we observe from a phenomenological viewpoint, and adequately set it in the context of globalization, this oblique, "asymmetrical" war fully describes Global War and its existing reality between the political and the military. The new, immediate relationship between war and politics in the global age and the subsequent filling up of the traditional "chasm between warfare and non-warfare" was better, or perhaps only first, conceptualized by Chinese culture, free from the intellectual weight of modernity, than by Western culture.[51] This, too, is globalization.

For a New Nomos of the Earth

Rather than denying the theoretico-political novelty of Global War, rather than closing our eyes to the fact that Global War radically challenges modern political philosophy and its categories, and rather than continuing to believe that globalization is not the horizon that determines our experience today, our task is to begin to think the novelties, the paradoxes, and the aporiae of globalization. We must ask ourselves about its possibilities—not in order to stabilize it, for that would be impossible—but in order to imagine routes within it that would make for a less tumultuous crossing of the sea the world has become.

If we do not want to make the mistake of applying old remedies to new illnesses, or to wander in vain in our own smug conceptuality (which has become nothing but ineffectual jargon), we must remember that we scholars need to apply a mix of good sense, humility, and theoretical radicalism. This will give us a renewed capacity for observation and analysis. Political philosophy should not institute itself primarily as a public elaboration of criteria of judgment, or as the rational production of a set of guiding values to be put into practice; it should not seek to be a discourse internal to the City. Before it takes on these tasks, it must first begin the radical deconstruction of its own concepts; it must clear the rubble of the Modern off the ground—for today, that rubble hinders more than it helps.

We are not likely to find the compass that can help us navigate this route in the universal concepts elaborated in the modern West. Globalization has reduced these universals to particulars and has revealed their partiality. Rights are universals; the conflict that denies them, and non-Western cultures' refusal of them, are global. The West that, along with Kant, thinks the conditions of pure humanity, of justice and cosmopolitical equality, is universal; the West wounded by those who ignored Kant and instead became students of the Western school of technological power is global.

And yet, just as we are unable to see the remedy for terrorist anarchy, or pandemic violence, or Global War in the modern Utopia of juridical universalism, we cannot resign ourselves to its supposed naturalness, nor can we justify it through Samuel Huntington's unconsciously neo-Schmittian perspective that proposes conflicts between closed greater spaces.[52] In short, we cannot respond to the lack of space either with Utopia (which is really an absence of space), or with the closure of space. Instead, we must find a "guiding image" that can reveal to us the concrete possibilities of the new political space we, in fact, already occupy.

It is impossible to see a Spirit of the world behind the image of the collapsing Twin Towers. There is no Spirit in that sight. Nor can we limit ourselves to chronicling and cursing the blindness of technology. Of course, we must know how to identify globalization and Global War, but we must also be able see a new land beyond them, and to make this land the final destination of our inescapable journey through globalization's seas. We must answer a crucial question: If modern institutions and concepts were oriented toward defending the Subject and Society, who in turn increasingly established themselves in liberal-democratic or social-democratic forms, toward what objective should we orient our new conceptual tools and our new institutions that are compatible with postmodernism today?

We need *terra firma*, certainly, but we cannot expect this land to be as secure as the State was. The dimension of danger and risk will remain insurmountable in the postmodern age—an age in which security has been lost, perhaps forever. If we maintain that postmodern politics, like modern politics, ought to be arranged around a juridical defense of Subject and Society, it is quite unlikely that we will be able to imagine the conditions that will allow us to exit this war without space, and to begin living instead in a space without war. At the end of this necessary undertaking—which is nothing less than the circumnavigation of globalization—even in the best possible scenario, we will be tied to an existence more unstable than was modern existence. The global age does not push us toward security, but toward freedom understood as "uncontrolled action."

The new conceptual tools and institutions that we must create should be oriented toward a goal, an end—the image, let us say, of a free humanity no longer miserably crushed in the coils of chaos. This humanity would be well aware of the seas of globalization, and would be able to cross them, if necessary, with acts of "piracy"—if by "piracy" we mean, in a strict etymological sense, *peirein*, the courage "*to attempt*."[53] As such, but only as such, this humanity will be able to structure the *terra firma* for itself. Our goal is aided by Goethe's image of the Netherlands—a space removed from the sea with harmonious effort—in the closing of *Faust, Part II.* In Faust's last appearance, we see him blinded but still engaged:

> What a delight to heart and ear
> This stir of spades at work to hear;
> All, that owe service for their land,
> Are active in the work at hand,
> Earth with itself to reconcile,
> Fix limits to the wild waves' race,
> And bind the sea with firm embrace.[54]

This image of draining the swamp and reclaiming the land—of making a new measure, or new *nomos*, for the Earth—this separation of water from the sea that is always risky and never definite (Mephistopheles, after all, will sarcastically respond to Faust by observing that "the Elements forevermore are doing/Our work,"[55] conspiring against man's labor) is neither a consolatory Utopia nor an idealistic model of a new world order. Rather, it is the viewpoint—vital for us to achieve, if we want to know how to criticize the present—of a secular promised land, a land that has been freed from obsessions of total security and that consists, instead, of open spaces that, as Faust puts it, "to many millions ample space would give,/not safe, indeed, from inroad of the sea,/But yet, in free activity to live."[56]

Faust dies, do not forget. As he utters his last words ("But stay, you are so beautiful!"), he contemplates this vision of a free people living on free land, exposed to danger, but removed from the sea through collective effort. Faust's death scene tells us that all attempts to possess the image he contemplates inevitably become banal. Its essence cannot be found in contemplation—a *logos* that is merely an object of *theoria*. It is a *practical objective*. It can only *be* what it *is* to the extent that it *becomes* action, hope, and struggle. After all, when Faust translates "In the beginning was the *Logos*," with "In the beginning was the Deed," he implies, precisely, that "action" is the correct translation of *logos*.[57]

The word we must try to hear over the roar of the collapsing towers is the din of Global War. But in this noise we can hear another word, it too immanent to the crisis of September 11: *freedom* as *action*, *action* for *freedom*. This is not an apocalyptic word that promises new skies and new earth. We already have too many of these—and they are part of the problem, not part of its solution. What we need today is a sober, collective action-image, postmodern and post-statual, that allows us to look into the gray of the global world and to see not a dawn or twilight of the Spirit, but simply—a fog. This fog is true and real, and it cannot be swept away by the light of reason like the Reign of Darkness (according to Hobbes, in his proto-Enlightenment optimism). However, we can at least refuse to this fog the right to present itself as the inscrutability of an antihuman destiny. If we manage to pierce and dispel this fog adequately by draining the swamps from which it rises, or through the construction of embankments to hold the sea as far back as possible, we may be able to see through the fog, and catch at least a glimpse of some recognizable configuration of risky freedom.

The duty with which Global War charges us, not too paradoxically, is that we cease to remain mere passive spectators to this chaos, and that we begin to define and practice liberty, both individual and collective, single, united, and agonal, in the global age. It is the duty of a generation.

Author's Note

Political Spaces originated in a paper called "Space and Politics: Notes on the Spatial Dimension of Political Thought" ("Spazio e Politica. Appunti sulla dimensione spaziale del pensiero politico") I presented at the Department of Politics, Institutions, and History seminar at the University of Bologna on December 16, 1998; and in a lecture on "Local/Global: Political Meanings of a New Categorial Couple" ("Locale/globale: significati politici di una nuova coppia categoriale") I delivered at the Idea of Community Conference organized by the Istituto Gramsci-Veneto in Mira on February 18, 2000.

Space and politics was also the subject of my course on the history of political doctrines in the academic year of 1999 to 2000 in the University of Bologna's Faculty of Political Sciences at Forlì. The didactic demands of that course contributed, in part, to the current expository form of this book.

The last chapter was anticipated, in quite different and abbreviated forms, in an article with the title "Space and Politics in the Global Age" ("Spazio e politica nell'età globale") in *Filosofia politica* 14:3 (December 2000), 357–78 (in the monographic section dedicated to globalization).

I give thanks to my students, collaborators, and colleagues, Furio Ferraresi, Maria Laura Lanzillo, Raffaele Laudani, and Sandro Mezzadra, for reading a first draft of this manuscript and for their kind suggestions.

The genesis of *Global War* can be found in my essay "War Without Space" ("Guerra senza spazio," *Micromega* 5 [2001]), which I have completely broadened and rewritten here. I further developed this theme in a paper on "World War and Global War: Structural Divergences and

Epochal Passage" ("Guerra mondiale e Guerra globale. Divergenze strutturali e passaggio epochale"), which I presented at the conference *Global War: Paradigms and Perspectives* (*Guerra globale. Paradigmi e prospettive*) held at the Istituto Suor Orsola Benincasa in Naples from November 23 to 24, 2001. The theoretical horizon in *Global War* is the same as the one outlined in *Political Spaces.*

Notes

Preface to the English Edition

1. [Latin for "boundary, limit, or frontier." —Ed.]

Editor's Introduction

I thank Joshua Barkan, Bruce Braun, Timothy Campbell, David Delaney, Amanda Minervini, Alberto Moreiras, Chris Tullis, and Christian Thorne for their comments on earlier drafts of this text. I owe special thanks to Gordon Bourjaily for his incisive and attentive reading of the penultimate draft, and to the librarians of Amherst College for acquiring and locating many of the texts I consider here. I thank Elisabeth Fay for reviewing my translations from the Italian. All mistakes and errors are mine.

1. For readers who are unfamiliar with Carl Schmitt, the most comprehensive introduction to his life and thought in English is Gopal Balakrishnan, *The Enemy: An Intellectual Portrait of Carl Schmitt* (New York: Verso Books, 2000).

2. Thalin Zarmanian, "Carl Schmitt and the Problem of Legal Order: From Domestic to International," *Leiden Journal of International Law* 19 (2006), 41. Michael Hardt and Antonio Negri, meanwhile, note that Galli's book is "the most extensive consideration of Schmitt's conception of the political that we know." See Michael Hardt and Antonio Negri, *Empire* (Cambridge, Mass.: Harvard University Press, 2000), 464 n6.

3. Carlo Galli, *Political Spaces and Global War*, trans. Elisabeth Fay (Minneapolis: University of Minnesota Press, 2010), Part II: "Global War ('On the "Political"')."

4. Carlo Galli, *Genealogia della politica: Carl Schmitt e la crisi del pensiero politico moderno*, second edition (Bologna: Il Mulino, 2010), x.

5. Carlo Galli, *Contingenza e necessità nella ragione politica moderna* (Rome-Bari: Laterza & Figli, 2009), v–viii.

6. Galli, *Political Spaces and Global War*, Part II: "Global War ('For a New Nomos of the Earth')"; Carlo Galli, "Editoriale. La pensabilità della politica. Vent'anni dopo," *Filosofia politica* 21:1 (April 2007), 9; Carlo Galli, *L'umanità*

multiculturale (Bologna: Il Mulino, 2008), 84–85; Galli, *Contingenza e necessità*, viii; Carlo Galli, *Perché ancora destra e sinistra* (Rome-Bari: Laterza, 2010), 67, 82–83.

7. Carlo Galli and Roberto Esposito, eds., *Enciclopedia del pensiero politico. Autori, concetti, dottrine*, second edition (Rome-Bari: Gius, Laterza, and Figli, 2005). The second edition has newly updated entries for biopolitics, conflict, disobedience, fundamentalism, globalization, war, multitude, and terrorism.

8. Barbara Cassin, ed., *Vocabulaire européen des philosophies: Dictionaire des intraduisibles* (Paris: Éditions du Seuil, 2004).

9. Nicola Matteucci and Norberto Bobbio, eds., *Il dizionario di politica* (Turin: UTET, 1976).

10. Otto Brunner, Werner Conze, and Reinhart Koselleck, eds., *Geschichtliche Grundbegriffe: Historisches Lexikon zur politisch-sozialer Sprache in Deutschland* (Stuttgart: E. Klett—G. Cotta, 1972–77).

11. Theodor Adorno, "The Meaning of Working through the Past," trans. Henry W. Pickford, in *Guilt and Defense: On the Legacies of National Socialism in Postwar Germany*, ed. Jeffrey Olick and Andrew Perrin (Cambridge, Mass.: Harvard University Press, 2010), 224.

12. See, on this point, Melvin Richter, "Conceptual History (*Begriffsgeschichte*) and Political Theory," *Political Theory* 14:4 (November 1986), 632–33. See also, more generally, Melvin Richter, "*Begriffsgeschichte* and the History of Ideas," *Journal of the History of Ideas* 48:2 (April–June, 1987), 247–63.

13. Barbara Cassin, "Présentation," in *Vocabulaire européen des philosophies*, xviii, xxi.

14. Roberto Esposito and Carlo Galli, "Prefazione all prima edizione," *Enciclopedia*, viii.

15. Maria Laura Lanzillo, "Europa," *Enciclopedia*, 275.

16. Galli and Esposito also share with Chakrabarty the conviction that the basic concepts of modern European political philosophy are as indispensable as they are inadequate—that, however globalized and inescapable they may be today, these concepts are nevertheless rife with contradictions and aporia, and cannot serve as foundations for universal norms. See Dipesh Chakrabarty, *Provincializing Europe: Postcolonial Thought and Historical Difference* (Princeton, N.J.: Princeton University Press, 2000), 16, 28, 43–45.

17. Roberto Esposito and Carlo Galli, "Prefazione all nuova edizione," *Enciclopedia*, vi.

18. Phillipe Raynaud, "Politique," in *Vocabulaire européen des philosophies*, 966.

19. Galli, "Politica," *Enciclopedia*, 649, 651.

20. Volker Sellin, "Politik," *Geschichtliche Grundbegriffe, Band 4*, 871–73; Norberto Bobbio, "Politica," *Il dizionario di politica*, 736.

21. Carlo Galli, "Politica: Una ipotesi di interpretazione," *Filosofia politica* 3:1 (June 1989), 19.

22. Galli, "La pensabilità della politica," 4.

23. Although Koselleck, Pocock, and Skinner are all members of the international editorial board of *Filosofia politica*, and all have contributed articles to it, it is the Koselleckian project that provides the journal with its main point of departure. See Nicola Matteucci, "Alla ricerca della filosofia politica," *Filosofia politica* 3:1 (June 1989), 15; Sandro Chignola, "History of Political Thought and the History of Political Concepts: Koselleck's Proposal and Italian Research," *History of Political Thought* 23:3 (Autumn 2003), 531–41.

24. Galli, "La pensabilità della politica," 8.

25. Galli, "La pensabilità della politica," 9.

26. Matteucci, "Alla ricerca della filosofia politica," 7. Topics in the *Materialia per un lessico politico Europeo* have included representation, prudence, police, the Good, politics, *metabolé* and *stasis*, nature, sovereignty, constitution, liberty, governance, the nation, body politic, State and federation, publicity and secrecy, decadence, technocracy and caretaker government, society and sociality, tyrannicide, totalitarianism, the history of concepts, republicanism and the republic, hermeneutics and politics, community, civil society, citizenship, globalization, justices and political forms, the Small State, empire, war, Europe, *ghenos* and race, the West, populism, the mixed constitution, rights, biopolitics, and democracy.

27. See, on this point, Nicola Matteucci, "Presentazione," *Filosofia politica* 1:1 (June 1987), 3–5. This work is, as Esposito puts it, "academic" in the best sense of the word. See Roberto Esposito, "La Politica al Presente," in *Impersonale. In dialogo con Roberto Esposito*, ed. Laura Bazzicalupo (Milan: Mimesis Edizioni, 2008), 17.

28. Adriana Cavarero, "Politicizing Theory," *Political Theory* 30:4 (August 2002), 518–19. Cavarero is a frequent contributor to *Filosofia politica*, and serves on its editorial board along with a number of other thinkers whose works are available in English (including Laura Bazzicalupo, Sandro Chignola, Filippo del Lucchese, Simona Forti, Sandro Mezzadra, and Pasquale Pasquino).

29. Carlo Galli, Edoardo Greblo, and Sandro Mezzadra, *Il pensiero politico del Novecento*, ed. Carlo Galli (Bologna: Il Mulino, 2005), 137.

30. See, for example, Roberto Esposito, "The *Dispositif* of the Person," trans. Timothy Campbell, *Law, Culture, and the Humanities* (forthcoming); Carlo Galli, *Political Spaces and Global War*, Part II: "Global War ('Global Time and Space')."

31. Roberto Esposito and Timothy Campbell, "Interview," trans. Anna Paparcone, *Diacritics* 36:2 (2006), 52. See also Roberto Esposito, "Storia dei concetti e ontologia dell'attualità," *Filosofia politica* 22:1 (April 2006), 8. On "imagination" as "the creation of concepts," see Galli, *Political Spaces and Global War*, Part II: "Global War ('Extreme Theology' and 'For a New Nomos of the Earth')."

32. David Harvey, *A Brief History of Neoliberalism* (Oxford: Oxford University Press, 2007), 12.

33. Peter Stein, *Roman Law in European History* (Cambridge, U.K.: Cambridge University Press, 1999), 45–54; Donald Kelley, *The Human Measure: Social Thought in the Western Legal Tradition* (Cambridge, Mass.: Harvard University Press, 1990), 113–18.

34. Harold Berman, *Law and Revolution: The Formation of the Western Legal Tradition* (Cambridge, Mass.: Harvard University Press, 1983), 123.

35. Maurizio Merlo, "Glossatori," *Enciclopedia*, 348–49.

36. Ernst Kantorowicz, "Kingship under the Impact of Scientific Jurisprudence," in *Selected Studies* (New York: J. J. Augustin Publisher, 1965), 151–66.

37. Karl Marx, *The Eighteenth Brumaire of Louis Bonaparte* (New York: International Publishers, 1994), 15–17; Hannah Arendt, *On Revolution* (New York: Penguin Books, 1963), 64, 190–206, but cf. 27–28, 65, 108–11, 181–82; Walter Benjamin, "Theses on the Philosophy of History," *Illuminations*, ed. Hannah Arendt, trans. Harry Zohn (New York: Schocken Books, 1968), 261. Roman Law also, of course, grounded the French National Assembly's opposition to the extension of the revolutionary principles of 1789 to French colonies. See, e.g., C. L. R. James, *The Black Jacobins: Toussaint L'Ouverture and the San Domingo Revolution*, second edition (New York: Vintage Books, 1989), 71–72.

38. Carl Schmitt, "The Plight of European Jurisprudence," trans. G. L. Ulmen, *Telos* 83 (1990), 65.

39. Schmitt, "The Plight of European Jurisprudence," 40.

40. Between 1964 and 1966, it is worth noting, Battaglia organized a lecture series at the University of Bologna in which a range of German intellectuals, including Theodor Adorno, Ernst Bloch, Hans-Georg Gadamer, and Leo Löwith, presented papers. See Albino Babolin, ed., *Filosofi tedeschi d'oggi* (Bologna: Il Mulino, 1967). For Battaglia's own account of his philosophic project, see Felice Battaglia, *La mia prospettiva filosofica* (Padova: Editoria Liviana, 1950), 51–69. Cf. Carlo Galli, "Felice Battaglia," *Enciclopedia*, 62.

41. Carlo Galli, "Alcune interpretazioni italiane della Scuola di Francoforte," *Il Mulino* 22 (1973), 648–71.

42. Martin Clark, *Modern Italy, 1871–1982* (New York: Longman Group Ltd., 1984), 374; Paul Ginsborg, *A History of Contemporary Italy: Society and Politics, 1943–1988* (New York: Penguin Books, 1990), 298; Robert Lumley, *States of Emergency: Cultures of Revolt in Italy from 1968 to 1978* (New York: Verso Books, 1990), 3; Yurii Colombo, "The Italian Left in the 1970s," *International Socialist Review* 26 (November–December, 2002), 57, 64; Giovanni Fasanella and Giovanni Pellegrino, *La guerra civile* (Milan: BUR, 2005), 62.

43. Norberto Bobbio, "Democracy and Invisible Government," *Telos* 52 (Summer 1982), 54–55; Norberto Bobbio, "Italy's Permanent Crisis," *Telos* 54 (Winter 1982–83), 123; Norberto Bobbio, *Ideological Profile of Twentieth-Century Italy*, trans. Lydia G. Cochrane (Princeton, N.J.: Princeton University Press, 1995), 169; but cf. Anna Cento Bull, *Italian Neofascism: The Strategy of Tension and the Politics of Nonreconciliation* (Oxford: Beghahn Books, 2007), 2–5.

44. Lumley, *States of Emergency*, 109–18; Colombo, "The Italian Left in the 1970s," 59.

45 Clark, *Modern Italy*, 384–85; Ginsborg, *A History of Contemporary Italy*, 333–37; Lumley, *States of Emergency*, 384–87; Colombo, "The Italian Left in the 1970s," 59–60.

46. Clark, *Modern Italy*, 388.

47. Ginsborg, *A History of Contemporary Italy*, 354–58.

48. Franco "Bifo" Berardi, "Anatomy of Autonomy," *Autonomia: Post-Political Politics*, ed. Sylvère Lotringer and Christian Marazzi (New York: Semiotext[e], 2007), 158.

49. Henri Weber, "In the Beginning was Gramsci," *Autonomia: Post-Political Politics*, 87. On the "Gentilian" interpretation of Gramsci that predominated in the PCI during these years, see Antonio Negri and Cesare Casarino, *In Praise of the Common: A Conversation on Philosophy and Politics* (Minneapolis: University of Minnesota Press, 2008), 46, 160–74.

50. Berardi, "Anatomy of Autonomy," *Autonomia: Post-Political Politics*, 153.

51. John Goodman, *Monetary Sovereignty: The Politics of Central Banking in Western Europe* (Ithaca, N.Y.: Cornell University Press, 1992), 162.

52. Piero Ignazi, "Italy in the 1970s between Self-Expression and Organicism," trans. Anna Cento Bull and Mark Donavan, *Speaking Out and Silencing: Culture, Society, and Politics in Italy in the 1970s* (Oxford: Legenda, 2006), 11.

53. Sylvère Lotringer, "In the Shadow of the Red Brigades," *Autonomia: Post-Political Politics*, xiv.

54. See, on this point, Bobbio, *Ideological Profile of Twentieth-Century Italy*, 170; Yann Moulier, "Introduction," in Antonio Negri, *The Politics of Subversion: A Manifesto for the Twenty-First Century*, trans. James Newell (Cambridge: Polity Press, 1989), 1–44; Sylvère Lotringer, "Foreward: We, The Multitude," in *A Grammar of the Multitude: For an Analysis of Contemporary Forms of Life*, trans. Isabelle Bertoletti, James Cascaito, and Andrea Casson, ed. Paolo Virno (New York: Semiotext[e] Foreign Agents Series, 2004), 8; Negri and Casarino, *In Praise of the Common*, 49–53.

55. Colombo, "The Italian Left in the 1970s," 60–62.

56. Ginsborg, *A History of Contemporary Italy*, 385–86; Lumley, *States of Emergency*, 279–93; Colombo, "The Italian Left in the 1970s," 63–64.

57. See, for example, Casarino and Negri, *In Praise of the Common*, 41–61.

58. See Lotringer, "In the Shadow of the Red Brigades," *Autonomia: Post-Political Politics*, xiii–xv; Berardi, "Anatomy of Autonomy," *Autonomia: Post-Political Politics*, 158–59.

59. See, for example, "Negri's Interrogation," *Autonomia: Post-Political Politics*, 188–94; Dario Fo, "The Sandstorm Method," *Autonomia: Post-Political Politics*, 214–16. According to Berardi, "The Bologna movement (the so-called 'creative wing') recognized without hesitation the contradiction between terrorism and the mass movement" (Berardi, "Anatomy of Autonomy," *Autonomia: Post-Political Politics*, 162). See also Lotringer, "In the Shadow of the Red Brigades," *Autonomia: Post-Political Politics*, xv.

60. See, in general, Alessandro Carrera, "On Massimo Cacciari's Disenchanted Activism," in *The Unpolitical: On the Radical Critique of Political Reason*, trans. Massimo Verdicchio, ed. Alessandro Carrera (New York: Fordham University Press, 2009), 1–43; Antonio Negri, *Books for Burning: Between Civil War and Democracy in 1970s Italy*, trans. Arianna Bove et al. (New York: Verso, 2005), 118–79; Antonio Negri, "Between 'Historic Compromise' And Terrorism: Reviewing the Experience of Italy in the 1970s," trans. Ed Emery, *Le Monde Diplomatique* (September 1998), http://mondediplo.com/1998/09/11negri (last checked January 19, 2009); Lucio Castellano et al., "Do You Remember Revolution?" in *Radical Thought in Italy: A Potential Politics*, ed. Paolo Virno and Michael Hardt (Minneapolis: University of Minnesota Press, 1996), 225–38.

61. See, on this point, Norberto Bobbio, *Left and Right: Significance of a Political Distinction*, trans. Allan Cameron (Chicago: University of Chicago Press, 1996), 18–19.

62. Bobbio, "Italy's Permanent Crisis," 128.

63. Carl Schmitt, *Le categorie del "politico": saggi di teoria politica*, ed. Gianfranco Miglio and Pierangelo Schiera (Bologna: Società editrice il Mulino, 1972).

64. Carlo Galli, "Carl Schmitt nella cultura italiana (1924–1978): Storia, bilancio, prospettive di una presenza problematica," *Materiali per una storia della cultura giuridica* 9:1 (1979), 120.

65. Galli, "Carl Schmitt nella cultura italiana," 82. See also, generally, Carlo Galli, "Carl Schmitt in Italia: Una Bibliografia," in *La political oltre lo Stato: Carl Schmitt,* ed. Giuseppe Duso (Venice: Aresnale, 1981), 169–81.

66. Galli, "Carl Schmitt nella cultura italiana," 137, see also 128 and 139. See also Galli, *Genealogia* (2010), 55–56; cf. Jan-Werner Müller, *A Dangerous Mind: Carl Schmitt in Post-War European Thought* (New Haven, Conn.: Yale University Press, 2003), 178.

67. Galli, "Carl Schmitt nella cultura italiana," 154.

68. Jürgen Habermas, *The New Conservatism: Cultural Criticism and the Historians' Debate*, trans. and ed. Shierry Weber Nicholsen (Cambridge, Mass.: Massachusetts Institute of Technology Press, 1997), 138.

69. Karl Löwith, "The Occasional Decisionism of Carl Schmitt," in *Martin Heidegger and European Nihilism*, trans. Gary Steiner, ed. Richard Wolin (New York: Columbia University Press, 1998), 141, 157.

70. Löwith, "The Occasional Decisionism of Carl Schmitt," 141, 146.

71. Löwith, "The Occasional Decisionism of Carl Schmitt," 138, 142.

72. Löwith, "The Occasional Decisionism of Carl Schmitt," 142–3, 158.

73. Löwith, "The Occasional Decisionism of Carl Schmitt," 144.

74. Löwith, "The Occasional Decisionism of Carl Schmitt," 137.

75. Löwith, "The Occasional Decisionism of Carl Schmitt," 158–59.

76. Carlo Galli, "Prefazione," in Karl Löwith, *Il nichilismo europeo: Considerazioni sugli antefatti spirituali della guerra europea*, ed. Carlo Galli (Rome-Bari: Editori Laterza, 2006), xxv.

77. See Carlo Galli, "Presentazione," in Carl Schmitt, *Romanticismo politico*, trans. and ed. Carlo Galli (Milan: Giuffrè, 1981), xxvii. On the relation between the concept of *kairòs* and the problem of "crisis" in Marxist thought, see Cesare Casarino, "Time Matters: Marx, Negri, Agamben, and the Corporeal," in *In Praise of the Common*, 219–45.

78. See, for example, Søren Kierkegaard, *Philosophical Fragments Or, a Fragment of Philosophy*, trans. Howard V. Hong and Edna H. Hong (Princeton, N.J.: Princeton University Press, 1985), 9–36, esp. 24–25.

79. Reinhart Koselleck, *Critique and Crisis: Enlightenment and the Pathogenesis of Modern Society*, trans. Maria Santos (Cambridge, Mass.: Massachusetts Institute of Technology Press, 1988), 174.

80. Immanuel Kant, *Critique of Pure Reason*, trans. and ed. Paul Guyer and Allen Wood (Cambridge, U.K.: Cambridge University Press, 1998), 271–77.

81. Carlo Galli, *Lo sguardo di Giano. Saggi su Carl Schmitt* (Bologna: Il Mulino, 2008), 121.

82. Galli, "Carl Schmitt nella cultura italiana," 150, 154; cf. Galli, *Lo sguardo di Giano*, 48. Galli draws on this same undersanding of criticism in his commentary on the political thought of Hannah Arendt. See Carlo Galli, "Hannah Arendt e le categorie politiche della modernità," in *La pluralità irrappresentabile. Il pensiero politico di Hannah Arendt*, ed. Roberto Esposito (Urbino: Edizioni QuattroVenti, 1987), 16.

83. Roberto Racinaro, "Carl Schmitt e la genealogia della politica," *Filosofia politica* 1:1 (April 1997), 130.

84. Galli, "Schmitt nella cultura italiana," 154.

85. Galli, "Schmitt nella cultura italiana," 92, 96, 101–2.

86. Galli, "Schmitt nella cultura italiana," 150, 154.

87. As Galli would put it in a 2005 summary of Schmittian thought, "'*The political*' and '*politics*' are not synonyms: the first term indicates a conflictual energy,

the second an institutional architecture. The Schmittian theory of the 'political' as the origin of politics thus signifies that *politics is always polemical*, never neutral, both in its concepts and in its institutional reality, and that the State, if it is really to be a political entity, should possess and exercise the capacity to distinguish friend from foe, the inside from the outside" (Galli, Greblo, and Mezzadra, *Il pensiero politico del Novecento*, 147, emphasis in original).

88. Löwith, "The Occasional Decisionism of Carl Schmitt," 147, 154.

89. Carlo Galli, "Il cattolicesimo nel pensiero politico di Carl Schmitt," in *Tradizione e Modernità nel pensiero politico di Carl Schmitt*, ed. Roberto Racinaro (Rome-Naples: Edizioni Scientifiche Italiene, 1987), 15.

90. Galli, "Carl Schmitt nella cultura italiana," 155.

91. Carl Schmitt, "Premessa all'edizione italiana," in *Le categorie del "politico"*, trans. Pierangelo Schiera, 25–26.

92. Carlo Galli, "La guerra nel pensiero politico di Carl Schmitt," *La Nottola* 1–2 (1986), 150.

93. Galli, *Lo sguardo di Giano*, 10.

94. Max Horkheimer and Theodor Adorno, "Preface (1944 and 1947)," *Dialectic of Enlightenment: Philosophical Fragments*, trans. Gunzelin Schmid Noerr (Stanford, Calif.: Stanford University Press, 2002), xvi. Compare Galli, *Political Spaces and Global War*, Chapter 5: "Dialectics and Equilibriums ('The Dialectical Structure of Place')" and Chapter 6: "The Twentieth Century ('Totalitarianism')."

95. Galli, "Carl Schmitt nella cultura italiana," 153.

96. Galli, "Carl Schmitt nella cultura italiana," 153.

97. Galli, *Genealogia* (2010), 847–48.

98. Hannah Arendt, "Organized Guilt and Responsibility," in *Essays in Understanding, 1930–1954: Formation, Exile, and Totalitarianism*, ed. Jerome Kohn (New York: Schocken, 1994), 128. According to Galli, "Since the end of 1936, the Nazi regime strongly suspected [Schmitt] not only because of power struggles in the highest levels and within the Ministry of Justice, but also for Schmitt's basic inability to assimilate, despite his own efforts, the regime's *völkisch* ideology. Schmitt nevertheless dedicated himself to serving that regime, although opportunistically, and only in 1944 did he begin to 'prudently' distance himself from his decision." See Galli, *Lo sguardo di Giano*, 120.

99. Hannah Arendt, *The Life of the Mind, Volume 1: Thinking* (New York: Harcourt, Brace, and Jovanovich, 1978), 4–5, 13, 179–80.

100. Theodor Adorno, *History and Freedom: Lectures 1964–1965*, trans. Rodney Livingstone, ed. Rolf Tiedemann (Cambridge, Mass.: Polity Press, 2006), 92.

101. See Galli, "Presentazione," *Romanticismo politico*, v–xxxi; Carlo Galli, "Presentazione dell'edizione italiana," in Carl Schmitt, *Amleto o Ecuba*, trans. Simona Forti (Bologna: Il Mulino, 1983), 7–35; Carlo Galli, "Introduzione," in Carl Schmitt,

Scritti su Thomas Hobbes, trans. and ed. Carlo Galli (Milan: Giuffrè, 1986), 1–44; Carlo Galli, "Presentazione," in Carl Schmitt, *Cattolicesimo romano e forma politica*, trans. and ed. Carlo Galli (Milan: Giuffrè, 1986), 3–27; Galli, "La guerra nel pensiero politico di Carl Schmitt," 145–58; Galli, "Il cattolicesimo nel pensiero politico di Carl Schmitt," 13–25; Carlo Galli, "Ernst Jünger e Carl Schmitt: per la ricostruzione di due modalità del nichilismo contemporaneo," *Studi politici in onore di Luigi Firpo*, ed. S. Rota Ghibaudi and F. Barcia (Milan: Angeli, 1990), 963–86.

102. Geminello Preterossi, "L'indeducibilità dell'origine: Tra Schmitt e Hegel," *Iride: Filosofia e discussione pubblica* 3 (1997), 574.

103. Galli, *Genealogia* (2010), xxv–xxvi, xxviii.

104. Galli, *Genealogia* (2010), xxvi.

105. Galli, *Genealogia* (2010), xiv–xv, xxv. Here too Galli's contribution may be understood in schematic terms as a radicalization of Löwith's 1935 critique of Schmitt in light of Löwith's own later writings on the problem of mediation in Kierkegaard, Marx, and Nietzsche. See Galli, "Prefazione," in Löwith, *Il nichilismo europeo*, ix–xv.

106. Galli, *Genealogia* (2010), xv.

107. Galli, *Genealogia* (2010), xvi.

108. On the "tragicity" of Schmittian thought, see Galli, "La guerra nel pensiero politico di Carl Schmitt," 146 n4. See also Galli, *Genealogia* (2010), xxxii, 10; Carlo Galli, "Contaminazioni: Irruzioni del Nulla" in *Nichilismo e politica*, ed. Roberto Esposito, Carlo Galli, and Vincenzo Vitiello (Rome-Bari: Gius, Laterza, and Figli, 2000), 156 n7; Galli, *Lo sguardo di Giano*, 9, 11. Reviewers of Galli's *Genealogia* have not failed to note Galli's emphasis on the tragic quality of Schmittian thought as one of the hallmarks of Galli's specific contribution to Schmitt scholarship. See Vittorio Dini, "Oltre la mediazione. Origine, decisione, forma: il 'politico' schmittiano come lettura del Moderno," *Iride: Filosofia e discussione pubblica* 3 (1997), 571, 574; Giovanni Messina, "Genealogia della politica. Carl Schmitt e la crisi del pensiero politico moderno (Review)," *Rivista internazionale di filosofia del diritto* 75:3 (1998), 498; Racinaro, "Carl Schmitt e la genealogia della politica (Review)," 127; Danilo Zolo, "Schmitt e la ragione politica moderna," *Iride: Filosofia e discussione pubblica* 3 (1997), 577–78. This is not an emphasis one generally finds in Anglophone scholarship on Schmitt. See, for example, Christian Thornhill, "Carl Schmitt after the Deluge: A Review of Recent Literature," *History of European Ideas* 26 (2000), 225–64; Peter Caldwell, "Controversies over Carl Schmitt: A Review of Recent Literature," *The Journal of Modern History* 77 (2005), 357–87.

109. Galli, *Genealogia* (2010), xiv.

110. Galli, *Genealogia* (2010), xiv.

111. Galli, *Genealogia* (2010), xvii.

112. Galli, "Schmit nella cultura italiana," 153.

113. Galli, *Political Spaces and Global War*, Chapter 6: "The Twentieth Century: Crisis and Restoration ('Schmitt')"; Carlo Galli, "Introduzione," in *Guerra*, ed. Carlo Galli (Rome-Bari: Laterza, 2004), xxv.

114. Galli, *Lo sguardo di Giano*, 123.

115. Galli, *Genealogia* (2010), 239–40, 244–45; cf. Galli, "Presentazione," *Cattolicesimo romano*, 13–14.

116. Galli, *Genealogia* (2010), 242, 245.

117. Galli, *Genealogia* (2010), 4–5.

118. Galli, *Genealogia* (2010), 11; cf. Carlo Galli, *Modernità: Categorie e profili critici* (Bologna: Il Mulino, 1988), 8.

119. Carlo Galli, "La 'macchina' della modernità: metafisica e contingenza nel moderno pensiero politico," in *Logiche e crisi della modernità* (Bologna: Il Mulino, 1991), 113–20.

120. Galli, "Presentazione," *Cattolicesimo romano*, 13.

121. Galli, "Presentazione," *Cattolicesimo romano*, 24.

122. Galli, *Genealogia* (2010), 254.

123. Carlo Galli, "Carl Schmitt's Antiliberalism: Its Theoretical and Historical Sources and Its Philosophical and Political Meaning," *Cardozo Law Review* 5–6 (May 2000), 1598, 1608–9, 1611; Carlo Galli, "Carl Schmitt on Sovereignty: Decision, Form, Modernity," in *Penser la Souveraineté à l'époque modern et contempporaine*, Vol. 2, ed. G. M. Cazzaniga and Y. C. Zarka (Pisa-Paris: Edizioni Ets-Libraire Philosophoque J. Vrin, 2001), 465.

124. Galli, "Carl Schmitt on Sovereignty," 469, 473.

125. See Galli, "Il cattolicesimo nel pensiero politico di Carl Schmitt," 21–23.

126. Galli, "Schmitt's Antiliberalism," 1599.

127. Galli, "Schmitt's Antiliberalism," 1604. See also Galli, "Carl Schmitt on Sovereignty," 463–64.

128. Galli, "Carl Schmitt on Sovereignty," 467, 470.

129. On these terms, there is no longer any contradiction or inconsistency (as Löwith and many after him have argued) between Schmitt's criticism of political romanticism and his affirmation of the exception. The speechlessness—the absence of morphogenetic power—that the political romantic disavows with endless chatter is the same "speechlessness" (or, in Kierkegaardian terms, the "inability to explain") that confronts reason each and every time it tries to think the exception. As Galli observes in his 1983 introduction to the Italian translation of Schmitt's "Hamlet or Hecuba," Schmitt's interest in Prince Hamlet is simply an attempt to inquire into this same speechlessness from the opposite side. In the silence of his indecisionism, Galli argues, "Hamlet is the tragic counterpart to Romantic indecisionism" (Galli, "Presentazione dell'edizione italiana," 12, 19, 34).

See also Galli, "Carl Schmitt nella cultura italiana," 89; Galli, *Genealogia* (2010), 212, 218; Galli, "Carl Schmitt on Sovereignty," 468–69.

130. Galli, *Lo sguardo di Giano*, 7.

131. Galli, *Genealogia* (2010), xi–xii. See also Balakrishnan, *The Enemy*, 259; Müller, *A Dangerous Mind*, 2; Ellen Kennedy, *Constitutional Failure: Carl Schmitt in Weimar* (Durham, N.C.: Duke University Press, 2004), 5.

132. Galli, *Genealogia* (2010), xiii–xiv.

133. Carl Schmitt, *Political Theology: Four Chapters on the Concept of Sovereignty*, trans. George Schwab (Chicago: University of Chicago Press, 2005), 5.

134. On this style of Schmitt commentary, see Andrew Norris, "*Sovereignty and Its Discontents: On the Primacy of Conflict and the Structure of the Political*, by William Rasch (Review)," *Constellations* 13:1 (2006), 131–34.

135. See, for example, Scott Horton, "State of Exception: Bush's War on the Rule of Law," *Harper's Magazine* 315 (July 2007), 80–81.

136. On this point, there is a pronounced difference between Galli's approach and the very best of Anglophone Schmitt studies. On the questions left open by Balakrishnan's interpretation of the relation between *Political Theology* and *Roman Catholicism and Political Form*, see Andrew Norris, "A Mine That Explodes Silently: Carl Schmitt in Weimar and After," *Political Theory* 33:6 (December 2005), 893.

137. Friedrich Nietzsche, *Jenseits von Gut und Böse: Vorspiel einer Philosophie der Zukunft* (Leipzig: Alfred Kröner, 1930), 4–5. This is not to imply that Schmitt is a direct disciple of Nietzsche, only that he writes in the wake of Nietzsche's critique of monotheism. See Galli, *Genealogia* (2010), 129–30.

138. Galli, *Genealogia* (2010), 153–55. See also Galli, *Political Spaces and Global War*, Chapter 6: "The Twentieth Century ('Negative Thought and the Space of Nothing')."

139. Martin Heidegger, *Basic Concepts of Ancient Philosophy*, trans. Richard Rojcewicz (Bloomington: Indiana University Press, 2008), 79; Martin Heidegger, *The Essence of Truth*, trans. Ted Sadler (New York: Continuum, 2002), 125–26.

140. Heidegger, *The Essence of Truth*, 69–84.

141. See, on this point, Roberto Esposito, *Categorie dell'impolitico*, second edition (Bologna: Il Mulino, 1999), 43.

142. Galli, *Genealogia* (2010), 342–43.

143. Galli, *Genealogia* (2010), xvi.

144. Galli, *Genealogia* (2010), xvi–xvii, emphasis in original.

145. Galli, *Genealogia* (2010), 876. Galli does not, to be clear, deny that the concept of the *nomos* marks a specific phase within Schmittian thought (see, for example, Galli, *Political Spaces and Global War*, Chapter 6: "The Twentieth Century ('Schmitt')"; Galli, *Lo sguardo di Giano*, 137). He simply dissents to the notion that this phase is discontinuous with Schmitt's earlier phases.

146. Galli, *Genealogia* (2010), 908 n43.

147. Galli, *Lo sguardo di Giano*, 140.

148. Frederic Jameson, "Notes on the *Nomos*," *The South Atlantic Quarterly* 104:2 (2005), 200.

149. Carl Schmitt, *The Nomos of the Earth in the International Law of Jus Publicum Europæum*, trans. G. L. Ulmen (New York: Telos Press Publishing, 2006), 326, 345–46.

150. Galli, *Genealogia* (2010), 880.

151. Galli, *Genealogia* (2010), 875.

152. Arturo Leyte puts it well: Schmitt's purpose in turning to this term is that "one can speak of *nomos* only to say that one cannot say anything about it," that "*nomos* is precisely that which in itself cannot be thematized." Arturo Leyte, "A Note on *The Nomos of the Earth*," trans. Virginia Tuma, *The South Atlantic Quarterly* 104:2 (2005), 289.

153. Galli, *Genealogia* (2010), 882.

154. Galli, "La guerra nel pensiero politico di Carl Schmitt," 146. On Heidegger's account of *polemos* and *polis*, cf. Martin Heidegger, *Hölderlin's Hymn "The Ister"*, trans. William McNeill and Julia Davis (Bloomington: Indiana University Press, 1996), 79–83; Galli et al., *Il pensiero politico del Novecento*, 144. Galli does not, in other words, agree with Emmanuel Faye's claim that there was "agreement" between Schmitt and Heidegger over the concept of *polemos*. See Emmannuel Faye, *Heidegger: The Introduction of Nazism into Philosophy in Light of the Unpublished Seminars of 1933–1935*, trans. Michael B. Smith (New Haven, Conn.: Yale University Press, 2009), 154.

155. Galli, "La guerra nel pensiero politico di Carl Schmitt," 151.

156. Galli, "La guerra nel pensiero politico di Carl Schmitt," 146–47.

157. Galli, "Introduzione," *Guerra*, xxvi.

158. Galli, *Lo sguardo di Giano*, 11–12.

159. Carl Schmitt, *Roman Catholicism and Political Form*, trans. G. L. Ulmen (Westport, Conn.: Greenwood Press, 1996), 5.

160. Galli, *Lo sguardo di Giano*, 7.

161. Galli, *Lo sguardo di Giano*, 7.

162. On "reliquefication," see Theodor Adorno, *Negative Dialectics*, trans. E. B. Ashton (New York: Continuum, 1981), 97.

163. Lucio Castellano, "Living with Guerilla Warfare," *Autonomia: Post-Political Politics*, 230–31.

164. Bobbio, "Italy's Permanent Crisis," 123.

165. Fasanella and Pellegrino, *La guerra civile*, 61.

166. Étienne Balibar, "What's in a War? (Politics as War, War as Politics)," *Ratio Juris* 21:3 (September 2008), 367–68.

167. Lanfranco Pace and Franco Piperno, "On the Recognition of the Armed Struggle," in *Autonomia: Post-Political Politics*, 240–43.

168. Massimo Cacciari, "Sorry, It's Exactly the Opposite," in *Autonomia: Post-Political Politics*, 245.

169. See Giorgio Agamben, "Du bon usage de la mémoire et de l'oubli," trans. Y. Moulier-Boutang, in Antonio Negri, *Exil* (Paris: Mille et une Nuits, 1998), 57–60.

170. Galli, *Lo sguardo di Giano*, 156.

171. Carl Schmitt, "La guerra civile fredda," *Il Borghese* 21 (November 1, 1951), 657. For the publication history of this little text, which first appeared anonymously in 1949, see Carl Schmitt, "Amnestie oder die Kraft des Vergessens," in *Staat, Grossraum, Nomos: Arbeiten aus den Jahren 1916–1969*, ed. Günter Maschke (Berlin: Duncker and Humblot, 1995), 220.

172. Galli, *Genealogia* (2010), 11.

173. According to Norberto Bobbio, the crisis of the 1970s was not limited to the spread of political violence, but extended to include the Italian government's response to that violence. For Bobbio, as for Agamben, the crisis of the 1970s remains incomprehensible if one forgets the degree to which the exception became the norm during these years. Bobbio argues that in the 1970s, there was a rapid increase in the dissolution of parliaments and the premature closing of legislature, the passage of emergency decrees (including preventative detention), and the passage of referenda. This "crisis of parliamentary democracy," Bobbio argued, resulted less in a "crisis of institutions" than in "an institutionalization of crisis." See Bobbio, "Italy's Permanent Crisis," 124–28.

174. Paul Virilio, *Speed and Politics: An Essay on Dromology*, trans. Mark Polizzotti (New York: Semiotext[e], 1986), 125.

175. Up to and including the bleached-out and exhausted rhetoric of "crisis" itself. As Robin Wagner-Pacifici has argued, the term "crisis" is so overused to describe this period of Italian politics that this very overuse—the exhaustion and meaningless of the very term "crisis"—is itself worthy of study (*The Moro Morality Play: Terrorism as Social Drama* [Chicago: University of Chicago Press, 1986], 22). Much the same holds for Weimar Germany, in which the concept of "crisis" also dominated thought (see, on this point, Peter Gordon, *Continental Divide: Heidegger, Cassirer, Davos* [Cambridge, Mass.: Harvard University Press, 2010], 43–44). In this respect, we may say that Galli's own turn in 1979 to the archaic concept of *occasio* is *itself* occasioned by this crisis of the term and concept "crisis," its inflation into meaninglessness.

176. Lotringer, "In the Shadow of the Red Bridges," *Autonomia: Post-Political Politics*, xiv; Sylvère Lotringer and Christian Marazzi, "The Return of Politics," *Autonomia: Post-Political Politics*, 12.

177. The United States, it is worth recalling, had a direct role in the making of the "years of lead." According to Timothy Weiner, in 1970, the Central Intelligence Agency (C.I.A.) received "formal approval from the Nixon White House" to oversee the distribution of $25 million to both Christian Democrats and Italian neofascists. "The money," Wiener writes, "helped finance right-wing covert operations—including terrorist bombings, which Italian intelligence blamed on the extreme left." See Timothy Weiner, *Legacy of Ashes: The History of the C.I.A.* (New York: Random House, 2007), 298–300.

178. Ashis Nandy, *The Intimate Enemy: Loss and Recovery of Self Under Colonialism* (Delhi: Oxford University Press, 1983), xiv.

179. Achille Mbembe, "Necropolitics," trans. Libby Meintjes, *Public Culture* 15:1 (Winter 2003), 24.

180 Compare, on this point, Roger Trinquier, *Modern Warfare: A French View of Counterinsurgency*, trans. Daniel Lee (New York: Praeger, 1963); Eqbal Ahmad, "Counterinsurgency," in *The Selected Writings of Eqbal Ahmad*, ed. Carollee Bengelsdorf, Margaret Cerullo, and Yogesh Chandrani (New York: Columbia University Press, 2006), 36–64.

181. See David Harvey, *Condition of Post-Modernity: An Enquiry into the Origins of Cultural Change* (Cambridge, Mass.: Blackwell, 1990), vii, 121–24, 141–97; Harvey, *A Brief History*, 1–2.

182. See George Schwab, *The Challenge of the Exception: An Introduction to the Political Ideas of Carl Schmitt between 1921 and 1936*, second edition (New York: Greenwood Press, 1989); Chantal Mouffe, ed., *The Challenge of Carl Schmitt* (New York: Verso Books, 1999).

183. Carlo Galli, *Spazi politici. L'età moderna e l'età globale* (Bologna: Il Mulino, 2001); Carlo Galli, *La guerra globale* (Rome-Bari: Laterza, 2002).

184. Galli, *Political Spaces and Global War*, Chapter 7: "Globalization ('Global Mobilization and "Glocalism"')" and Part II: "Global War ('Extreme Theology')."

185. Alexandre Koyré, *From the Closed World to the Infinite Universe* (New York: Harper & Row, 1957), 5–27; Michel Foucault, *The Order of Things: An Archaeology of the Human Sciences*, trans. Alan Sheridan (New York: Vintage Books, 1970), 67–71.

186. Galli, *Political Spaces and Global War*, Chapter 1: "Premodern Political Spaces and Their Crises ('Political Geographies')," Chapter 2: "Responses from Political Thought ('Hobbes')."

187. Galli, *Political Spaces and Global War*, Chapter 1: "Premodern Political Spaces and Their Crises."

188. Galli, *Political Spaces and Global War*, Chapter 3: "Political Geometries."

189. Benjamin, "Theses on the Philosophy of History," 261.

190. James Scott, *Seeing Like a State: How Certain Schemes to Improve the Human Condition Have Failed* (New Haven, Conn.: Yale University Press, 1998), 11–52.

191. Galli, *Political Spaces and Global War*, Chapter 2: "Responses from Political Thought ('Hobbes')."

192. Galli, *Political Spaces and Global War*, Chapter 4: "Modern Universals ('The Universal Categories of Modernity and Their Contradictions')," Chapter 7: "Globalization," and Part II: "Global War ('Two Empires, One Question' and 'War and Space')."

193. Galli, *Political Spaces and Global War*, Chapter 7: "Globalization ('Politics')." See also Carlo Galli, "On War and the Enemy," trans. Amanda Minervini and Adam Sitze, *CR: The New Centennial Review* 9:2 (2009), 214.

194. Galli, *Political Spaces and Global War*, Chapter 6: "The Twentieth Century: Crisis and Restoration ('Total Mobilization')."

195. Galli, *Political Spaces and Global War*, Chapter 7: "Globalization ('Global Mobilization and "Glocalism"')."

196. Theodor Adorno, *Hegel: Three Studies*, trans. Shierry Weber Nicholsen (Cambridge, Mass.: Massachusetts Institute of Technology Press, 1993), 44, 82–87.

197. Michael Hardt and Antonio Negri, *Multitude* (New York: Penguin Books, 2002), 3–95, 360 n9.

198. For non-presentist accounts of emergency power in U.S. law and politics, see William Scheuerman, "Globalization and Exceptional Powers: The Erosion of Liberal Democracy," *Radical Philosophy* 93 (January/February 1999), 14–23; William Scheuerman, "The Economic State of Emergency," *Cardozo Law Review* 21 (5/6), 1869–94; Nasser Hussain, "Beyond Norm and Exception: Guantanamo," *Critical Inquiry* 33:4 (2007), 734–53; Bonnie Honig, *Emergency Politics: Paradox, Law, Democracy* (Princeton, N.J.: Princeton University Press, 2009), 65–86 ("Decision").

199. Schmitt, "The Plight of European Jurisprudence," 36–37.

200. William Scheuerman, *Liberal Democracy and the Social Acceleration of Time* (Baltimore, Md.: Johns Hopkins University Press, 2004).

201. On the necessary relation between the "spirit of commerce" and perpetual peace, see Immanuel Kant, "Toward Perpetual Peace: A Philosophical Project," in *Practical Philosophy*, trans. and ed. Mary Gregor (Cambridge, U.K.: Cambridge University Press, 1996), 331–37 ("First Supplement: On the Guarantee of Perpetual Peace"). For an early neoliberal reiteration of this claim, see Ludwig von Mises,

Liberalism: The Classical Tradition (Indianapolis, Ind.: The Liberty Fund, 2005), 81–87. On the necessary connection between free trade and perpetual war in the thought of von Mises, see Warren Montag, "War and the Market: The Place of the Global South in the Origins of Neo-Liberalism," *The Global South* 3:1 (Spring 2009), 126–38. See also Galli, *Political Spaces and Global War*, Part II: "Global War ('Indistinctness and Asymmetry')."

202. Paul Virilio and Sylvère Lotringer, *Pure War*, trans. Mark Polizzotti (New York: Semiotext[e], 1997), 9–17.

203. See, on this point, Norris, "A Mine That Explodes Silently," 887–88.

204. See Carl Schmitt, *Hamlet or Hecuba: The Intrusion of the Time into the Play*, trans. David Pan and Jennifer R. Rust (New York: Telos Press, Ltd., 2009); Carl Schmitt, *Political Theology II: The Myth of the Closure of any Political Theology*, trans. Michael Hoelzl and Graham Ward (Malden, Mass.: Polity Press, 2008); Carl Schmitt, *The Leviathan in the State Theory of Thomas Hobbes: Meaning and Failure of a Political Symbol*, trans. George Schwab and Erna Hilfstein (Chicago: University of Chicago Press, 2008); Carl Schmitt, *The Concept of the Political: Expanded Edition*, trans. George Schwab (Chicago: University of Chicago Press, 2007); Carl Schmitt, *Constitutional Theory*, trans. Jeffrey Seitzer (Durham, N.C.: Duke University Press, 2007); Carl Schmitt, *Theory of the Partisan: Intermediate Commentary on the Concept of the Political*, trans. G. L. Ulmen (New York: Telos Press, 2007); Schmitt, *Political Theology*; Schmitt, *Nomos of the Earth*; Carl Schmitt, *Legality and Legitimacy*, trans. Jeffrey Seitzer (Durham, N.C.: Duke University Press, 2004); Carl Schmitt, *On the Three Types of Juristic Thought*, trans. Joseph Benderesky (Westport, Conn.: Greenwood Press, 2004).

205. Galli, "La pensabilità della politica," 8. See also Galli, "Carl Schmitt's Antiliberalism," 1617; Galli, *Political Spaces and Global War*, Chapter 7: "Globalization ('Liberty')."

206. And in this, Galli's text constituted a response *avant la lettre* to Derrida's 2003 call for a "*critical* reading of Schmitt." See Jacques Derrida, "Autoimmunity: Real and Symbolic Suicides," in Giovanna Borradori, *Philosophy in a Time of Terror: Dialogues with Jürgen Habermas and Jacques Derrida* (Chicago: University of Chicago Press, 2003), 100–1, emphasis in original. See also, on this point, Balibar, "What's in a War?," 370.

207. Galli, *Lo sguardo di Giano*, 11–12.

208. In this respect, "and" is both the most opaque *and* the most important word in the subtitle of Galli's *Spazi politici*: "The Modern Age and the Global Age."

209. For various iterations of this claim, see Galli, "Carl Schmitt's Antiliberalism," 1617; Galli, "Carl Schmitt on Sovereignty," 477; Galli, "La pensabilità della politica," 8; Galli, *Lo sguardo di Giano*, 12–13, 166–72. Galli's claim to this effect extends and

intensifies a similar critique of Schmitt set forth by Hans Blumenberg. See Hans Blumenberg, *The Legitimacy of the Modern Age*, trans. Robert Wallace (Cambridge, Mass.: Massachusetts Institute of Technology Press, 1985), 91.

210. Étienne Balibar, "Europe as Borderland," *Environment and Planning D: Society and Space* 27:2 (2009), 190.

211. Horkheimer and Adorno, "Preface (1944 and 1947)," *Dialectic of Enlightenment*, xvi.

212. Theodor Adorno, *Minima Moralia: Reflections on Damaged Life*, trans. Edmund Jephcott (New York: Verso Books, 1999), 192.

213. Adorno, *Minima Moralia*, 132.

214. Adorno, "Working Through the Past," 214, 222–23.

215. See Renato Cristi, "Hayek and Schmitt on the Rule of Law," *Canadian Journal of Political Science* 17:3 (1984), 521–35; William Scheuerman, "The Unholy Alliance of Carl Schmitt and Friedrich A. Hayek," in *Carl Schmitt: The End of Law* (Boston: Rowman & Littlefield Publishers, Inc., 1999), 209–24; Ralf Ptak, "Neoliberalism in Germany: Revisiting the Ordoliberal Foundations of the Social Market Economy," in *The Road from Mont Pèlerin: The Making of the Neoliberal Thought Directive*, ed. Philip Mirowski and Dieter Plehwe (Cambridge, Mass.: Harvard University Press, 2009), 111–22. For the opposite view, see Joseph Benderesky, "The Definite and the Dubious: Carl Schmitt's Influence on Conservative Political and Legal Theory in the U.S.," *Telos* 122 (2002), 33–47. On Hayek's influence on the Chicago School of Economics, see Rob van Horn and Philip Mirowski, "The Rise of the Chicago School and the Birth of Neoliberalism," in *The Road from Mont Pèlerin*, 139–78.

216. Naomi Klein, *The Shock Doctrine* (New York: Random House, Inc., 2007), 154.

217. Scheuerman, "The Unholy Alliance of Carl Schmitt and Friedrich A. Hayek," 224.

218. Antonio Negri, "Cartografie per muoversi del presente," *Il Manifesto* (May 4, 2001), 13.

219. Giorgio Agamben, *Homo Sacer: Sovereign Power and Bare Life*, trans. Daniel Heller-Roazen (Stanford, Calif.: Stanford University Press, 1998), 166–80.

220. Thomas Hobbes, *On the Citizen*, ed. Richard Tuck and Michael Silverthorne (Cambridge, U.K.: Cambridge University Press, 1998), 151; Thomas Hobbes, *Leviathan*, ed. Richard Tuck (Cambridge, U.K.: Cambridge University Press, 1996), 239–40.

221. See, on this point, David Harvey, "Space as a Key Word," in *Spaces of Global Capitalism: Towards a Theory of Uneven Development* (New York: Verso Books, 2006), 129.

222. There is, for example, no entry for Schmitt in Phil Hubbard, Rob Kitchin, and Gill Valentine, eds., *Key Thinkers on Space and Place* (London: Sage

Publications, Ltd., 2004). For an exception, see David Delaney, *The Spatial, the Legal and the Pragmatics of World-Making: Nomospheric Investigations* (New York: Routledge, 2010).

223. Carl Friedrich, *The Philosophy of Law in Historical Perspective*, second edition (Chicago: University of Chicago Press, 1963), 18–19; J. M. Kelley, *A Short History of Western Legal Theory* (Oxford: Oxford University Press, 1992), 19, 22, 25.

224. Hans-Georg Gadamer, *Dialogue and Dialectic: Eight Hermeneutical Studies on Plato*, trans. P. Christopher Smith (New Haven, Conn.: Yale University Press, 1980), 71.

225. See, for example, Schmitt, *Nomos of the Earth*, 329.

226. Huizinga's critique of Schmitt takes place in Johann Huizinga, *Homo Ludens: A Study of the Play-Element in Culture* (Boston: Beacon Press, 1950), 208–11. On Schmitt's esoteric polemic against Huizinga, see Galli, "Presentazione dell'edizione italiana," *Amleto o Ecuba*, 30–32. On Huizinga's reading of "play" in Plato's *Laws*, see *Homo Ludens*, 18–19, 27, 37, 159–60, 162, 211–12.

227. Plato, *Laws*, 714a (*"tēn toû noû dianomēn eponomazontas nomon"*).

228. See Plato, *Laws*, Volume 1: Books 1–6, trans. and ed. R. G. Bury (New York: G. P. Putnam's Son, 1926), 286–87 n1.

229. Eric Voegelin, *Plato* (Columbia: University of Missouri Press, 2000), 239 n8.

230. Schmitt, *Nomos of the Earth*, 70, 326–27, 345.

231. Plato, *Republic*, 525b1–c6.

232. Plato, *Laws*, 811d.

233. Plato, *Laws*, 817b–c.

234. Plato, *Laws*, 803c.

235. See, variously, Hannah Arendt, *Origins of Totalitarianism* (New York: Harcourt, Brace, and Jovanovich, 1972), 299; Leo Strauss, *The Argument and Action of Plato's Laws* (Chicago: University of Chicago Press, 1975), 129; Leo Strauss, *Philosophy and Law: Contributions to the Understanding of Maimonides and His Predecessors*, trans. E. Adler (Albany, N.Y.: SUNY Press, 1995), 76; Jacques Rancière "Ten Theses on Politics," *Theory & Event* 5:3 (2001), para. 17, cf. para. 9–10, http://muse.jhu.edu/journals/theory_and_event/v005/5.3ranciere.html (last checked January 2010).

236. See Cicero, *De Legibus*, trans. Clinton Walker Keyes (Cambridge, Mass.: Harvard University Press, 1928), 317, 321. Although Cicero explicitly positions Plato's *Laws* as the primary model for his *De Legibus*, he nevertheless departs from Plato quite markedly throughout his text. The passages we here consider, for example, derive much from Zeno's *Republic*. See, on this point, Andrew Dyck, *A Commentary on Cicero, De Legibus* (Ann Arbor: University of Michigan Press, 2004), 12, 46, 120.

237. Arendt, *On Revolution*, 178–80.

238. Learned men, Cicero argues, have determined that "law [*lex*] is the highest reason, implanted in Nature, which commands what ought to be done and forbids the opposite. This reason, when firmly fixed and fully developed in the human mind, is law [*lex*]. And so they believe that Law is intelligence, whose natural function it is to command right conduct and forbid wrongdoing. They think that this quality has derived its name in Greek from the idea of granting to every man his own, and in our language I believe it has been named from the idea of choosing [*legendo*]. For as they have attributed the idea of fairness [*aequitatis*] to the word law, so we have given it that of selection [*dilectus*], though both ideas properly belong to law" (I.vi.19). As Dyck notes, "Cicero does not specify how, if at all, … the etymologies of the Greek and Latin terms … are meant to relate to each other" (111).

239. On which point, see Jean-Pierre Baud, "Lex," in *Vocabulaire européen des philosophies*, 713.

240. Galli, *Genealogia* (2010), 769–71.

241. Schmitt, *Nomos of the Earth*, 76.

242. Schmitt, *Nomos of the Earth*, 71–72; Schmitt, "The Plight of European Jurisprudence," 36–37.

243. Schmitt, *Nomos of the Earth*, 342, cf. 71.

244. Schmitt, *Nomos of the Earth*, 67.

245. Ramona Nadoff, *Exiling the Poets: The Production of Censorship in Plato's Republic* (Chicago: University of Chicago Press, 2002), 37–66.

246. Schmitt, *Nomos of the Earth*, 76–77.

247. Schmitt, *Nomos of the Earth*, 77.

248. Schmitt, *Nomos of the Earth*, 78.

249. Schmitt, *Nomos of the Earth*, 343.

250. On Schmitt's reading of Spinoza, see Galli, *Lo sguardo di Giano*, 115–24.

251. Schmitt, *Nomos of the Earth*, 343–45, cf. 70 n10.

252. For Galli, we should note, Platonic political philosophy remains a privileged point of reference for the comprehension of the tragicity of Schmittian thought. As Galli puts it, "Politics is, for Plato, the 'royal science' that has no real object, but is nevertheless certain, because it not only has authority over science and its opportunities, but also supervises all the laws and their relation to justice. For Schmitt, by contrast, the only political science is knowledge of the origin—this origin that at once constructs and destroys political order. It is therefore precisely in contact with the thought of Plato that we see quite clearly what the tragedy of modernity is for Schmitt: it is the impossibility of identifying an ontological objectivity in politics, in the knowledge of politics, and therefore too of the relations between politics and war" (Galli, *Genealogia* (2010), 771). In other words, just

as "the objectivity of conflict implies the non-objectivity of science," so too does the non-objectivity of science imply the tragic impossibility of a politics free from war (or, in other words, the objectivity of conflict).

253. Schmitt, *Nomos of the Earth*, 70 n10.

254. Kant, *Critique of Pure Reason*, 677.

255. Cavarero, "Politicizing Theory," 506.

256. Arendt, *Life of the Mind, Volume 1*, 199.

257. Plato, *Republic*, 484b–484d4, 517b8, 520a5–520d4, 540a3–540c.

258. Galli, *Genealogia* (2010), xv; Galli, "Carl Schmitt's Antiliberalism," 1614. Cf. Löwith, "The Occasional Decisionism of Carl Schmitt," 144.

259. See, for example, Schmitt, *Nomos of the Earth*, 50 n1 (the political space of rhetoric is the *agora*; the political space of dialectics is the lyceum and the academy), 59 (there is no concept of peace absent a concrete political space), 66 (even nihilism itself has a *topos*), etc. The original German title of Schmitt's 1943 "testament" ("*Die geschichtliche Lage der europäischen Rechtswissenschaft*") also bears witness to this point. "*Lage*" has a distinct spatial sense (literally translated, it refers to a "situation" or "position") that Schmitt himself emphasizes in his opening critique of legal positivism (here, as in *Nomos of the Earth*, Schmitt's objection to positivism is that it dissolves any "spatial concreteness" to European international law [37]). The existing English translation ("The Plight of European Jurisprudence") captures the tone of Husserlian crisis that suffuses Schmitt's text, but only at the cost of replicating, in its obliteration of the spatial, the very crisis that Schmitt himself diagnosed and lamented.

260. Leo Strauss, *The City and Man* (Chicago: University of Chicago Press, 1964), 59.

261. Kelley, *The Human Measure*, 3.

262. Donna Haraway, "Situated Knowledges: The Science Question in Feminism and the Privilege of Partial Perspective," in *Simians, Cyborgs, and Women: The Reinvention of Nature* (New York: Routledge, 1991), 183–201; Gilles Deleuze and Félix Guattari, *What is Philosophy?*, trans. Hugh Tomlinson and Graham Burchell (New York: Columbia University Press, 1994), 85–113.

263. Arendt, *Life of the Mind, Volume 1*, 199.

264. David Harvey, "Cosmopolitanism and the Banality of Geographical Evils," *Public Culture* 12:2 (2000), 538, emphasis added.

265. Galli, *Political Spaces and Global War*, Introduction.

266. Kant, *Critique of Pure Reason*, 273. See also, on this point, Slavoj Žižek, *Welcome to the Desert of the Real! Five Essays on September and Related Dates* (New York: Verso Books, 2002), 109–10.

267. Immanuel Kant, "What Is Orientation in Thinking?" in *Political Writings*, trans. H. B. Nisbet, ed. Hans Reiss (Cambridge, U.K.: Cambridge University Press, 1991), 240, 243.

268. Gilles Deleuze, *Kant's Critical Philosophy*, trans. Hugh Tomlinson and Barbara Habberjam (Minneapolis: University of Minnesota Press, 1984), 18.

269. See, on this point, Rodolphe Gasché, "The Partisan and the Philosopher," *CR: The New Centennial Review* 4:3 (Winter 2004), 31 n3.

270. Saskia Sassen, *Territory, Authority, Rights: From Medieval to Global Assemblages* (Princeton, N.J.: Princeton University Press, 2006), 1–2, 7, 11–13.

271. Sassen, *Territory, Authority, Rights*, 5–6.

272. Sassen, *Territory, Authority, Rights*, 1–2.

273. Peter Sahlins, "*Territory, Authority, Rights: From Medieval to Global Assemblages*, by Saskia Sassen (Review)," *American Journal of Sociology* 112:6 (May 2007), 1934–35.

274. Schmitt, *Theory of the Partisan*, 85.

275. On this point, compare Jacques Derrida, *Politics of Friendship*, trans. George Collins (New York: Verso Books, 1997), 162–63 and Gasché, "The Partisan and the Philosopher," 26, but cf. 15.

276. Galli, *Political Spaces and Global War*, Introduction.

277. Carlo Galli, "Introduzione," Max Horkheimer and Theodor Adorno, *Dialettica dell'illuminismo* (Turin: Einaudi, 1997), vii–xliii. Reprinted as "Dialettica dell'illuminismo," in Galli, *Contingenza e necessità*, 167–208.

278. Galli, "Dialettica dell'illuminismo," 204.

279. Galli, "Dialettica dell'illuminismo," 181–82, emphasis added.

280. Galli, "Dialettica dell'illuminismo," 194.

281. Galli, "Dialettica dell'illuminismo," 181, emphasis added.

282. Galli, *Contingenza e necessità*, 4.

283. Galli, "Dialettica dell'illuminismo," 176.

284. Roberto Unger, *False Necessity: Anti-Necessitarian Social Theory in the Service of Radical Democracy*, New Edition (New York: Verso Books, 2001).

285. In the closing pages of his 1950 book *Ex Captivitate Salus*, which he wrote while imprisoned by American authorities in Germany, Schmitt wrote, "I am the last conscious advocate of the *jus publicum europæum*, its last teacher and researcher in an existential sense, and I experience its end like Benito Cereno experienced the voyage of the pirate ship. There is silence in this place and at this time. We do not need to be afraid of it. By being silent, we reflect upon ourselves and upon our divine origin" (*Ex Captivitate Salus. Erfahrungen der Zeit 1945/7* [Druck: Greven & Bechtold, Köln, 1950], 75).

286. Gayatri Chakravorty Spivak, "What Is Gender? Where Is Europe? Walking with Balibar," The Ursula Hirschmann Annual Lecture on Gender and Europe, European University Institute, Florence, Italy, April 21, 2005, 6, http://cadmus.iue.it/dspace/bitstream/1814/8066/1/RSCAS_DL_2006_UHL_Spivak.pdf (last checked February 19, 2010).

287. See, on this point, Esposito, *Categorie dell'impolitico*, 65–68.

288. Galli, *Political Spaces and Global War*, Introduction ("Objectives, Hypotheses, and Method").

289. Giorgio Agamben, *Profanations*, trans. Jeff Fort (New York: Zone Books, 2007), 74.

290. Agamben, *Profanations*, 87. Cf. Giorgio Agamben, *The Open: Man and Animal*, trans. Kevin Attell (Stanford, Calif.: Stanford University Press, 2004), 87, 92; Giorgio Agamben, *State of Exception*, trans. Kevin Attell (Chicago: University of Chicago Press, 2005), 64; Giorgio Agamben, *What Is an Apparatus?*, trans. David Kishik and Stefan Pedatella (Stanford, Calif.: Stanford University Press, 2009), 19.

291. Karl Marx, *The Communist Manifesto*, ed. Phil Gasper (Chicago: Haymarket Press, 2005), 44.

292. To avoid any misunderstandings, let us clarify here what Galli does *not* mean when he calls for a "new *nomos* of the Earth." There is in Fascism, as Klaus Theweleit has shown, a very clear and distinct mode of anxiety about the ability of floods to exercise a sort of "castrating fluidity." It does not follow from this, however, that all anxieties over fluidity are therefore also necessarily Fascist at root. Totalitarianism, as Hannah Arendt argued, operated on the assumption that, for it, "everything is possible." Galli's call for a "new *nomos* of the earth," by contrast, invites us to imagine a political space, and therefore too an experience of borders, in which "*not* everything is possible." This is less an invitation to "stabilize" space (as Arendt might put it) than a call to resist the alarming experience of "global mobilization," in which economic globalization sweeps up and drowns scores of "superfluous people" in its undertow. In theoretical terms, meanwhile, Galli's "new *nomos*" invites us to resist what Doreen Massey has called the new orthodoxy of "openness, movement, and flight"—to rethink, that is to say, the superficial valorization of Deleuzian "smooth space" that became fashionable in some academic circles during the 1990s, and that is today all the rage for the theorists of urban warfare. Indeed, the very fact that some readers may recoil at the very mention of a "new border" is itself symptomatic: It signifies the impoverishment of our ability today to think the conjunction of *nous* and *nomos* (as if the only two "schemata" available to us for the imagination of political space were completely bounded places, on the one hand, or absolutely wide-open deserts or seas, on the other), and confirms the extent to which the smooth space of "global mobilization" has today come to serve as a form of domination (as if borderlessness were somehow inevitable or even mandatory). See, variously, Klaus Theweleit, *Male Fantasies, Volume 1: Women, Floods, Bodies, History*, trans. Stephan Conway with Erica Carter and Chris Turner (Minneapolis: University of Minnesota Press, 1987), 229–309; Arendt, *Origins of Totalitarianism*,

427, 437, 440, 459, 463; Doreen Massey, *For Space* (London: Sage, 2005), 172–75; Eyal Weizman, *Hollow Land: Israel's Architecture of Occupation* (London: Verso, 2007), 187, 208–10.

293. Galli, *Political Spaces and Global War*, Introduction.

294. See, on this point, Andrea Fumagalli (on behalf of the UniNomade group in Bologna), "Nothing Will Ever Be the Same," in *Crisis in the Global Economy: Financial Markets, Social Struggles, and New Political Scenarios*, trans. Jason Francis McGimsey, ed. Andrea Fumagalli and Sandro Mezzadra (New York: Semiotext[e], 2010), 246–47.

295. Étienne Balibar, "Europe: Final Crisis? Some Theses," *Theory & Event* 13:2 (2010), para. 5, http://muse.jhu.edu/journals/theory_and_event/summary/ v013/13.2.balibar.html (last checked July 2010).

296. Balibar, "Europe: Final Crisis?," 5.

297. Étienne Balibar, *Politics and the Other Scene*, trans. Christine Jones, James Swenson, and Chris Turner (New York: Verso Books, 2002), 82; Étienne Balibar, *We, The People of Europe? Reflections on Transnational Citizenship*, trans. James Swenson (Princeton, N.J.: Princeton University Press, 2004), 43–45.

298. Aimé Césaire, *Discourse on Colonialism*, trans. Joan Pinkham (New York: Monthly Review, 1972), 11, 60–61.

299. See, for example, G. W. F. Hegel, *Hegel's Philosophy of Mind: Part 3 of the Encyclopædia of Philosophical Sciences*, trans. William Wallace and A. V. Miller (Oxford: Clarendon Press, 1971), 44–47; Galli, *Political Spaces and Global War*, Chapter 7: "Globalization ('Politics')."

300. For Galli's account of this concept, see *Contingenza e necessità*, 144–49.

301. Galli, *L'umanità multiculturale*, 48–49, 79–81. On multiculturalism as a problematization of the categories of modern political rationality, see also Carlo Galli, "Introduzione," *Multiculturalismo. Ideologie e sfide*, ed. Carlo Galli (Bologna: Il Mulino, 2006), 9, 20–21.

302. As Galli construes it, the concept of the "unpolitical" is not an "evasion of the logics of the political" (which are, Galli insists, "impossible to ignore"), but rather a "realistic acceptance of those logics that empties them of the necessity and the value they pretend to exhibit." The "unpolitical" is not, then, a synonym for the "post-political" or "apolitical" (and indeed, in Galli's view, the conflict between left and right over the meaning and force of the principle of equality is only going to intensify with the passage of the Modern). Put positively, the unpolitical is an attempt to think that which, in the contemporary experience of politics, political philosophy itself is, by virtue of its commitment to the necessity of the concept of the political, unable to think. In particular, as Giuseppe Cantarano has written, the concept of the unpolitical is "an invitation … not to elude the tragic dimension of the political."

This implies, above all, attention to the conflict that the tragic has always entailed, and that political philosophy has always sought to repress. See, variously, Esposito, *Categorie dell'impolitico*, vii–xxxii; Esposito, "La Politica al Presente," 14–19; Galli, "Pensare la politica," 5; Galli, "Dialettica dell'illuminismo," 205; Galli, *Perché ancora destra e sinistra*, 65; Giuseppe Cantarano, *Immagini del nulla. La filosofia italiana contemporanea* (Milan: Mondadori Bruno, 1998), 375 n117.

303. Schmitt, "Plight of European Jurisprudence," 39.

304. Schmitt, "Plight of European Jurisprudence," 43–44.

305. Theodor Adorno, *Kierkegaard: Construction of the Aesthetic*, trans. Robert Hullot-Kentor (Minneapolis: University of Minnesota Press, 1989), 95–105.

306. Søren Kierkegaard, *Fear and Trembling/Repetition*, trans. and ed. Howard V. Hong, Edna H. Hong (Princeton, N.J.: Princeton University Press, 1983), 82–83, 149; Benjamin, "Theses on the Philosophy of History," 261.

Introduction

1. Carl Schmitt, *Glossarium: Aufzeichnungen der Jahre 1947–1951* (Berlin: Duncker & Humblot, 1991), 236 (26/IV/1949), my translation.

2. The terms "mondialization" and "globalization" are sometimes used as synonyms and sometimes used in opposition. The distinction I note here, which links them quickly in succession, is akin to the three phases of the process of *mondialization* in the twentieth century proposed by Samir Amin in *Spectres of Capitalism: A Critique of Current Intellectual Fashions*, trans. Shane Henry Mage (New York: Monthly Review Press, 1998).

3. David Harvey, *Justice, Nature, and the Geography of Difference*, (Oxford: Blackwell, 1996). Robert David Sack, *Homo geographicus* (Baltimore, Md.: Johns Hopkins University Press, 1997); Nicholas Blomley, *Law, Space and the Geographies of Power* (New York: Guilford Press, 1994).

4. [Fernand Braudel, "Is There a Geography of Biological Man?" in *On History*, trans. Sarah Matthews (Chicago: University of Chicago Press, 1982), 115. —Ed.]

5. As occurs in the valuable work of geographer and sociologist Jacques Lévy, *L'espace légitime: Sur la dimension géographique de la fonction politique* (Paris: Presses de la Fondation nationale des Sciences Politiques, 1994).

6. On the distinction between potamic, thalassic, and Atlantic civilizations, see Sergio Ortino, *The Nomos of the Earth: A Short History on the Connections Between Technological Innovation, Anthropological Space and Legal Order* (Baden-Baden: Nomos, 2002), 54–75.

7. Stein Rokkan, *Citizens, Elections, Parties: Approaches to the Comparative Study of the Processes of Development* (New York: McKay, 1970), esp. 251–351.

While the predominance of many powerful cities in the countryside rendered state construction difficult in the center of Europe, from Rhenian Germany to northern Italy, it facilitated it in lateral areas; the same state construction was made much more difficult the nearer it got to the Church of Rome (South) and much easier the further away it got (in the North).

8. Max Jammer, *Concepts of Space: History of Theories of Space in Physics* (Cambridge, Mass.: Harvard University Press, 1969).

9. Alexander von Humboldt, *L'invenzione del mondo nuovo: Critica della conoscenza geografica* (1836–37) (Florence: La Nuova Italia, 1992); Manfred Büttner, *Wandlungen im geographischen Denken von Aristoteles bis Kant* (Paderborn: Schoeningh, 1979). See also "L'officina geografica. Teorie e metodi tra moderno e postmoderno," ed. Franco Farinelli, *Geotema* 1 (1995), 1–156. As far as deconstruction is concerned, see the work, a little adventurous but stimulating, of Marcus Doel, *Poststructuralist Geographies: The Diabolical Art of Spatial Science* (Lanham–Boulder–New York–Oxford: Rowman & Littlefield, 1999), which is an attempt to refound spatial disciplines based on the theoretical stimuli of Jacques Derrida, Gilles Deleuze and Félix Guattari, Jean Baudrillard, and Luce Irigaray.

10. Phillipe Moreau Defarges, *Introduzione alla geopolitica* (Bologna: Il Mulino, 1996); Carlo Jean, *Geopolitica* (Rome-Bari: Laterza, 1995).

11. Carl Schmitt, *Land and Sea*, trans. Simona Draghici (Corvalis, Ore.: Plutarch Press, 1997).

1. Premodern Political Spaces and Their Crises

1. Robert Nisbet, *The Social Philosophers, Community and Conflict in Western Thought* (London: Heinemann, 1974), 23–24. Compare Sergio Ortino, *The Nomos of the Earth: A Short History on the Connections between Technological Innovation, Anthropological Space, and Legal Order* (Baden-Baden: Nomos, 2002), 37–54.

2. Lewis Mumford, *The City in History: Its Origins, Its Transformations, and Its Prospects*, Vol. 1 (New York: Harcourt, Brace & World, 1961), 29–182.

3. On Cain, see Genesis 4:17. See also René Girard, *Violence and the Sacred*, trans. Patrick Gregory (Baltimore, Md.: Johns Hopkins University Press, 1977); Andrea Caradini, *La nascita di Roma* (Turin: Einaudi, 1997).

4. Georges Dumezil, *Jupiter Mars Quirinus* (Turin: Einaudi, 1955); Louis Dumont, *Homo Hierarchicus: The Caste System and Its Implications*, trans. Mark Sainsbury, Louis Dumont, and Basia Gulati (Chicago: University of Chicago Press, 1981); M. L. Picascia, ed., *La società trinitaria: Un'immagine medioevale* (Bologna: Zanichelli, 1980).

5. Aristotle, *Politics* VII, 1327a (arguing that Greeks are the happy medium between the peoples of the North, who are brave and independent but not that intelligent, and Asian peoples, who are intelligent but subject to political slavery).

6. Santo Mazzarino, *Fra Oriente e Occidente: Ricerche di storia greca arcaica* (Milan: Rizzoli, 1989); on conflict, Massimo Cacciari, *Geo-filosofia dell'Europa* (Milan: Adelphi, 1994); Massimo Cacciari, *L'Arcipelago* (Milan: Adelphi, 1997); on pluralism, Renato Cristin and Sandro Fontana, *Europa al plurale* (Venice: Marsilio, 1997); on the opposition between "Western rationalism" as exactness and "Southern rationalism" as *phronesis*, Serge Latouche, *La sfida di Minerva* (Turin: Bollati Boringhieri, 2000); on the relationship between Europe and the world as thought in terms of *oikoumēnē* and hermeneutics, Martin Heidegger and Hans-Georg Gadamer, *L'Europa e la filosofia* (Venice: Marsilio, 1999).

7. Massimo Bonanni, *Il cerchio e la piramide: L'epica omerica e le origini del politico* (Bologna: Il Mulino, 1992).

8. Oddone Longo, "Atene: Il teatro e la città," in *Mito e realtà del potere nel teatro: dall'antichità classica al Rinascimento*, ed. Maria Chiabò and Federico Doglio (Rome: Centro Studi sul Teatro Medievale e Rinascimentale, 1988), 17–31. Compare Pierre Levéque and Pierre Vidal-Naquet, *Cleisthenes the Athenian: An Essay on the Representation of Space and Time in Greek Political Thought from the End of the Sixth Century to the Death of Plato*, trans. David Ames Curtis (Atlantic Highlands, N.J.: Humanities Press International, 1996).

9. Xenophon, "Constitution of the Athenians," in *Scripta Minora*, trans. E. C. Marchant and G. W. Bowerstock (Cambridge, Mass.: Harvard University Press, 1971), 459–507.

10. Plato, *Timaeus*, 29e–69a.

11. [The Greek *oikoumēnē* designates inhabited areas of the world, in distinction to areas that are sparsely or not at all inhabited. —Ed.]

12. See Galli, "Cittadino/Straniero/Ospite," *Filosofia e Teologia* 2 (1998), 223–43, which is based on Michel Serres, *Rome: The Book of Foundations*, trans. Felicia McCarren (Stanford, Calif.: Stanford University Press, 1991).

13. Carl Schmitt, "Raum un Rom: Zur Phonetik des Wortes Raum," *Universitas* 6 (1951), 963–67. Schmitt also, however, makes a nod to Rome as an example of spatialized politics in *Nomos of the Earth*, 87.

14. [Anubis is the ancient Egyptian god of the dead. He is usually represented as a jackal or as a man with the head of a jackal. —Ed.]

15. Carlo Galli, "Autorità," in *Enciclopedia delle Scienze Sociali*, Vol. 1. (Rome: Istituto per l'Enciclopedia Italiana, 1991), 432–43.

16. [Rutilii Claudii Namatiani, *De Reditu Suo, Libri Duo,* trans. George F. Savage-Armstrong, ed. Charles Haines Keene (London: George Bell & Sons, 1907), 112–13. —Ed.]

17. Eric Voegelin, *The New Science of Politics, An Introduction* (Chicago: University of Chicago Press, 1952); Eric Voegelin, *Anamnesis,* trans. and ed. Gerhart Niemayer (Notre Dame, Ind.: University of Notre Dame Press, 1978). Compare Carlo Galli, "Eric Voegelin: La rappresentazione, la trascendenza, la storia," in *Aspetti e problemi della rappresentanza politica dopo il 1945,* ed. C. Carini (Florence: Centro Editoriale Toscano, 1998), 73–107.

18. Philippians 3:20 (*nostra conversatio in caelis est* [our *patria* is in heaven]).

19. [Schmitt, *Roman Catholicism and Political Form,* 56, 59 n5. —Ed.]

20. Schmitt, *Political Theology II,* 65, emphasis in original.

21. Berman, *Law and Revolution.*

22. Eusebius, *Life of Constantine,* trans. Averil Cameron and Stuart George Hall (Oxford: Oxford University Press, 1999); Eusebius, "In Praise of Constantine," in Harold Allen Drake, *In Praise of Constantine: A Historical Study and New Translation of Eusebius' Tricennial Orations* (Berkeley: University of California Press, 1976), 83–102, esp. 87; Pope Gelasius I, "Epistola XII: Aeonium Arelatensem Episcopum," in Jacques-Paul Migne, *Patrologia Latina,* Vol. 59 (London: Chadwyck-Healey, Inc., 1996), col. 41–47. On the dualism, which is constitutive of Western experience, between divine and earthly justice, Church and Empire, and in the Modern, between state and individual conscience, see Paolo Prodi's important book *Una storia della giustizia: Dal pluralismo dei fori al moderno dualismo tra coscienza e diritto* (Bologna: Il Mulino, 2000).

23. Paolo Grossi, *L'ordine giuridico medievale* (Rome-Bari: Laterza, 1995).

24. See Emmanuele Morandi and Riccardo Panattoni, eds. *Ripensare lo spazio politico: quale aristocrazia?* (Padua: Il Poligrafo, 1998), particularly the essays by Plinio Corrêra de Oliviera and Pio Filippani Ronconi.

25. Matthew 28:19.

26. Schmitt, *Nomos of the Earth,* 58–59; Paul Alphandéry and Alphonse Dupront, *La cristianità e l'idea di crociata* (Bologna: Il Mulino, 1974).

27. Vito Fumagalli, *Landscapes of Fear: Perceptions of Nature and the City in the Middle Ages,* trans. Shayne Mitchell (Cambridge, Mass.: Polity Press, 1994).

28. Hasso Hofmann, *Bilder des Friedens, oder, die vergessene Gerechtigkeit: Drei anschauliche Kapitel der Staatsphilosophie* (Munich: Siemens Stiftung, 1997).

29. Max Weber, "The Plebeian City," in *Economy and Society: An Outline of Interpretive Sociology,* Vol. 2, ed. Guenther Roth and Claus Wittich (Berkeley: University of California Press, 1978), 1302.

30. Schmitt, *Land and Sea*, 33–49.

31. Martin Luther, *The Freedom of a Christian*, trans. Mark D. Tranvik (Minneapolis, Minn.: Fortress Press, 2008); Schmitt, *Roman Catholicism and Political Form*, 10.

32. Michel de Montaigne, *The Complete Works: Essays, Travel Journal, Letters*, trans. Donald Murdoch Frame (Stanford, Calif.: Stanford University Press, 1943), 693.

33. Antonello Gerbi, *The Dispute of the New World: The History of a Polemic, 1750–1900*, trans. Jeremy Moyle (Pittsburgh, Penn.: University of Pittsburgh Press, 1973); J. H. Elliott, *Il vecchio e il nuovo mondo: 1492–1650* (Milan: Il Saggiatore, 1985).

34. Sergio Landucci, *I filosofi e i selvaggi* (Bari: Laterza, 1972); Giuliano Gliozzi, *Adamo e il Nuovo Mondo* (Florence: La Nuova Italia, 1976); Giuliano Gliozzi, *Le teorie della razza nell'età moderna* (Milan: Angeli, 1986); Giuliano Gliozzi, *Differenze e ugualianza nella cultura europea moderna* (Naples: Vivarium, 1993); Tzvetan Todorov, *The Conquest of America: The Question of the Other* (New York: Harper & Row, 1984); Tzvetan Todorov, *On Human Diversity: Nationalism, Racism, and Exoticism in French Thought* (Cambridge, Mass.: Harvard University Press, 1993); Pierre-André Taguieff, *The Force of Prejudice: On Racism and Its Doubles*, trans. Hassan Melehy (Minneapolis: University of Minnesota Press, 2001); Pierre-André Taguieff, *Il razzismo. Pregiudizi, teorie, comportamenti* (Milan: Cortina, 1999).

35. Montaigne, *Essays*, 150–59.

36. Montaigne, *Essays*, 693.

37. [Galli's use of the term "artificio" implies both a talent for strategy and the kind of cunning or deception necessary to effect it. Here and elsewhere in this text, this will be rendered "artifice." —Trans.]

38. Blaine Pascal, *Pensées and Other Writings*, trans. Honor Levi (Oxford: Oxford University Press, 1999), 23.

39. On the "abstract relativism" of Montaigne, see Todorov, *On Human Diversity*, 32–45.

40. Roman Schnur, *Individualismo e assolutismo* (Milan: Giuffre, 1979); Emanuele Castrucci, *Ordine convenzionale e pensiero decisionista* (Milan: Giuffre, 1981).

41. Todorov, *The Conquest of America*, 185–201. Anthony Giddens, by contrast, maintains that perspective, an invention of early modernity, quickly withdraws when faced with independent depictions of space (world maps); but this is a matter of the difference between a political level (that which is under discussion here) and a cartographic, or even artistic, level of discourse. See Anthony Giddens, *Consequences of Modernity* (Stanford, Calif.: Stanford University Press, 1990), 19. Compare Erwin Panofsky, *Perspective as Symbolic Form*, trans. Christopher S. Wood (New York: Massachusetts Institute of Technology Press, Zone Books,

1997); as well as Hubert Damisch, *The Origin of Perspective*, trans. John Goodman (Cambridge, Mass.: Massachusetts Institute of Technology Press, 1994).

42. Alphonse Dupront, *Spazio e umanesimo: L'invenzione del Nuovo Mondo* (Venice: Marsilio, 1993).

43. Dupront, *Spazio e umanesimo*, 36–60. For Dupront, America is invented as Other, not as Europe's equal.

44. Adriano Prosperi and Wolfgang Reinhard, eds. *Il Nuovo Mondo nella coscienza italiana e tedesca del Cinquecento* (Bologna: Il Mulino, 1992). Humboldt also argues that it is classicism that supplies the first interpretative schema for the discovery of America. On this, compare Lyle McAlister, *Spain and Portugal in the New World, 1492–1700* (Minneapolis: University of Minnesota Press, 1984).

45. Dupront, *Spazio e umanesimo*, 67–71.

46. Dupront, *Spazio e umanesimo*, 95ff.

47. Schmitt, *Nomos of the Earth*, 50–51, 214–39.

2. Responses from Political Thought

1. Niccolò Machiavelli, *The Prince*, trans. and ed. Angelo M. Codevilla (New Haven, Conn.: Yale University Press, 1997), 54–56. On the relation between "good laws" and "good arms," see *The Prince*, 45, 89.

2. Carlo Galli, "Il volto demoniaco del potere? Momenti e problemi della fortuna continentale di Machiavelli," in *Contingenza e necessità nella ragione politica moderna* (Rome-Bari: Laterza & Figli, 2009), 5–37. Compare Gennaro Sasso, *Niccolo Machiavelli*, Vols. 1 and 2 (Bologna: Il Mulino, 1993); Giuseppe Cambiano, *Polis: Un modello per la cultura europea* (Rome-Bari: Laterza, 2000), 60–93.

3. Machiavelli, *The Prince*, 55.

4. Under discussion here is the spatiality implicit in Machiavelli's thought, and not his "scientific" methodology. Nonetheless, there are strong links between the two, and I therefore disagree with the reading presented by Mario Martelli ("Il buon geometra di questo mondo," Machiavelli, *Tutte le opere* [Firenze, Sansoni, 1971], especially xxviii–xxix). Martelli sees Machiavelli arguing platonically— nearly *more geometrico* ("in a geometric way")—passing from the universal to the particular, giving life to a "geometric" image of the world.

5. Machiavelli, *The Prince*, 91–92.

6. Machiavelli, *The Prince*, 67.

7. Machiavelli, *The Prince*, 55. For Machiavelli, even the study of history is (as he says in the "Epistle Dedicatory" to *The Prince*, writing on the topic of his studies

of the ancients) subject to the same hyperpoliticism, one that strips it of any and all disinterested humanistic usability.

8. Niccolò Machiavelli, *Discourses on Livy*, trans. Harvey Mansfield and Nathan Tarcov (Chicago: University of Chicago Press, 1996), 10–12.

9. Machiavelli, *Discourses on Livy*, 302–3.

10. Niccolò Machiavelli, *Art of War*, trans. Christopher Lynch (Chicago: University of Chicago Press, 2003), 58–59.

11. [Galli is here using the concept of the "bracketing of war" (and, later, the "limitation of interstate war") in the sense that Schmitt uses it in *Nomos of the Earth*. Schmitt argues that the "bracketing of war"—which is to say, its "rationalization, humanization, and legalization"—has been "the great, core problem of every legal order" (74, 100). Schmitt claims that the great accomplishment of European international law was to have achieved this bracketing through a spatial order, which is to say, "a balance of territorial states on the European continent in relation to the maritime British Empire and against the background of vast *free spaces*" (140). —Ed.]

12. Machiavelli, *Discourses on Livy*, 17–23. On the "causes of expansion," see Machiavelli, *Discourses*, 21.

13. Gerhard Ritter, *The Corrupting Influence of Power*, trans. F. W. Pick (Essex: Hadleigh, 1952).

14. Thomas More, *Utopia*, trans. Clarence H. Miller (New Haven, Conn.: Yale University Press, 2001), 22–23 (on enclosures), 47–48 (on common property of land).

15. On enemies and on humanitarian war to liberate neighboring communities from tyranny, see More, *Utopia*, 105–7.

16. Hans Freyer, *Die politische Insel: Eine Geschichte der Utopien von Platon bis zur Gegenwart* (Leipzig: Bibliographisches Institut AG, 1936).

17. Pier Paolo Portinaro, *Il realismo politico* (Rome-Bari: Laterza, 1999).

18. Compare Roberto Esposito, *Ordine e conflitto: Machiavelli e la letteratura politica del Rinascimento* (Naples: Liguori, 1984).

19. Hobbes, *Leviathan*, 86–90 (Chapter 13: "Of the Naturall Condition of Mankind, as concerning their Felicity, and Misery").

20. Hobbes, *Leviathan*, 100–11 (Chapter 15: "Of Other Lawes of Nature").

21. Hobbes, *Leviathan*, 89–90.

22. Carlo Galli, "Ordine e contingenza: Linee di lettura del 'Leviatano,'" in *Percorsi della libertà: Scritti in onore di Nicola Matteucci*, ed. Nicola Matteucci and Giovanni Giorgini (Bologna: Il Mulino, 1996), 81–106 (reprinted in Galli, *Contingenza e necessità*, 38–71); Galli, "Contaminazioni: Irruzioni del Nulla," 139–58.

23. On the Nothing and its geometric containment, see Horst Bredekamp, "Thomas Hobbes's Visual Strategies," in *The Cambridge Companion to Hobbes's*

Leviathan, ed. Patricia Springborg (Cambridge, U.K.: Cambridge University Press, 2007), 29–60.

24. Hobbes, *Leviathan*, 145–47. Isaiah Berlin, "Two Concepts of Liberty," in *The Proper Study of Mankind: An Anthology of Essays*, ed. Henry and Roger Hausheer (New York: Farrar, Straus and Giroux, 1998), 191–242.

25. Martin Heidegger, "The Age of the World Picture," in *The Question Concerning Technology, and Other Essays*, trans. William Lovitt (New York: Harper & Row, 1977), 115–24. On representation as a symbolic form, see also Damisch, *The Origin of Perspective*, 29.

26. Hobbes, *Leviathan*, 28.

27. [Galli's allusion to a "crystal" is a reference to the diagram of Hobbesian political thought that appears in the long endnote Schmitt appended to Section 7 of the 1963 reprint of his 1927 treatise *Concept of the Political*. Because Schmitt's note has been omitted from the existing English translation of *Concept of the Political* (see George Schwab, "Introduction," in Schmitt, *Concept of the Political*, 5 n8), we here reproduce the portion of it to which Galli alludes.

The much-admired system of Thomas Hobbes leaves a door open to transcendence. The truth that *Jesus is the Christ*, which Hobbes had so often and so strongly confessed as his faith, is a truth of the public faith, *public reason* [English in the original], and public worship in which the citizen participates. In the mouth of Thomas Hobbes, this claim is not merely a tactic of protection, without any purpose or necessity except to bring him security against persecution and censorship. It is also something else, something like the *morale par provision* through which Descartes remained with traditional belief. [Schmitt here makes reference to the Third Part of Descartes's *Discourse on Method*. There Descartes argues that just as one must build a provisional dwelling in which to live while one is tearing down and rebuilding one's own house, so too must one construct a "provisional code of morals" while one is subjecting one's traditional moral system to hyperbolic doubt. The *morale par provision* Descartes then proceeds to outline consists of three maxims: obey the laws and customs of the country in which I live; retain the religion of my childhood; and govern myself through moderation and not excess. —Ed.] In the transparent structure of the political system of "The Matter, Form, and Power of the Commonwealth Ecclesiastical and Civil" [Schmitt here makes reference to the subtitle of Hobbes's *Leviathan*], this truth is more of a keystone, in which public worship presents God with a name under the saying *Jesus is the Christ*. Of course,

Above

Open for Transcendence

↙ 1 *Veritas: Jesus Christus* 5 ↖

↙ 2 *Quis interpretabitur?* 4 ↖

↙ 3 *Autoritas, non veritas, facit legem* 3 ↖

↘ 4 *Potestas directa, non indirecta* 2 ↗

↘ 5 *Obœdientia et* 1 ↗

↘ *Protectio* ↗

→ → → →

Under

Closed; System of Needs

the gruesome civil war between the Christian confessions immediately raises the question: Who interprets, and enforces in a legally binding manner, this continually interpretable truth? Who decides what true Christianity is? Whence the inevitable *Quis interpretabitur*? ["Who is to interpret?"] and the incessant *judicabit Quis* ["Who is to judge?"]. Who mints the truth into a *bona fide* coin? These questions are answered with the maxim *Autoritas, non veritas, facit legem*. The truth does not execute itself; it requires executable commands. These are the *potestas directa*, which—in contrast with the *indirecta potestas*—authenticate the execution of the command, require obedience, and are able to protect those who obey. The result of all of this is a series that runs from top to bottom, from the truth of public worship and obedience to protection of the individual. If we now instead proceed from the bottom up, beginning with the system of the material needs of the individual, then the series starts with the "natural" need for protection and safety on the part of helpless individuals, and consequently too with their obedience to the commands of the *potestas directa*, and leads in reverse order, but *via* the same route, to the door to transcendence. In this way, we arrive at a diagram, which in its five axes—with the 3–3 formula as its central axis—gives us the *crystal-system*.

This "Hobbes-crystal" (the fruit of lifelong labor on the big
issues in general and on the work of Thomas Hobbes in particular)
deserves a moment of reflection and serious thought. Obviously,
the first formula (the 1–5 axis) already contains a neutralization
of the opposites of inner-Christian religious war. Immediately
the question arises whether this neutralization over the framework of the common faith in God could be expanded, so that this
first sentence could also read, "Allah is great," or even further to
include some of the many contestable truths, social ideals, high
values, and principles whose interpretation, implementation, and
enforcement have also been a source of strife and war (such as, for
example, "Liberty, Equality, and Fraternity," "the good of humanity," or "to each according to needs," etc.). I do not think that
Hobbes intended so total a neutralization. But the question here
is not about Thomas Hobbes's individual subjective psychology
or conviction; it is about a systematic and fundamental problem
within his political doctrine as a whole, namely, that in it the door
to transcendence is by no means closed. It is the question of the
interchangeability or non-interchangeability of the formula, *that
Jesus is the Christ* [English in the original].

From Carl Schmitt, *Der Begriff des Politischen: Text von 1932 mit einem
Vorwort und drei Corollarien* (Berlin: Duncker and Humblot, 1963), 121–23, my
translation. —Ed.]

28. Carlo Galli, *Genealogia* (1996), 1–175 (Chapter 1: "La mediazione razi-
onalistica e la mediazione dialettica," Chapter 2: "La crisi della medazione," and
Chapter 3: "La dissoluzione della mediazione").

29. Bredekamp, "Thomas Hobbes's Visual Strategies," 35–38. On the problem
of representation, compare the monographic section of *Filosofia politica* 1 (1987),
as well as Giuseppe Duso, ed., *Il contratto sociale nella filosofia politica moderna*
(Milan: Adelphi, 1993).

30. Hobbes, *Leviathan*, 152 (on freedom as the "Silence of the Law"), 171–74
(on the sovereign distribution of land). On the way in which modernity is ear-
marked by the *homo faber*, see Arendt, *The Human Condition*, 79 & ff.

31. Hobbes, *Leviathan*, 244.

32. [Galli is here using the word "discriminatory" in the sense that Schmitt
uses it in *Nomos of the Earth*: "In the modern, discriminatory concept of war,

the distinction between the justice and injustice of war makes the enemy a felon, who no longer is treated as a *justis hostis*, but as a criminal. Consequently, war ceases to be a matter of international law, even if the killing, plundering, and annihilation continue and intensify with new, modern means of destruction" (*Nomos*, 124). —Ed.]

33. Marina Lalatta Costerbosa, "Guerra e libertà in Jean-Jacques Rousseau: L'impossibilità di un progetto per la pace internazionale," *Teoria politica* 1 (1999), 125–41.

34. Charles de Secondat Montesquieu, *The Spirit of the Laws*, trans. and ed. Anne M. Cohler, Basia Carolyn Miller, and Harold Samuel Stone (Cambridge, U.K.: Cambridge University Press, 1989), 231–35; Julia Kristeva, *Strangers to Ourselves*, trans. Leon Roudiez (New York: Columbia University Press, 1991), 133.

35. Montesquieu, *The Spirit of the Laws*, 27–29, 283–84. On Europe and Asia, see Alberto Burgio, "Un'apologia della storia: Con Montesquieu tra Ancien Régime e modernizzazione," in Louis Althusser, *Montesquieu, la politica e la storia* (Rome: Manifestolibri, 1995), 7–41; Karl August Wittfogel, *Il dispotismo orientale* (Milan: Sugar Co, 1980).

3. Political Geometries

1. Giddens also discusses empty modern space separated from time and from "place" (that is, from concrete determination) as a condition of dynamism. See Giddens, *Consequences of Modernity*, 17–20. In what follows, however, we will adopt a political perspective, and go beyond dynamism in order to demonstrate how empty space is also the precondition for state "stability."

2. Galli, *Genealogia* (1996), 331–459 (Chapter 9: "Teologia politica: sovranità e secolarizzazione").

3. [On the concept of the "crystal," see Chapter 2, Note 27. —Ed.]

4. Galli, "La 'macchina' della modernità," 83–141.

5. ["Whose is the territory, his is the religion." Galli is using this in the sense that Schmitt discusses it *Nomos of the Earth*. There, Schmitt argues that this maxim expressed "the new relation between religious belief and a spatially closed territorial order" that emerged in Europe in the sixteenth century (128). —Ed.]

6. As Giovanni Botero ably demonstrates in his 1591–96 text *Le Relazioni Universali* (*Relations of the Most Famous Kingdomes and Common-wealths Thorowout the World*, trans. Robert Johnson [London: John Hauiland, 1630]).

7. Michael Stolleis, *Stato e ragion di Stato nella prima età moderna* (Bologna: Il Mulino, 1998); A. Enzo Baldini, ed., *La ragion di Stato dopo Meinecke e Croce: Dibattito su recenti pubblicazioni* (Genoa: Name, 1999). On the problem of the "police," see the monographic section by the same name in *Filosofia politica* 1 (1988).

8. Schmitt, *Nomos of the Earth*, 140–68.

9. Ludwig Dehio, *Equilibrio o egemonia: Considerazioni sopra un problema fondamentale della storia politica moderna* (Bologna: Il Mulino, 1988); Maurizio Bazzoli, ed., *L'equilibrio di potenza nell'età moderna* (Milan: Unicopli, 1998).

10. Schmitt, *Land and Sea*, 19–26.

11. Schmitt, *Nomos of the Earth*, 172–75; see also Carl Schmitt, "Sovranità dello Stato e libertà dei mari," in *L'unità del mondo e altri saggi* (Rome: Pellicani, 1994), 217–52.

12. Schmitt, *Nomos of the Earth*, 188–89.

13. Gilles Deleuze and Félix Guattari, *A Thousand Plateaus: Capitalism and Schizophrenia*, trans. Brian Massumi (Minneapolis: University of Minnesota Press, 1987).

14. [Galli is using the term "in form" here in the sense that Schmitt uses it in *Nomos of the Earth*. Schmitt argues that war turns into a "war-in-form" in the sixteenth and seventeenth centuries, when European international law managed to "[limit] war to conflicts between territorially defined European states." This spatial order enabled "each side to recognize the other as *justi hostes*," which, in turn, allowed European international law "to neutralize and, thereby to overcome the conflicts between religious factions" and "to end both religious and civil wars" (142). —Ed.]

15. Schmitt repeatedly talks of England's "decision" for naval existence. See Schmitt, *Land and Sea*, 51–52 (on the way that England completes its spatial revolution by deciding itself for naval existence). See also Carl Schmitt, *Hamlet or Hecuba: The Intrusion of Time into Play*, trans. Simona Draghici (Corvallis, Ore.: Plutarch Press, 2006), 58.

16. Schmitt, *Nomos of the Earth*, 42–49. On *Ordnung und Ortung*, see Enrique Dussel, *The Invention of the Americas: Eclipse of "the Other" and the Myth of Modernity*, trans. Michael Barber (New York: Continuum, 1995) for opposite political and geographical perspectives; he only sees the discovery of America as the chance for the constitution of a worldwide system in which Europe is the center and the rest of the world is periphery.

17. Galli, "Cittadino/Straniero/Ospite," 223–43. See also Carlo Galli, "Guerra e politica, modelli d'interpretazione," *Ragion pratica* 14 (2000), 163–95; Rogers Brubaker, *Citizenship and Nationhood in France and Germany* (Cambridge, Mass.: Harvard University Press, 1992).

18. Ernst Kantorowicz, *The King's Two Bodies: A Study in Mediaeval Political Theology* (Princeton, N.J.: Princeton University Press, 1957).

19. Charles Howard McIlwain, *Constitutionalism, Ancient and Modern* (Ithaca, N.Y.: Cornell University Press, 1940).

20. Nicola Matteucci, *La rivoluzione americana: Una rivoluzione costituzionale* (Bologna: Il Mulino, 1987); Tiziano Bonazzi, "Un 'costituzionalismo' rivoluzionario: Il 'demos basileus' e la nascita degli Stati Uniti," *Filosofia politica* 2 (1991), 283–302.

21. It is a matter of the result of traditional society's evolution, which does not immediately fit within the coordinates supplied by Roberto Scazzieri, "Modelli di società civile," *Filosofia politica* 3 (1999), 363–78, but which constitutes the antecedent of his "commercial model" of civil society.

22. Marcus Buford Rediker, *Between the Devil and the Deep Blue Sea: Merchant Seamen, Pirates, and the Anglo-American Maritime World, 1700–1750*, (Cambridge, U.K.: Cambridge University Press, 1989).

23. Michel Foucault, *Microfisica del potere: Interventi politici*, ed. Alessandro Fontana and Pasquale Pasquino (Turin: Einaudi, 1977); Michel Foucault, "Different Spaces," in *Essential Works of Michel Foucault, Volume 2: Aesthetics, Epistemology, Methodology*, ed. James D. Faubion (New York: The New Press, 1998), 175–85; Pierangelo Schiera, *Specchi della politica: Disciplina, melanconia, socialità nell'Occidente moderno* (Bologna: Il Mulino, 1999); Vittorio Dini, *Il governo della prudenza: Virtù dei privati e disciplina dei custodi* (Milan: Angeli, 2000).

24. Gianfranco Miglio, "L'unità fondamentale di svolgimento dell'esperienza politica occidentale," in *Le regolarità della politica: Scritti scelti raccolti e pubblicati dagli allievi*, Vol. 1 (Milan: Giuffre, 1988), 325–50.

25. This is the "political" model of civil society, according to the coordinates outlined by Scazzieri in "Modelli di società civile."

26. [A concordat is "an agreement between church and state, esp. between the Roman See and a secular government relative to matters that concern both" (OED). —Ed.]

27. Antonio Negri, *Spinoza* (Rome: Derive Approdi, 1998); Riccardo Caporali, *La fabbrica dell'imperium: Saggio su Spinoza* (Naples: Liguori, 2000)

28. Alain Laurent, *Storia dell'individualismo* (Bologna: Il Mulino, 1994).

29. Alexis de Tocqueville, *Democracy in America*, trans. and ed. Harvey Mansfield and Delba Winthrop (Chicago: University of Chicago Press, 2000), 483.

30. Michel Foucault, *Discipline and Punish: The Birth of the Prison*, trans. Alan Sheridan (New York: Pantheon Books, 1977), 195–228. See also Zygmunt Bauman, *Globalization: The Human Consequences* (New York: Columbia University Press, 1998), 49.

31. On the distinction between border and frontier, see Piero Zanini, *Significati del confine: I limiti naturali, storici, mentali* (Milan: Bruno Mondadori, 1997).

32. Arendt, *On Revolution*; Karl Griewank, "Emergence of the Concept of Revolution," in *Revolutions in Modern European History*, ed. Heinz Lubasz (New York: Macmillan, 1966), 55–61.

33. [Galli here makes reference to Virgil's Fourth Eclogue: "*Magnus ab integro saeclorum nascitur ordo*," which is often translated as, "a new world order is born" or "a great order of the ages is born anew." —Ed.]

34. Ambrogio Santambrogio, *Destra e Sinistra: Un'analisi sociologica* (Rome-Bari: Laterza, 1998). Santambrogio's account is quite unlike the perspective of Bobbio, *Left and Right.*

35. Tommaso Campanella, *Thomas Campanella, an Italian Friar and Second Machiavel—His Advice to the King of Spain for Attaining the Universal Monarchy of the World: Particularly Concerning England, Scotland and Ireland: Also for Reducing Holland by Procuring War Betwixt England, Holland, and Other Sea-Faring Countries*, trans. Edmund Chilmead (London: Printed for Philemon Stephens, 1659).

36. Daniel 2:31–45 and 7:11–27.

37. Jacques Bénigne Bossuet, *An Introduction to, or a Short Discourse Concerning, Universal History Faithfully Compar'd with, and Done (with Some Little Alterations) from the Original of ... James Bénigne Bossuet* (London: Printed by Richard Reily, 1728).

38. Cambiano, *Polis*, 261–311.

39. Francesca Rigotti, *L'onore degli onesti* (Milan: Feltrinelli, 1998).

40. Maurizio Viroli, *Republicanism*, trans. Antony Shugaar (New York: Hill and Wang, 2002); Philip Pettit, *Republicanism: A Theory of Freedom and Government* (Oxford: Clarendon Press, 1997). For a careful interpretation of the republican element in Rousseau, see Maurizio Viroli, *Jean-Jacques Rousseau and "the Well-Ordered Society,"* trans. Derek Hanson (Cambridge, U.K.: Cambridge University Press, 2003).

41. Jean-Jacques Rousseau, "Of the Social Contract," in *The Social Contract; and Other Later Political Writings*, trans. and ed. Victor Gourevitch (Cambridge, U.K.: Cambridge University Press, 1997), 74. Rousseau's discourse on the "small State" pertains as much to lawgiving as it does to governing. On the proportion between monarchy and extension, see Rousseau, "Of the Social Contract," 91, and esp. 100–4.

42. Rousseau, "Of the Social Contract," 78–80.

43. Jean-Jacques Rousseau, "Constitutional Project for Corsica," in *Political Writings*, trans. and ed. Frederick Watkins (Edinburgh: Thomas Nelson and Sons, Ltd., 1953), 277–330.

44. Rousseau, "Considerations on the Government of Poland," in *The Social Contract; and Other Later Political Writings*, 193.

45. Rousseau, "Considerations on the Government of Poland," 194.

46. Johannes Althusius, "Politica methodice digesta of Johannes Althusius (Althaus)," *Harvard Political Classics, Volume 2* (Cambridge, Mass.: Harvard University Press, 1932). On Althusius, see Otto Von Gierke, *The Development of Political Theory*, trans. Bernard Freyd (New York: W. W. Norton, 1939) (which

paints Althusius as a theoretician of popular sovereignty, "modernizing" him); K. W. Dahm, W. Kaiwetz, and D. Wyuduckel, eds., *Politische Theorie des Johannes Althusius* (Berlin: Duncker & Humblot, 1988); Giuseppe Duso, "Sulla genesi del moderno concetto di società: la 'consociatio' in Althusius e la 'socialitas' in Pufendorf," *Filosofia politica* 10:1 (1996), 5–31. Giuseppe Duso, Werner Krawietz, and Dieter Wyduckel, eds., *Konsens und Konsoziation in der politischen Theorie des frühen Föderalismus* (Rechtstheorie, Beiheft 16) (Berlin: Duncker and Humblot, 1997).

47. Daniel Judah Elazar, *Exploring Federalism* (Tuscaloosa: University of Alabama Press, 1987), 33–79.

48. Elazar, *Exploring Federalism*, 34–38.

49. On the modern history of federalism, see Elazar, *Exploring Federalism*, 128–53.

4. Modern Universals

1. Hendrik Spruyt, *The Sovereign State and Its Competitors* (Princeton, N.J.: Princeton University Press, 1994).

2. Alois Dempf, *Sacrum Imperium: La filosofia della storia e dello Stato nel medioevo e nella rinascenza politica* (Florence: Le Lettere, 1988).

3. Tiziano Bonazzi, "'Gli uomini come i fiori e le piante se trapiantate prendono dal terreno in cui crescono.' Riflessioni sull'alterità e la politica a proposito delle origini degli Stati Uniti d'America," in *Percorsi della libertà*, 107–29.

4. Eric Leed, *Shores of Discovery: How Expeditionaries Have Constructed the World* (New York: Basic Books, 1995).

5. Koselleck, *Critique and Crisis* (Cambridge, Mass.: Massachusetts Institute of Technology Press, 1988). This thesis emerged first, however, in Schmitt, *The Leviathan in the State Theory of Thomas Hobbes*, 53–64. There Schmitt establishes a genetic link, strongly colored by anti-Semitism, between absolutism and liberalism, and presents the latter as having exited from the interior of the former.

6. Tiziano Bonazzi, *Il sacro esperimento, Teologia e politica nell'America puritana* (Bologna: Il Mulino, 1970); Pietro Adamo, *La libertà dei santi, fallibilismo e tolleranza nella rivoluzione inglese 1640–1649* (Milan: Angeli, 1998).

7. Voltaire, *An Essay on Universal History, the Manners, and Spirit of Nations, from the Reign of Charlemaign to the Age of Lewis XIV*, trans. Thomas Nugent (London: J. Nourse, 1759), 3 ("When you consider this globe as a philosopher, you first direct your attention to the east, the nursery of all arts, and from whence they

have been communicated to the west"). See also Maria Laura Lanzillo, *Voltaire, La politica della tolleranza* (Rome-Bari: Laterza, 2000), 133 & ff.

8. Felice Battaglia, *Le carte dei diritti* (Reggio Calabria: Larugga, 1998), 117 & ff.

9. François-Dominique Toussaint Louverture, *La libertà del popolo nero, scritti politici*, ed. Sandro Chignola (Turin: La Rosa, 1997).

10. In his *Origins of Totalitarian Democracy* (London: Secker & Warburg, 1952), Jacob Talmon institutes a link which is probably too direct between "subjective" criticism and the eighteenth-century revolution on the one hand, and "objective" ideologies and nineteenth-century totalitarianism on the other. See also Carlo Galli, "Presentazione," in *Le origini della democrazia totalitaria*, ed. Jacob Talmon (Bologna: Il Mulino, 2000), xi–xxxi, esp. xxvi & ff.

11. Battaglia, *Le carte dei diritti*, 535–41.

12. Otto Brunner, "La 'casa come complesso' e l'antica 'economica' europea," *Per una nuova storia costituzionale e sociale* (Milan: Vita e Pensiero, 1970), 133–64.

13. See John Locke, *Two Treatises of Government; and, A Letter Concerning Toleration*, ed. Ian Shapiro (New Haven, Conn.: Yale University Press, 2003), 154–55 (§123–4 of Chapter 9: "Of the Ends of Political Society and Government").

14. On colonialism, see Adelino Zanini, *Adam Smith, economia, morale, diritto* (Milan: Bruno Mondadori, 1997), 260 & ff.

15. Locke, *Two Treatises of Government*, 164–65 (§145–6 of Chapter 12: "Of the Legislative, Executive, and Federative Power of the Commonwealth").

16. See, in general, Immanuel Wallerstein, *The Modern World-System, Volume 1: Capitalist Agriculture and the Origins of the European World-Economy in the Sixteenth Century* (New York: Academic Press, 1974); *The Modern World-System, Volume 2: Mercantilism and the Consolidation of the European World-Economy, 1600–1750* (New York: Academic Press, 1980); *The Modern World-System, Volume 3: The Second Great Expansion of the Capitalist World-Economy, 1730–1840s* (San Diego, Calif.: Academic Press, 1989).

17. Robert Morrison MacIver, *The Modern State* (Oxford: Oxford University Press, 1926), 227. Cf. Schmitt, *Nomos of the Earth*, 256 n12.

18. Kant, "Toward Perpetual Peace," 338–51. On the nonagreement between politics and law, see Giuliano Marini, *Tre studi sul cosmpolitismo kantiano* (Pisa-Rome: Instituti Editorili e Poligrafici Internazionali, 1998).

19. Kant, *Critique of Pure Reason*, 672–76; Immanuel Kant, *Critique of the Power of Judgment*, trans. Paul Guyer and Eric Matthews (Cambridge: Cambridge University Press, 2001), 331–46 (§91).

20. Immanuel Kant, "Critique of Practical Reason," in *Practical Philosophy*, 162–63 (§6).

21. André Tosel, *Kant rivoluzionario: Diritto e politica* (Rome: Manifestolibri, 1999).

22. Kant, "Toward Perpetual Peace," 317–20.

23. Kant, "Toward Perpetual Peace," 325–28. We here set aside the *vexata quaestio* of Kant's provisional choice in favor of the *foedus gentium* of the *Volkerbund*, and not the *civitas maxima*, *Weltrpublik*, or *Volkerstaat*. On this problem, see Marzia Ponso, "'Zum ewigen Frieden': Letture interpretative del pacifismo kantiano," *Teoria politica* 1 (1999), 143–62.

24. Kant, "Toward Perpetual Peace," 331–37.

25. Kant, "Toward Perpetual Peace," 319–20.

26. Kant, "Toward Perpetual Peace," 328–31.

27. Heinrich Heine, *On the History of Religion and Philosophy in Germany and Other Writings*, trans. Howard Pollack-Milgate, ed. Terry P. Pinkard (Cambridge, U.K.: Cambridge University Press, 2007), 115.

28. Schmitt, *Nomos of the Earth*, 168–71.

5. Dialectics and Equilibriums

1. Hannah Arendt, *The Life of the Mind* (New York: Harcourt, Brace, and Jovanovich, 1978).

2. G. W. F. Hegel, *Elements of the Philosophy of Right*, trans. H. B. Nisbet, ed. Allen Wood (Cambridge, U.K.: Cambridge University Press, 1991), 282–83 (§260).

3. Hegel, *Elements of the Philosophy of Right*, 290–304 (§270).

4. Hegel, *Elements of the Philosophy of Right*, 267–69 (§246–8).

5. Hegel, *Elements of the Philosophy of Right*, 372–80 (§341–60).

6. Giuseppe Duso, "La libertà politica nella 'rechtsphilosophie' hegeliana: Una traccia," in *Le libertà nella filosofia classica tedesca: Politica e filosofia tra Kant, Fichte, Schelling e Hegel*, ed. Giuseppe Duso and Gaetano Rametta (Milan: Angeli, 2000), 171–85.

7. Hegel, *Elements of the Philosophy of Right*, 275–81 (§258).

8. See Hegel, *Hegel's Philosophy of Mind*, 29 (§ 388), 35–54 (§§ 391–5), 195–98 (§448), and 277 (§548), among others. See also Pietro Rossi, *Storia universale e geografia in Hegel* (Florence: Sansoni, 1975).

9. G. W. F. Hegel, *Lectures on the Philosophy of World History*, trans. Hugh Barr Nisbet (Cambridge, U.K.: Cambridge University Press, 1975), 152–209 (on the geographical basis of world history).

10. G. W. F. Hegel, *Phenomenology of Spirit*, trans. A. V. Miller (Oxford: Oxford University Press, 1977), 355–63 (para. 582–95). In a letter to Friedrich Immanuel Niethammer from Nuremberg on April 29, 1814, Hegel commented

on these same passages (which refer to Absolute Freedom passing, together with its self-destructive actuality, into "another land") by emphasizing that "I had in mind here a specific *land*" ("*Ich hatte dabei ein Land in Sinne*"), namely, Protestant Germany. See G. W. F. Hegel, *Hegel: The Letters*, trans. Clark Butler and Christiane Seiler (Bloomington: Indiana University Press, 1984), 307.

11. Hegel, *Elements of the Philosophy of Right*, 374 (§346) and 376 (§351, on Euro-centric space).

12. Karl Marx and Friedrich Engels, *The Communist Manifesto*, ed. David McLellan (Oxford: Oxford University Press, 1992), 7.

13. Harvey, *Justice, Nature, and the Geography of Difference*, 62–68.

14. Harvey, *Justice*, 291–326.

15. Carlo Galli, "Etologia, sociobiologia e le categorie della politica," in *L'analisi della politica, tradizioni di ricerca, modelli, teorie*, ed. Angelo Panebianco (Bologna: Il Mulino, 1989), 423–46.

16. Emmanuel-Joseph Sieyès, *What Is the Third Estate?*, trans. M. Blondel (New York: Frederick A. Praeger, 1963). See also Francesco Tuccari, *La nazione* (Rome-Bari: Laterza, 2000).

17. Sieyès, *What Is the Third Estate?*, 119–39.

18. Max Weber, "Politics as a Vocation," in *From Max Weber: Essays in Sociology*, trans. and ed. Hans Heinrich Gerth and Charles Wright Mills (New York: Oxford University Press, 1946), 78, emphasis altered.

19. Max Weber, "Territorial Political Organizations," in *Economy and Society, Volume II*, 903.

20. Sieyès, *What Is the Third Estate?*, 59–60.

21. Konrad Lorenz, *On Aggression*, trans. Marjorie Kerr Wilson (New York: Routledge, 2002); Robert Ardrey, *The Territorial Imperative: A Personal Inquiry into the Animal Origins of Property and Nations* (New York: Atheneum, 1966); Robert Ardrey, *The Hunting Hypothesis: A Personal Conclusion Concerning the Evolutionary Nature of Man* (New York: Atheneum, 1976). On the fear/border relationship based on Gehlen and Canetti, see also Roberto Escobar, *Metamorfosi della paura* (Bologna: Il Mulino, 1997).

22. See, for example, Anthony Smith, *The Ethnic Origins of Nations* (New York: Wiley-Blackwell, 1986). On this phenomenon, see Sanjay Seth, "Rethinking the State of the Nation," Irimline Veti-Brause, "The Authentic State: History and Tradition in the Ideology of Ethnonationalism," and Stephanie Lawson, "The Stars on China's Flag: Appropriating the Universe for the Nation," in *The State in Transition: Reimagining Political Space*, ed. Joseph Camilleri, Anthony Jarvis, and Albert Paolini (Boulder-London: Lynne Rienner, 1995).

23. Carl Schmitt, *Political Romanticism*, trans. Guy Oakes (Cambridge: Massachusetts Institute of Technology Press, 1986); Carl Schmitt, "Der Gegensatz von Gemeinschaft und Gesellschaft als Beispiel einer zweigliedrigen Unterscheidung, Betrachtungen zur Struktur und zum Schiksdal solcher Antthesen," in *Estudios juridico-sociales: Homenaje al Profesor Luis Legaz y Lacambra*, Vol. 2 (Galicia: Universidad de Santiage de Compostela, 1960), 165–78. Schmitt's thesis is that community and society are originally, from the romantics to Tönnies, not alternative ideas but instead defer to a "third superior" (the State) or a synthetic mix of the two. Only late positivism defined the "irrational" community and, drawing both terms into a nihilistic dual logic, transformed them into conflictual values, in which Schmitt recognized intrinsic destructivity.

24. Ferdinand Tönnies, *Community and Civil Society*, trans. Jose Harris and Margaret Hollis, ed. Jose Harris (Cambridge, U.K.: Cambridge University Press, 2001), 28–30, 39–43 (on the "place," the house, the neighborhood), 45–48 (on the house and the field), 62–63 (on citation), 66–68 (on the centripetal and centrifugal action of the world market).

25. Renato Treves, "Introduzione" to Ferdinand Tönnies, *Comunità e società* (Milan: Edizioni di Comuntia, 1963), xx. See also Furio Ferraresi, "Ferdinand Tönnies interprete di Hobbes: strategie politiche nella modernità," *Filosofia politica* 2 (1994), 209–32. See also Maurizio Ricciardi, *Ferdinand Tönnies sociologo hobbesiano* (Bologna: Il Mulino, 1997).

26. George L. Mosse, *The Crisis of German Ideology: Intellectual Origins of the Third Reich* (New York: H. Fertig, 1998); Furio Jesi, *Cultura di destra* (Milan: Garzanti, 1993), 11–66.

27. Mauro Barberis, *Benjamin Constant: Rivoluzione, constituzione, progresso* (Bologna: Il Mulino, 1988); Maurizio Fioravanti, *Constituzione* (Bologna: Il Mulino, 1999), 124–39.

28. David Harvey, "Time-Space Compression and the Rise of Modernism as a Cultural Force," in *The Condition of Postmodernity: An Enquiry into the Origins of Cultural Change* (Oxford: Blackwell, 1989), 260–83; Stephen Kern, *Il tempo e lo spazio: La percezione del mondo tra Otto e Novecento* (Bologna: Il Mulino, 1995).

29. Dolf Sternberger, *Panorama of the Nineteenth Century*, trans. Joachim Neugroschel (Oxford: Blackwell, 1977).

30. Foucault, *The Order of Things*, 387.

6. The Twentieth Century

1. Franz Kafka, *The Castle*, trans. Mark Harmon (New York: Schocken Books, 1998); Franz Kafka, "In the Penal Colony," in *The Metamorphosis and Other Stories*, trans. Malcolm Pasley (New York: Penguin Books, 2000), 111–36. On the

latter, see Walter Müller-Seidel, *Die Deportation des Menschen: Kafkas Erzählung "In der Strafkolonie" im europäischen Kontext* (Stuttgart: Metzler, 1986).

2. Bruno Accarino, *Mercanti ed Eroi: La crisi del contrattualismo tra Weber e Luhmann* (Naples: Liguori, 1986), 89 & ff.

3. Karl Dietrich Bracher, *The Age of Ideologies: A History of Political Thought in the Twentieth Century*, trans. Ewald Osers (New York: St. Martin's Press, 1984).

4. Ernst Jünger, "Total Mobilization," in *The Heidegger Controversy: A Critical Reader*, ed. Richard Wolin (Cambridge, Mass.: Massachusetts Institute of Technology Press, 1993), 119–39.

5. Galli, *Modernità*, 79–105; Galli, *Genealogia* (1996), 123–75 (Chapter 3: "La dissoluzione della mediazione"); Pietro Barcellona, *Lo spazio della politica: Tecnica e democrazia* (Rome: Editori Riuniti, 1993); Michela Nacci, *Pensare la tecnica: Un secolo di incomprensioni* (Rome-Bari: Laterza, 2000).

6. Carlo Galli, "Strategie della totalità: Stato autoritario, Stato totale, totalitarismo, nella Germania degli anni Trenta," *Filosofia politica* 1 (1997), 27–62.

7. Ernst Jünger, *The Worker: Dominion and Gestalt*, trans. Dirk Leach (Albany, NY: SUNY Press, 1990).

8. Eric Leed, *No Man's Land: Combat and Identity in World War I* (Cambridge, U.K.: Cambridge University Press, 1981), 73–114.

9. Arendt, *Origins of Totalitarianism*.

10. Schmitt, *The Concept of the Political*.

11. Schmitt, *Political Theology: Four Chapters*.

12. Schmitt, *Constitutional Theory*, 125–66. See also on this point Galli, *Genealogia* (1996), 575–633 ("Chapter 12: Democrazia e forma politica: il potere costituente e la costituzione"), and Geminello Preterossi, *Carl Schmitt e la tradizione moderna* (Rome-Bari: Laterza, 1996).

13. Carl Schmitt, *Il Custode della Costituzione* (Milan: Giuffrè, 1981); Schmitt, *Nomos of the Earth*, 227–39.

14. Carl Schmitt, "L'unità del mondo," in *L'unità del mondo e altri saggi*, ed. Alessandro Campi (Rome: Pellicani, 1994), 303–19; Galli, *Genealogia* (1996), 839–912 ("Dal nazismo al 'nomos' della Terra"); Caterina Resta, *Stato mondiale e "nomos" della terra: Carl Schmitt tra universo e pluriverso* (Rome: Pellicani, 1999).

15. Carl Schmitt, "Dialogo del nuovo spazio," in *Terra e Mare* (Milan: Giuffrè, 1986), 85–109, particularly 108.

16. Carl Schmitt, *Il concetto d'Impero nel diritto internazionale: Ordinamente dei grandi spazi con esclusione delle potenze estranee* (Rome: Istituto nazioanle di cultura fascista, 1941); Schmitt, *Nomos of the Earth*, 281–294.

17. Schmitt, "Appropriation/Distribution/Production: An Attempt to Determine from *Nomos* the Basic Questions of Every Social and Economic Order," in *Nomos of the Earth*, 324–35.

18. Schmitt, *Glossarium*, 34 (22/X/1947).

19. Ernst Jünger and Carl Schmitt, *Il nodo di Gordio: Dialogo su Oriente e Occidente nella storia del mondo* (Bologna: Il Mulino, 1987).

20. Schmitt, *Nomos of the Earth*, 308.

21. On the *civitas maxima*, see Hans Kelsen, *Il problema della sovranità* (Milan: Giuffrè, 1989), 365 & ff.

22. Ernst Jünger and Martin Heidegger, *Oltre la linea* (Milan: Adelphi, 1989); Roberto Esposito, *Nove pensieri sulla politica* (Bologna: Il Mulino, 1993), 207 & ff; see also the essay by Umberto Regina, Caterina Resta, and Riccardo Panattoni in *Ripensare lo spazio politico*. ed. Emmanuele Morandi and Riccardo Panattoni (Padua: Il Poligrafo, 1998).

23. Ernst Jünger, *Trattato del ribelle* (Milan: Adelphi, 1990), 53 & ff.; Ernst Jünger, *Al muro del tempo* (Milan: Adelphi, 2000); Luisa Bonesio and Caterina Resta, *Passaggi al bosco: Ernst Jünger nell'era dei Titani* (Milan: Mimesis, 2000).

24. Ernst Jünger, *Lo State mondiale: Organismi e organizzazione* (Parma: Guanda, 1998), 17. A thesis ideologically opposite to Jünger's may be found in Hardt and Negri, *Empire*, on which see also Chapter 7.

25. Horkheimer and Adorno, *Dialectic of Enlightenment*, 1.

26. Martin Heidegger, *Being and Time*, trans. John Macquarrie and Edward Robinson (New York: Harper and Row, 1962), 145–148 (§24: "Space and *Dasein's* Spatiality"). On the expression "it is not the world that is in space, but rather, it is space that is in the world," see Schmitt, *Land and Sea*, 58.

27. Roberto Esposito, "Nichilismo e comunità," in *Nichilismo e Politica*, ed. Roberto Esposito, Carlo Galli, and Vicenzo Vitiello (Rome-Bari: Gius, Laterza and Figli, 2000), 25–40.

28. The reference is to Jünger and Heidegger, *Oltre la linea*, and to the introductory essay by Franco Volpi, "Itinerarium mentis in nihilum," in *Oltre la linea*, 9–45.

29. Martin Heidegger, *L'arte e lo spazio* (Genoa: Il Melangolo, 1979); but above all, Martin Heidegger, *Saggi e discorsi* (Milan: Mursia, 1980).

30. Paolo Godani, *Il Tramonto dell'essere: Heidegger e il pensiero della finitezza* (Pisa: ETS, 1999), 104; Caterina Resta, *Il Luogo e le Vie: Geografie del pensiero in Martin Heidegger* (Milan: Angeli, 1996).

31. Karl Popper, *The Open Society and Its Enemies* (New York: Routledge, 2003).

32. See Andre Gunder Frank, "The Development of Underdevelopment," Fernando Henrique Cardoso, "Dependency and Development in Latin America," and Immanuel Wallerstein, "The Rise and Future Demise of the World Capitalist

System: Concepts for Comparative Analysis," in *From Modernization to Globalization: Perspectives on Development and Social Change*, ed. J. Timmons Roberts and Amy Hite (Oxford: Blackwell, 2000), 159–68, 169–78, 190–209. See also, in general, Wallerstein's three-volume *Modern World-System*.

33. Ennio DiNolfo, *Storia delle relazioni internazionali, 1918–1999* (Rome-Bari: Laterza, 2000), 595 & ff.

34. Trevor Marshall, "Citizenship and Social Class," in Trevor Marshall and Tom Bottomore, *Citizenship and Social Class* (London: Pluto Press, 1992), 3–51.

7. Globalization

1. Samir Amin, "The Challenge of Globalization," *Review of International Political Economy* 3:2 (1996), 216–59; Bruno Amoroso, *Della globalizzazione* (Molfetta: La Meridiana, 1995); Giovanni Arrighi, *The Long Twentieth Century: Money, Power and the Origins of Our Times* (London: Verso, 1994); *Globalizzazione e transizione* (Proceedings of the Conference "Beyond Capital: Globalization and Transition," held in Milan on December 13–14, 1997) (Milan: Edizioni Punto Rosso, 1998); Raffaele Laudani, "Marxismo e globalizzazione: La filosofia politica di Istvan Meszaros a partire da 'Beyond Capital,'" *Filosofia politica* 3 (2000), 397–402.

2. Kate Nash, *Contemporary Political Sociology: Globalization, Politics and Power* (Oxford: Blackwell, 2000), 64 & ff.

3. On the central role of technology, authors who are usually distant from one another reach agreement. See, for example, Pietro Barcellona, *Il declino dello Stato* (Rome-Bari: Dedalo, 1998) and Luisa Bonesio, "Terra, singolarità, paesaggi," in *Orizzonti della geofilosofia: Terra e luoghi nell'epoca della mondializzazione*, ed. Luisa Bonesio (Bologna: Arianna, 2000), 5–25.

4. See, generally, Sakari Hänninen and Jussi Vähämäki, eds., *Displacement of Politics* (Jyvaskyla: SoPhi, 2000). A number of the essays in this volume, along with a few others, were also published in *Aut Aut* 298 (July–August 2000).

5. For the essential bibliography regarding these signs of globalization, with slight differences in use from author to author, see Michael Porter, *Competition in Global Industries* (Boston: Harvard Business School Press, 1986); Mike Featherstone, ed., *Global Culture, Nationalism, Globalization and Modernity* (London: Sage, 1991); François Chesnais, *La mondialisation du Capital* (Paris: Syros, 1995); James Mitteleman, ed., *Globalization: Critical Reflections* (Boulder, Colo.: Lynne Rienner Publishers, 1996); Eugenia Parise, ed., *Stato nazionale, lavoro, e moneta nel sistema mondiale integrato* (Naples: Liguori, 1997); Eugenia Parise, "Gli incerti sentieri della globalizzazione: Note di letteratura economica,"

Filosofia politica 3 (2000), 379–95; Mario Arcelli, ed., *Globalizzazione dei mercati e orizzonti del capitalismo* (Rome-Bari: Laterza, 1997); Paul Hirst and Grahame Thompson, *Globalization in Question: The International Economy and the Possibilities of Governance* (Cambridge, Mass.: Polity Press, 2000); Robert Schaeffer, *Understanding Globalization: The Social Consequences of Political, Economic and Environmental Change* (New York: Rowman & Littlefield, 1997); Kenichi Ohmae, *The Evolving Global Economy* (Boston: Harvard Business School Press, 1995); Ulrich Beck, *What Is Globalization?*, trans. Patrick Camiller (Cambridge, Mass.: Polity Press, 2000); Timmons and Hite, ed., *From Modernization to Globalization*; Frank Lechner and John Boli, ed., *The Globalization Reader* (Oxford: Blackwell, 2000); Sandro Mezzadra and Agostino Petrillo, eds., *I confini della globalizzazione: Lavoro, cultura, cittadinanza* (Rome: Manifestolibri, 2000); Nash, *Contemporary Political Sociology*; Giddens, *Consequences of Modernity*, 63 & ff.

6. Dominique Méda, *Società senza lavoro: Per una nuova filosofia dell'occupazione* (Milan: Feltrinelli, 1997); Jeremy Rifkin, *The End of Work: The Decline of the Global Labor Force and the Dawn of the Post-Market Era* (New York: G. P. Putnam's Sons, 1996); Luc Boltanski and Eve Chiapello, "Dismantling the World of Work," in *The New Spirit of Capitalism*, trans. Gregory Elliott (London: Verso, 2005), 217–72.

7. Benjamin Coriat, *Ripensare l'organizzazione del lavoro: Concetti e prassi nel modello giapponese* (Rome-Bari: Dedalo, 1991); Taiichi Ohno, *Lo spirito Toyota: Il modello giapponese della qualità totale* (Turin: Einudi, 1994); Marco Revelli, "Economia e modello sociale nel passaggio tra fordismo e toyotismo," in *Appuntamenti di fine secolo*, ed. Pietro Ingrao and Rossana Rossandra (Rome: Manifestolibri, 1995), 161–224.

8. Paolo Savona and Carlo Jean, eds., *Geo-economia: Il dominio dello spazio economico* (Milan: Angeli, 1995); Suzanne Berger and Ronald Philip Dore, *National Diversity and Global Capitalism* (Ithaca, N.Y.: Cornell University Press, 1996).

9. Susan Strange, *The Retreat of the State: The Diffusion of Power in the World Economy* (Cambridge, U.K.: Cambridge University Press, 1996); Saskia Sassen, *Losing Control?: Sovereignty in an Age of Globalization* (New York: Columbia University Press, 1996). On the "network" and the jump in quality that this organizing form constitutes, see Boltanski and Chiapello, *The New Spirit of Capitalism*, 55–164.

10. Saskia Sassen, *Cities in a World Economy: Sociology for a New Century* (Thousand Oaks, Calif.: Pine Forge Press, 2000); Kenichi Ohmae, *The End of the Nation State: The Rise of Regional Economies* (London: HarperCollins, 2008); Paolo Perulli, *La città delle reti: Forme di governo nel postfordismo* (Turin: Bollati Boringhieri, 2000).

11. John H. Goldthorpe, *Order and Conflict in Contemporary Capitalism* (Oxford: Clarendon Press, 1984); Sabino Cassese, Francesco Galgano, Giulio Tremonti, and Tiziano Treu, eds., *Nazioni senza ricchezza, richezze senza nazione* (Bologna: Il Mulino, 1993); Lester Thurow, *The Future of Capitalism: How Today's Economic Forces Shape Tomorrow's World* (New York: William & Morrow Company, 1996); Ankie Hoogvelt, *Globalization and the Postcolonial World: The New Political Economy of Development* (Baltimore, Md.: The Johns Hopkins University Press, 1997); Luciano Galliano, *Globalizzazione e disuguaglianza* (Rome-Bari: Laterza, 2000).

12. Jean-François Bayart, "Finishing with the Idea of the Third World: The Concept of the Political Trajectory," in *Rethinking the Third World Politics*, ed. James Manor (London–New York: Longman, 1991), asserts the need to go beyond the development/dependence dichotomy and to think the Third World as "history"; Hoogvelt, *Globalization and the Postcolonial World*; Immanuel Wallerstein, "C'était quoi, le tiers-monde?" *Le Monde Diplomatique* 47:557 (August 2000), 18–19.

13. Alessandro Dal Lago, *Non-persone: L'esclusione dei migranti in una società globale* (Milan: Feltrinelli, 1999).

14. ["*Jus cogens*" refers to "a principle of international law which cannot be set aside by agreement or acquiescence. So, in modern use, as laid down by the Vienna Convention on the Law of Treaties (1969), 'a peremptory norm of general international law'" (OED) —Ed.]

15. Joseph Camilleri, Anthony Jarvis, and Albert Paolini, eds., *The State in Transition: Reimagining Political Space* (Boulder, Colo.: L. Rienner, 1995); Pier Paolo Portinaro, "Il futuro dello Stato nell'età della globalizzazione: Un bilancio di fine secolo," *Teoria politica* 3 (1997), 17–36; David Smith, Dorothy Solinger, and Steven Topik, eds., *States and Sovereignty in the Global Economy* (London–New York: Routledge, 1999); Bertrand Badie, *Un monde sans souveraineté: Les états entre ruse et responsabilité* (Paris: Fayard, 1999); Pietro Barcellona, *L'individuo e la comunità* (Rome: Edizioni Lavoro, 2000); Giacomo Marramao, *Dopo il Leviatano: Individuo e comunità nella filosofia politica* (Turin: Bollati Boringhieri, 2000); Barbara Henry, ed., *Mondi globali: Identità, sovranità, confini* (Pisa: ETS, 2000) (on the dimension of globalization that is "volumetric" and not "planar").

16. Davina Cooper, *Governing out of Order: Space, Law and the Politics of Belonging* (London–New York: Rivers Oram Press, 1998).

17. Charles Taylor, Amy Gutmann, and Charles Taylor, *Multiculturalism: Examining the Politics of Recognition* (Princeton, N.J.: Princeton University Press, 1994); Rainer Bauböck, ed., *From Aliens to Citizens: Redefining the*

Status of Immigrants in Europe (Aldershot, UK: Avebury, 1994); Will Kymlicka, *Multicultural Citizenship: A Liberal Theory of Minority Rights* (Oxford: Clarendon Press, 2003); John Rundell and Rainer Bauböck, ed., *Blurred Boundaries: Migration, Ethnicity, Citizenship* (Aldershot, UK: Ashgate, 1998); Saskia Sassen, *Migranti, coloni, rifiugiati: Dall'emigrazione di massa alla fortezza Europa* (Milan: Feltrinelli, 1999) (a history of migration models).

18. Bauman, *Globalization*, 27–54.

19. John Breuilly, *Nationalism and the State* (Chicago: University of Chicago Press, 1994).

20. Nash, *Contemporary Political Sociology*, 92 & ff.

21. Sandro Mezzadra and Agostino Petrillo, "Introduzione: I confini della globalizzazione," in *I confini della globalizzazione*, 7–38.

22. Beck, *What Is Globalization?*, 74.

23. Mathias Albert, Lothar Brock, and Klaus Dieter World, ed., *Civilizing World Politics: Society and Community Beyond the State* (Lanham–Boulder–New York–Oxford: Rowman & Littlefield, 2000), where it is emphasized, among other things, that the ideal type of "world society" implies a much higher rate of integration between the actors than the "international society."

24. George Ritzer, *The McDonaldization of Society: An Investigation into the Changing Character of Contemporary Social Life* (Thousand Oaks, Calif.: Pine Forge Press, 1996); Douglas Kellner and Ann Cvetkovich, eds., *Articulating the Global and the Local: Globalization and Cultural Studies* (Boulder, Colo.: Westview Press, 1996); Frederic Jameson and Masao Miyohoshi, eds., *The Cultures of Globalization* (Durham, N.C.–London: Duke University Press, 1998); Tony Spybey, *Globalizzazione e società mondiale* (Trieste: Asterios, 1997); Joana Breidenbach and Ina Zukrigl, *Danza delle culture: L'identità culturale in un mondo globalizzato* (Turin: Bollati Boringhieri, 2000), 32 & ff (arguing that an authentic, non-American culture exists, making cultural differentiations possible). For Clifford Geertz, meanwhile, culture is not a compact substrata of consensus, but a "variety of participation in a collective life, which occurs simultaneously on a dozen different levels, in a dozen different dimensions and circles," in which conflict—far from being regressive or irrational—entails a problem of identity (*Mondo globale, mondi locali: Cultura e politica alla fine del ventesimo secolo* [Bologna: Il Mulino, 1999], 68, my translation—Trans.).

25. Beck, *What Is Globalization?*, 87–113; Robert Gilpin, *War and Change in World Politics* (Cambridge, U.K.: Cambridge University Press, 1981); James Rosenau, *Turbulence in World Politics* (Princeton, N.J.: Princeton University Press, 1990); Pierre Lellouche, *Il Nuovo Mondo: Dall'ordine di Yalta al disordine delle*

nazioni (Bologna: Il Mulino, 1994); Charlotte Bretherton and Geoffrey Ponton, eds., *Global Politics: An Introduction* (Oxford: Blackwell, 1996); Zbigniew Brzezinski, *The Grand Chessboard: American Primacy and Its Geostrategic Imperatives* (New York: Basic Books, 1997); Vittorio Emanuele Parsi, *Interesse Nazionale e Globalizzazione: I Regimi Democratici nelle Trasformazioni del Sistema Post-Westfaliano* (Milan: Jaca Book, 1998); Stanley Hoffmann, *World Disorders: Troubled Peace in the Post–Cold War Era* (Lanham–Boulder–New York–Oxford: Rowman & Littlefield, 1998); Paul Close and Emiko Ohki-Close, *Supranationalism in the New World Order: Global Processes Reviewed* (London: Macmillan Press, 1999).

26. Samuel Huntington, *The Clash of Civilizations and the Remaking of World Order* (New York: Simon & Schuster, 1996); Mary Kaldor, *New and Old Wars: Organized Violence in a Global Era* (Cambridge, Mass.: Polity Press, 1999).

27. A case study (Iraq, Somalia, Bosnia, Rwanda, Haiti) is in Thomas George Weiss, *Military-Civilian Interactions: Intervening in Humanitarian Crises* (Lanham–Boulder–New York–Oxford: Rowman & Littlefield, 1999). Strong criticism of the new forms of discriminatory war can be found in Danilo Zolo, *I signori della pace: Una critica del globalismo giuridico* (Rome: Carocci, 1998); Danilo Zolo, *Chi dice umanità: Guerra, diritto e ordine globale* (Turin: Einaudi, 2000); Alessandro Dal Lago, "Polizia globale? Note sulle trasformazioni della guerra in Occidente," in *Il confini della globalizzazione*, 241–65. See also Rita Di Leo, *Il primato Americano: Il punto di vista degli Stati Uniti dopo la caduta del muro di Berlino* (Bologna: Il Mulino, 2000).

28. There is a divergence on this point from Mario Tronti, *La politica al tramonto* (Turin: Einaudi, 1998). See Carlo Galli, "Politica e politico nella fine del Moderno," *Filosofia politica* 3 (1999), 497–504.

29. Zygmunt Bauman, *La solitudine del cittadino globale* (Milan: Feltrinelli, 2000). See also Bauman, *Globalization*; and Zygmunt Bauman, *La società dell'incertezza* (Bologna: Il Mulino, 1999).

30. Dupront, *Spazio e umanesimo*, 95 & ff. See also Schmitt, "L'unità del mondo."

31. Arjun Appadurai, *Modernity At Large: Cultural Dimensions of Globalization* (Minneapolis: University of Minnesota Press, 1996).

32. Ulrich Beck, *Risk Society: Towards a New Modernity*, trans. Mark Ritter (London: Sage Publications, 1992); Giddens, *Consequences of Modernity*, 131 & ff. On risk, see also Anthony Giddens, *Runaway World: How Globalization Is Reshaping Our Lives* (New York: Routledge, 2000).

33. Giddens, *Consequences of Modernity*, 36–44; Anthony Elliott, "Symptoms of Globalization: Or, Mapping Reflexivity in the Postmodern Age," in *The State*

in Transition, 157–72; Ulrich Beck, Anthony Giddens, and Scott Lash, *Reflexive Modernization: Politics, Tradition and Aesthetics in the Modern Social Order* (Stanford, Calif.: Stanford University Press, 1994).

34. Serge Latouche, *The Westernization of the World: The Significance, Scope and Limits of the Drive Towards Global Uniformity*, trans. Rosemary Morris (Cambridge, Mass.: Polity Press, 2005); Serge Latouche, *La megamacchina: Ragione tecnoscientifica, ragione economica e mito del progresso* (Turin: Bollati Boringhieri, 1995); Armand Mattelart, *La communicazione-mondo* (Milan: Il Saggiatore, 1995); Armand Mattelart, *The Invention of Communication*, trans. Susan Emanuel (Minneapolis: University of Minnesota Press 1997); Paul Virilio, *The Information Bomb*, trans. Chris Turner (London: Verso, 2000).

35. Bauman, *Globalization*, 52–53.

36. Maria Rosaria Ferrarese, *Le istituzioni della globalizzazione* (Bologna: Il Mulino, 2000). Globalization is the particular interest that makes itself universal, and the triumph of the juridical forms of private right's contract over public right.

37. Bauman, *Globalization*, 77–102.

38. Ignacio Ramonet, *Geopolitica del caos* (Trieste: Asterios, 1998).

39. For reactions to the ideological justifications of the war in Kosovo, see Raffaella Gherardi, "Nell'Europa della Guerra: sovranità e diritti tra politica e dottrine," *Scienza e politica* 21 (1999), 21–46.

40. We use this term, of course, in the sense that Schmitt uses it in *Political Romanticism*.

41. Zygmunt Bauman, "On Glocalization: Or, Globalization for Some, Localization for Some Others," in *The Bauman Reader*, ed. Peter Beilharz (Malden, Mass.: Blackwell Publishers, Inc., 2001), 298–310; Roland Robertson, *Globalizzazione: Teoria sociale e cultura globale* (Trieste: Asterios, 1999), 137 & ff.

42. Clifford Geertz, "The World in Pieces: Culture and Politics at the End of the Century," *Focaal* 32 (1998), 91–117.

43. Ignacio Ramonet, Fabio Giovannini, and Giovanna Ricoveri, *Il pensiero unico e i nuovi padroni del mondo* (Rome: La strategia della lumaca, 1995); Ramonet, *Geopolitica del caos*.

44. Ferrarese, *Le istituzioni della globalizzazione*, 159 & ff. See Norberto Bobbio, *The Age of Rights*, trans. Allan Cameron (Cambridge, Mass.: Polity Press, 1996); Daniele Archibugi and David Beetham, *Diritti umani e democrazia cosmopolitica* (Milan: Feltrinelli, 1998); Tim Dunne and Nicholas Wheeler, eds., *Human Rights in Global Politics* (Cambridge, U.K.: Cambridge University Press, 1999).

45. Otfried Höffe, *Demokratie im Zeitalter der Globalisierung* (Munich: Beck, 1999).

46. Zolo, *I signori della pace*; Edoardo Greblo, "Globalizzazione e diritti umani," *Filosofia politica* 3 (2000), 421–31.

47. Jürgen Habermas and Max Pensky, *The Postnational Constellation: Political Essays* (Cambridge, Mass.: Polity Press, 2007).

48. David Held, *Democracy and the Global Order: From the Modern State to Cosmopolitan Governance* (Stanford, Calif.: Stanford University Press, 1995). Compare Gilda Manganaro Favaretto, "Globalizzazione e democrazia: considerazioni si D. Held, 'Democrazie e ordine globale,'" in *Etica e politica* 1 (2000) http://www2.units.it/~etica/2000_1/index.html (last checked April 14 2009).

49. David Held, "Democracy: From City-States to a Cosmopolitan Order?" *Political Studies* 40:1 (August 1992), 10–39.

50. An attempt to use the term/concept "community" in the circle of international relations is offered by Emanuel Richter, "'Community' in the Global Network: A Methodological Exploration," in *Civilizing World Politics*, 69–90, but with still uncertain results, if not for the acquisition of evidence that "community" entails levels of inclusion and exclusion that are more intense than those of "society."

51. John Rawls, *A Theory of Justice* (Cambridge, Mass.: Belknap Press of Harvard University Press, 2003); John Rawls, *Political Liberalism* (New York: Columbia University Press, 1993); Michael Walzer, *Spheres of Justice: A Defense of Pluralism and Equality* (New York: Basic Books, 1983); Charles Taylor, *Sources of the Self: The Making of the Modern Identity* (Cambridge, Mass.: Harvard University Press, 1989). See also, in general, Alessandro Ferrara, "Beyond Liberalism and Communitarianism: Towards a Critical Theory of Social Justice," in *Universalism vs. Communitarianism: Contemporary Debates in Ethics*, ed. David Rasmussen (Cambridge, Mass.: Massachusetts Institute of Technology Press, 1990).

52. Martha Nussbaum, *Women and Human Development: The Capabilities Approach* (Cambridge, U.K.: Cambridge University Press, 2000).

53. Martha Nussbaum, *The Fragility of Goodness: Luck and Ethics in Greek Tragedy and Philosophy* (Cambridge, U.K.: Cambridge University Press, 2007).

54. Zanini, *Significati del confine*; Étienne Balibar, *Le frontiere della democrazia* (Rome: Manifestolibri, 1993); Bertrand Badie, *La fine dei territori: Saggio sul disordine internazionale e sull'utilità sociale del rispetto* (Trieste: Asterios, 1996); Étienne Balibar, "Qu'est-ce qu'une 'frontiere'?" in *La crainte des masses: Politique e philosophie avant e après Marx* (Paris: Galilée, 1997).

55. Sandro Mezzadra, "Cittadini della frontiera e confini della cittadinanaza," *Aut Aut* 298 (July–August 2000), 133–53.

56. Jean-Luc Nancy, "A la frontière, figures et couleurs," in *Europes de l'Antiquité au XXe siècle: Anthologie critique et commentée*, ed. Yves Hersant and Fabienne Durand-Bogaert (Paris: Laffont, 2000), 821–29.

57. Jean-Luc Nancy, *The Experience of Freedom*, trans. Bridget McDonald (Stanford, Calif.: Stanford University Press 1993). See also Roberto Esposito, "Introduction," in Jean-Luc Nancy, *L'esperienza della liberta* (Turin: Einaudi, 2000).

58. In the sense Esposito gives to the term in his *Categorie dell'impolitico*.

59. Jean-Luc Nancy, *The Sense of the World*, trans. Jeffrey S. Librett (Minneapolis: University of Minnesota Press, 1998), 37–45, 54–58, 88–93, 103–17. [In a prefatory note published in the 2007 English translation of his 2002 book *La création du monde ou la mondialisation*, Nancy distinguishes between *mondialisation* and "globalization." "The French language," Nancy writes, "has used the word *mondialisation* since the middle of the twentieth century—which seems to me slightly before the term *globalization* appeared in English. The reasons for this neologism should be studied for their own sake. Whatever those reasons may be, the connotation of the term *mondialisation* gives it a more concrete tonality than that of *globalization*, which designates, in French, a more abstract process leading to a more compact result: the 'global' evokes the notion of a totality as a whole, in an indistinct integrality. Thus, there has been in the English *globalization* the idea of an integrated totality, appearing for example with the 'global village' of McLuhan, while *mondialisation* would rather evoke an expanding *process* throughout the expanse of the *world* of human beings, cultures, and nations. The usage of either term, or the search for an English translation that would keep the semantics of 'world' are not without a real theoretical interest: the word *mondialisation*, by keeping the horizon of a 'world' as a space of possible meaning for the whole of human relations (or as a space of possible significance) gives a different indication than that of an enclosure in the undifferentiated sphere of a unitotality. In reality, each of the terms carries with it an interpretation of the process, or a wager on its meaning and future. This also means that it is understandable that *mondialisation* preserves something untranslatable while *globalization* has already translated everything in a global idiom" (Jean-Luc Nancy, *The Creation of the World or Globalization*, trans. François Raffoul and David Pettigrew [Albany: State University of New York Press, 2007], 27–28). For Galli's own distinction between "globalization" and "mondialization," see Introduction, page 14, note 3. —Ed.]

60. Hardt and Negri, *Empire*.

61. Hardt and Negri, *Empire*, 1–66.

62. Hardt and Negri, *Empire*, 13 & ff, 183 & ff.

63. Hardt and Negri, *Empire*, 304 & ff.

64. Hardt and Negri, *Empire*, 221 & ff.

65. Hardt and Negri, *Empire*, 219 & ff.

66. Hardt and Negri, *Empire*, 205 & ff, 271 & ff.

67. David Harvey, *Spaces of Hope* (Berkeley–Los Angeles: University of California Press, 2000), esp. 196.

68. Elazar, *Exploring Federalism*, 223–65 (that which is defined as "postmodern epoch" is globalization); Daniel Elazar, *Constitutionalizing Globalization: The Postmodern Revival of Confederal Arrangements* (Lanham–Boulder–New York–Oxford: Rowman & Littlefield, 1998).

69. James Anderson, Chris Brook, and Allan Cochrane, eds., *A Global World? Re-ordering Political Space* (Oxford: Oxford University Press, 1995).

70. Dante Alighieri, *Inferno*, trans. Robert Hollander and Jean Hollander (New York: Anchor Books, 2002), 93.

71. Edmund Husserl, "Philosophy and The Crisis of European Man," in *Phenomenology and the Crisis of Philosophy: Philosophy as a Rigorous Science, and Philosophy and the Crisis of European Man*, trans. Quentin Lauer (New York: Harper & Row, 1965), 191.

72. Arno Baruzzi, *L'autonomia dell'Europa* (Venice: Marsilio, 2000).

Global War

1. [Anonymous, *De rebus bellicis*, trans. and ed. Robert Ireland (Oxford: B.A.R. International Series, 1979). —Ed.]

2. [*De rebus bellicis*, 28–36. —Ed.]

3. [In *Theory of the Partisan*, Schmitt writes "*Der Feind is unsre eigene Frage als Gestalt*," which, as Gary Ulmen notes, "literally means that the enemy is the shape or configuration of our own question" (*Theory of the Partisan*, 85 n89). —Ed.]

4. [Hegel, *Hegel: The Letters*, 114. —Ed.]

5. [The text in which Hegel here expresses interest is Guibert de Nogent's *The Deeds of God through the Franks*, trans. Robert Levine (Rochester, N.Y.: Boydell Press, 1997). —Ed.]

6. [Adorno, *Minima Moralia*, 55. —Ed.]

7. [Adorno, *Minima Moralia*, 55. —Ed.]

8. [On "war-in-form" see Chapter 3, Note 14. —Ed.]

9. [Carl von Clausewitz, *On War*, trans. and ed. Michael Howard and Peter Paret (Princeton, N.J.: Princeton University Press, 1976), 89. —Ed.]

10. [Jünger, "Total Mobilization," 128–29. —Trans.]

11. [Jünger, "Total Mobilization," 126. —Trans.]

12. [Jünger, "Total Mobilization," 128. —Trans.]

13. [Jean Baudrillard, *The Spirit of Terrorism*, trans. Chris Turner (New York: Verso Books, 2003), 8, 41, 60. —Ed.]

14. [Osama Bin Laden, *Messages to the World: The Statements of Osama Bin Laden*, trans. James Howarth, ed. Bruce Lawrence (New York: Verso Books, 2005), 146. —Ed.]

15. [*Revelation* 18:2–23. —Trans.]

16. [See Chapter 5, Note 5. —Ed.]

17. [Compare Elaine Scarry, "Citizenship in Emergency," *Boston Review* 27:5 (October/November, 2002) http://www.bostonreview.net/BR27.5/scarry .html (last checked May 18, 2009). —Ed.]

18. [Oriana Fallaci (1929–2006) was an Italian journalist and author whose 2001 book, *The Rage and the Pride*, grew out of a highly emotional editorial piece for the Italian newspaper *Corriere della sera*. In both the article and the book, Fallaci uses her personal experience of the September 11 attacks and her belief in the superiority of Western culture as a basis for harsh criticism of Islam and of Western apathy in the face of Islamofascism. Both *The Rage and the Pride* and 2004's *The Force of Reason* sparked controversy in Italy and abroad, and were seen by many as Islamophobic justifications of Western intervention in Muslim regions. See Oriana Fallaci, *The Rage and the Pride* (New York: Rizzoli International Publications, 2002); *The Force of Reason* (New York: Rizzoli, 2006). —Trans.]

19. [*What We're Fighting For: Sixty Scholars Make the Moral Case for the War on Terrorism* (New York: Institute for American Values, 2002). —Ed.]

20. [Edward Luttwak, *Winners and Losers in the Global Economy* (London: Weidenfeld and Nicolson, 1998). —Ed.]

21. [Karl Marx and Friedrich Engels, *The Communist Manifesto*, trans. Samuel Moore (New York: Penguin Books, 2002), 223. —Ed.]

22. [Zygmunt Bauman, *Liquid Modernity* (Oxford: Polity Press, 2000). —Ed.]

23. [See Chapter 7, page 113. —Ed.]

24. [This is a reference to the "Hobbes-Crystal" Schmitt appended to Section 7 of the 1963 reprint of his 1927 treatise *The Concept of the Political*. See Chapter 2, Note 27. —Ed.]

25. [For more on escaping subjects, see Sandro Mezzadra, "The Right to Escape," trans. Tania Rajanti, *Ephemera* 4(3) November 2004, http://www.ephemeraweb .org/journal/4-3/4-3mezzadra.pdf (last checked April 27, 2009). —Trans.]

26. [See Chapter 7, pages 110–12. —Ed.]

27. [Clausewitz, *On War*, 89. —Ed.]

28. [Clausewitz, *On War*, 77, 79, 83. —Ed.]

29. [See Carl Schmitt, "*Inter pacem et bellum nihil medium*," *Lo Stato* X (1939), 541–48. —Ed.]

30. [Hugo Grotius, *The Rights of War and Peace*, trans. A. C. Campbell (Washington, D.C.: M. Walter Dunne, 1901), 17. —Ed.]

31. [Kaldor, *New and Old Wars*. —Ed.]

32. [Henry de Montherlant, *La guerre civile* (Paris: Gallimard, 1965), 13. —Ed.]

33. [Frantz Fanon, *Black Skin, White Masks*, trans. Richard Philcox (New York: Grove Press, 2008), 191–97. —Ed.]

34. [Coen To Heren XVII, 27 December 1614 (from Bantam in Java), quoted by H. T. Colenbrander, *Jan Pieterszoon Coen: Levensbeschrijving* (The Hague: M. Nijhoff, 1934), 64 (*"den handel sonder d'oorloge, noch d'oorloge sonder den handel nyet gemainteneert connen werden"*). —Ed.]

35. [Remarks as delivered by Secretary of Defense Donald Rumsfeld, National Defense University, Fort McNair, Washington, D.C., Thursday, January 31, 2002, http://www.defenselink.mil/speeches/speech.aspx?speechid=183 (last checked on January 16, 2009). —Ed.]

36. [H. J. Mackinder, "The Geographical Pivot of History (1904)," *The Geographical Journal* 170:4 (December 2004), 298–321. —Ed.]

37. [Carl Schmitt, *Theory of the Partisan*, 71. —Ed.]

38. [Carl Schmitt, *State, Movement, People: The Triadic Structure of the Political Unity*, ed. and trans. Simona Draghici (Corvallis, Ore.: Plutarch Press, 2001), 35. —Ed.]

39. [Raymond Aron, *Le Grand Schisme* (Paris: Gallimard, 1948), 13–31. —Ed.]

40. The collapse of modern and late-modern political space revealed itself nearly perfectly in the anthrax scares, a counterpoint of the "external" war on the "internal" front of security. It is as though the perpetrator, still unknown today, had wanted to give life to one of Poe's stories; his *Masque of the Red Death* describes death's appearance within the heart of a fortress's closed space, and death's spectral gait as it empties the space around it from within, until the space is reduced to the same Nothing that rages outside. The perpetrator of the anthrax scares realized an interior annihilation of the primary defensive, immune function

of political space, which should be read in parallel with the exterior annihilation of international political space.

41. [Cicero, *De Officiis*, trans. Walter Miller (London: William Heinemann, 1913), 384–85 (3.29.107). —Ed.]

42. [Galli is referring to the first stanza of the Marines' Hymn: "From the Halls of Montezuma/To the shores of Tripoli;/We fight our country's battles/On the land as on the sea." See http://www.marineband.usmc.mil/learning_tools/library_and_archives/resources_and_references/marines_hymn.htm (last checked November 7, 2009). —Ed.]

43. [*Unrestricted Warfare* was first published in 1999 by the People's Liberation Army Literature and Arts Publishing House in Beijing, China. Three years later, it was translated into English as *Unrestricted Warfare: China's Master Plan to Destroy America* (Panama City, Panama: Pan American Publishing Company, 2002). Although this translation shows signs of being unreliable, it is nonetheless the only English edition of the text held by the Library of Congress and most university libraries, and it is consequently from this edition that we shall quote in what follows. —Ed.]

44. [Liang Qiao and Xiangsui Wang, *Unrestricted Warfare*, 5. —Trans.]

45. [Liang Qiao and Xiangsui Wang, *Unrestricted Warfare*, 37–38. —Trans.]

46. [Liang Qiao and Xiangsui Wang, *Unrestricted Warfare*, 82–87. —Trans.]

47. [Liang Qiao and Xiangsui Wang, *Unrestricted Warfare*, 110. —Trans.]

48. [Liang Qiao and Xiangsui Wang, *Unrestricted Warfare*, 114. —Trans.]

49. [Liang Qiao and Xiangsui Wang, *Unrestricted Warfare*, 144. —Trans.]

50. [Liang Qiao and Xiangsui Wang, *Unrestricted Warfare*, 153. —Trans.]

51. Though, recently, Umberto Rapetto and Roberto Di Nunzio in their work *Le nuove guerre: Dalla Cyberwar ai Black Bloc, dal sabotaggio mediatico a Bin Laden* (Milan: Rizzoli, 2001) have collected a great deal of convincing empirical material with good interpretative points.

52. [Huntington, *The Clash of Civilizations*. —Ed.]

53. [The Latin *pīrāta*, which gives rise to the English "pirate" and the Italian "*pirata*," is formed from the Greek root πειρα, which means "trial, attempt, endeavor" (OED). See also Schmitt, *Nomos of the Earth*, 43. —Ed.]

54. Johann Wolfgang von Goethe, *The Second Part of Goethe's Faust*, trans. John Anster (London: Routledge, 1886), 265.

55. Goethe, *The Second Part of Goethe's Faust*, 265.

56. Goethe, *The Second Part of Goethe's Faust*, 266.

57. Johann Wolfgang von Goethe, *Faust, A Tragedy*, trans. Walter Arndt, ed. Cyrus Hamlin (New York: W. W. Norton and Co., 2001), 34.

Index

absent Idea, xl, xli, xliii
absolutism-liberalism link, 232n5
Adorno, Theodor: critique of
 Heidegger, xlvii; *Dialectic of
 Enlightenment*, lxxviii–lxxix, 96;
 Galli compared, xii; interpretation
 of Hegel, Galli on, xvii; the knight
 of faith, lxxxiv–lxxxv; *Minima
 Moralia*, 142; on Schmittian
 thought, xxviii–xxix, lxii–lxiii;
 seeing the world Spirit, 142
Afghanistan, U. S. war in, 152, 169, 177
Agamben, Giorgio, xlix–l, lxiv, lxxxi
age of consumption, 96
age of individualism, 110
agonal freedom, 124
agoraphobia, 107, 184
alienation, 74, 111
Al Jazeera, 149
Allende, Salvador, xviii
al Qaeda, 139, 151, 172
alternative spaces: the federation,
 52–53; to globalization, European,
 130–33; the small State, 48–52
Althusius, Johannes, 52
Althusser, Louis, xlvii
America: alterity of, 19, 27; discovery
 of, 17–20, 37; empty space of,
 lvi; independence, 55; invention
 of, 19; open spaces for political

theology, 59; the state of nature, 27.
 See also United States
American identity, 150–51, 153–54
amnesty, xlix–li, lii
An der Zeitmauer (At the Wall of
 Time) (Jünger), 95
anarchy, 10, 155–56
Anglo-Saxon nations, 42–43, 55,
 64–65, 97
anthrax scares, 249n40
"anything can happen", 39–40, 67,
 116, 158
apartheid, lxxi, lxxxii
Appadurai, Arjun, 111
Ardrey, Robert, 80
Arendt, Hannah, xxix, lxxii–lxxiii, 69,
 89, 216n292
aristocracy-democracy, 11
aristocratic system, 14, 46, 77
armed peace, xliv–xlv
Aron, Raymond, 183
artificial space of politics, 29–32, 36,
 42–43, 45–46, 76
artificio, 222n37
Of the Art of War (Machiavelli), 23
asymmetrical war, 168, 169, 187–88
Athenaion Politeia (pseudo-Xenophon),
 11, 77
atomic war, 90, 181
axis of evil, 178

CARLO GALLI teaches History of Political Thought in the Faculty of Letters and Philosophy at the University of Bologna. He has written extensively on Carl Schmitt and is a leading Italian political philosopher.

ADAM SITZE is assistant professor of law, jurisprudence, and social thought at Amherst College.

ELISABETH FAY is completing a PhD in Italian Studies at Cornell University. She is the translator of Carlo Galli's "Carl Schmitt and the Global Age."